Dissolving Royal Marriages

Dissolving Royal Marriages provides for the first time a comparative overview of royal marriage dissolutions from the early Middle Ages through to the end of the sixteenth century, on the basis of original translations and editions of key source documents. The book sheds new light on some of the most prominent marriage cases in Western history, from Lothar II v. Theutberga to Henry VIII v. Catherine of Aragon and Henri IV v. Marguerite of Valois. The distilled commentary that accompanies these materials allows readers to grasp, for the first time, how the constructs of canon law helped shape the legal arguments on which specific cases were founded, and to understand the inner side of the events that unfolded in the courtrooms. In his case-by-case exploration of elaborate witness statements, extensive legal negotiations and political wrangling, the author shows us how little the canonical law for the dissolution of marriage changed over time in this fascinating new study of Church—State relations and papal power over princes.

D. L. D'AVRAY is Professor of History at University College London. A Fellow of the British Academy since 2005, he has published widely on religious and social history.

Dissolving Royal Marriages

A Documentary History, 860–1600

D. L. d'Avray

CAMBRIDGE UNIVERSITY PRESS

CAMBRIDGE
UNIVERSITY PRESS

University Printing House, Cambridge CB2 8BS, United Kingdom

One Liberty Plaza, 20th Floor, New York, NY 10006, USA

477 Williamstown Road, Port Melbourne, VIC 3207, Australia

4843/24, 2nd Floor, Ansari Road, Daryaganj, Delhi - 110002, India

79 Anson Road, #06-04/06, Singapore 079906

Cambridge University Press is part of the University of Cambridge.

It furthers the University's mission by disseminating knowledge in the pursuit of
education, learning and research at the highest international levels of excellence.

www.cambridge.org
Information on this title: www.cambridge.org/9781107643994
DOI: 10.1017/9781107477148

First published 2014
Reprinted 2017
First paperback edition 2017

A catalogue record for this publication is available from the British Library

Library of Congress Cataloging in Publication data
D'Avray, D. L.
Dissolving royal marriages : a documentary history, 860-1600 / D. L. d'Avray.
    pages   cm
Includes bibliographical references and index.
ISBN 978-1-107-06250-4 (hardback)
1. Marriages of royalty and nobility – History.   2. Royal houses – Europe – History.
3. Divorce – Europe – History.   4. Europe – Kings and rulers.   5. Europe – Politics
and government.   I. Title.
D107.D38   2014
929.7094'0902 – dc23   2013048909

ISBN   978-1-107-06250-4   Hardback
ISBN   978-1-107-64399-4   Paperback

To Julia

Contents

Preface	*page* ix	
Acknowledgements	xi	
A note on the text	xii	
Introduction	1	
1	Lothar, Theutberga and Waldrada	11
2	Robert II of France and Bertha	44
3	Philip I of France and Bertrada	47
4	Eleanor of Aquitaine and Louis VII of France	50
5	King John of England and Isabella of Gloucester	53
6	Philip II Augustus of France and Ingeborg of Denmark	58
7	Pere II of Aragon and Maria of Montpellier	69
8	Jaume I of Aragon and Lyonor	76
9	Sancho of Portugal and Mécia Lopes de Haro ('Mentia Lupi')	79
10	Henry III of England and Jeanne of Ponthieu	81
11	Plaisance of Cyprus and Balian	99
12	Alfonso III of Portugal and Mathilda of Boulogne	108
13	Jaume I of Aragon and Teresa	112
14	Charles IV of France and Blanche: the law of godparenthood	116
15	Charles IV and Blanche: the annulment process	119
16	Maximilian I, Anne of Brittany and Charles VIII of France	183

17 Louis XII and Jeanne of France   190

18 Margaret of Scotland and Archibald Douglas,
    the Earl of Angus   220

19 Henry VIII and Catherine of Aragon   227

20 Henri IV of France and Marguerite of Valois   239

    Appendix 1: Paris, Archives nationales, J.682.1   249
    Appendix 2: Paris, Archives nationales, J.682.2   267
    Appendix 3: London, British Library, Add. 20917   285
    Appendix 4: London, British Library, Add. 37154   288
    Appendix 5: Glossary of technical terms   295
    Bibliography   300
    Index of manuscripts   307
    General index   308

Preface

The present volume has its own *raison d'être* as a collection of texts, freshly translated and also in some cases edited for the first time, bearing on marriage cases where both kings and the papacy were involved; it also prepares the way for a second, analytical volume on *Papacy, Monarchy and Marriage, 860–1600*, now in press, which develops an interpretation of the intersection of these three themes on the basis of the cases presented here and other data. Translation is of course itself interpretation – above all of the thought processes behind these marriage disputes.

Since the mid 1990s I have been trying to work out the rationalities under the surface of the *causes célèbres* presented in this book. Marriage was on the border of royal and papal power, and in these cases 'events history' can be integrated with the study of long-term patterns and structural changes. The best way to understand the cases was to edit key documents not yet in print and to translate them and others that are already in adequate editions. This process is what one could call 'research translation', because it involves penetrating terminology and concepts not adequately explained in the scholarly literature. There is a big difference between this and (say) translating famous classical texts, nearly all of which have been the object of much reflection over several centuries. With the documents translated here the interpretation of a word or phrase may not be obvious to anyone, however expert, and in such cases, and in others where the Latin is not so much hard as ambiguous, I have given the original in a footnote. In a way, this is even more useful to the scholarly reader than a dual-language edition would be, because it draws attention to passages on which the attention of the learned should be especially focused. The translations are of course for the intelligent unlearned as well, and especially for students who want to go straight into source work. Another way to read the book, however, would be to skip most of the translations and concentrate on the general introduction and the introductions to individual cases. Read that way, the book becomes a very short guide to royal marriage cases involving the papacy. A third way to use this book is as the underpinning of the study of *Papacy Monarchy and Marriage* (covering the same dates), which will attempt an overall interpretation of royal dissolutions taken together with papal dispensation documents. So it is a multi-purpose book. However it is read or used, the nature of the cases it contains ensures that it is full of human interest.

Acknowledgements

I would like to thank John Baldwin, Joe Bergin, Barbara Bombi, Elizabeth A. R. Brown, Ghislain Brunel, Jean-Pierre Brunterc'h, David Carpenter, Emily Corran, Michael Crawford, Stephen Davies, Jane Dawson, Camille Dechelotte, Charles Donahue, Roswitha Dotterweich, Thomas Frenz, Liz Friend-Smith, Murielle Gaude-Ferragu, Shiru Lim, Peter Linehan, Alexander Murray, Janet Nelson, Marigold Norbye, John Sabapathy, Alexandra Sanmark, Maartje Scheltens (who chose the title), Marc Smith, Rachel Stone, Nicholas Vincent, Julia Walworth, Benedict Wiedemann, Lucy Wooding, Patrick Zutshi and many students, in addition to some listed above, who have taken the 'Marriage and Monarchy' course.

A note on the text

#: The hash sign followed by a date, e.g. **# 1104**, is a reference to one of the documents translated in the volume. When there is only one document for a given year, only the year is given. When there are several in the same year, the dates within the year are given: e.g. **# 863, c. October 30**. If the precise date is not known, the heading can take other forms: e.g. **# 863 (early) (b)**. When the date does not distinguish between the two documents translated, then they are distinguished in other ways, say by the archive reference of the document: e.g. **# 1322, J.682.1**. The principle is: **#** followed by as much information as is needed to distinguish the documents from others translated. These **#** references are used in the introduction as a quick way of referring to documents, and they will also be used in the interpretative book on *Papacy, Monarchy and Marriage*, which will follow the present volume and explain its data. The **#** references are used as running heads to facilitate quick reference to a given document.

{}: passages between braces are documents contained within documents. **{{ }}** indicates a document within a document within a document, etc.

Introduction

The triangle of Henry VIII, Catherine of Aragon and Anne Boleyn is an instance of a structure with a long history. A king wants to change wives but is hampered by the need to get papal permission. Lothar II, Theutberga and Waldrada in the ninth century; Robert II, Rozala and Bertha at the end of the tenth; Philip I, Bertha and Bertrada at the turn of the eleventh and into the twelfth; King John of England, Isabella of Gloucester and Isabelle of Angoulême, and Philip Augustus, Ingeborg and Agnes of Meran around 1200; later in the thirteenth century Pere II of Aragon, Maria of Montpellier and Marie of Montferrat; Jaume I of Aragon, Lyonor and Violant; Alfonso III of Portugal, Mathilda and Beatrice; Jaume I of Aragon (again), Teresa Gil de Vidaure and Berenguera Alfonso; in the fourteenth century Charles IV of France, Blanche of Burgundy and Marie of Luxembourg; and in the fifteenth Louis XII of France, Jeanne and Anne of Brittany – it is quite a list.

Sometimes the queen was quite happy for the marriage to be annulled. In the middle of the twelfth century Eleanor of Aquitaine was probably at least as keen as her husband Louis VII of France to be free. In the thirteenth century Plaisance of Cyprus was the petitioner for the annulment of her marriage to Balian, and Jeanne of Ponthieu certainly had no desire to go back to Henry III. In the late fifteenth century, Anne of Brittany had given up on Maximilian of Habsburg. Margaret of Scotland, Henry VIII's sister, tried and succeeded in getting her marriage with Archibald Douglas, Earl of Angus, annulled. Marguerite of Valois did not mind breaking up finally with Henri IV of France if the terms were right.

These lists leave out many dissolutions, for this book concentrates on cases where the pope became involved; and it largely looks at them with the following question in mind: what were Pope X's options when confronted with this situation? This has the advantage of being an answerable question, as some others are not. Perhaps we can guess plausibly on the basis of human nature at the feelings of the husbands and wives involved: a powerful man wanting to ensure his succession and attracted to another woman, a wife deserted for the same reasons – but it is the task of historical novelists and popular writers to articulate such intuitions. The private thoughts of popes are equally inaccessible, but we do know that their authority rested on the consent to it of the educated clergy and that they needed to legitimate their decisions to the latter. If we know the case and the canon law, we are consequently less dependent on intuition. The idea that the need to legitimate is a constraint on action[1] underlies the brief analyses before the documents, and the companion volume on *Papacy, Monarchy and Marriage*, for which the present volume provides the main documentation. We have enough to understand the papacy's 'official mind' – a research end in itself. These documents can also supply contextual material for biographers who reconstruct events from the point of view of the king or queen involved, but that is a secondary objective here.

In all the cases documented below the papacy is drawn into a royal marriage crisis. There seems to have been no law requiring papal involvement, and up until Innocent III it was not uncommon for kings to break up with their wives without involving the pope. Even after Innocent, Ottokar of Bohemia managed to get an annulment in 1262 at diocesan level, during a papal vacancy.[2] Enrique IV of Castile and Blanca of Aragon had their marriage annulled by a local tribunal in 1453, on the grounds of impotence induced by magic.[3] Anne of Brittany and Maximilian (see **# 1491** or **1492**) seem to have taken care to keep the papacy out of their break-up, and indeed to conceal the evidence of their marriage. There may be other cases, but for the later Middle Ages the pattern first found in the ninth century, when Pope Nicholas I was called in to judge between Lothar II and Theutberga, had become entirely normal.

This history documents occurrences from the Lothar II case, around 860, to the end of the sixteenth century. Such cases will not be found in

---

[1] Perhaps the most important single idea of the intellectual historian Quentin Skinner. See Quentin Skinner, 'Some Problems in the Analysis of Political Thought and Action', *Political Theory* 2 (1974), pp. 277–303, at p. 299; also his *Visions of Politics*, vol. I: *Regarding Method* (Cambridge, 2002), ch. 8, 'Moral Principles and Social Change', especially p. 156: 'any course of action will be inhibited to the degree that it cannot be legitimised'. But above all: Quentin Skinner, 'The Principles and Practice of Opposition: The Case of Bolingbroke versus Walpole', in Neil McKendrick (ed.), *Historical Perpectives: Studies in English Political Thought and Society* (London, 1974), pp. 93–128.

[2] Jörg K. Hoensch, *Premysl Otakar II. von Böhmen: der goldene König* (Graz, 1989), pp. 124–5. The grounds were that she had sworn a vow of chastity after the death of her first husband.

[3] *Colección de documentos inéditos para la Estoria de Espana*, vol, XL, ed. Marqueses de Pidal y de Miraflores y D. Miguel Salva (Madrid, 1862), pp. 444–50. This is an annulment on the grounds of impotence due to magic, fitting exactly into the type of case which is the subject of Catherine Rider's *Magic and Impotence in the Middle Ages* (Oxford, 2006).

the history of any other civilisation. In no other culture has divorce been banned at the same time as polygamy, and in no other culture have the sexual lives of monarchs been subject to constraints by a religious power outside their domains. Furthermore, power was transmitted to children from legitimate marriages in most Western European kingdoms, so a monarch's marriage was a public political affair. Thus the cases to be analysed represent a major long-term theme in Church–State relations.

Changing contexts

The structural similarities between these cases are so striking that the changes in context can easily slip to the back of the observer's mind. Yet these changing settings must be kept in mind while reading the documents translated here. The next few pages aim to set the individual cases against the background of changes over some six centuries of European history.

The sequence begins with Lothar II of Burgundy's attempt to leave his wife Theutberga for his former partner Waldrada (see **# 862, November 23 – 867, October 31**). Though the Carolingian empire had broken up, the Christianisation programme initiated by Charlemagne helps explain why the series starts here. By our next case, the remains of the empire had become the geographical area that is now France, only a small part of which was controlled by the Capetian King Robert II.

The Capetian dynasty was still a minor power at the time of our next marriage case, that of Philip I of France (**# 1104**). The case dragged out over years around 1100 (so about a century had elapsed since Robert II's case). It coincided with the First Crusade, in which Philip did not participate, and which raised papal prestige.

Eleanor of Aquitaine's divorce from King Louis VII of France half a century later marked a temporary lurch in the balance of power away from a French monarchy otherwise slowly growing in strength. Eleanor went on to marry Henry, Count of Anjou and Duke of Normandy, and heir to the English throne which he duly inherited two years later.

The twelfth was a century of frequent annulments because the extensive laws of 'forbidden degrees' enabled great men to work the Church's own system to change wives almost at will. If they wanted a change there was a probability of 'discovering' a relationship within the forbidden degrees. Or, like King John, one could simply refrain from seeking a dispensation, so that an annulment was possible at any time (see **# 1199/ 1200**). Or again, a genealogy could be faked – it was hard to check in the absence of registers of births, marriages and deaths. But things were about to change. Philip II of France's frustrated attempts to get

Pope Innocent III to approve of his break with Ingeborg of Denmark (see **# 1202, c. June 1–5**) anticipate a new, more rigorous, matrimonial world. Innocent took an equally hard line with Pere II of Aragon, in the end ruling against the dissolution of his marriage to Maria of Montpellier (see **# 1211, May 21**). What makes his intransigence more surprising is that both kings were his allies. Pere II was a hero of the Reconquest of Spain from Islam, and Philip II was the most powerful king in Europe, a man not to be alienated lightly. Innocent meant business. The Fourth Lateran Council changed the 'forbidden degrees' in such a way as to make annulment harder, at the same time tightening up the rules of proof in annulment cases, and generalising the system of banns, designed to flush out impediments before the actual marriage. In the history of marriage this pontificate is a landmark.

Given Innocent III's determination to prevent the subversion of the indissolubility principle, it may be surprising that there are quite a few thirteenth-century cases from after his pontificate in the pages of this book: far more than for the preceding period. That impression is misleading for several reasons. The book deals with cases where the papacy was involved, and in the preceding period that was much less normally the case. Furthermore, we have much more documentation of papal action from the thirteenth century than before: above all papal registers, mostly lost for the period before Innocent III.

Another reason is the attitude to marriage in Spain, from which several of the thirteenth-century cases come (see **# 1245, # 1263, # 1266**). An attitude akin to that of early medieval times seems to have remained strong in the peninsula: the assumption that important people might be expected to have several official or semi-official sexual partners in their lifetime. One could describe this as successive polygamy for both sexes, with the possibility of secondary wives for men. In fact it may be that the most studied countries of Europe – France, Germany, England and Italy – were exceptional in the degree to which the elite internalised the Church's double ban on polygamy and divorce. That is broadly the argument of Jan Rüdiger.[4]

Thirteenth-century English kings (after John) were more respectful of Church rules. The case involving Henry III (see **# 1254**) is a sharp contrast with those easy twelfth-century annulments. He took a lot of

---

[4] Jan Rüdiger, 'Married Couples in the Middle Ages? The Case of the Devil's Advocate', in Per Andersen et al. (eds.), *Law and Marriage in Medieval and Early Modern Times: Proceedings of the VIIIth Carlsberg Academy Conference on Medieval Legal History* (Copenhagen, 2012), pp. 83–109. For illustrations from the medieval period as a whole of the range of liaisons other than marriage as understood by the Church, see Ruth Mazo Karras, *Unmarriages: Women, Men and Sexual Unions in the Middle Ages* (Philadelphia, 2012).

trouble to get the pope to annul a *de facto* union to which, probably, no one would have given a second thought a century before. The heavy documentation of the dissolution of his proxy marriage with Jeanne of Ponthieu seems like overkill with a marriage contract so obviously invalid to anyone conversant with the facts. The best explanation is that the aim was to kill rumours among the ill-informed, to make sure the succession to the throne was unchallenged.

Across the Channel in France, we have no thirteenth-century royal annulments. France was now the great power of Europe. In two conflicts with Pope Boniface VIII *c.* 1300 the French king emerged on top. Between this humiliation and our next big marriage case, that of Charles IV, the papacy did its best to stay on the right side of the Capetian kings. Furthermore, Pope John XXII had moved the curia to Avignon, not then part of France but close to it. All this makes it easy to assume that deference to Capetian needs was the key to papal policy, but this works less well for Pope John XXII than for his predecessor Clement V. When the last of this long-lived royal line needed an annulment to get an heir, one might assume that political exigency was everything and due process just a charade. The documents transcribed and edited in this volume (see **# 1298, # 1322**) show that view to be simplistic, as will be argued more fully in *Papacy, Monarchy and Marriage*.

Throughout the period of the Hundred Years War there were no royal annulment cases on either side of the Channel – or indeed elsewhere that I can find, at least with papal endorsement. Significantly, Casimir of Poland's efforts to get his marriage with Adelheid of Hesse dissolved were rebuffed by Pope Urban V, though the pope was prepared to play politics by legitimating Casimir's daughters by his new partner: as with Innocent III and Philip Augustus, legitimation of children was in the realm of instrumental rationality, indissolubility a non-negotiable value.[5] As in that previous case, the pope in the end went out of his way to keep good relations with Casimir. A papal bull had actually been forged to legitimate Casimir's new marriage, and Urban was prepared to exonerate him from responsibility for preparing it. But he explicitly refused to annul the marriage.[6] (Casimir's dubious case seems never to have come to trial.) In any case, readers will be struck by the gap between 1322 and 1491 in the texts translated here.

---

[5] Dieter Veldtrup, *Zwischen Eherecht und Familienpolitik: Studien zu den dynastischen Heiratsprojekten Karls IV* (Studien zu den Luxemburgern und ihrer Zeit II; Warendorf, 1988), pp. 255, 393–6. In this 'instrumental' spirit, Urban subsequently backtracked, as his own military situation changed: details *ibid.*, pp. 395–6.

[6] Paul W. Knoll, *The Rise of the Polish Monarchy: Piast Poland in East Central Europe, 1320–1370* (Chicago, 1972), pp. 219–22.

By the last decades of the fifteenth century, 'old' powers that had been in partial eclipse were reasserting themselves. The papacy's prestige probably increased. This is not the textbook picture, but it is significant that there is far more preaching about the papal office in the fifteenth than in the thirteenth century; nor is the preaching sponsored by popes.[7] After the blood-letting of the Wars of the Roses, England achieved stability under the Tudor dynasty, partly because all possible contenders were eliminated. Above all, France emerged once again as the greatest power on the continent, much strengthened by victory over England in the Hundred Years War, and by the recovery of the duchy of Burgundy, which for three generations had been joined to industrially wealthy Flanders as part of the emergent but transient Burgundian state.

Flanders went by marriage to the man next in line to rule the Holy Roman Empire, Maximilian of Habsburg. He had many irons in the fire, including an ambition to rule Hungary. To these he added Brittany, by marrying its heiress Anne after the male line died out (see **# 1491** or **1492**). For a moment it looked like a master stroke against his great rival the French king, but the latter turned the situation upside down by conquering Brittany and 'stealing' Anne, at a time when Maximilian had his hands full in Hungary.

Such was the obsession with Brittany in what one might call the 'official mind' of the French monarchy that on the early death of Charles VIII, his cousin and successor Louis of Orleans resolved to have his own marriage to Charles's sister dissolved and to marry Anne himself, ensuring that Brittany stayed in the family (see **# 1498**). As a result of ruthless *Realpolitik*, the duchy did indeed become a permanent part of France.

A generation later it was the turn of the Tudors. Henry VII's daughter Margaret had married the King of Scotland, and remarried after his death, fast and informally. This second marriage was eventually dissolved (see **# 1528**). We do not have the records of the case, so lack the detail that takes us so close to the reasoning behind other late medieval and early modern cases.

The divorce of Henry VIII (see **# 1529–31**), on the other hand, hardly needs introducing. It was set against the background of the continental Reformation, which created the special circumstances of the last marriage discussed in this book, that of Henri of Navarre, later Henri IV of France, and Marguerite of Valois (see **# 1599**). The second, Calvinist, wave of reform had made dramatic progress in France, and war

---

[7] D. L. d'Avray, 'Papal Authority and Religious Sentiment in the Late Middle Ages', in Diana Wood (ed.), *The Church and Sovereignty, c. 590–1918: Essays in Honour of Michael Wilks* (Studies in Church History Subsidia IX; Oxford, 1991), pp. 393–408.

between Calvinists and Catholics seemed impossible to stop – or for either side definitively to win. The marriage between Marguerite and the Protestant Henri was an attempt to patch things up. The massacre of St Bartholomew's Eve following closely on the wedding showed the instability of the situation. To stay safe, Henri briefly converted on the surface to Catholicism.

After Henri inherited the throne himself he reconverted in a more definitive way, increasing the odds for peace, and he brokered a skilful compromise between the warring parties (the Edict of Nantes, 1598). But he and Marguerite had no children. He also had a series of other love interests, but a stable succession to ensure peace was the driving force behind his successful effort to get his marriage annulled (enabling him to marry Marie de Medici). Once again, closer knowledge of the documents, with the ideal-type of 'constraint by legitimation' in mind, shows that the surface impression is deceptive.

Legal formality

Rules about the reception of dispensations turned out to be the key to the Henri IV–Marguerite dissolution. The Council of Trent had decreed that the local bishop must have sight of dispensations before they could take effect. With the dispensation for Henri IV and Marguerite this formality had been ignored. Their wedding took place before the dispensation arrived, and when it did the bishop had not been informed. As a Protestant at heart, Henry would not have taken papal permission seriously in any case. He may not even have bothered to tell Marguerite.

Though the Council of Trent had added this extra legal requirement, a formally rational marriage dispensation law had been operating since the thirteenth century. Plaisance of Cyprus got her annulment because the law (and indeed theological logic) required a fresh consent after the dispensation had arrived. But by that time she and Balian had broken up.

The seriousness of these situations aside, modern students of these marriage cases are like people observing a game with complicated rules which they have to take seriously if they want to know what is going on and whether the game is being played fairly. A Martian watching Association Football would have to grasp the 'off-side' rule, or the referee's decisions would seem arbitrary and incomprehensible. The decisions were in fact far from arbitrary in the cases from the last four centuries covered in this book. By the pontificate of Innocent III we are in an age of formal legal rationality.

The setting in life of this mode of thought is the professionalisation of canon law. It is part of a wider process. Roman law was spreading from universities to the courts, and in England an indigenous legal profession was growing up around the Inns of Court, still flourishing today. But canon law seems to have led the trend towards legal professionalisation, as a recent magisterial study has convincingly argued.[8] By the mid-thirteenth century there was a well-developed legal profession. Canon law was a higher faculty at universities and a network of ecclesiastical courts covered Europe. Increasingly they were staffed by men with at least some university training. Canon law culture naturally spread beyond the world of professional lawyers, just as some knowledge of the common law and its processes is current in England and the USA today.

The rigour of legal formality in dispensation practice will be a pivotal theme in *Papacy, Monarch and Marriage*, the companion volume to the present study. There it will be argued that the combination of formality and easy availability in dispensation practice became a factor favouring indissoluble marriage. The more readily dispensations were granted, and the more precisely they were framed, the fewer the annulments.

Here, however, a more immediate concern is with another concomitant of the legal revolution: namely, the creation of a new kind of 'due process' for marriage cases (among others).[9] The originality of this form of due process has perhaps not been perfectly grasped by historians. There are excellent analyses of canon law procedure from start to finish,[10] but it is still worth highlighting those components of the system that seem to have been 'made in the Middle Ages' – though of course there are analogues if one moves up to a high enough level of abstraction.

When historians think of later medieval legal procedure in lands where law had been professionalised, they tend to imagine judge-led questioning or *inquisitio* on the one hand, and the adversarial common law system on the other. What we find in most of the documents after 1200 edited and/or translated in this volume is a combination of both sorts, in an original mix. It does have strong analogues to the 'deposition' or 'examination before trial' system in North American common law jurisdictions. Any analogues in medieval English common law seem rather remote and unrelated, and there seems no evidence of a classical Roman law origin.

---

[8] James A. Brundage, *The Medieval Origins of the Legal Profession: Canonists, Civilians and Courts* (Chicago, 2008).

[9] Here I provide a brief summary in anticipation of a fuller and documented account in *Papacy, Monarchy and Marriage*.

[10] R. H. Helmholz, *Marriage Litigation in Medieval England* (Cambridge, 1974), pp. 123–40 (close to practice on the ground in local ecclesiastical jurisdiction); James A. Brundage, *Medieval Canon Law* (London, 1995), pp. 129–35; Brundage, *The Medieval Origins of the Legal Profession*, pp. 430–55.

This combination was not a canon law invention. It seems to have arisen in Italian cities by the late twelfth century. Though its origins require further investigation, the match between still earlier medieval systems and the canon law method is much more approximate. In any case it was canon law that gave this procedure a European-wide diffusion. Understanding it is an essential part of the 'Diplomatic' of the documents it left behind.[11]

In essence it is simple: the plaintiff and the defendant both listed propositions they wanted to have tested by documentary evidence or witnesses. Some propositions on either side might be eliminated – say, if the other side did not contest them. Then a consolidated list was drawn up, which could incorporate propositions from either side. The two sides each gave the names of the witnesses they wanted to be called. Then the list of propositions was run by each person on the list of witnesses, who would respond to questions where their testimony was relevant. Witnesses could be deposed away from court by an authorised person. This had the advantage of providing a written record of considered replies given in tranquil circumstances to carefully thought-out questions, deriving from both parties, put by a neutral person, without courtroom tricks and manipulation. (Against that, the absence of courtroom cross- examination made it less likely that the kind of unexpected results common in television courtroom dramas, if not in reality, would be produced.[12]) This was an 'inquisitorial' system – except that the enquiries came not from the judge but from the adversaries.

A final relevant feature of the legal revolution was the use of proctors. Anyone who has applied for power of attorney in a modern jurisdiction knows how technical the process can be. The proxy system in canon law also involved many formal technicalities, as a glance at **# 1322, J.682.1 (b)** (pp. 126–8) makes clear.

Marriage law had not been free from elaborate rules before the transformation that went with professionalisation, but these rules had not been about dispensations, or the procedure for testing truth, or proxy. They did not form a coherent rational whole, apart from the forbidden degrees rule which was extended by a logic in danger of losing contact with reality. The earlier technicality of canon law expertise had tended to be an instrument for advocates of annulment. We see this in the Lothar II case, where the pope simply refused to deal with the sophisticated and – he doubtless felt – sophistical dossier produced by Lothar's legal team. We see it in the eleventh and twelfth centuries, when the elaborate forbidden

---

[11] 'Diplomatic' as in 'the discipline which elucidates the structures and settings in life of documents'.

[12] Pointed out to me by my pupil Camille Dechelotte.

degrees rule helped great men play the system. The new formality was a force for internal coherence and for indissolubility as understood by the medieval Church. To help modern readers handle it, a short glossary of technical terms is to be found in Appendix 5.

The structure of the book

The other four appendices all contain transcriptions from manuscripts on which translations in the main body of the book are based. Though the body of the book is divided into chapters, the real points of reference are the sections marked by a # sign followed by a date. Within each section, there is a rapid overview of the marriage case, followed by a discussion of the scholarly (and occasionally not so scholarly) literature; then details of the text used for the translation, if it is not from a fresh transcription.

Translation policy

'As near to the original as possible and as far from it as necessary', was the advice of the great philologist Edward Ullendorff. My policy has been to stay as close to the original as I can without writing bad English, but I do not count as 'bad English' very long and complex syntactical structures, which are not to my personal taste but which mirror the Latin. Complex syntax is part of the character of the source, to be rendered faithfully wherever possible, especially since this makes it easier to match up the English with the Latin, as some readers may wish to do. With the same scholarly readers in mind, I have included in the notes lemmata of Latin counterparts to words or phrases the translation of which is not obvious. This gives the English translations some of the advantages of a dual language text: indeed, this system has the advantage over a dual language text of pinpointing the places where the meaning might be debated. With texts like some of these there are two kinds of translators: those who find them hard in places, and bluffers. Thus it is worth drawing attention to the hard parts.

For the section about Eleanor of Aquitaine, Louis VII and Eugenius III, I have done my own translation rather than using that of Marjorie Chibnall in John of Salisbury, *Historia Pontificalis* (London, 1956) – simply to keep the copyright situation simple. I have tried to acknowledge help received from colleagues in the relevant places.

1   Lothar, Theutberga and Waldrada

Lothar II ruled a middle kingdom north of the Alps and between France and Germany. The Carolingian polity was in pieces but the Christianisation programme had affected attitudes and perhaps this celebrated case, the first one in which a king answered to prelates for his marital behaviour. Lothar gave up his partner Waldrada for a political marriage (855) to Theutberga, whose brother could block an attack over the Alps. As fears of that faded, Lothar went back to Waldrada, but he had to justify breaking off his marriage. His wife was accused of crimes so awful as to free him, it was argued, but she survived a trial by ordeal (858) and Lothar had to turn to an ecclesiastical tribunal. Things moved fast in 860. Theutberga's confessor (a very senior prelate) claimed she had revealed the heinous crimes to him. She decided or was pressured into saying she wanted to become a nun, which Lothar claimed would entitle him to remarry. However, she escaped to her brother who ruled the kingdom to the west (roughly modern France), and appealed to the pope, the first such appeal by a queen that we know of, though not the last. The greatest prelate of that kingdom, Hincmar of Reims, wrote a treatise on 'the divorce', more or less in her favour.

In his own middle kingdom Lothar's faithful bishops backed him up. In 862 a council of clergy and laymen found in his favour and he married Waldrada. In the same year Pope Nicholas I was gearing up to put a stop to it all. He thought Theutberga had been wronged, and sent legates to a synod in Lothar's kingdom where the case would be judged afresh. His instructions to them focused on the question of whether a genuine marriage to Waldrada had preceded the union with Theutberga. This reformulated the issue: it was no longer whether she had committed sodomy with her brother or would become a nun (**# 862–863**). Around that time, Lothar changed his line. Previously, he had concentrated on Theutberga's infamy. Now he argued that Waldrada had indeed been his wife, not just a partner. To Nicholas I's fury, the synod found in Lothar's favour and sent two great prelates to the pope with a little book full of their legal arguments. Nicholas was not interested: it looks as though he trusted his instinct that the whole thing was a set-up and that even his legates had been corrupted by bribes, but he did not trust the legal resources in Rome to rebut the king's case. This explains much about the character of the letters by Nicholas translated below (**# 862, November 23 – 867, October 31**). They are rhetorical narratives designed to win over the clerical elites north of the Alps, and the great laymen who might listen to these learned clerics.

Most of the passages translated are transmitted by a manuscript (Paris, Bibliothèque nationale de France, Lat. 1557) containing letters to top people in Frankish kingdoms and collected in the circle of a man who must have been following the controversy, Hincmar of Laon, nephew of Hincmar of Reims who wrote about the divorce. The aim must have been to win elite opinion by telling the tale with passionate force, rather than to allow due process to take its course – because due process hardly existed as yet. Nicholas had some success: Lothar was forced to take Theutberga back, though he seems to have gone on working to get her sidelined, and clearly still hankered after Waldrada.

The letters of Nicholas translated below should ideally be read in conjunction with the following passages from the *Chronicle* of Regino of Prüm, which are easily available in a good recent translation with scholarly annotation: Simon MacLean, *History and Politics in Late Carolingian and Ottonian Europe: The Chronicle of Regino of Prüm and Adalbert of Magdeburg* (Manchester, 2009): under year 864, pp. 140–1 (relating to 862); under year 865, pp. 141–3. See also his introduction pp. 43–4.

Historiographical highlights

The bibliography on this famous case is enormous, so the following highlights have to be more than usually selective. There is a recent full-scale monograph by Karl Heidecker, *The Divorce of Lothar II: Christian Marriage and Political Power in the Carolingian World* (Ithaca, NY, 2010), translated by Tanis M. Guest from a fuller Dutch version. 'Act V', pp. 149–72, deals with Nicholas I's role. Heidecker provides a substantial bibliography of earlier studies. Among the more recent ones two are notable for robustly arguing that there was a strong case for dissolving Lothar II's marriage to Theutberga, the implication being that Nicholas I was mainly interested in asserting papal power: Thomas Bauer, 'Rechtliche Implikationen des Ehestreites Lothars II.: Eine Fallstudie zu Theorie und Praxis des geltenden Eherechts in der späten Karolingerzeit. Zugleich ein Beitrag zur Geschichte des frühmittelalterlichen Eherechts',

Zeitschrift der Savigny Stiftung f. Rechtsgeschichte, kanonistische Abteilung 80 (1994), pp. 41–87, and Raymond Kottje, 'Kirchliches Recht und päpstlicher Autoritätsanspruch. Zu den Auseinandersetzungen über die Ehe Lothars II.' in H. Mordek (ed.), *Aus Kirche und Reich. Studien zu Theologie, Politik und Recht im Mittelalter: Festchrift für Friedrich Kempf zu seinem fünfundsiebzigsten Geburtstag und fünfzigjährigen Doktorjubiläum* (Sigmaringen, 1983), pp. 97–103. I am not convinced by their interpretations which will be discussed (on the basis of the letters translated below) in *Papacy, Monarchy and Marriage*. Stuart Airlie, 'Private Bodies and the Body Politic in the Divorce Case of Lothar II', *Past and Present* 161 (1998), pp. 3–38, makes a point that tells against the views of Kottje and Bauer: namely, that the (non-royal) name 'Hugh' given to Lothar's son by Waldrada suggests that he did not regard their partnership as the definitive one (p. 17). Airlie develops other thought-provoking ideas, notably that once Lothar II had moved the argument into the religious realm, to his own ends, he found himself constrained by logic that he might not otherwise have bothered about, and that his argument that he could not be expected to live without sex turned against him, because a man who could not control his own body could not be trusted to control the body politic. For good general background in the same scholarly tradition as Airlie, see Rachel Stone, *Morality and Masculinity in the Carolingian Empire* (Cambridge, 2012), ch. 8, 'Marriage'. Ruth Mazo Karras, *Women, Men and Sexual Unions in the Middle Ages* (Philadelphia, 2012), pp. 38–42, discusses the case as illustrating the range of possibilities beyond indissoluble marriage as conceived by the likes of Nicholas I. The fine edition by Letha Böhringer of Hinkmar of Reims, *De Divortio Lotharii regis et Theutbergae reginae*, MGH Concilia IV, Supplementum I (Hannover, 1992), is a central background source. In my view the best account of Nicholas I's part in the events reflected in the letters translated below is in a book nearly a century old: Ernst Perels, *Papst Nikolaus I. und Anastasius Bibliothecarius: Ein Beitrag zur Geschichte des Papsttums im neunten Jahrhundert* (Berlin, 1920), a balanced interpretation with a first-hand feel – unsurprisingly since he was also the scholarly editor of the *Monumenta Germaniae Historica* (*MGH*) edition of the letters.

The translation

Unless otherwise indicated, the translations that follow are from 'Nicolai I. Papae Epistolae de Rebus Franciae, Praecipue de Divortio Lotharii II. Regis', *Monumenta Germaniae Historica Epistolarum*, ed. Ernst Perels, vol. VI: *Karolini Aevi* (Berlin, 1925), pp. 268–351.

862, November 23, Letter 3, pp. 268–70

In Paris, Bibliothèque nationale de France, Lat. 1557. Nicholas I urges the bishops assembled in Metz to reach a just judgement under the presidency of the legates he is sending.

Nicholas, bishop, servant of the servants of God, to all the most reverend and holy archbishops our brothers and bishops present at the council which is being celebrated at Metz.

Due honour is rendered to the reverence of the sacerdotal office when we see that they hold the scales of mercy with the balance of rectitude in all things that ought to be done by them taking full account of equity, and in holding it, be not turned away from the path [**'iustitiae quoquomodo'** **p. 269**] of justice by any man's favour or moved by terrors of anyone whatsoever or even by great quantities of money or by having honours heaped upon them. For, in proportion to the responsibility[1] which is conceded to them in watchfully monitoring[2] their neighbours, should, without doubt, be the magnitude of the anxious attention which should be applied by them[3] to this responsibility,[4] without privileging anybody,[5] with zeal for righteousness, lest they seem to forget the text of St Paul: 'Let each get his reward according to his labour.' For since[6] our apostolic spirit is extended among cases of many different ecclesiastical affairs which are seen to pertain to the salvation and the firmness of the faith of the people of God, the account of a dispute between certain women, namely, Theutberga and Waldrada, as also between certain men who recounted it,[7] won our full attention, since our pastoral care had moved us to listen, and – lest the flock of the Lord be tormented by any sickness of violence on account of inaction – lead us with the fire of charity burning up intensely, to restore health by healing. For the aforesaid Theutberga has made great efforts again and again to appeal to the apostolic see with tearful letters,[8] in which she says, her words full of grief, that she is pure and innocent of the crime of which she is accused. For this matter and

---

[1] 'cura'.   [2] 'discutiendo'.

[3] 'his': ablative pronoun standing for the bishops, rather than dative standing for the neighbours.

[4] 'sui'.

[5] 'sine personarum acceptione' (Stone, whose preferred translation would be 'without respect for persons', points out that 'this is a frequently used phrase in Carolingian discussions of secular justice').

[6] 'cum': one could also translate as 'although', with the sense that, busy as he was, the pope found time for this dispute between the two women.

[7] 'sicut quorundam referentium': the phrase is thrown into the sentence rather awkwardly. The best way to interpret it seems to be that controversy extended to divergent accounts given to the pope.

[8] It or they do not survive: cf. Perels, *MGH* edn, p. 269, note 2.

for a discriminating judgement, as we recently decided to remind you, brothers, through an apostolic letter,[9] we want you and in our apostolic office urge you that you should, endowed with apostolic authority, unite to celebrate a synod there,[10] with the legates[11] who are coming from us in our office as pope presiding together with your brotherly selves, and that together with them you may give every effort with their consent to defining and establishing without doubt, what you are able to find together with the aforesaid legates to be more just or true, doing this with great vigilance, without the stain of deceit or the heat of envy or being consumed by hatred, all of which can twist men away from the path of truth and, alas, deflect them from the road of righteousness; having God always before your eyes, despising the persons of princes and terrors which arise for a time and end in time; fearing the words that the prophet says [Isa. 5:20]: 'Woe to you who call good evil and evil good, who put darkness for light and light for darkness, who call sweet bitter and bitter sweet.' For the words of the Gospel, among other things that instruct us on how to live well, remind us, saying [John 7:24]: 'Judge not according to the appearance, but judge just judgement'; and the Psalmist too says [57: 2]: 'If in very deed you speak justice: judge right things, ye sons of men.' Therefore, though there are many things of which we can put you in mind, brothers, not passing judgement on you as being forgetful or ignorant, but giving ourselves over fully to our charitable zeal, we think that these suffice, because[12] we have no doubt that in such matters you can be transported by memory beyond them to many teachings found by reading the Gospel, St Paul,[13] and the prophets. This is the whole thing: that with equitable justice in the present investigation, without any deceit or stain of ill-will, as we said above, since you are assembled in the presence of God, you should, together with our aforementioned legates, strive to decide in a God-fearing manner the cases of your neighbours in so just and irreproachable manner that their[14] and your own holinesses' agreed decision and judgement may be seen to shine out with its equity. For if we see you or them falling away from the rules[15] established in the canons and by the Holy Fathers to favour one party for the sake of a favour from anyone whatsoever – and we hope it will not be so – we will not hesitate to pursue the matter. If however in this same council matters relating to other needs of the Church should come up, deal with them as they deserve with attention and strive to settle them in a God-fearing

---

[9] Dr Rachel Stone pointed out to me that 'apices' could refer to more than one letter.

[10] 'synodicam ... celebrationem ... adunare': literally bring together the celebration of a synod. The sense of this convoluted sentence would seem to be that the council already meeting at Metz should be transformed into a synod led by papal legates.

[11] 'missis'.   [12] 'ideo ... quia' construction.   [13] 'apostolicae'.

[14] i.e. the legates'.   [15] 'institutionibus'.

way. But if any dispute should arise in it in respect of which you may perchance be unable to reach a definitive judgement, we rule that it be reserved to our judgement. We order, however, that you should inform us as supreme authority[16] without delay in the order in which it happened of everything that is done or decided in the same council, so that if we see them to have been decided [**'ea iustitiae pulchritudine' p. 270**] in the beauty of justice and by a decree which can meet with approval, we may give thanks to Almighty God, but if things have been done in a spirit of injustice – and we hope this will not be the case – and contradiction – we may absolutely order that they be done again.[17] We were indeed unable to send the legates[18] from our pontifical office that we referred to in our first letter to your beloved selves, because of certain needs of the Church with which we were kept busy. But with Christ's help we have now decided to send as legates men endowed with great ability and worthy of the utmost reverence on account of their knowledge and teaching, namely, Radoald and John, bishops, who enjoy our favour and give us counsel, who are keen to celebrate the aforesaid council, as I have said above, with your holy selves. May Almighty God, through whom you adorn the highest office of sacred government, fill your blessed hearts with the brightness and beauty of rectitude and justice, so that in all your acts you may be seen to sparkle with the fullness of equity.

Given on the 9th Kalends of December, indiction 11.

863 (early) (a), Letter 10, pp. 275–6

In Paris, Bibliothèque nationale de France, Lat. 1557. Nicholas commands all the archbishops and bishops in France and Germany to reach a canonical judgement on the Lothar marriage dispute.

Nicholas, bishop, servant of the servants of God, to all the archbishops and bishops throughout France and Germany.

We do not believe it is unknown to you how, on account of the two wives of Lothar the king, the face of God's Church has been spattered with the stain of an illicit marriage, or how the same king rejected one and most wickedly joined the other to himself. The first of them, Theutberga by name, grieving bitterly because she had been repudiated, sought the judgement of our see by having a message brought to me[19] about this

---

[16] 'nostro praesulatui'.
[17] 'ea renovare': I would have expected 'renovari'.   [18] 'missos'.
[19] 'per emissam legationem'. Stone suggests 'a legation sent', on the grounds that 'Theutberga had fled to West Francia, under Charles the Bald's protection, by this point, so might have had access to legates'.

matter. On that account, it was our view that it would be entirely uncanonical to judge the case of one party without the other. We therefore ordered that you, brothers,[20] collected at Metz, together with our legates,[21] should hear the case of the same Lothar and agree on a canonical judgement. And so, when, in accordance with our decision, we sent those two bishops our brothers to those regions, it happened to come to our attention, that Lothar, after rejecting his legitimate and first woman,[22] had taken to himself a second wife, neither awaiting the judgement of our see that had been asked and promised, nor submitting in any way to canonical judgement. How else can this be interpreted than that where he anticipates the judgement of many, he judges himself to be guilty by his own judgement.[23] And therefore, as an open message[24] we send this letter endowed with apostolic authority to you, brothers, so that, burning with zeal for the Christian faith, you may set out to Metz, like[25] our legates, and, summoning Lothar there, you may give him a hearing and pass a canonical judgement on him. And if he puts off coming and absents himself from the synod when our legates are present, and makes absolutely no effort to return to penance and satisfaction by hastening to the synod in person to come before our legates to do satisfaction and to cease to do wrong, we will excommunicate him from then on, and, as long as he remains excommunicate, we will exclude him from any part in the fellowship of the whole Church.

863 (early) (b), Letter 11, pp. 276–7

The letter is edited by Perels from Paris, Bibliothèque nationale de France, Lat. 1458, minus the memorandum for the investigation (*Commonitorium*), though the original must have included it. He edits the *Commonitorium* from Berlin Lat. fol. 197, fol. 84.

Here Nicholas I instructs his legates what to do at the Synod in Metz

To the most reverend and holy Radoald and John, bishops.

As you are faithful men of the holy Roman Church and columns of the apostolic see, keep it so,[26] hurry to carry out everything in accordance with our previous order, and at Metz at the synod summoned by apostolic authority, carry out our commands. But if the synod of bishops fails to

---

[20] 'fraternitatem vestram'.   [21] 'legatis'.   [22] 'muliere'.
[23] 'iudicium . . . iudicio . . . iudicat'.   [24] 'universaliter'.
[25] 'pariter cum': probably going with 'set out' ('profiscamini'), rather than 'burning with' ('accensi').
[26] 'ita custodite'.

gather there, or Lothar puts off coming to it, then you should make every effort to go to him and to declare our commands and what we have laid down; and then, when you have gone on to Charles [the Bald] for the sake of the Baldwin case, show to that glorious king, in the presence of all, the synodal letters[27] and the letter we are sending you now together with the memorandum for the investigation; and making this known not only to him but to all the bishops and all the faithful make every effort to read them and announce them openly. Know besides that two letters have been sent by us to your holy selves in place of the ones taken away,[28] one to King Charles and the second to his wife. We send another[29] [no. 10, above] however to the bishops of France and Germany together with this one addressed to you.

Memorandum for investigating the case of King Lothar II

King Lothar claims that he received[30] Waldrada from her father[31] and afterwards took[32] the sister of Hucbert. Here first inquire with diligent investigation and, if you find, in all respects, that the same glorious king received Waldrada with a dowry being given beforehand, and in front of witnesses, according to the law and the customary rite for celebrating weddings, and the same Waldrada was taken as his wife publicly and openly,[33] it remains for you to examine why she was repudiated or the daughter of Boso [father of Theutberga] was taken. But since the same king says that he took Theutberga out of fear, you remember those words of the Gospel where the Lord says [Matt. 10:28]: 'Do not fear those who kill the body', and again he says [Matt. 16:26]: 'What does it profit a man, if he gains the whole world, but suffers loss to his own soul?' In these texts of our Lord one should consider that if those who slay the body are not to be feared when they drive man against justice, and if the gain of the whole world does not benefit a man if his soul is lost, how much less ought so great a king out

---

[27] Perels, *MGH* edn, p. 276, note 11, identifies these with letters 3–6 in his edition.

[28] Perels, *MGH* edn, p. 277, note 1, identifies these with Letters 7 and 8 in his edition (not translated here). They deal with another marital cause célèbre, the elopement of Baldwin, Count of Flanders, with Judith, daughter of King Charles the Bald of West Francia: for a good summary see Janet L. Nelson, *Charles the Bald* (Harlow, 1992), 203–4.

[29] Perels, MGH edn, p. 277, note 2, refers to Letter 10; see above **# 863 (early) (a)**.

[30] 'accepisse'.

[31] her father: no possessive pronoun, so grammatically could be 'his father'.

[32] 'admisisse'.   [33] 'publica manifestatione . . . in matrimonium ipsius admissa'.

of fear of one man, against the Lord's command, be plunged into a dreadful precipice! Without doubt he showed himself to be more reprehensible in that he puts the love of God after the love of the World. If that is where the matter stands,[34] the only command we give you, if the king is convicted[35] by what he has himself revealed,[36] is that you should judge his case definitively in accordance with canon law,[37] acting on our behalf. But if on the other hand it is by no means proved that Waldrada was the legitimate wife nor that she was joined to our son Lothar by[38] a marriage celebrated in accordance with custom, with the blessing of a priest that is, put it to him, that he should not object to his legitimate wife being reconciled with him, if she should be seen to be innocent; nor in this should he submit to the voice of the flesh, but rather, in obedience with the Lord's commands, he should be ashamed, and indeed very afraid, to rot away in the ordure of lust and by following his own will to render a strict account before the tribunal of Christ. Besides, we want you to know that the aforesaid Theutberga has twice and three times appealed to the apostolic see[39] and complained that she had been unjustly cast away by the aforesaid glorious king and that, compelled by force, she had composed a false confession of crime.[40] For at the time[41] when she sent her appeal[42] to the apostolic see, in which she made it clear that she had not indeed yet confessed, but that she was being forced to make a false accusation against herself, adding furthermore [= she furthermore added]:[43] 'And if I am forced to undergo further compulsion, know that I may say[44] what they want not because it is true but out of fear of death and in the desire to escape, because I cannot do so otherwise. You should remember my saying this to you.' Therefore I command you that when the same Theutberga comes to the synod that has been arranged, as I laid down, you should subject her case to

---

[34] 'Ubi': the translation tries to bring out the undoubted fact that Nicholas was sceptical of Lothar's story.

[35] Literally 'the . . . king having been convicted': my translation supplies the conditional from context.

[36] 'manifestatione sua'.   [37] 'secundum canonicam auctoritatem'.

[38] The Latin is a simple ablative, so one could also translate: '*in* a marriage . . . '

[39] Perels, *MGH* edn, p. 277, note 7, here refers to Letter 10; see above # 863 (early) (a).

[40] 'confession of crime': 'piaculum'.   [41] 859 (Perels, *MGH* edn, p. 277, note 8).

[42] Not extant, according to Perels, *MGH* edn, p. 277, note 9.

[43] The Latin seems to lack a main clause.   [44] dicam] future or subjunctive.

diligent examination; and if the objection is made to it[45] that
that she had confessed that she admitted[46] to some crime,
and, on the contrary, she proclaims that she has had to bear
violence, or if she testifies that those judges were her enemies,
then make a fresh judgement according to the norm of equity,
so that she may not be oppressed by the might of injustice.

863, *c.* October 30, Letter 18, pp. 284–6

Here Nicholas I narrates what happened at Metz and afterwards: the
rude awakening of the two archbishops who presented the synod's decisions to him in Rome and the sanctions against those involved. The letter
is not in Paris, Bibliothèque nationale de France, Lat. 1557, but note
that it is transmitted in Bibliotheca Apostolica Vaticana, Reg. Lat. 566,
compiled by Ado of Vienne, in Lotharingia.[47] The Annals of St-Bertin
report that Nicholas sent the decisions translated below to 'Hincmar
of Reims, Wenilo of Rouen and . . . the archbishops and bishops established in the realm of the glorious King Charles': see Janet L. Nelson, *Ninth-century Histories*, vol. I: *The Annals of St-Bertin* (Manchester,
1991), pp. 107. Nelson provides a different (but good) translation of
the decisions *ibid.*, 107–110. Nicholas also sent the same letter to the
prelates of the kingdoms of Lothar's uncle, Charles the Bald, in West
Francia (Perels, *MGH* edn, Letter 19, p. 286) and Ludwig the German
in East Francia (Perels, *MGH* edn, Letter 20, p. 287), and also to those
of France,[48] Germany and Italy generally (Perels, *MGH* edn, Letter
21, p. 287). Thus he is attempting to win over the episcopate of all the
Carolingian successor states.

Nicholas, bishop, servant of the servants of God, to our most
reverend and holy brother Ado archbishop of Vienne.

The crime is known to all that was committed in respect of two women,
namely Theutberga and Waldrada, by King Lothar – if indeed someone
can truly be called a king who does not restrain the appetites of his
body with any healthy control, but instead yields with sinful weakness
to its illicit impulses. But also, recently, almost all the world, streaming
from all sides to the papal court[49] or apostolic see, reports that he had
as guides and supporters in this deed the bishops Theutgaud [of Trier]
and Gunther [of Cologne], with people also informing us in our official
apostolic capacity in writing from afar of the same thing. Our refusal to

---

[45] 'ei': so 'to her' is also possible.
[46] ' confessed that she admitted': the pleonasm is in the Latin.
[47] See Jasper, in Detlev Jasper and Horst Fuhrmann, *Papal Letters in the Early Middle Ages*
(History of Medieval Canon Law) (Washington, DC, 2001), p. 111.
[48] 'Galliam', as elsewhere.   [49] 'ad limina'.

believe this was in proportion to our expectation never to hear such a thing of bishops, until they themselves came to us at Rome at the time of the council, and in front of us and the holy synod were found to be exactly as they had so often been described by many, in such a way that they were convicted[50] by the text[51] which they had endorsed with their own hands[52] and which they wanted us to confirm with our chirograph, and, in their eagerness to set a trap for the innocent, they were caught in their own ambush. Thus God brought it about that the words of Proverbs were fulfilled: 'But a net is spread in vain before the eyes of them that have wings.' For those men were tied up and fell, while we, who were falsely said to have fallen into this scandalous business,[53] with God's help rose again with the defenders of justice and stood upright. Therefore by the judgement of the holy synod, together with ourselves, they are undoubtedly at present[54] deposed and excommunicated from their sacerdotal office and removed from official authority[55] as bishops; therefore you, brothers, upholding the norm of the canons and true to the sanctions laid down by the decrees,[56] should take care lest you presume to receive in the catalogue of priests those whom we have cast out. But the sentence of deposition, which we passed on the aforesaid Theutgard and Gunther, together with the other chapters that we have promulgated, the holy synod together with ourselves declaring them to be binding, is shown in the appendix below.

Chapter I. On altogether nullifying the synod in the town of Metz called by archbishops Theutgaud and Gunther

The synod that was summoned recently, that is, under the most pious emperor Louis,[57] indiction 11, in June, in the town of Metz, by bishops who pre-empted our judgement, and who rashly violated the commands of the apostolic see, and which then and now and in eternity we judge to be void and repudiated together with the Robbers' Council of Ephesus,[58] by

---

[50] 'caperentur'.

[51] Perels, *MGH* edn, p. 284, note 5, identifies this with the acts of the synod held at Metz in June 863.

[52] 'stipulaverant manibus'.

[53] 'in hoc flagitium falso cecidisse dicebamur'. Nicholas's point here is not obvious: perhaps that people falsely said that his intervention had vindicated Lothar.

[54] 'in presentia'.   [55] 'regimine'.   [56] 'decretorum sanctiones'.

[57] Emperor Louis II (d. 875), brother of Lothar II. His share of the Carolingian inheritance was south of the Alps.

[58] A council of 449 rejected by both the Latin and Greek Churches: see *Oxford Dictionary of the Christian Church* (3rd edn, 1997), ed. E. A. Livingstone, s.v. *Latrocinium*.

apostolic authority we judge it to be condemned in perpetuity
and to be denied the name of synod, but we determine that it
be called a brothel, as being favourable to adulterers.

*Chapter II. The deposition of the archbishops Theutgaud
and Gunther*

We now[59] judge that archbishops Theutgaud of Trier, the
primate of the Belgian[60] province, and Gunther of Cologne –
currently, in our presence and that of the holy synod, by way of
an account of how they acted[61] in taking cognisance of and
judging[62] the case of Lothar and his two women, Theutberga
that is and Waldrada – offering a written report[63] about it,
confirmed by their own hands, and affirming by their own lips,
in the presence of many people there, that they had done
nothing more, or less, or differently; and confessing in public
orally that they had violated the sentence that our most holy
brother the archbishop of Milan Tado and our other fellow
bishops asked to be promulgated by the holy see against
Ingiltrude the wife of Boso[64] and that we, burning with godly
zeal, had passed in accordance with canon law, calling down an
anathema[65] – in all of which things we find that they have
transgressed the apostolic and canonical ordinances in many
respects and evilly broken the norm of equity – should remain
removed[66] altogether from the exercise of any priestly office:
and we rule,[67] by the judgement of the Holy Spirit and by the
authority of St Peter[68] working through us, that they are to be
deprived of all the governmental authority that goes with the
episcopal office. And if following previous custom they should
dare to touch in the manner of bishops anything related to the
sacred ministry, it shall not in any way be permitted to them to

---

[59] Taking 'nunc' with 'iudicamus' rather than with the clauses about the archbishop's
actions at the synod.
[60] 'Belgicae': the translation should obviously not be read anachronistically.
[61] 'sub gestorum insinuatione': the sense is probably that the archbishops gave a verbal
account as well as handing over the 'scriptum' to which Nicholas goes on to refer.
[62] 'qualiter . . . recognoverint and iudicaverint'.   [63] 'scriptum'.
[64] Ingiltrude 'had gone off with one of her husband's vassals and found protection with
Lothar II . . . She later threatened to seek refuge with the Northmen' (Nelson, *Annals*,
p. 109, note 16).
[65] 'sub anathematis obtestatione'.   [66] 'alienos'.   [67] 'diffinientes'.
[68] 'by the judgement . . . St Peter': I have taken this with 'definientes' rather than 'judica-
mus'.

have the hope or any place where they may make amends[69] even in another synod, but all those who communicate with them are to be cast out[70] of the Church, and especially if, after they learn that sentence has been passed against the aforesaid men, they attempt to communicate with them.

Chapter III. On the other bishops

But the other bishops, who are said to be accomplices, or followers, of these men, Theutgard namely and Gunther, if, in combination with them, they plot or cabal or conspire with them or, choosing[71] them, dissent from the head, that is from the see of Peter, let them be held as bound by the condemnation equally with them. But if they declare, in person or through messengers sent to us with writings from them, that they[72] will in the future think with the apostolic see, from which it is clear that their episcopal authority[73] originated, they should know that pardon will not be denied to them by us, and that the loss of their honours through our action, on account of past presumptions or written adherence, for which in their profane deeds they were responsible, need in no way be feared.

864 *Annales Xantenses*

But the aforesaid Gunther archbishop of Cologne and Theutgaud archbishop of Trier, in the same year, at the command of Pope Nicholas, came to Rome because of the adultery which King Lothar had previously committed, because in this they had been consenting with him, as had their suffragans, without good grounds,[74] contrary to the Christian religion:[75] bringing with them sentences put together as if by canonical authority. After they and all they had asserted had been condemned at the Synod of Rome,[76] they were altogether confuted,[77] and after they had been barred for the time being[78] from all exercise of the sacerdotal office, they were sent away.

---

[69] 'locum habere satisfactionis'.   [70] 'abici', without a main verb.   [71] 'haerendo'.
[72] 'se professi extiterint'.   [73] 'episcopatus'.
[74] 'uniusta occasione'.   [75] 'religionem Christianitatis'.
[76] 'Quibus in sinodo Romanensi cum omni assertione illorum condempnatis'.
[77] 'refutati'.
[78] 'ad tempus'. De Simson, *MGH* edn, p. 22, note 1, points out that the ban was not merely temporary.

(*Annales Xantenses et Annales Vedastini*, ed. B. de Simson (*MGH*, SS rer. Germ., 'in usum scholarum' XII; Hannover, 1909), pp. 21–2)

867, January 25, Letter 47, pp. 325–8

In Paris, Bibliothèque nationale de France, Lat. 1557. The letter is addressed to the archbishops and bishops of Lothar's kingdom. It contains the third announcement of Waldrada's excommunication and tells them to proclaim it on pain of being excommunicated themselves; and asks for a report on relations between Lothar and Theutberga. The passage translated is a summary of Lothar's previous climb-down.

But, that said, we now for the third time indicate to you by our letter[79] that Waldrada, the most evil rival of our daughter Queen Theutberga, is excluded from all company of Christians and from communion. In the end, after Lothar had as you know, with our legate[80] nearby,[81] rejected Waldrada and obediently given himself back to Theutberga the queen his wife, and, thanks to the very sure guarantee[82] that a given oath provides, could be justifiably believed to have put an end to his crime, it was decided that the distance separating Waldrada from the same king should be the greater in proportion to the cunning of the ancient enemy which we know not to be lacking in such people.[83] It was also determined that this woman should stay in Italy for the time being and wait to hear what we say by way of censure, and that, if we should think it necessary for her to come to Rome, she should hurry without delay, that she might stand before us and either, if she could, show her innocence, or confess what she has done and beg for mercy. Indeed, she did come to Italy, though not voluntarily, but overcome by her obstinacy of mind she did not deign to set out for Rome, indeed, as if her conscience were beyond reproach, she turned back and hastened towards the province[84] (p. 326).

867, October 30, Letter 51, pp. 334–8

In Paris, Bibliothèque nationale de France, Lat. 1557. In the passages translated from this letter to Louis the German, Nicholas I complains that Lothar has only physically separated himself from Waldrada, while remaining under her influence, and failing to treat Theutberga as a wife, and asks Louis to exercise a positive influence on his nephew.

[79] 'epistolis'.   [80] Bishop Arsenius (Perels, *MGH* edn, p. 326, note 2).
[81] 'imminentia missi nostri'.   [82] 'satisfactione certissima'.
[83] 'talibus' – could be 'such cases'.   [84] 'provintiam'.

[**p. 335**]: you say you sent to him [Lothar] your . . . brother King Charles together with one of the bishops of your kingdom in order that he might, as we enjoined on you through the letter[85] we sent to you,[86] be admonished by them to obey all our orders in all respects. In that, both loving justice like pious princes and seeking in your charity the salvation of your neighbour, you have nonetheless[87] done as we exhorted you, we give you thanks, despite the fact that, I confess, it is not yet clear what has been actually gained by your or our admonitions so far as the same King Lothar is concerned. But you do say that both when he was absent and afterwards in your presence[88] he had taken the same admonition from you in good part and had then claimed that he was going to obey our commands in all respects. Because we have often heard this but not noticed any perceptible result we are not a little distressed, and we are more afflicted than we can say, thanks to this business . . . [**p. 336** . . . **p. 337** . . .] . . . For if it is permitted for your excellency to know on what grounds Lothar boasts that he has entirely fulfilled our will, we will explain it clearly. Namely because he obeyed us and indeed our God and received Theutberga as his wife, and rightly distanced Waldrada from himself as being an adulteress, and did not go to her after the return of our legate. But the prudence of your glorious self can already see what good it does if he has access to her not with bodily feet and yet with strides of the mind . . . What does it profit our beloved daughter Queen Theutberga, since he seems not to be absolutely separated from her with his body,[89] when he nevertheless proves to be in no way bound to her in his mind. What does it profit her to enjoy conjugal union or the royal dignity in name alone, when she lacks all the things which seem to be the badges[90] of perfect love and equal power. For who but her rival, that is Waldrada, who is bound by the chains of excommunication not only for the adultery she committed but also for her impenitent heart, controls the heights of the kingdom's power[91] together with Lothar, enjoys the glory, controls the rights,[92] and orders everything as she wants? For although she may seem in appearance to be separated from his company,[93] she is as powerful with

---

[85] 'epistolas'.   [86] Perels, *MGH* edn, Letter 49, pp. 332–4.

[87] 'nichilominus': presumably: 'despite Lothar's absence'.

[88] Perels, *MGH* edn, p. 335, note 3, indicates a meeting at Frankfurt, and gives further references.

[89] 'non ex toto ab illa . . . corpore prolongatus': I have taken 'ex toto' as an adverbial phrase. Grammatically one could also take 'toto' with 'corpore': separated with his entire body.

[90] 'ad . . . pertinere videntur insignia'.   [91] 'regni . . . culmina possidet'.

[92] 'iura'.   [93] 'colloquio eius'.

him – if not even more powerful – through intermediaries and various aides, as she would be if she could be in any way held to be a legitimate wife. For no-one is enabled to get to the king's inner circle[94] except through her; scarcely anyone is said to suffer injury anywhere except because of her. For it is she who normally obtains pardon[95] from him for petitioners, and she alone distributes benefits to the people it suits her to favour. Now, however, if it is not as we say, that is, if Queen Theutberga is not suffering all this injury and disgrace at his hands, and if the whore Waldrada is not enjoying such glory: why then, when he writes to us[96] or justifies himself to others, does he not match his assurance with regard to Waldrada – that since the return of our messenger he has not been with her – with a similar one about his wife Theutberga: that he is treating her and keeping her in accordance with the content of the oaths given – unless because he has nothing to boast about? And is not acting towards her in such a way that he can give us a truthful report about it and receive our thanks? Since she is not only not receiving any generosity at his hands, but even wasting away, treated without any respect and, as we said, in the greatest need. Therefore, dear friend, you say to him, and do your best to bring your wise personal influence to bear to persuade him[97] that, when he sends to us the message that since the return of our messenger he has not been in Waldrada's company at all, he should also send a message that he is treating his wife Theutberga kindly in accordance with the oaths he swore and that he is keeping her as royal dignity requires; in such a way, specifically,[98] that we can know from the testimony of others also that the message corresponds with the truth. In addition, furthermore, let him send a message to say that in the aforesaid churches[99] bishops are to be ordained in a proper way along the orderly lines which we laid down above:[100] and then we will believe him when he says he wishes to carry out our instructions, and we will give suitable thanks to God. For as long as that land does not keep Theutberga in a style befitting royalty, and lets her live without conjugal love, and permits Theutgaud or Gunther to get

---

[94] 'regium apicem'.   [95] 'gratiam': this could also be translated as 'favour'.
[96] 'Cf. Lotharii epis. laud., supra p. 238' in edition.
[97] 'et vestra sagaci conventione suadere contendite'.
[98] 'dumtaxat'.   [99] Trier and Cologne.
[100] This is about replacing the two archbishops, Theutgaud and Gunther, whom he had deposed for their role on Lothar's side in the dispute. Earlier in the letter he had written: 'Hinc etiam ut novi Treverensi et Coloniensi ecclesiis antistites darentur iniunximus, videlicet qui nec per Theutgaudi et Guntharii dudum episcoporum nec per iam fatae Waldradae favorem proveherentur, sed canonice a filiis et de filiis iam nominatarum ecclesiarum electi ab his, qui earundem ecclesiarum antistites soliti sunt consecrare, regulariter ordinarentur' (p. 335, lines 30–4).

and occupy[101] the churches which were recently[102] taken away from them together with the priestly office,[103] even though he may not see Waldrada, yet these are the steps, though they plunge towards the depths,[104] down which any discerning man clearly recognises that Lothar is gradually moving towards her, since he both favours the men who were clearly guides towards such wrongdoing,[105] and afflicts the woman, whom [**p. 338: praemissa Christo**] with Christ's help, he received back after due correction.[106] We do indeed find that the accusers[107] of Lothar are none other[108] than the person called in Revelation [12:10] 'the accuser of our brethren',[109] and his own deeds, and the original impulse of these same deeds can also[110] be traced back to our Ancient Enemy the Devil.[111] In truth, the deeds that your nephew King Lothar does are such that no accuser is required. As St Paul indeed bears witness, 'the works of the flesh are manifest, which are fornication, impurity, lust and the rest'. We hope that your glorious self will prosper now and always, dearest son. Given on 30 October, first indiction.

(pp. 335–8)

A further paragraph is added (p. 338), but it is about collecting revenue.

867, October 31, Letter 53, pp. 340–51

In Paris, Bibliothèque nationale de France, Lat. 1557. In this letter to archbishops and bishops in the realm of Louis the German Nicholas I deploys all his powers of rhetorical narrative to convince them of his interpretation of the cause célèbre.

---

[101] 'obtinere . . . occupatas'.
[102] Perels, *MGH* edn, p. 337, note 3: 'Anno 863; v. supra p. 285 c. II.'
[103] 'sacerdotio': probably not to be understood as meaning that they ceased to be priests.
[104] Presumably an allusion to Virgil, *Aeneid* 6.126.
[105] 'quos ad pronefas ductores habuisse claret'.
[106] 'debita correctione praemissa'.
[107] Lothar had complained of accusers whom he compares to the evil accuser in Rev. 12:10: cf. Perels, *MGH* edn, p. 338, note 2: '*Cf. litteras Lotharii ad Nicolaum directas, supra p. 232:* De nostris igitur accusatoribus et inimicis luculenter rescribentes, qui penes vos famam nostram acriter et mendose laesere, super malignos spiritus interpretari libuit, quorum caput accusator fratrum appellatur.' Nicholas I's thought is convoluted here because the 'accuser' in the verse of Revelation is an entirely negative figure, Satan in fact. The idea would seem to be that the Devil is behind Lothar's deeds, which bear witness against him.
[108] 'nonnisi'.
[109] Nicholas may have slipped here, as the implication from the quotation would be that Lothar was unjustly accused.
[110] To catch the 'quae et ipsa'.   [111] 'antiqui hostis'.

[**p. 342**]: Meanwhile the scandal created by King Lothar in abandoning Theutberga and taking Waldrada began to grow and to become more generally notorious, spread by the adulation and iniquitous defence of it by these men [Theutgaud and Gunther]. Learning the fact of this matter, we forbade as earnestly as we could and tried – both through certain faithful men and through writings – to argue against the commission of so great a crime. King Lothar sent two counts to us, through whom, in writing[112] and orally, he indicated that the bishops of his kingdom together with certain others were authorising him to reject Theutberga and choose Waldrada as a spouse, but that [**p. 343 'se, ut ordo custodiretur'**] he, to do things properly,[113] was seeking from us by preference this authority and judgement, and waiting for advice. When we heard this, we replied that we were not indeed able to send legates[114] at such short notice for this business, but we gave a most definite promise instead to send them later, warning that in the meantime no-one at all should engage in any deliberation whatsoever about this case. Lothar however, relying as afterwards became clear on the authority of these men, Theutgaud and Gunther, at that time bishops, did not wait for our legates and in a public celebration of the marriage rite[115] joined Waldrada to himself by the law of matrimony. Nevertheless the legates of the apostolic see, who had already set out for Gaul, came to Lothar and said that they had been sent to him in accordance with our promise, and made every effort to bring home to the king that he should as we had ordered have pairs of bishops[116] from the realms of the most glorious kings, Louis, namely, Charles the Greater [Charles the Bald] and Charles the Younger [King of Provence] to come together with them[117] together with those of his kingdom, and they stated verbally[118] that we had ordered Theutberga, who had appealed to the apostolic see, to be present at the same assembly, after a suitable safe conduct had been given her by King Lothar. For they were not able to have with them the letters that we had sent to you and the bishops of your kingdoms,[119] since they had, as was well known, already been taken off them by friends of Lothar. King Lothar however,

---

[112] 'in scriptis' – texts now lost.   [113] 'ut ordo custodiretur'.   [114] 'missos'.
[115] 'publico festoque nuptiarum ritu celebrato'.
[116] 'binos': i.e. two from each realm. Cf. Perels, *Papst Nikolaus I. und Anastasius*, p. 71.
[117] 'secum'.   [118] 'verbis asseruerunt'.
[119] This is an odd phrase considering that the letter translated here is addressed to the 'archbishops and bishops' in just Ludwig's kingdom. Perhaps he has momentarily forgotten the original *inscriptio* – the addressees of the letter – and is in his mind addressing the archbishops of all three kingdoms: East Francia, West Francia and Provence.

under the instruction of these two masters, neither wanted to give to Queen Theutberga definite assurance that justice would be done or that she would not be subjected to violence, nor waited at all for anyone but the prelates of his kingdom, that is those whom he had already bent to his wishes either by benefits[120] or threats, to come to the assembly that was being gathered at the town of Metz: but after he had corrupted our legates and indeed got them on to his side[121] he did what he wanted with no resistance from anyone. When the assembly had gathered together the prelates who had convened, among whom Theutgaud and Gunther retained the place of special eminence and enjoyed the greater power, anticipating, indeed usurping and arrogating to themselves our judgement, namely the one that we had already promised to pass, moved first by Queen Theutberga's appeal and then by the petition of King Lothar, and which we could be seen quite clearly to have begun both through our legates and through our letters,[122] they believed Theutberga to be guilty and thought that she should be condemned in her absence. An unholy document[123] was written concerning the things that had at the king's wish come out of the throat of iniquity, and thinking that these things would thus be kept in full force, they confirmed them with their own signatures, with Theutgaud first of all and Gunther leading the way, and poisonously compelling the others to follow them, in signing as in their other deeds. They made a solemn and comprehensive commitment[124] to come to Rome soon and to render an account of what they had done. Finally they arrived [**p. 344 'nostro sunt conspectui'**] and presented themselves to our sight in the presence of the whole Church, and when we asked how those things had been done, they offered the aforesaid

---

[120] 'beneficiis', which can also be translated as 'fiefs' or 'benefices'.

[121] 'ad favorem suum traductis legatis'.

[122] 'incoatumque tam per missos quamque per epistolas nostras habere luce clarius videbamur': the construction seems to be close to the modern vernacular: 'habere incoatum' roughly corresponds to 'aver iniziato', 'avoir commencé'.

[123] 'libello': here not a 'writ'-type document starting the case, since Nicholas's point is that they have pre-empted him and judged it. The 'libellus' has not survived but see the translation of chronicle extracts from the *Annales Xantenses* (above, # 864), and Regino of Prüm: see MacLean, *History and Politics,* under the year 865, p. 142: 'they thought they could deceive with some perverse doctrine the see of Peter, which has never been mistaken nor could ever be deceived by any heresy. Therefore when they came into the presence of Pope Nicholas they presented a document containing the acts of the synods they had organised at Metz and Aachen.' Perhaps these 'acts' (*gesta*) included canon law authorities on which they based their decisions. Maclean comments, p. 142 note 85: 'This booklet is no longer extant. Regino could have taken this information from Nicholas, *Epistolae,* no. 53: 343–4.'

[124] 'se per omnia spoponderunt'.

document and said that they had done nothing more or less than or different from what the document they were offering seemed to contain. It was taken and its contents detailed in the presence of the gathering of our bishops that was with us and of Theutgaud and Gunther themselves, and we explained very precisely in their hearing in how many ways we reprehended it and judged it to be altogether reprehensible and how inimical to justice and hateful to God were the things in it which were read as having been done. Although not all the passages worthy of censure in those unholy acts[125] were then discovered, nor can all the things found be recalled to our mind and rehearsed again now:[126] they were none the less so great and of such a kind, that the holy synod sitting together with me repeatedly cried out that on account of them Theutgaud and Gunther ought rightly to undergo the canonical sentence of deposition. At this we were moved – we say it here before God – by divine zeal, and, wishing only to carry out a just judgement, by common consent, after the council that favoured the adulterers, which we noted above had met in the town of Metz, had first been declared invalid, on those men – we are distressed to record this – we imposed the sentence of deposition; and, if they were perchance thenceforth to touch anything relating to their sacred ministry in accordance with previous custom, we excommunicated them. Firstly, indeed, because they refused contemptuously to obey our salutary orders with respect to Ingiltrude or Theutberga, or to Waldrada; for disobedience is such a horrendous evil that it is rightly compared to idolatry, for as Samuel says [1 Kgs 15:23] 'To resist is like the sin of divination and to refuse to obey is like the crime of idolatry', so St Paul rightly says [2 Cor. 10:6] 'having in readiness to revenge all disobedience'... [The passage omitted deals with another case, that of Ingiltrude.] Fourthly, since they not only put up no pastoral resistance to the couple in the grip of adultery [Lothar and Waldrada] and failed as watchmen to announce the coming sword [Ezek. 33:2–7] but even, by giving them their consent and support, gave them the confidence to persist in their evil doing, and attempted with all their strength to defend so great a crime to the end. Therefore the Lord rightly made their tongue cleave to their palate,[127] namely so that those who had no tongue to rebuke crime [**p. 345 'ad bona quoque praedicandum**] could not even have it to preach good things, in accordance with the words of the chant[128] in a different place 'God said to the sinner' up to 'and you will place your portion with

---

[125] 'gestis': acts keeps the double meaning of what they did and the written account of it.
[126] 'nec rursus omnia, quae inventa sunt, nunc ad memoriam nostram valeant repedare'.
[127] The mixture of singulars and plurals is in the original.
[128] 'iuxta quod alias cantatur'.

adulterers' [Ps. 49:16–18]. A man indeed puts his portion with adulterers when he becomes like them in respect of both crimes and punishments by consenting or favouring or not rebuking them, in accordance with what St Paul too wrote about such people [Rom. 1:32] 'Since those who are responsible for such things are worthy of death – not only those who do them, but those who consent to those who do them.' Fifthly, because they audaciously presumed to reach a definitive judgement, without any authority from us, in a case, surreptitiously arrogated to themselves, in which an appeal had been lodged by each side, that is by Theutberga and by Lothar, as we have already noted – acting contrary to the canons: for indeed, concerning appeals, which take place by the tomb of St Peter,[129] the sacred laws[130] committed anything requiring judgement[131] to the decision and council[132] of the bishop of Rome.[133] But these men, ignoring the reverence due to St Peter, with audacious presumption both passed the definitive judgement which each party had beseeched us to give, and which we had begun to carry out, and judged that Theutberga, even as she sought refuge with the Church, should be crushed by condemnation. Sixthly, because they did this in [her] absence, contrary to the metaphorical saying:[134] 'Do not verbally abuse a deaf man.' Indeed, it is verbal abuse of a deaf man when a person is condemned *in absentia.* For in a manner of speaking a person is deaf when they are absent and cannot hear what is objected against them; although that absence was rightly ensured, not because Theutberga sought it willingly, or because she had a bad conscience, as those men[135] think, but from fear of the king, who refused to grant her an appropriate safe conduct, and out of suspicion of counsel biased against her.[136] Seventhly, since the same men not only acted profanely[137] by subscribing to all the things that had been evilly compiled, and thus lending them authority,[138] to the detriment of the respect due to the apostolic see, but also, by compelling others to subscribe to them, became responsible for the transgression of all involved, and became criminally responsible for as many souls as they had in their role as ringleaders[139] plunged into the depths of transgression by word or by deed.[140]

---

[129] 'apud memoriam sancti Petri'. This seems to be 'Memoria' in the sense studied by the Munster School of the later twentieth century: namely, the community of the living and the dead.

[130] 'sacrae regulae'. [131] 'iudicandum'. [132] 'arbitrio et consilio'.

[133] 'siquidem de appellationibus, quae apud memoriam sancti Petri fiunt, iudicandum Romani praesulis arbitrio et consilio sacrae regulae commiserunt'.

[134] 'Quod tropice dicitur'. [135] 'isti'. [136] 'factiosi consilii'.

[137] 'in profanis gestis'. [138] 'roboraverunt'. [139] 'utpote praeminentes'.

[140] The 'by word or deed' could apply either to the two ringleaders or to those whom they led.

But if it is our wish[141] to reveal more fully in writing all the things which it was clear to us and the holy synod, both from the document[142] and from other evidence, that they had done, we would run out of parchment before we ran out of words. Therefore let it be enough to have listed seven charges[143] which especially gave rise to the deposition of Theutgaud and Gunther; for it is customary for the number seven to stand for the entirety.[144] Besides, who would be able to relate all of the things that they did wrong either before or after the condemnation? Namely how they lied in saying that our case against them was groundless,[145] contrary to the words said to God: 'You will destroy all who tell a lie'! How, contrary to divine and human law, they had not the slightest hesitation in attacking Theutberga again after she had first been found innocent through the judgement they had selected. How, after that, they condemned this lady without an accuser, a thing forbidden by both laws![146] How indeed they allowed certain witnesses who were at the king's beck and call to contribute, contrary to the public laws, to her condemnation – as also certain servants of the ruler![147] How, contrary to the standards of the priestly order,[148] they committed to writing,[149] and showed openly to everyone, all sorts of obscene things,[150] things [**p. 346 'adversus apostolum'**] contrary to St Paul,[151] and full of slander,[152] and also[153] words filling everyone with revulsion and embarrassment;[154] even though, as the Lord testifies, men will give an account of every careless word they utter [Matt. 12:36]! Or how, when they had already been condemned, they importuned the emperor's[155] ear to turn him against[156] the sacred canons![157] Or how they resisted

---

[141] 'volumus' in the indicative.   [142] 'libellum'.   [143] 'capitula'.   [144] 'universitas'.

[145] 'qualiter videlicet nos se frustra redarguisse mentitit sint'.

[146] i.e. given the immediately preceding context, 'divine and human laws'.

[147] 'imperantis'.   [148] 'reverentiam sacerdotalem'.

[149] *MGH* note: '*Cf. infra nominata capitula obtrectationum guntharii et Theutgaudi, quae tradita sunt in Ann. Bertin. a. 864 p. 69 sq., in Ann. Fuld. a. 863 p. 60 sq.*'

[150] 'turpia quaeque'.

[151] 'adversus apostolum'. This could mean 'against the pope', but 'Apostolus' tends to mean St Paul, and the latter's letter to Titus, ch. 1 lists standards of behaviour that a bishop should meet.

[152] 'criminosa'.

[153] Taking the sentence structure as: [turpia . . . criminosa] necnon [pudorem . . . inferentia verba] rather than [turpia] ac [criminosa necnon . . . pudorem . . . inferentia verba].

[154] 'pudorem'. 'Shame' is closer but in modern speech that tends to mean shame at what the one who feels it has done, not the 'blush of shame to the cheek of modesty' sort.

[155] A reference to Ludwig II, who 'invaded Rome early in 864 at their instigation' (Perels, *MGH* edn, p. 346, note 2, my trans.).

[156] 'auribus imperatoris adversus sacras regulas molesti fuerint'.

[157] Perels, *MGH* edn, p. 346, note 3 refers to: 'Cf. Conc. Antioch. c.11; Mansi [*Sacrorum Conciliorum . . . Collectio*] II, [col.] 1323 sq.', which reads 'Si quis episcopus, aut presbyter, aut quilibet regulae subjectus ecclesiae, praeter consilium & literas episcoporum

the sacred authority of God[158] conferred on the Roman Church in St Peter,[159] and published charges[160] contrary to the privileges of his see, and spread them throughout almost all of the West,[161] and how, through these, even after they had been cast down for their very great crime, their influence was a source of strength enabling Lothar to persist in his crime.[162] Or how they tyrannically afflicted us, pressed upon us, and wearied us in every evil way they could, when we were by the very tomb of St Peter, to such an extent that their men broke through the doors of St Peter and shed blood in his church! How too, at night, when we were saying matins,[163] they plotted and conspired with their accomplices and supporters, contrary to the Council of Chalcedon,[164] and in the most important places of our dioceses, they divisively[165] organised gatherings and decision-making about specific items of business, and despicable little councils, despite the fact that the canons forbid this, even against us, and also, together with our suffragans, put together[166] evil tracts and fictions of various sorts! Lastly, how they presume still to hold on to the churches which they have occupied – churches once entrusted to them and afterwards lost together with the priestly office – and to rule them arbitrarily as tyrants. See what Theutgaud and Gunther have done and are doing in the Church, aside from that of which Gunther specifically is guilty, with respect to the sacred ministry,[167] for which he is altogether forbidden by canon law[168] even from any opportunity to make amends.[169] In truth, when they were just initiating their

---

provinciae, & praecipue metropolitani, adierit imperatorem, hunc reprobari & abjici oportere, non solum a communione, verum & ab honore', etc.

[158] 'ordinationi Dei'.   [159] 'ordinationi Dei in beato Petro ecclesiae Romanae collatae'.

[160] 'capitula obtrectationum'.   [161] 'occidentale clima'.

[162] 'Hlothario in scelere perdurandi robur dari suaserint'.

[163] 'matutinales hymnos celebrantibus'.

[164] Perels, *MGH* edn, p. 346, note 5: '*C. 18 (Mansi VII, 398)*'.

[165] 'factiose'.   [166] 'texuerint'.

[167] Perels, *MGH* edn, p. 346, note 7: '*Ann. Bertin. a. 864 p. 71:* Guntharius – Coloniam veniens missas celebrare et sacrum chrisma conficere, ut homo sine Deo, praesumpsit; Theutgaudus vero a ministerio, sicut ei fuerat praeceptum, se reverenter abstinuit. – *De speciali Guntharii inoboedientia v. etiam supra ep. n. 26 (p. 291), infra ep. n. 66*'.

[168] 'a sacris regulis'.

[169] 'etiam locum habere satisfactionis penitus interdicitur'. Cf. Perels, *MGH* edn, p. 346, note 8: '*V. conc. Antioch. c. 4; Mansi* [*Sacrorum Conciliorum . . . Collectio*] *II,* [col.] *1322*'. The text reads 'Si quis episcopus damnatus a synodo, vel presbyter, aut diaconus ad suo episcopo, ausi fuerint aliquid de ministerio sacro contingere, sive episcopus juxta praecedentem consuetudinem, sive presbyter, aut diaconus; nullo modo liceat ei, nec in alia synodo restitutionis spem, aut locum habere satisfactionis, sed communicantes ei omnes abjici de ecclesia, & maxime, si posteaquam didicerint adversum memoratos prolatam fuisse sententiam, eisdem communicare tentaverint.' By 'satisfactionis' the council fathers at Antioch may have meant 'doing public penance', or, alternatively, justifying himself.

action,[170] which they did at the often mentioned pernicious meeting at Metz, they made their inclinations absolutely evident. For although our representatives there afterwards went astray, they began the first part of what they had to say in moderately conciliatory manner. Those men, however, because they heard a hint of criticism being expressed in their regard, immediately lost their temper entirely and reported that we had said words that we had in no way uttered about them, and asserted that we had called them fosterers, and planters and irrigators of vices. And for sure, we as yet had no knowledge of the deplorable things which we described above, such that we might be able to say those things about them with confidence at that time. And yet these men were driven by their guilty conscience[171] to prate that we made assertions[172] that would have been quite improper on our part, since those things were unknown to us. What is going on here, if not that even as we held our peace, the Holy Spirit already wanted to show that they were planters and irrigators of vices not by the mouths of others but by their very own? And just as once the Spirit made public through Caiaphas that which had to take place, so too, through those men, even though not of their own volition,[173] he expressed what needed to be made clear. For the things that they maintained that we would in no way say about them if we had knowledge of their life and character, these very things out of their own mouths and with their own lips they asserted,[174] while trying to seem in all respects men of praiseworthy life and character.[175] Now however, if you want [**p. 347 'liquido nosse'**] to see through the ridiculous games they played and the parts they acted out, find and read the acts of the aforesaid Council of Metz, a council which we thought fit to call a brothel, when we voided it, because it gave support to adulterers. This 'brothel' did indeed favour adulterers, as it gave its backing to Lothar, Waldrada and Ingiltrude in all things,[176] and presented models of adultery to others following these in their footsteps.

Behold the things for which you asked so often, behold the things which you indefatigably sought! – though we too felicitate your charitable self[177] in no small way, when we see that you feel compassion for

---

[170] 'prosecutionis'.   [171] 'conscientia stimulante'.   [172] 'astruere'.
[173] 'licet non ex se'.   [174] 'asserere': historic infinitive.
[175] 'Quae tamen isti nos de se loqui penitus denegabant, si vitam eorum moresque cognitos haberemus, haec videlicet ore suo et labiis propriis asserere procurantes, ut laudandae vitae ac morum esse per omnia viderentur.' The punctuation in Perels's edition suggests that he thinks 'procurantes' governs 'asserere' rather than the clause that follows it after his comma, but if he is right the sentence lacks a main verb.
[176] 'Hlothario . . . cuncta pro voto consenserit'.
[177] 'caritati vestrae': less probably: 'your charity'.

your neighbours in their grief, since we too feel no small grief on their account and are shaken by frequent sighs for their sake.[178] And truly we should weep for them, since – while they were originally the head among their peers[179] – by teaching untruth they have become the tail, namely by causing the Church of the Lord to plunge into such heavy seas and to be put to so many troubles. Therefore let us weep for them, and, clearly, for the Church of God, which has undergone such trials through their doing. For thus it is read that Saul was mourned by the prophet Samuel.[180] And indeed the Lord, foreseeing that Jerusalem would be utterly overthrown above all through the fault of the priests, is described by the evangelist as having wept.[181] We, however, who are members,[182] do not want to hold on to the memory of injuries done to us or contemplate repaying them with revenge, as they perhaps believe we do. But because they have especially provoked to anger our Head[183] by casting out an innocent woman and allowing in a harlot, we mourn and weep for them, to such an extent[184] that, in the written account of the aforesaid actions, their intervention[185] alone may be noted, so that we leave out the rest. In[186] this same account we find the writer saying openly that:[187] 'Theutgaud and Gunther, who examined and judged the case of Theutberga'; and again, King Lothar saying openly of them that: 'In whatever I have done in this case, I have taken counsel from these most holy bishops.' Indeed, furthermore, while the assembled bishops – in the midst of the aforesaid foul acts,[188] among the innumerable detestable things which they presumed to put together from here and there to legitimate the position of that evil harlot – confirmed the same acts – and indeed through them, the crime – by adding their signatures, there came the turn of a certain brother and fellow bishop of ours, who subscribed to the effect that the acts were to be held to be valid[189] only until we had considered them.[190] Seeing this, those men, Theutgaud that is and Gunther,

---

[178] 'crebris urguemur pro eis gemitibus'. The sentence beginning with 'Quamvis' appears to lack a main verb, but can be taken as an appendage to the previous one.

[179] 'suos'.

[180] 'per prophetam Samuhel Saulem legitur deplorasse': one would expect 'deploratum esse' to correspond to the clear sense of 1 Reg. 15:35: did Nicholas think it was Saul who did the mourning?

[181] Luke 19:41–4.   [182] Members of Christ's body, presumably.

[183] Presumably meaning: Christ.   [184] 'Adeo'.   [185] 'interlocutio'.

[186] Note that I divide the sentences in this passage and punctuate them differently from Perels, who may have slightly misunderstood the sense here – a Homeric nod.

[187] Perels, *MGH* edn, p. 347, note 5, suggests that the passages in quotation marks that follow are taken from the lost acts of the Synod of Metz.

[188] 'in iamdictis fetidis gestis'.   [189] 'subscripsit eadem esse gesta servanda'.

[190] 'tantum usque ad nostram deliberationem'.

natched a knife and erased everything which the wise bishop had identified as to be kept for our consideration,[191] leaving only the name of the bishop, and audaciously writing out the rest just as they wanted. The same bishop informed us of this, and it is absolutely evident in the physical manuscript of the acts that this was done:[192] for one can easily see which part of the document has not been tampered with.[193] Indeed, to legitimate[194] the crime they sharpened heart and tongue and pen to such an extent that everything that they had once laid down to confirm it,[195] orally or in writing, they would try with all their power to defend even in our presence, until they fell. In truth, to what purpose should we dwell on details and attempt to [**p. 348 '-rentia narrare conamur**] recount those acts[196] of theirs that brought peremptory condemnation down on their heads,[197] when it is impossible for the tongue to state or even the memory to retain these things But, since you, brothers,[198] are writing to us out of kindness in a zealous attempt to implore mercy for these men, and asking for them to receive the consolation of having their previous status restored, it is not inappropriate that we also attend to granting that which is licit, and reasonably requested. In the end, if the aforesaid men, Theutgaud that is and Gunther, should behave patiently, and if the wrongdoing which in the eager pursuit of favour for themselves they have allowed to happen,[199] be destroyed at the root, and if they should try hard to obliterate it, with complete internal humility[200] and with appropriately grief-stricken penance, but to such an extent too[201] that the peace that they have disturbed be returned to the Church of Christ; then, assuredly, they would[202] for the sake of God alone, and through the affection that you, brothers, bear for them, be deemed worthy to have with our consent and the help of our power the other benefits of the ecclesiastical ministration – however, the futile hope of the honour of their former ministry or any

---

[191] 'omne quod antistes providus ad deliberationem nostram servandam esse descripserat'.
[192] 'id ita gestum esse in ipsis authenticis gestis luce clarius patet'.
[193] 'ubi sanum est, evidentissime claret': the sense would seem to be that the contrast between the part of the document which was erased and rewritten and the original writing is easy to see in the physical document.
[194] 'roborandum'.   [195] 'in eius confirmatione diffinierant'.
[196] 'gesta . . . narrare': here the sense of deeds may have shifted from 'acts' (of the synod) to the actions generally of the offending bishops, since the rest of the sentence suggests he means more than what the document recording the 'acts' contained.
[197] 'eorum gesta peremptoriam illis dampnationem inferentia'.
[198] 'fraternitas vestra'.   [199] 'malum, quod sui favoris studio perficere passi sunt'.
[200] 'perfecta in se humilitate': conceivably, given Nicholas I's penchant for reshuffling words, the 'in se' might instead go with 'abolere', so: 'to obliterate within themselves'.
[201] 'quin et'.   [202] 'egerint . . . extiterit . . . studuerint . . . potuerint'.

kind of priestly office they will indeed be able to cherish,[203] but they will never, ever, be able to resume it.

Therefore, my wise brothers, let your skilful and persistent representations to us on this matter now cease,[204] and let there finally be an end to what cannot be. For a decision of the apostolic see is conceived always with such restrained deliberation, matured with such slow patience, and afterwards pronounced with such deep solemnity,[205] that it does not need to be withdrawn, nor does it deem any alteration to be required, unless perchance it be pronounced in such a way that it could be withdrawn or should be changed[206] in accordance with the terms of a condition stated in advance. Let them therefore bear the disgrace of their deposition, since, as scripture says [Ecclus. 4:25], 'there is a shame that bringeth glory'. In the meantime let them be a 'sign and a wonder' [Isa. 20:3] to all those whom they deceived or to whom they exhibited their temerity in persisting in evil, so that the latter,[207] covered in such great confusion, might hold in their heart too what they profess with their lips, and be saved, and the former[208] might openly recognise that it was not good that they were so tricked[209] as to fall into such wrongdoing. For the evil still presses upon us, it is fostered still, it is waiting still to be unleashed, and for a time of licence. Proof of this is[210] the ascendant glory of Waldrada even after the public crime of adultery, and the casting down of Queen Theutberga, our beloved daughter, to below the status of serf girls,[211] even after oaths had been sworn. Finally, when King Lothar took back his true wife, the oft-mentioned Theutberga, in the presence of our emissary, he commanded, as you have heard, twelve illustrious counts to swear an oath in turn[212] that he would from then on keep and treat Theutberga in such a way as it befits a legitimate king to keep and treat his legitimate wife the queen. But alas! As you are perhaps not unaware, he makes her endure such contumely and such great hatred and, a terrible thing even to say, he subjects her to such indigence that, let alone helping the necessity of those suffering, even in the person of one

---

[203] 'prioris tamen ministerii vel cuiuscumque sacerdotalis officii dignitatem frustra quidem sperare poterunt'.

[204] 'Cesset itaque vestrae fraternitatis iam nos super hoc pulsare solertia'.

[205] 'deliberationis gravitate'.   [206] 'immutanda . . . existat'.

[207] 'isti': the people to whom they exhibited their temerity.

[208] 'illi': the people deceived.   [209] 'sibi subreptum fuisse'.

[210] 'probat hoc' in the singular, though there are two subjects.

[211] 'nec ancillarum qualitati coaequata deiectio'.

[212] 'sua vice repromittere'. On this use of oath-helpers see Perels, *MGH* edn, p. 348, note 5; and Nelson, *Annals*, pp. 124–5 and note 10, where she points out that 'This legal procedure is widely attested in the early medieval West.'

individual,[213] she is utterly unable to provide either for herself or for her own small entourage.[214] Waldrada on the other hand, a harlot and excommunicated, although she appears to separated – purely physically – from Lothar, in whose heart however she is shown by many signs to be always present, both holds the heights of royal authority[215] and [**p. 349 'omnimodam optinet potestatem'**] total power to harm or help whomsoever she wants. Behold, brothers, the buds, behold the fruits, which have grown up from the seed scattered by Theutgaud and Gunther. If however, brothers, you grieve about these men truly and in a productive way, and want to give them some help, you must take care, together with us,[216] to cut in to and earnestly work at curing the wound, on which those men have not only utterly failed to perform surgery with the blade of justice, but have even – with the oil of evil adulation and persuasion keeping it open[217] – caused to spread in all directions.[218] Although these same aforesaid men, as we made clear before, would not, so far as the priestly office is concerned, be able to have any hope of receiving it. For if we were to build up again that which we have destroyed in them, we will beyond doubt be turned into renegades in the Lord's eyes, and seem as if, repenting of inappropriate actions, we had changed our mind for the better.[219] And, through this, those men would not reform, being unafraid of a punishment like that; and men who have not yet externalised a sin which is in its initial stages[220] will not expect it to be punished; nor, learning from the latter what is good for them, will the other people who are in a position to relapse into this sinful activity be wise enough to let themselves be deterred from doing something which they see to be pardoned with such lax indulgence.

Therefore, brothers, come back to your senses[221] and look into your heart[222] and accept your official duty to combat vices,[223] correcting and admonishing with a more fervent zeal and with greater urgency the man

---

[213] 'aliquem penes virum'.   [214] 'propriis . . . homunculis'.   [215] 'cacumen regium'.

[216] 'nobiscum pariter': but 'pariter' could also be taken with the words that follow, in which case the translation would be: 'to at the same time (*pariter*) cut in to and earnestly work at curing'.

[217] 'fovente'. This can mean: keeping it warm, in which case the sense is that they keep the wound open with hot oil – but this would be a puzzling sense: see next note.

[218] This is rather an unfortunate metaphor, in that one might suppose that oil would be good for a wound.

[219] Probably preferable to the (possible): 'commuted the sentence to a lighter one'.

[220] A debatable interpretation of: 'qui actenus inchoatum scelus introrsus retinent': from context, it seems preferable to the alternative sense: 'who retain within the sin they have so far initiated'.

[221] 'Revertimini . . . ad vos'.   [222] 'redite at cor'.

[223] 'recognoscite contra vitia ministerium vestrum'.

through whom the Church of God has endured such a scandal, namely King Lothar, that he might do what is in his interests, that he might also act in the interests of those wretched men whom he bound by oath-taking on his behalf, and treat the queen, namely Theutberga, his wife, as the oath sworn lays down, covering himself against leaving the men swearing oaths on his behalf in the state of being (rightly) accused of a crime;[224] let him also send to us Waldrada, so that through all this[225] he may lead a safe[226] life from now on and we may no longer be put to so much trouble on her[227] account. For it is unjust for a legitimate wife to suffer such discomfort and dishonour from him and for the distinction that goes with her rank to be stolen by an adulteress. If King Lothar denies that this is happening and says that he has truly taken in and wants to carry out what we have told him to do – as our beloved son Ludwig the glorious king indicates on the basis of his assertion[228] – we ask that the question be put, by you or at your instigation,[229] to the aforesaid pious king, why, when he writes to us or convinces others that, as he states in respect of Waldrada, he has not been with her since our emissary returned, he does not in the same way state in respect of his wife Theutberga, that he treats her and keeps her according to the terms of the oaths sworn? – If not because he has nothing to boast about and has not acted towards her in such a way that he can relate it to us truthfully and to be able to receive our thanks for it, since she not only receives no generous treatment at his hands, but rather instead languishes in conditions disgraceful in all respects and in the greatest need. Therefore let him be told by the pious prince [Ludwig] or persuaded by your priestly efforts that when he sends to us to say that he is never with[230] Waldrada contrary to our prohibition, he should also send to tell us that he treats Theutberga his wife with kindness in accordance with the oaths sworn and that he maintains[231] her as her royal rank requires: provided, indeed,[232] that we may recognise that what he sends to tell us is also supported by others who back it up. Finally, when Waldrada has

---

[224] 'et se a reatu vice sua iurantium tegens'. The translation was suggested to me by Janet Nelson. Another possibility, also viable, arose from a suggestion by Jim Binns: 'and covering himself against reproach from those swearing on his behalf'. My thanks to both colleagues. My own initial translation was: 'covering himself against the incurring by his oath-helpers of guilt on his behalf'.

[225] 'per haec'.   [226] Safe from temptation, presumably.

[227] 'illius': so it might conceivably refer not to Waldrada but to 'his [Lothar's] account'.

[228] 'ex ipsius assertione': presumably, Lothar's assertion to Ludwig. Cf. Perels, *MGH* edn, p. 349, note 2, and *ibid.*, p. 335, lines 8–10.

[229] 'studio vestrae suggestionis'.   [230] 'accedere'.

[231] 'retineat'.   [232] 'ita dumtaxat'.

been driven away and the same King Lothar has taken back Theutberga as his wife, it is a settled thing that the decision was taken[233] that the same Waldrada should be sent to Italy, to await our definitive decision on whether or not she had to come to Rome. For when it comes to people [**p. 350 'quorum sedes apostolica'**] with whose business the apostolic see has begun specially to concern itself, as we started to follow the dispute between the king and queen[234] Lothar and Theutberga and Waldrada the concubine,[235] no one has the authority to transfer the case[236] or to decide anything, unless perchance someone commanded to do so by the apostolic see itself. Waldrada therefore, who is well known to have been taken away from Lothar's side at our instigation and in accordance with our commands, is also under an especial obligation to submit herself to our judgements, to make appropriate satisfaction to the Church which she has injured. As long as Lothar does not take action to this effect,[237] then, just as we will have no rest and Theutberga no security, so too no secure peace will be possible for him, nor any confidence that he will be saved.[238] Therefore, the more attentively you read that [Jas. 5:20]: 'he who causes a sinner to be converted from the error of his way shall save his soul from death and cover a multitude of sins', the more diligently you should apply yourselves to correcting him, and the more earnestly you should not only admonish him, that he ought to obey us, but also as well encourage our beloved son Ludwig the most excellent king, that he may constantly press Lothar to hear our admonitions. But hence you must not only approach your glorious king, but also plead with him especially to admonish and persuade the same Lothar not to presume to come to Rome unless he has purified himself,[239] and when we give our assent. For if he does not first, in obedience to us, take care to wash away the stain of suspicion and ill fame, he should watch out lest perchance he be driven away in the greatest confusion as lepers are from the castles of their lords.[240] We will briefly indicate, however, how he might be able to get rid of those stains: namely, if he were to treat his wife Theutberga kindly, as the sworn oaths demand and maintain[241] her as her royal rank requires, and compel Waldrada to hasten to us, and permit bishops to be ordained in the aforementioned churches following the steps[242] we laid

---

[233] 'diffinitum fuisse constat'.   [234] 'regum'.   [235] 'pellicis'.   [236] 'removere'.
[237] This could mean: 'as long as he does not make Waldrada submit', or: 'as long as he fails to make similar satisfaction': probably the former: Nicholas writes below, line 20: 'ad nos accelerare conpellat'.
[238] 'fiducia salutis'.   [239] 'nonnisi purgatus'.
[240] 'leprosorum more de castris dominicis'.   [241] 'retineat'.
[242] 'in ordine': by which he probably means: election by bishops of the dioceses, consecration, request for pallium: see Perels, *MGH* edn, p. 350, note 2, referring to Letter

down.[243] For so long as he lets Waldrada remain in this way, as is evident to all,[244] he will not be treating Theutberga either with the honour due to royalty or with conjugal love, and so long as he also allows[245] Theutgaud or Gunther to hold the churches taken away from them together with their priesthood, he will not be able to be free from the leprosy of unjust evil-doing nor from the stains of the worst kind of repute – that is, of bad reputation or suspicion – nor will he be able to walk into a church of Christ without pollution,[246] nor indeed will it be freely or safely possible for the priests of Christ to touch him or receive him within the camp.[247]

Therefore work with us in this, dearest brothers, and fight alongside us,[248] since, just as we face all kinds of labour on earth, so too a rich reward will last for ever in heaven. Nor can it be doubted that this young man has many people who are currently consenting to him because of his power or lordship,[249] and the conversion and salvation of all of these would indeed make us all rejoice together[250] if their leader, thanks to our common efforts inspired by God's grace, should more perfectly mend his ways.[251] Besides, your holy selves[252] may know[253] that his great highness your aforementioned king has written to us on behalf of Theutgaud and Gunther with the same affection as you have.[254] Since we replied to him about this in a brief note, if he wishes to have a fuller knowledge of the opinion we have crystallised with regard to them, we indicated to his conscientious self that he should examine the content of this letter which [**p. 351 'destinavimus'**] we have sent to you, brothers. For this reason may your holy selves act in such a way that with due reverence and[255] speedy diligence it may be taken to be read by his pious eyes. If however there are perhaps any persons who might be saying that Waldrada is free and therefore the necessity of coming here should not be imposed on her,

---

50, p. 334, where Nicholas urges Lothar to get the clerics of the churches of Trier and Cologne to appoint bishops and sets out the sequence of actions to be followed.

[243] Perels, *MGH* edn, p. 350, note 2, cross-refers to the fragment of a letter of Nicholas I to Lothar which he had printed as Letter 50, p. 334.

[244] 'sicut omnibus liquet': in the Latin as in the English the phrase could go either with the preceding or the following clause.

[245] 'dimiserit . . . tractaverit . . . permiserit': future perfect rather than the perfect subjunctive (the forms are the same); the future perfect is not normally translated literally into English.

[246] 'puris gressibus'.

[247] 'castra': an allusion to the exclusion of lepers from the camp in the Old Testament: cf. Lev. 13:46.

[248] 'pariter'.   [249] 'dominatu'.   [250] 'simul'.   [251] 'perfectius emendabitur'.

[252] 'sanctitas vestra' – he is not writing to a single person, so not: 'your holiness'.

[253] 'noverit': which could also be 'should know', or 'will know'.

[254] 'ea qua vos nobis affectione scripsisse'.   [255] 'seu'.

they should know that a woman is not free when, after being conquered by sin, she is also a serf girl bound to it,[256] for as Peter the apostle says [2 Pet. 2:19]: 'For by whom a man is overcome, of the same also he is the serf', and again, in another passage[257] [John 8:34]: 'whosoever commits sin is the serf of sin': namely, while she has not yet been freed from sin, assuredly one must hold her to be a servile woman and through this she needs to be purified by our special judgement – by the decree of which her iniquity began to be assailed with reproach[258] – and, if Christ allows, to receive its quietus. For if we had not known that she was not yet free from wrongdoing, we would by no means have made her come to Italy, for her own liberation and that of her supporters, even though afterwards Satan through his servants prevented her from coming.[259] Now however, if she thinks that to carry out our commands or orders makes her a serf girl, King Lothar ought consequently to be called a serf, as he is known to have done to some extent[260] what we told him to do. Therefore one should regard this woman as a lady with authority,[261] when she remains disobedient, and dominates Lothar, who to some extent tries to obey our decrees?![262] This is completely absurd and absolutely wrong. In truth, if it were the case that King Lothar wanted to deliver the adulteress Waldrada to us, for her case to be decided by us according to the law,[263] as much as he wanted to send his legitimate wife Theutberga to us to relate falsehoods against herself and crimes to which she had confessed under duress, then perhaps a little peace or rest might be restored to us. And indeed, would that he might make an effort to deliver Waldrada to us, when she has things that she could tell us about her wrongdoing, in the way in which he pressured Queen Theutberga, who did not indeed have anything to reveal about wrongdoing, but who would have a lot to say[264] about the violence and endless suffering inflicted on her, and

---

[256] 'quae a peccato superata ipsius et ancilla addicta est'.   [257] 'alibi'.   [258] 'agitari'.

[259] This seems to be an allusion to an attempt made a couple of years earlier to get Waldrada to Rome. Perels, *MGH* edn, p. 351, note 2, cross-refers to *ibid.*, p. 336, note 6, to the phrase 'nisi Waldrada Romam, sicute coeptum fuerat' [dirigatur]. The note indicates that the papal legate Arsenius was behind an abortive attempt in 865.

[260] 'utcumque'.

[261] 'domina' – 'mistress' is the obvious translation but it would be a confusing translation in context: Nicholas I does think she is Lothar's mistress but that is not the point he is making here.

[262] This is a (slightly confusing) *reductio ad absurdum*: the idea that Waldrada cannot be summoned to Rome because she is free would entail that the king is a serf, because he is under her thumb and because he obeys the pope to some extent.

[263] 'legitime'.   [264] Taking 'multipliciter' with 'enarraret'.

whom he sent [to us][265] contrary to our will and compelled in a variety of ways falsely to accuse herself before us of wrongdoing. We wish you very well, brothers, in Christ, now and always.

Given on 31 October, first indiction.

(pp. 342–51)

---

[265] Following Perels, *MGH* edn, p. 351, who rightly notes in his apparatus, at 'invitis', '*suppleas:* nobis'.

2   Robert II of France and Bertha

Robert II was the second of the Capetian kings of France, whose dynasty stretched from the tenth to the fourteenth century. At this formative point the king did not actually control more than a fraction of France, though he had a lot of ritual prestige. In 992 he repudiated his much older wife Rozala (also called Susanna) and shortly afterwards married Bertha, who was closely related to him by blood and through 'spiritual relationship' (he was godfather to one of her sons). Contrary to what historians thought until recently, this was genuinely shocking to contemporaries. Aside from the repudiation, the couple had transgressed against the contemporary incest taboo much more gravely than was realised before the recent study by Karl Ubl.[1] The case started a chain reaction. A relatively reform-minded pope, Gregory V, had the union condemned (# 997), and another conciliar condemnation (# 998–9) impressed itself on the mind of a man who would soon afterwards become Emperor Henry II, and who used an anti-incest campaign as a way to mark his new exalted identity. Henry worked with the influential canonist Burchard of Worms and the outcome was a vastly extended range of forbidden degrees. Meanwhile Robert II held out for a long time against the condemnations, but eventually backed down, perhaps because Bertha had not given him a son.

The first of the documents translated is a short report in a letter by Gregory V to Archbishop Willigis of Mainz on the decisions of the Council of Pavia. It is the fuller of two versions – neither of which gives the council's decisions verbatim – and was chosen for the recent edition in the *Monumenta Germaniae Historica* series, where there is a scholarly discussion of the synod.[2]

---

[1] Karl Ubl, *Inzestverbot und Gesetzgebung: die Konstruktion eines Verbrechens (300–1100)* (Millennium-Studien XX; Berlin, 2008).

[2] For this analysis, see *MGH Concilia*, vol. VI: *Die Konzilien Deutschlands und Reichsitaliens 916–1001*, ed. Ernst-Dieter Hehl, 2, 962–1001 (with Carlo Servatius) (Hannover, 2007), pp. 534–9. (The edition of the letter to Willigis follows.)

The second document shows the 998–9 Council of Rome endorsing this decision and also excommunicating the archbishop who had married the couple and the bishops who had been present at and consented to the ceremony.

Historiographical highlights

The critical edition of both documents in the *MGH* includes a useful apparatus of footnotes on the individuals involved and scholarly bibliography on the Robert–Bertha affair.[3] Perhaps the best-known discussions of the case are in Georges Duby's *Medieval Marriage: Two Models from Twelfth-Century France*, trans. Elborg Forster (Baltimore, MD, 1978), pp. 45–53; and *The Knight, the Lady and the Priest: The Making of Modern Marriage in Medieval France* (Harmondsworth, 1983, 1984), ch. IV, 'Robert the Pious'. These attempt an explanation in terms of political manoeuvring: Robert bigamously married Bertha to get control of Tours and the county of Blois. There is no doubt some truth in this, though Duby's confidence in his own intuitions may make some readers feel uneasy. The straightforward account from the sources in Charles Edward Smith, *Papal Enforcement of Some Medieval Marriage Laws* (Baton Rouge, LA, 1940, reissued Port Washington, NY, 1972), pp. 77–83, is still a useful corrective to Duby. The most important recent treatment, because it traces the domino effect following from the condemnation of Robert, is that of Karl Ubl, *Inzestverbot und Gesetzgebung: die Konstruktion eines Verbrechens (300–1100)* (Millennium-Studien XX; Berlin, 2008), ch. 7.

The translation

The passages are translated from the critical editions in the recent *Monumenta Germaniae Historica* volume: see below.

997

Letter of Gregory V concerning the Synod of Pavia

2. It is also decreed that King Robert, who married his relative contrary to a papal prohibition, should be summoned to do penance,[4] together

---

[3] *Ibid.*, p. 540, note 27 and p. 574, notes 32–7.   [4] 'ad satisfactionem'.

with the bishops who consented to this incestuous marriage. But should they refuse let them be deprived of communion.

(*MGH Concilia*, vol. VI: *Die Konzilien Deutschlands und Reichsitaliens 916–1001*, ed. Ernst-Dieter Hehl, Part 2: *962–1001* (with Carlo Servatius) (Hannover, 2007), no. 55, p. 540)

998–9

Synod of Rome

I. It is judged that King Robert should leave his relative Bertha, whom he married contrary to the laws, and do seven years of penance according to the ecclesiastical scale laid down.[5] If he does not do this, let him be an anathema. The same is commanded to be done with respect to Bertha.

II. We suspend from sacred communion Erchembald, archbishop of Tours, who consecrated such a marriage, together with all the bishops who were present and consenting at this incestuous wedding of the king and Bertha his relative, until they come to this apostolic see to do penance.

(*MGH Concilia*, vol. VI: *Die Konzilien Deutschlands und Reichsitaliens 916–1001*, ed. Ernst-Dieter Hehl, Part 2: *962–1001* (with Carlo Servatius) (Hannover, 2007), no. 59, p. 574)

---

[5] 'secundum praefixos ecclesiasticos gradus'.

3   Philip I of France and Bertrada

About a century after the scandal of Robert II's relationship, another French king repudiated his wife and married a woman whom he should not have touched, at least according to high-minded churchmen. The king was Philip I, the woman Bertrada. His own political position was not much stronger than his ancestor's, but the world had changed around the dynasty. The Gregorian reform had been convulsing Church–State relations for decades. The Normans had ruled England for a generation. A commercial revolution was beginning. Within the timespan of the scandal, the First Crusade was launched and reached Jerusalem. Philip I's marital problems, however, fitted a structural pattern transcending periods.

In 1092 Philip I repudiated his wife Bertha. A helpful synod annulled the marriage on grounds of relationship within the forbidden degrees, but it was hard to legitimise his affair with and marriage to the wife of the Count of Anjou, one of his greatest vassals and in some ways politically stronger than he was. The count had been through a couple of marriages, but his union with Bertrada was probably valid in contemporary canon law and anyway she was related to Philip through the count himself (who was a blood relative of Philip's), by 'affinity', and so off limits for marriage. Thus the death of Philip's first wife did not remove the problem. A sequence of censures, pseudo-submissions and recidivism followed. At the same council where the First Crusade was launched (Clermont, 1095) the excommunication was renewed. It dragged on for years. In 1104 Philip did public penance, as described in the document translated. If he continued his relationship with Bertrada after that, he was discreet about it. His son by his first marriage may have become afraid of losing out to Philip's children with Bertrada, and may have pushed the king into a more serious conversion. The ritual certainly sent a strong public signal about indissolubility.

Historiographical highlights

The case is treated at length, though perhaps more eloquently than rigorously, by Georges Duby, in *Medieval Marriage*, pp. 29–45, and in *The Knight, the Lady and the Priest*, ch. 1. He makes dramatic claims for the case as a turning point, arguably over-interpreting his data. Smith, *Enforcement*, pp. 85–98, is a more clear-headed account in my view. There is a detailed analysis of the canon law issues in Christopher Rolker, *Canon Law and the Letters of Ivo of Chartres* (Cambridge, 2010), 230–46.

The translation

The document translated is a letter from Lambert of Arras to the pope, describing Philip's public penance.[1]

1104, December 2

Lambert of Arras to Paschal II: Philip I of France has separated himself from Bertrada

To the most reverend and lord father of fathers Paschal the pope, Lambert, by the grace of God bishop of Arras, due subjection with prayers. At Paris, by your authority the archbishop, Lord Daimbert of Sens, Rodolphus of Tours, and also the bishops Ivo of Chartres [a list of other bishops follows], convened and had recited the letters sent by your see for the penitential satisfaction[2] and absolution of the king. When the letters had been read and understood, they sent to the king bishops John of Orleans and Gualo of Paris, to find out if the king would do penance[3] as laid down in the letter, and had determined to abjure the sin of carnal and illicit union. He replied in a friendly way and said that he was more than willing to perform penitential satisfaction for God and the holy Roman Church, and to accept the command of the apostolic see and also the counsel of the archbishops and bishops present. Therefore in the presence of the aforesaid bishops, and also of the abbots [list follows], and also of very many archdeacons, and honourable clerics and laypeople standing around, the king arrived in a devout enough manner, and with great humility, his feet bare, renouncing sin, and putting right the cause of the excommunication,[4] and thus he deserved to receive absolution by

---

[1] The date given in the Bouquet–Delisle edition is 2 December 1104, but see their p. 198, note (a), for a discussion of dating problems.
[2] penitential satisfaction: 'satisfactione'.   [3] 'satisfaceret'.
[4] 'putting right the cause of the excommunication': 'excommunicationem emendans'.

your authority. When these things had been done, he swore on the holy gospels to give up the sexual union and scandalous crime of an illicit partnership, in these words:

May you hear, O Lambert bishop of Arras, who represents the pope in this place, and may the archbishops and bishops present hear, that I Philip King of the French, will no longer commit the sin and the habit of carnal and illicit union which I have practised hitherto with Bertrada: but I abjure this sin and scandalous crime altogether and without any reservation. Also, I will not converse or keep company with the same woman unless people who are above suspicion are present.[5] All these things, as stated in the pope's letter and understood by yourselves,[6] I will observe without any bad faith. So help me God, and these most holy Gospels of Jesus Christ.

Similarly, too, Bertrada, when she was released from the bond of excommunication, swore this same oath on the holy gospels in her own person.

May the Holy Trinity, our God, keep your Holiness safe for a very long time, as you work and pray for the Catholic Church; and since you, with the holy Roman Church, have stood with us 'in judgement and justice',[7] may you receive your reward at the resurrection of the just. Given at Paris . . .

> (Epistolae Lamberti Atrebatensis Episcopi, XLVII. *LAMBERTI AD PASCHALEM II Papam*, in Martin Bouquet and Leopold Delisle, *Recueil des historiens des Gaules et de la France*, vol. XV (Paris, 1878), pp. 197–8)

---

[5] 'nisi sub testimonio personarum minime suspectarum'.

[6] 'sicut literae Papae dicunt, et vos intelligitis'.

[7] 'in judicio et justitiam' (*sic*): this apparently ungrammatical phrase is from the 'Liber Comitis' – 'book containing passages to be read at Mass' (*Oxford Dictionary of the Christian Church*, s.v. *Comes*) printed in J. P. Migne's *Patrologia Latina*: '*usque* in judicio et justitiam dicit Dominus omnipotens' (*PL*, vol. XXX, col. 498).

4   Eleanor of Aquitaine and Louis VII of France

Philip I's son by his marriage duly succeeded, unthreatened by children of Bertrada, and in his reign royal authority began to matter more in French politics. His son succeeded in turn as Louis VII, and hugely augmented his lands by marrying Eleanor of Aquitaine in 1137. By the customary law of the time she had inherited it in the absence of brothers. He was enamoured of her but she may have been, or became, less committed to him. She went on the Second Crusade with him but there were tensions between them, publicly noted. Louis and Eleanor were within the forbidden degrees and there was talk of an annulment. On the way back from the crusade, however, when they stopped at the papal court, Eugenius III made emotional and temporarily successful efforts to reconcile them, giving them what sounds like some kind of dispensation, both verbally and in writing (**# 1149**). It has not survived and appears to have had no impact on the annulment of their marriage by a council of French prelates at Beaugency in 1152. In consequence Louis lost all of Aquitaine to Eleanor's new husband, Henry II of England. This suggests that the problem between them was more personal than political. It is true that Eleanor had not yet given him a son, but they had not been married so long, and both had male offspring later. Without the tension between them, Louis might well have settled for hanging on to Aquitaine and trying a little longer for an heir.

Historiographical highlights

Eleanor of Aquitaine is one of the select band of historical figures who attract popular historians like magnets. Such historians perform a service by popularising the field but cannot be expected to grasp the technicalities of medieval marriage law. An example of the perils of popularisation is the completely misleading account of the annulment in Alison Weir, *Eleanor of Aquitaine: By the Wrath of God, Queen of England* (London, 2000), pp. 90–1. Some professional scholars are more cautious, skirting adroitly round the difficult problems: D. D. R. Owen, *Eleanor of*

Aquitaine, Queen and Legend (Oxford, 1993, 1996), p. 31; Jean Flori, *Aliénor d'Aquitaine: la reine insoumise* (Paris, 2004), pp. 79–80; Ralph V. Turner, *Eleanor of Aquitaine, Queen of France, Queen of England* (New Haven, CT, 2009), pp. 97, 104–7. That they are difficult should not be in doubt: they seem to have left confused the important Munich medievalist Eduard Hlawitschka, in his 'Weshalb war die Auflösung der Ehe Friedreich Barbarossas und Adelas von Vohburg möglich?', *Deutsches Archiv für die Erforschung des Mittelalters* 61 (2005), pp. 509–536, at p. 519. Hlawitschka is discussing another royal annulment, that of Frederick Barbarossa's marriage. He infers that the papal curia must have been counting the degrees in the Roman law way. (To explain: by the Roman law reckoning one counted up to the common ancestor and down again, so that a first cousin would be related in the fourth degree – rather than just counting up to the common ancestor, so that a first cousin would be related in the second degree, on both sides.) If not, according to Hlawitschka, the pope would never have tried to get Eleanor of Aquitaine and Louis VII to stay together. This is a very surprising claim for two reasons. Firstly, it is more or less common ground among historians of medieval marriage that by this date the Church no longer counted degrees the Roman law way. Secondly, popes had been experimenting with quasi-dispensations for marriages within the forbidden degrees for some time before this.[1] Two scholarly treatments of the annulment stand out. The most recent is Constance Brittain Bouchard, 'Eleanor's Divorce from Louis VII: The Uses of Consanguinity', in Bonnie Wheeler and John Carmi Parsons (eds.), *Eleanor of Aquitaine, Lord and Lady* (New York, 2002), pp. 223–35. Best of all, however, is the relevant endnote in John W. Baldwin, *Masters, Princes and Merchants: The Social Views of Peter the Chanter and his Circle*, 2 vols. (Princeton, NJ, 1970), vol. II, note 182 to ch. XVI, pp. 225–6 – a wonderful note that brings past scholarship to bear and disentangles the issues.

The translation

The source extract is from John of Salisbury's *Historia Pontificalis*, apparently firsthand evidence for the history of the papal court during his time there.

---

[1] Ubl, *Inzestverbot und Gesetzgebung*, pp. 467–8. Cf. James Brundage, 'The Canon Law of Divorce in the Mid-Twelfth Century: Louis c. Eleanor of Aquitaine', in Bonnie Wheeler and John Carmi Parsons (eds.), *Eleanor of Aquitaine, Lord and Lady* (New York, 2002), pp. 213–21, at p. 217.

1149

Eugenius III's informal 'dispensation' for Louis VII of France and Eleanor of Aquitaine

The cardinals and curial officials[2] met the king there [at Ceprano], and, making available everything he wanted, led him to the lord pope at Tusculum. The king was received by the pope with such courtesy and enthusiasm that it was as if he were receiving no ordinary mortal but an angel of the Lord. After hearing separately the complaints of the king and queen [i.e. about each other], he altogether laid to rest the quarrel which had begun at Antioch, forbidding any further mention of consanguinity between them; and, confirming the marriage both verbally and in writing, he commanded under pain of anathema that nobody attacking it should be heard, and it should in no circumstances[3] be dissolved. This decision[4] seemed to please the king a great deal, because he loved the queen ardently and in an almost childish way. The pope made them lie in the same bed, and he himself provided bedclothes of the most precious kind to adorn it.[5] And every day of their short stay he did his best to restore their love[6] with friendly conversation. He paid them honour with presents and finally, when taking his leave of them, even though he was a rather stern man, he was unable to contain his tears; and sending them away he blessed them and the kingdom of the Franks.

(John of Salisbury, *Historia Pontificalis*, ed. and trans. M. Chibnall (London, 1956), section xxix, pp. 61–2)[7]

---

[2] 'ministri ecclesie': this might also just mean 'clergy'.   [3] 'quacunque . . . occasione'.
[4] 'constitutio'.   [5] 'quem de suo preciosissimis uestibus fecerat exornari'.
[6] 'caritatem'.
[7] I have retranslated the passage for copyright reasons, but this is no criticism of Chibnall's version, memories of which have probably influenced my own translation.

5　King John of England and Isabella of Gloucester

The future King John of England and his first wife Isabella of Gloucester were related in the third degree of consanguinity on each side.[1] Even twelfth-century canonists disposed to allow marriages within degrees closer than the seven forbidden by formal law were not prepared to go so far as that.[2] When the couple were betrothed, there appears to have been uncertainty whether it would be allowed. 'Should the pope prevent the marriage on grounds of the couple's close affinity, the king [Henry II] pledged to arrange the best marriage possible for Isabella' (so Isabella's biographer).[3]

The source extracts are from three near-contemporary chronicle sources that give contradictory accounts of the annulment of King John's first marriage to Isabella of Gloucester, prior to the marriage to another Isabelle, of Angoulême, which provided a pretext for the French king's confiscation of most of John's continental domains, including Normandy. They had got married in 1189 and the marriage was annulled in 1199. Ralph of Diceto claims that the papal court was annoyed at the dissolution of a union made with its authority, while Ralph of Coggeshall tells exactly the opposite story: the annulment was on the pope's orders. Neither is right. The marriage was within the forbidden degrees, and John was pressed by the archbishop of Canterbury to get it validated by a dispensation, but he prevaricated and thus had a free canon law pass out of the marriage when it suited him.

The extracts translated are from Ralph of Diceto, Ralph of Coggeshall and Roger of Howden. The first two are both misleading. The evidence that shows this is a remark in the document translated below (**# 1202**)

---

[1] Cf. Robert B. Patterson, 'Isabella, *suo jure* countess of Gloucester', in *Oxford Dictionary of National Biography*, vol. XXIX (Oxford, 2004), pp. 416–17, at p. 417: 'Through her father she was first cousin once removed of Henry II.'

[2] Hubert Kroppmann, *Ehedispensübung und Stauferkampf unter Innozenz IV.: Ein Beitrag zur Geschichte des päpstlichen Ehedispensrechtes* (Abhandlungen zur Mittleren und Neueren Geschichte LXXIX; Berlin, 1937), pp. 8, 9 and 11, note 3.

[3] Patterson, 'Isabella', p. 416.

to illustrate the effort of Philip Augustus of France to get his marriage to Ingeborg of Denmark annulled – he complains that other kings have been treated more leniently and Innocent III replies à propos of John and Isabella of Gloucester that the papal court had never been involved.

Historiographical highlights

The truth about John's marriage to Isabella of Gloucester emerged *en passant* from a twentieth-century controversy about the events leading up to the loss of Normandy by King John in 1204. To get at the decisive evidence on the annulment one must read through the following papers: H. G. Richardson, 'The Marriage and Coronation of Isabelle of Angoulême', *English Historical Review* 61 (1946), pp. 289–314; Fred A. Cazel Jnr and Sidney Painter, 'The Marriage of Isabelle of Angoulême', *English Historical Review* 63 (1948), pp. 83–9; H. G. Richardson, 'King John and Isabelle of Angoulême', *English Historical Review* 65 (1950), pp. 360–71; Cazel and Painter, 'The Marriage of Isabelle of Angoulême', *English Historical Review* 67 (1952), pp. 233–5. Richardson was a British career civil servant who published much more serious research than most professors. Painter and Cazel were Americans, the former the leading specialist of his day on King John. Many scholars today will find the marriage issue more interesting than the hotly disputed details at the centre of the controversy. The debate is only worth summarising because the papers just listed are excruciatingly unfriendly to a rapid reader, who might be grateful for a little help.

The loss of Normandy and other continental territories hitherto held by the English crown was certainly a major turning point in medieval history, but the minutiae of the tensions preceding the war matter less. Such a war had been on the cards for a long time. Philip Augustus of France had great wealth at his disposal and clearly wanted to use his power to expand French territory. The standard view is that the war was triggered by King John's marriage to Isabelle of Angoulême when she had promised to marry one of Philip's vassal's, Hugh of Lusignan the Elder, who appealed to the French king as his overlord, providing a pretext for war. Richardson attacked this story. He argued that the quarrel between John and Hugh was not over Isabelle but about something else entirely ('a wrong done to Ralf of Lusignan': Richardson, 'The Marriage and Coronation', p. 299). To demonstrate this he argued for a different chronology of events, and his rearrangement depends on evidence that by very early in 1200 John was engaged to Isabelle of Angoulême with the agreement of her former fiancé, so without irritating either the Lusignan clan or the French king. To prove they were engaged Richardson makes much of the words *uxor sua desponsata* (*ibid.*, 300–3). His critics, on the other hand, say that the phrase was a legal formula, one which did not necessarily refer to a man betrothed and not yet married. It did not have to be a reference to an actual fiancé. In my view they were right and Richardson wrong, for all the huffing and puffing which was his typical modus operandi.

All of this is without direct relevance to our problem: the annulment of his marriage to Isabella of Gloucester. What is relevant is the comment in Cazel and Painter, 'The Marriage of Isabelle of Angoulême' (1948), p. 89, that Richardson's 'argument that John never received a dispensation for his marriage to Isabella of Gloucester and that as a result the marriage was always "voidable" is completely convincing'. Richardson, 'The Marriage and Coronation', pp. 291–4, had discredited the remark by Diceto implying that the marriage to Isabella of Gloucester had received a dispensation (cf. also Richardson, 'King John and Isabelle', p. 361), and by Coggeshall that the pope was outraged at the annulment. His evidence is the letter of Innocent III which is also a key document for the marriage trials of Philip II Augustus of France (below, **# 1202**). Richardson is also probably right in thinking that there were two judgements in favour of annulment. This would reconcile Ralph of Diceto's list of Norman bishops passing judgement, which may be a factual element in his inaccurate account, and Roger of Howden's list (the archbishop of Bordeaux, William of Poitiers and Henry of Saintes). Richardson, 'King John and Isabelle', also puts forward arguments for dating: 'it would be unsafe to put John's release from his putative marriage later than 1199' (p. 362). I wonder, though, whether this has to apply to the second judgement: Roger of Howden puts a dissolution in 1200. Again, Richardson thinks that two sets of judges delegate were required to reach this outcome but that, after the second one reached a decision, Isabella of Gloucester 'did not appeal to the apostolic see'. Again, while agreeing that she did not try to take the case to Rome on a final appeal, I am not sure that Richardson can prove the existence of two sets of papal judges delegate. The bishops mentioned by Ralph of Diceto could be an episcopal council. Perhaps Isabella of Gloucester appealed against this first judgement, lost again before papal judges delegate, the bishops mentioned by Roger of Howden, and then refrained from taking the case to the papal curia, where the judges delegate phase was forgotten.

However it may be with these details, the salient fact would seem to be that John never got around to obtaining a dispensation for his relationship to Isabella of Gloucester, with the possibly intended consequence that it was easy to have the marriage annulled. Thus Richardson's obstinate defence of a trivial and untenable thesis about feudal manoeuvring before the loss of Normandy left as a side effect an analysis of John's annulment which still holds the field.

Nicholas Vincent, 'Isabella of Angoulême: John's Jezebel', in S. D. Church, *King John: New Interpretations* (Woodbridge, 1999), pp. 165–219, is, as its title suggests, mainly about John's second marriage, but note p. 175: 'in 1200 King John appears to have gone out of his way to obtain letters from the bishops of Bordeaux, Saintes, Périgueux, Limoges, Angoulême and Waterford, testifying to the legitimate nature of his marriage to Isabella', and the corresponding note 30: 'For the episcopal letters, testifying *quod omnia in matrimonio canonice contrahendo processerunt*, see *Rot. Norm.*, 36'. This indirectly supports Richardson's case for thinking that the annulment was by the book.

The translations

The translations are from editions in the Rolls Series.

1199/1200

Ralph of Diceto, on the year 1199

John King of England, immediately after his coronation,[4] visiting St Thomas and afterwards St Edmund, spent Pentecost at Northampton. Afterwards, gathering a multitude of knights and foot soldiers and ships at Shoreham,[5] he crossed the sea on 19 June. The dissolution of the marriage of King John of England and the daughter of the Count of Gloucester, was officialised[6] in Normandy by the bishops of Lisieux, Bayeux, Avranches, and other bishops who participated.[7] He had married her in his father's day with the Roman Church's permission, acquiring the counties of Gloucester, Somerset, Devonshire and Cornwall, and very many other fiefs[8] throughout England. But he, carried away by the hope of a more illustrious marriage, drove her away, counselled by evil men, and so incurred the great indignation of the pope, that is, of Innocent III, and of the whole Roman curia, for he had audaciously presumed to dissolve, contrary to the laws[9] and canons, that which had been joined together by their authority.

> (*Radulphi de Diceto Decani Lundoniensis Opera Historica*, ed. William Stubbs, vol. II (Rolls Series 68) (London, 1876), pp. 166–7)

[4] 'sub ipso coronationis suae initio'.   [5] 'Sorham'.   [6] 'Celebratum est divortium'.
[7] 'interfuerunt'.   [8] 'honoribus'.   [9] 'leges'.

Ralph of Coggeshall

Therefore after paying the King of France those 30,000 marks, and with all his enemies subdued and pacified, he returns to England around the Feast of St Michael, together with his wife, the daughter that is of the Count of Angoulême, whom he had married on the other side of the Channel by the counsel of King Philip; for he had sent away[10] his first wife, that is the daughter of the Count of Gloucester, on the order of the lord pope, because of the relationship of consanguinity.

(*Radulphi de Coggeshall Chronicon Anglicanum*, ed. J. Stevenson (Rolls Series 66) (London, 1875), p. 103)

Roger of Howden

In the same year [1200] the marriage of John King of England and Hawis [= Isabella] his wife, daughter of William, Count of Gloucester, was dissolved[11] by Elias archbishop of Bordeaux and William of Poitiers and Henry of Saintes: for they were related in the third degree of affinity.

(*Chronica Magistri Roberi de Houedene*, ed. William Stubbs (Rolls Series, 51 IV; London, 1871), p. 119)

[10] 'dimiserat'.   [11] 'Facto . . . divortio'.

6 Philip II Augustus of France and Ingeborg of Denmark

Philip Augustus was on the way to becoming Europe's most powerful king when he made a political marriage with Ingeborg of Denmark. After their wedding night (1193) he wanted to walk away from it all with the kind of annulment that other kings had been granted in the twelfth century. He was not to have such an easy time of it. The case that resulted is perhaps the most closely studied royal marriage conflict between Lothar II and Henry VIII.

The procedure that usually worked so well was followed. A genealogy was worked out to show that he and Ingeborg were within the forbidden degrees, and a council of French bishops judged the marriage to be null (1194). Then things got difficult.

Ingeborg appealed and the genealogy was shown to be unfit for purpose. In 1195 Celestine III told the archbishop of Reims to prevent Philip from remarrying, but Philip nonetheless married Agnes of Meran in 1196. When Celestine died Philip found himself dealing with a firm believer in the indissolubility of marriage, Innocent III. Innocent would later change marriage law to close the loophole which had proved so useful to kings and nobles in the eleventh and twelfth centuries (even if Philip Augustus himself did not manage to exploit it). In the meantime Innocent's energetic efforts led to a Council at Soissons (1201) under a papal legate, but Philip muddied the waters and ended the council by apparently taking Ingeborg back, though she was soon in prison again. Innocent went out of his way to help by legitimising Philip's children by Agnes of Meran, but the letter to Philip translated here (**# 1202**) shows that the pope was disinclined to cut any corners when it came to judging the marriage itself. Innocent III actually alluded to the Lothar–Theutberga–Waldrada case as a precedent, and in his way he was as tough as Nicholas I had been, but his tone and whole modus operandi were strikingly different. Where Nicholas poured out passionate rhetoric, Innocent writes with sovereign calm, explaining rather patronisingly that it is in Philip's own interests to follow all the procedures that canon law and Innocent prescribe for him. The stand-off continued for years, but in 1213 Philip backed down publicly, probably because he wanted full papal support against England.

The letter translated is interesting for earlier royal marriage cases as well as for Philip's, since Innocent rebuts claims that earlier kings had been given an easier time of it.

Historiographical highlights

Arguably,[1] the best analysis is in R. H. Tenbrock, 'Eherecht und Ehepolitik bei Innocenz III.' (doctoral dissertation for the University of Münster, Dortmund-Hörde [1933?]). He comments thus on the variable tempo of Innocent's handling of the case:

> He may well have slackened his pace on this steep and rough road, to keep an eye out for paths leading off the main route, which would not lead him away from his goal, but which permitted him to gain many an advantage for the Church. Admittedly, that often meant backing off in the face of difficulties, and an anxiety about abandoning certain external successes, the successes of the politician, of the man who is 'orientated towards' this world. But it was precisely in this way that he managed 'to translate his idea of the papacy into a genuine reality, and to raise the papacy to the highest possible point'. (p. 99, my translation)

The language is flowery but the assessment is justified. Tenbrock is no doubt reacting against the emphasis of the nineteenth-century historian Davidsohn's assessment of the cause célèbre: 'When the duty of the supreme pastor would have called for quick action, the interest of political predominance required clever delaying tactics' (R. Davidsohn, *Philipp II. Augustus von Frankreich und Ingeborg* (Stuttgart, 1888), p. 75). Davidsohn's mistake was his failure to distinguish between the 'value rational' and 'instrumentally rational' elements in Innocent's thinking: indissolubility of marriage was an absolute value, whereas 'timing, tone, and sanctions were the objects of instrumental calculation' (d'Avray, *Medieval Marriage*, p. 103, note 97). More recent scholars too seem to have failed to understand the relation between conviction and instrumental calculation in Innocent's decision-making. Duby, *Medieval Marriage*, p. 78, suggested that 'the most important consideration for Rome was the increase in power that might accrue to it from the ascension to the French throne of a bastard legitimized by the pope'. The legitimation of bastards was a pragmatic matter, not a question of principle like indissolubility. As I commented elsewhere:

---

[1] In the following paragraphs I borrow freely from my own earlier historiographical survey in *Medieval Marriage. Symbolism and Society* (Oxford, 2005), pp. 103–4, notes 96–8.

This is an instance of Duby's tendency to over-explain. The desire to please Philip at that critical time is a sufficient explanation. Anyway, it was not as if legitimation could be withdrawn, so it would not have given a future pope much of a hold over a future king who might not inherit anyway (and did not: in the event, Philip's son by a previous marriage to a wife who had died succeeded him as Louis VIII). Again, what of the power that would have accrued to Rome from the marriage of the king to a mistress turned into a queen by the pope's decision?[2]

As so often in the latter part of his career, Duby was on thin ice. But far more reckless are the speculations of M. B. Bruguière, 'Le mariage de Philippe-Auguste et d'Isambour de Danemark: aspects canoniques et politiques', in Université des Sciences Sociales de Toulouse, *Mélanges offerts à Jean Dauvillier* (Toulouse, 1979), pp. 135–56. (Cf. also her 'Canon Law and Royal Weddings, Theory and Practice: The French Example, 987–1215', in S. Chodorow (ed.), *Proceedings of the Eighth International Congress of Medieval Canon Law* (Monumenta Iuris Canonici, Series C, Subsidia IX) (Vatican City, 1992), pp. 473–96; my thanks to Alexandra Sanmark for bringing both papers to my attention.) Bruguière believes that Innocent III knew that Philip II and Ingeborg really were related within the forbidden degrees, chose to keep quiet about it, but could not go so far as to endanger the succession to the throne of France, so legitimated Philip's children by Agnes of Meran.

This is an implausible hypothesis. Firstly, it ignores the simple explanation, which is that Innocent III believed that a ruler (not just the pope) had the power to legitimise bastards, while even the pope could not dissolve a valid marriage. Secondly, it depends on Bruguière's bizarre theory that the papal court must have been able to work out that Philip II and Ingeborg really were related within the forbidden degrees. She devotes much learning to showing that they were. The demonstration is marred by what looks like a misunderstanding of the nature of affinity (relation by marriage) in the 'second and third genus'. *Nisi fallor*, she seems to take this to mean that one could not marry anyone whose family was already related to one's wife's family by marriage, or whose family was related by marriage to a family related to one's wife's family through marriage. Extraordinarily large though the circle of forbidden degrees may have been, it was not as large as that. The key point about affinity is that it only arose when a sexual relationship with a relative of someone with whom one had already had sex was in question. (Cf. Bruguière's own footnote 13, 'Le mariage', p. 152; admittedly the technicalities of the

---

[2] *Ibid.*, p. 103, note 96.

impediment of affinity in the second and third *genera*, abolished by the Fourth Lateran Council in 1215, could put anyone in difficulty.) Where royal marriages are concerned, this means in practice that it was only created when a widow or widower remarried. However, Bruguière does herself seem to have shown that they shared common ancestors within the outer reaches of the forbidden degrees. If correct, this is a considerable feat of genealogical research on her part, and the criticisms levelled against the rest of her argument should not distract from this major positive contribution, but the more one admires it the less it seems likely that the papal curia could have easily done the same on its own, as if they had some great database of the noble families of Europe (in this case including Russia) to tap into in Rome. It was precisely to provide the opportunity to establish the genealogy that Innocent III patiently laid out a plan to hear witnesses in France and in Denmark. All that is set out in the letter translated below.

The knock-down argument against Bruguière's view that any fool could have discovered the forbidden degree relationships between Ingeborg and Philip II is that the king and all his advisers failed to do so. She ties herself in knots trying to explain this away by suggesting that they were not really trying. Almost equally implausible is her hypothesis (p. 147) that Innocent III was more worried about offending the King of Denmark, a relatively minor kingdom at that time, than the superpower of France. For a more balanced view of these events from a Danish perspective, see Frederik Pedersen, 'The Danes and the Marriage Break-up of Philip II of France', in Paul Brand, Kevin Costello and W. N. Osborough (eds.), *Adventures of the Law*, Proceedings of the Sixteenth British Legal History Conference, Dublin, 2003 (Dublin, 2005), pp. 54–69. The few lines of John Baldwin's *Masters, Princes and Merchants*, vol. I, p. 335 and vol. II, p. 225 are, as usual, spot on.[3]

The translation

The letter is translated in its entirety from the critical edition by O. Hageneder with C. Egger, K. Rudolf and A. Sommerlechner, *Die Register Innocenz' III* (Österreichische Akademie der Wissenschaften – historisches Institut beim Österreichischen Kulturinstitut in Rom) (Vienna, 1993).

---

[3] I have also benefitted from reading an article submitted to me by a journal for assessment, and unpublished at the time this book goes to press, entitled: 'Neither "Bewitched" nor Beguiled: Philip Augustus's Alleged Impotence and Innocent III's Response'.

1202, *c.* June 1–5

Innocent III to Philip II Augustus of France

The sharp point of sadness has penetrated into the depths of our mind and unexpected grief has poured into our heart, since your royal serenity is complaining, as we have heard, about us, concerning something for which we deserved and expected thanks from him. For our beloved sons Master Fulk, dean of Orleans, and William, treasurer of St Frambaldus, your messengers, have in an audience made a complaint to us on behalf of your Royal Highness, asserting with great firmness, as they were – so we believe – commanded to do – that in the marriage case we treated you more severely than other princes in a similar situation have customarily been treated. For in times past your father Louis of famous memory,[4] and Frederick,[5] the late emperor, and recently our most dear son in Christ John the illustrious King of the English,[6] before the prelates based in their own lands, pursued the matter in dispute[7] against the women who were their wives in appearance within the limits of due process,[8] and were separated from them by ecclesiastical judgement: and this the apostolic see did not in any way retract afterwards. Besides, if you look at the facts, though the aforesaid emperor was separated from the woman who was called his wife within the kingdom of Germany, this was nevertheless done by legates of the apostolic see;[9] we too took care to send our legates into your kingdom,[10] so that they might take cognisance of the marriage

---

[4] Hageneder edn, p. 94, note 5: 'Louis VII, King of France 1137–1180. His marriage contracted in 1137 with Eleanor, heiress of Aquitaine was dissolved on grounds of forbidden degrees of kinship in 1152 at a Synod in Beaugency.' Here and below the translation of notes in the edition by Hageneder *et al.* is my own.

[5] *Ibid.*, p. 94, note 6: 'Emperor Frederick I, 1152–1190. His first marriage with Adela, the daughter of the Margrave Diepold of Vohburg, was broken up on grounds of forbidden degrees of kinship in 1153.'

[6] *Ibid.*, p. 94, note 7: 'See Letter V 19 (20) note 1. King John of England had the English bishops declare the nullity of his marriage with Isabella of Gloucester – for which no dispensation had been obtained despite kinship in the third degree' (with further references).

[7] 'questionem . . . intenderunt'.

[8] 'servato iuris ordine'. Innocent III's emphasis on the phrase is significant and its recurrence is noted below.

[9] 'imperator predictus ab ea, que coniunx dicebatur ipsius, licet in regno Teutonico, fuit tamen per legatos sedis apostolice separatus'. Hageneder edn, p. 94, note 8, comments that: 'The dissolution of the marriage of Frederick I took place in the Choir of Konstanz cathedral before the papal legates in the presence of the bishop of Konstanz.'

[10] Innocent III's point is that Frederick Barbarossa's case and that of Philip Augustus had not been handled differently: in both cases, jurisdiction had been delegated by the pope to legates who could pass judgement in the respective countries.

case and bring it to a conclusion in accordance with due process.[11] But although the aforesaid Louis, your late father, and the present King of England too, were separated from the women whom they had united to themselves by the judgement of the prelates of their land, yet no complaint about the divorce was brought to the apostolic see; and so it did not wish to revoke what had been done by the same prelates, since no-one made any complaint whatsoever about it.[12] But I would that your Royal Serenity would understand more fully yourself, or that those who are your counsellors and members of your household and who are expert in both civil and canon law[13] would teach your Royal Serenity better, whether the apostolic see is able to ignore the cries for justice of the oppressed and of women, especially women[14] who need to be protected and supported in their just cause all the more in that they are of weaker condition. Since however our predecessor Pope Celestine of good memory judged that that sentence of divorce should be revoked, as having been pronounced[15] contrary to order, we wanted to accommodate you through our legates,[16] whom we sent to the kingdom of the French,[17] lest too much worry cause distress to the royal heart, if your case were to remain for very long in suspense; they would perhaps today have brought the matter to a close in accordance with your desires after the truth had been discovered, had you not refused to accept their judgement. For the withdrawal from judgement was on your side, after our most dear daughter in Christ I[ngeborg], the illustrious Queen of the French, had withdrawn her appeal.[18] We know, however, and in this we also

---

[11] 'servato iuris ordine'.

[12] Innocent III is implicitly replying to the question: 'Why couldn't you leave this to the French bishops to decide, as with Louis VII and King John of England?' with the answer: 'Because in those cases there was no appeal to the pope.' (In the case of Philip Augustus the queen had appealed to Rome.) The (possible) involvement of papal judges delegate in John's case could have slipped off the pope's radar.

[13] 'utroque sunt iure periti': a significant allusion to the now professionalised legal class.

[14] 'quae'. One could also (perhaps a little less plausibly) translate the passage as: 'especially those women who': making the women in a weaker condition a subset of women generally.

[15] Hageneder edn, p. 94, note 10: '1193 at Compiègne. See Letter V 48 (49) note 3.'

[16] 'per legatos...expedire'.   [17] 'Francorum'.

[18] Hageneder edn, p. 95, note 12: 'The Legates Octavian (Cardinal-)Bishop of Ostia and Velletri, and John of St Paul, Cardinal Priest of S. Prisca, had in April/May 1201, at an assembly in Soissons, started the legal proceedings afresh. In these Ingeborg had at the beginning probably agreed to an appeal made by the Danish ambassadors to the pope, but had asked again to be heard in the trial, probably trusting the impartiality of Cardinal John, who only arrived in the course of the proceedings, to which the two legates also agreed. At this point King Philip caused astonishment by leaving Soissons

feel compassion for your Serenity, that this complaint does not indeed proceed from reason but from sensuality, since you call equity severity and find justice hard to take, as if it were violence. Beside, the apostolic see could, had it not shown consideration for your honour, not only have cancelled the aforesaid verdict which had been passed without due process,[19] but also imposed canonical retribution on the man who passed it,[20] as it is read that our predecessor Pope Nicholas of good memory did with Gunther archbishop of Cologne and Theutgaud archbishop of Trier in a case that was very much like this one: he both revoked the sentence they had passed and deposed those archbishops from their pastoral office; indeed he even pronounced a sentence of excommunication against King Lothar and his mistress,[21] because the same king, on the pretext of the sentence passed by the same archbishops, after leaving Theutberga, whom he had joined to himself legitimately, kept Waldrada, whom he had taken as a mistress, as his wife.

We, however, wishing to show respect to your Royal Serenity so far as we could without offending God, have taken no legal measures[22] against the man who passed sentence, since he is a blood relative of yours,[23] nor have we thought fit to pass any sentence against the person of your mistress[24] or your own person, but have only, after frequent warnings, put the land under interdict.[25] Therefore since we judged that you should be treated not according to the full force of the law but rather in accordance with equity,[26] we believed that we had deserved, rather than diminished,[27] the devotion of your Serenity, nor did we think you had been harmed if we pursued justice justly, but rather helped. Now however we would like you at least to accept wiser counsel and wait patiently for a short time and allow us to get you and ourselves through the difficulties[28] of this business which is of such great moment, so far as

---

and taking Ingeborg with him. See in addition King Philip's letter to Innocent III [references follow].'

[19] 'iuris ordine non servato'.

[20] Hageneder edn, p. 95, note 13: 'Archbishop Guillaume de Reims'.

[21] 'superinductam'.   [22] 'nec...processimus'.

[23] Hageneder edn, p. 96, note 18: 'Archbishop Guillaume de Reims was the king's uncle, the brother of Adèle de Champagne, the wife of King Louis VII.'

[24] *Ibid.*, p. 96, note 19: 'Agnes, a daughter of Berthold IV, count of Andechs and Duke of Meran, whom the king had married in 1196. She died in 1201.'

[25] *Ibid.*, p. 96, note 20 (with a further reference): 'On 13 Jan. 1200'.

[26] 'iuris...equitatem': for further thoughts on the 'law/equity' distinction in medieval religious thought, see David d'Avray, *Medieval Religious Rationalities: A Weberian Analysis* (Cambridge, 2010), pp. 116–17.

[27] 'non demereri sed promereri'.   [28] 'tam te quam nos...expediremus'.

is consistent with the heavy responsibility[29] of the pastoral office. For we believe that we are no less inconvenienced than you by this matter, since it is burdensome for us to be burdensome to your Royal Highness, and to depart from the royal road[30] is not safe, lest we incur the displeasure of the heavenly king on account of an earthly king.

We will however explain to you in this letter the offer we have thought fit to make to your messengers, for the sake of the honour of your Royal Serenity, lest perchance it be twisted by an inaccurate interpretation. For the offer we made to them, subject to your Majesty's approval, was to send two honest, sensible and faithful men to your presence, to hear the case about the impediment of affinity or consanguinity[31] or the other things that might be proposed and take care to depose your witnesses[32] – not outside the kingdom of the French but even at Étampes,[33] where the aforesaid queen is staying, whether she should wish to contest the case[34] in their presence, or be unwilling to answer it, and so contumacious.[35] Then, assuming that the queen was not contumacious, but rather, contesting the case, asked for her witnesses to be received, since this is something we would be unable to deny her legally,[36] as your Royal Prudence knows, the same men would hasten at our expense – lest our dearest son in Christ, Canute, illustrious King of the Danes, her brother,[37] were he to be summoned by them, should excuse himself as he has so far on account of the difficulty of coming at that time, the storms at sea, and the dangers of the journey[38] – to receive the witnesses that he might introduce and to receive and hear any arguments[39] he might think fit to propose. If it were your good pleasure that some honest, prudent and faithful man from your kingdom should be joined to them for the examination of this matter,[40] they should, also together with[41] some such man from the kingdom of Denmark, take the witness statements[42] on the side of the queen; and, returning immediately in haste to France, if the will of the queen could

---

[29] 'gravitate'.   [30] An allusion to Num. 21:22, 'we will walk along the royal road'.

[31] Hageneder edn, p. 96, note 22 gives a cross-reference to Letter 48 (49) note 8.

[32] On witnesses in the Romano-canonical legal procedure that Innocent III is invoking, see Brundage, *Medieval Origins of the Legal Profession*, pp. 435–9.

[33] Hageneder edn, p. 96, note 21: 'Étampes (Dep. Essonne), where Queen Ingeborg of France had been brought after the day at Soissons'.

[34] 'litem . . . contestari':   and   in   the   following   sentence: 'contest   the   case': 'lite . . . contestata': a technical term for the formal opening of the trial. See Brundage, *Medieval Origins of the Legal Profession*, pp. 433–4.

[35] 'ut contumax'.   [36] 'de iure'.

[37] Hageneder edn, p. 96, note 23: 'Knut VI., King of Denmark 1182–1202, Ingeborg's brother'.

[38] 'viarum discrimina'.   [39] 'recepturi et audituri rationes'.   [40] 'facti'.

[41] 'ipsi quoque cum'.   [42] 'testes reciperent'.

be persuaded without compulsion, they should publish the depositions of the witnesses; and after the matter had been examined they would not delay to pass sentence without possibility of appeal.[43] Otherwise they should make sure to take the case back with them to our presence, set out in adequate form,[44] since in our presence the same queen would not be able through her proctor to allege either that the place gave reason for suspicion or that an advocate was lacking or any other objection as a subterfuge, nor to appeal.[45] And if you should even so prefer to reveal the sentence in your kingdom, we could send it after it has been decided in secret[46] with the counsel of our brothers to be solemnly published in your kingdom; nor would we allow the decision in this matter to be deferred, but indeed we would take care to get it done with the utmost expedition so far as this lay in our power.

We have been inclined to favour you to the point that when our messengers arrive in your presence, some men of judgement from your kingdom would have been selected to bring this case to a conclusion with the consent of the parties as justice determines, if this were done in accordance with the free will of the same queen. But you should know that it was prudently decided that without the free consent of the same queen we did not wish to entrust this case to persons only from your kingdom, or for the sentence to be decided[47] by the same in your kingdom, for two reasons: both on account of justice, which cannot allow that the judge or the place should be suspect to one of the parties, especially to the defence;[48] and as a precaution,[49] lest such a sentence might be able to be revoked because of a valid suspicion, in order to avoid in this way both scandal reflecting on ourselves and a loss to yourself. But although the same messengers of yours did not form the view that what we offered them should be accepted, nevertheless, if, as we believe, it seems to your Serenity[50] that it is the best thing for you to do, we will do it when we are asked by letter and messengers from you, since we

---

[43] Innocent III's use of the subjunctive indicates that he does not think Ingeborg is especially likely to give her free agreement to this.

[44] 'sufficienter instructam'.

[45] Innocent III knows that Philip would prefer to keep the whole case within his kingdom, where he could exercise pressure, and is giving reasons why it is actually in Philip's interest for the final stage of the case to take place at the papal court. In essence, his argument is that if justice is seen to be done then the case will come to an end, whereas otherwise the queen would be able to reopen it.

[46] 'occulte formatam'.   [47] 'formari'.

[48] Hageneder edn, p. 97, note 24, 'Letter V. 48 (49) note 4 and Decretum Gratiani C. 33.q.2.c.4 (Friedberg, *Corpus Iuris Canonici*, I... [col.] 1151'. The decretal cited actually deals with the Lothar–Theutberga case.

[49] 'cautelam'.

[50] 'Serenitati tue... visum fuerit [future perfect rather than perfect subjunctive] expedire'.

would not like to deny you anything that we are able to concede without loss of our integrity. And so that you may fully understand how determined we are to do what is best for you,[51] in our presence, with your messengers watching, we received a corporal oath[52] from those who are to be sent by us to carry out this business that they would without delay proceed to dispatch it in good faith to the best of their ability.

We admonish your Royal Serenity and exhort you earnestly that you hold firmly before your mind[53] the affection and paternal love that we bear you, giving careful thought to the fact that no other way in which this business could be more quickly dispatched occurs to us at present. For it often happens, that excessive haste creates excessive delay, and as you have already learned this by experience once in matrimonial litigation, be careful not to experience it again. For if due process[54] had been observed in this case[55] from the beginning, it is possible that today no shred of doubt[56] would be left. May you therefore pay careful attention to what may be allowed, what may help,[57] and for what may be fitting; have a care for the salvation of your soul and do what pleases the will of God! In addition to these things we most earnestly warn and urge your Royal Highness to ensure that the aforesaid queen is treated honourably, as befits you and her, since, even if she had not been joined[58] to you, but had found her way to the kingdom of the French out of some necessity, it would have been right and proper to show her honour. And this you should do above all to prevent the progress of your case from being impeded in any way.

(O. Hageneder with C. Egger, K. Rudolf and A. Sommerlechner, *Die Register Innocenz' III*, vol. V, 5. *Pontifikatsjahr, 1212/1203 Texte* (Österreichische Akademie der Wissenschaften – historisches Institut beim Österreichischen Kulturinstitut in Rom) (Vienna, 1993), 49 (50) [Potthast Reg. 1713], pp. 93–7)

For other important letters of Innocent III bearing on this case, in this great and as yet uncompleted edition, see vol. I: *1. Pontifikatsjahr 1198/99* (Graz, 1964), Letter 4, pp. 9–12, Letter 171, pp. 243–6, Letter 347, p. 518, Letter 348, pp. 519–20; vol. VI: *6. Pontifikatsjahr, 1203/1204* (Vienna, 1995), Letter 85, pp. 132–4, Letter 86, pp. 134–7, Letter 180 (182), pp. 299–301; vol. VIII: *8. Pontifikatsjahr, 1205/1206* (Vienna, 2001), Letter 114 (113), pp. 200–2; vol. X: *10. Pontifikatsjahr,*

---

[51] 'intelligas nostre propositum voluntatis, per quod te cupimus expedire'.
[52] Cf. *Oxford English Dictionary Online*, 'Corporal', 5a: 'an oath ratified by corporally touching a sacred object'.
[53] 'intendas'.   [54] 'ordo . . . iudiciarius'.   [55] 'in ea', standing for 'causa'.
[56] 'nullius dubitationis scrupulus'.   [57] 'quid expediat'.   [58] 'copulata'.

1207/1208 (Vienna, 2007), Letter 42, pp. 66–7, Letter 176, pp. 292–3; vol. XI: *11. Pontifikatsjahr, 1208/1209* (Vienna, 2010), Letter 82 (86), pp. 117–18, Letter 176 (181), pp. 285–6, Letter 177 (182), pp. 286–93 (very rich). (The editorial teams are not identical from volume to volume.)

7   Pere II of Aragon and Maria of Montpellier

Pere II became King of Aragon and Count of Catalonia in 1196, and he married Maria of Montpellier in 1204. They did not stay together long, though their union did produce the eventual successor, the future Jaume II. These documents reveal a world in which royal and noble men and women moved easily from one more or less legitimate partner to another. That made it difficult to untangle who was really married to whom. Pere II wanted to marry Marie of Montferrat (heiress of Jerusalem) and to get his marriage to Maria annulled, and he seemed to be on strong ground in arguing that when they had got married she already had a husband, so could not get married again. Maria could, however, reply that the husband in question had two wives alive at the time she married him. Thus her marriage to him was invalid and she had been free to marry Pere II. Working out which marriages actually were valid and so capable of invalidating subsequent marriages was a complex business. Nevertheless, Pere II might have thought he had every prospect of success. The preceding century was full of encouraging precedents, and he had been an ally of the current pope, Innocent III. In 1204 Pere II had been crowned by Innocent himself; in 1212, when the annulment process was already going on, he and the King of Castile won a decisive battle against the Moslem Moors at Las Navas de Tolosa. Though Pere would end up fighting with the Count of Toulouse, who was suspected of being soft on heretics, against the Albigensian Crusade, that was a very late turn of events – too late to explain the outcome of this marriage case. For the outcome was surprising, at least to anyone who had not reflected on the marital trials of Philip Augustus. Maria of Montpellier appealed to the pope, who examined the dossier and found in her favour. The age of easy annulments was over.

Historiographical highlights

J. Vincke, 'Der Eheprozeß Peters II. von Aragon (1206–1213), mit Veröffentlichung der Prozeßakten', in H. Finke *et al.*, *Gesammelte Aufsätze*

zur Kulturgeschichte Spaniens: Spanische Forschungen der Görresgesellschaft,
series 1, vol. V (Münster in Westfalen, 1935), pp. 108–89, is funda-
mental. There is an excellent analysis of the case and the whole context by Martin Aurell in his *Les noces du comte: mariage et pouvoir en
Catalogne (785–1213)* (Paris, 1995), pp. 427–58. Also useful is Damian
J. Smith, *Innocent III and the Crown of Aragon: The Limits of Papal Authority* (Aldershot, 2004), pp. 70–4, 107–10, 127–30.

The translations

The translations are from documents edited by J. Vincke (see above).

1210, February 16

'*1210, February 16, Rome: Innocent III commissions his legates
(Bishop Hugh of Riez and Abbot Arnold of Citeaux) and the
Bishop Raymond of Usez, to investigate and decide the annulment
plea [Scheidungsklage] of Peter II.*'[1]

Innocent, bishop, servant of the servants of God, to his venerable brothers
the bishop of Riez, legate of the apostolic see, and[2] the bishop of Usez,
and his beloved son[3] the abbot of Citeaux, legate of the apostolic see,
greetings and apostolic blessing. In a courteous communication[4] sent to
us, our most dearly beloved son in Christ the illustrious King Peter of
Aragon has shown that, when he had contracted[5] a *de facto* marriage with
our beloved daughter in Christ the noblewoman Maria, daughter of the
late William of Montpellier, it finally came out[6] that he had previously
had sexual intercourse with a certain woman related to the same noble
lady [i.e. Maria] by a close line of consanguinity. Also indeed that the
same Maria has a living husband, with whom she had contracted marriage
previously, namely the noble man the Count[7] of Comminges.[8] On this
account the same king, as a Catholic and God-fearing man, who has
a guilty[9] conscience concerning this and who fears that his soul is in
imminent danger because of it, decided that he should have recourse
without delay to the oracle of the apostolic see.

---

[1] When, as here, the summary of the document is in italics and in quotation marks, it is a
translation of Vincke's German summary; otherwise, it is a paraphrase of Vincke.
[2] Preceded by double dot.   [3] Preceded by double dot.   [4] 'insinuatione'.
[5] 'cum . . . copulasset'.   [6] 'apparuerit'.   [7] Preceded by double dot.
[8] 'Convenarum'.   [9] 'cauteriatam'.

Consequently we command your sagacious selves[10] by apostolic writings that, if the plaintiff[11] appears to be of such a sort that his plea[12] may be admitted in law, you should convoke the parties and hear the case and bring it to a canonical conclusion, if the parties consent, with no appeal.[13] Otherwise you should make written records of all that has been done,[14] with a covering letter from you as authentication,[15] and faithfully dispatch them to us, fixing in advance for the parties in the case a suitable date by which they should present themselves before us through suitable proctors,[16] to receive just judgement that God will inspire.[17] If you are not all able to take part in carrying these things out, let two of you carry them out nonetheless. Given at the Lateran, 16 February, twelfth year of our pontificate.

(Vincke, 'Der Eheprozeß', document no. 2, p. 167)

1211, May 21

'King Pere II informs the papal judges delegate that he has appointed Bernard Amell as his proctor in the current marriage suit.'

Reverend fathers and friends the most dear[18] Raymond by the grace of God bishop of Uzès, legate of the apostolic see, and Hugues de Riez, bishop, Pere, by the same [grace of God][19] King of Aragon, Count of Barcelona, greetings and love. We make known to you, fathers,[20] that in the matrimonial case which is at issue between us and the Lady Maria of Montpellier, we make our beloved and faithful man Bernard Amell our proctor, treating as ratified and confirmed[21] whatever he does for us legally[22] in the same case, whether by acting or replying and accepting the sentence. Given at Perpignan, 21 May 1211.

(Vincke, 'Eheprozeß', document no. 3, p. 167)

---

[10] 'discrecioni vestre'.   [11] 'accusator'.   [12] 'accusatio'.

[13] 'sublato appellationis obstaculo': this seems to imply that the parties would be asked in advance if they were prepared to accept the delegates as judges and waive any right to appeal, rather than taking the case on to the pope himself.

[14] 'gesta omnia conscribentes'. One could also translate as 'should record the acts of the trial'.

[15] 'sub testimonio litterarum vestrarum'.

[16] 'per procuratores idoneos nostro se conspectui representent'.   [17] 'auctore deo'.

[18] 'karissimis', which could also be taken with 'amicis'.   [19] 'eadem'.

[20] 'vestre . . . paternitati'.   [21] 'firmum'.   [22] 'de iure'.

1211, May 25 and 26

'Narbonne, 25 and 26 May 1211: the Litis contestatio, the establishment of the articles to be proved, the setting of the latest date for proofs [Beweisfrist].'

AD 1211, 25 May, the Lord Peter the King of the Aragonese brought suit[23] before the lords R. of Uzès legate of the apostolic see and Hugues of Riez,[24] bishops, judges delegated by the lord pope, against the marriage between himself and the Lady Maria of Montpellier, asserting that it had been contracted between them *de facto*, not *de iure*, since, before he contracted the marriage with her, she had contracted marriage 'in the eyes of the Church'[25] with the Count of Comminges, who is still alive. He appointed as proctor, to conduct the suit[26] or the entire case, Bernard Amell, promising that he would ratify whatever might be done with or through him in the aforesaid case. The Lady Maria admitted[27] that she did once contract marriage 'in the eyes of the Church' with the Count of Comminges. But she said it had been contracted *de facto* not *de iure*, because there was a blood relationship between her and the said count, and because he had had a blood relative of hers as a wife, and, besides her, he had two [wives] alive. Again, she admitted that the Count of Comminges, with whom she had contracted marriage, was still alive. On the same day, and before the aforesaid Lord Hugues bishop of Riez and B. de Bloye,[28] a judge delegated by the Lord R. of Uzès in this case to conduct the hearing,[29] again the Lady Maria admitted that the marriage, if it had been such, between the Count of Comminges and the daughter of Arnaud Uillelmi de Barta[30] had been dissolved[31] by a judgement of the Church, but immediately and in the same place she said that it could be so, but that she has her doubts, and she said that the said count keeps the same woman, which the king admits to be true. After objections[32] had been put forward on the part of the Lady Maria, namely that the Count of Comminges was her blood relative, and had had a blood relative of hers as his wife, and that at the time when he contracted marriage with her the said Count of Comminges had two wives, the reply was given by the king's side that the court ought not to accept these objections, and that the king's side was not bound to reply to them. Finally, 'without

---

[23] 'accusavit'.   [24] 'Regensi'.   [25] 'in facie ecclesie'.   [26] 'accusationem'.
[27] 'Confessa est'.   [28] 'Blaudiaco'.   [29] 'ad audiendum': this particular hearing only?
[30] 'Arnaldi Uillelmi de Barta'.   [31] 'separatum'.
[32] 'exceptionibus': a technical term in the *Ius Commune*, but close in meaning to 'objection' in common law systems.

prejudice' to the king's side, that is, saving his option to oppose it as before,[33] it was the court's pleasure that the king should reply. And with respect to the aforesaid three objections he replied that he did not believe so.

On the following day Bernard Amell, the proctor of Lord Peter King of the Aragonese, with the same king present and expressly consenting, said that he would prove that a marriage had been contracted previously between the aforesaid Lady Maria and the Count of Comminges, and that the marriage, if such it was, between the Count of Comminges and the daughter of Arnaud Uillelmi de Barta had been dissolved[34] by a judgement of the Church. Again he says that he would prove that there had been a blood relationship between the lord king and the daughter of the Count Bigore who was the wife of the Count of Comminges. And he requested a delay[35] to prove these things. The Lady Maria said that she would prove that the Count of Comminges is her blood relative, and that he had had a wife who was a blood relative of hers, that is of the Lady Maria, and that, at the time at which he got married to her, the said Count of Comminges had two wives. Finally, at the wish of both parties, since the Lady Maria similarly asked for a delay, a delay was granted to both parties and a day assigned, namely the next Feast of St Andrew, and Narbonne as the place, namely in such a way that each party promised that they would never again ask for a delay for the purpose of proving some fact or proposing anything else in the whole of that case, renouncing explicitly and of their certain knowledge[36] all right[37] to ask for a delay that pertains or will pertain to them. To the Lady Maria however a delay was granted for proving the aforesaid things, namely in such a way that she should make the same proof without prejudice to the party of the lord king, that is, with the reservation that his party might still, just as from the beginning, be able to oppose this proof legally,[38] because it had not been admissible.[39] The aforesaid proofs can however be given and should be received in this case in the meantime[40] up to the deadline fixed in advance at the discretion of the aforesaid judges delegate or those

---

[33] 'eo salvo quod adhuc liceret idem opponere sicut antea'.   [34] 'separatum'.

[35] 'dilationem' – also a semi-technical term, which one might also translate as 'adjournment'.

[36] 'ex certa scientia' – a technical term, though here it would seem only to mean that their promise is not formulaic and could not be taken back.

[37] 'iuri'.   [38] 'opponere de iure'.

[39] 'quod non fuerat admittenda' – the gender of 'admittenda' suggests it has to go with 'probationi'. We should take this clause to mean that the king's side claimed that the evidence was not admissible, rather than that the court necessarily accepted the claim.

[40] 'in hoc medio'.

delegated by them. These things were done at Narbonne in the town[41] in the monastery of St Mary.

(Vincke, 'Der Eheprozeß', document no. 4, pp. 167–9)

1212, March 10

'Maria von Montpellier nominates the knight Raimund Aerra as her proctor in the marriage case.'

In the name of our Lord Jesus Christ. In the year of the incarnation of the same Jesus 1211, 10 March, I, Maria, by the grace of God Queen of the Aragonese and Lady Ruler[42] of Montpellier, being prevented by many adversities, lest I seem to be negligent, make and constitute as proctor you Raymond Arra,[43] knight, in the matrimonial case which is at issue between the lord King of the Aragonese, and his proctors, and me; promising that I will ratify and confirm[44] whatever is done in that aforenamed case with him, together with my said proctor,[45] and lest any doubt be able to arise concerning these things, I corroborate this deed[46] with my seal. All these things were done at Montpellier in the house of Anania,[47] in the presence and with the testimony of the witnesses invited, namely [names follow]. And of Bertrand Arcolen, public notary of Montpellier, who wrote these things at my request.

(Vincke, 'Der Eheprozeß', document no. 16, pp. 182–3)

1212, March–April

'. . . the Abbot of Feuillans deposes the witness statements which were to be made concerning the marriage of the Count of Comminges and Beatrice of Lomagne.'

To his venerable lords and brothers Raymond [as above], A. abbot of Feuillans sends greetings, obedience, reverence and honour. We received the witnesses produced before us by Master P. de Auarsonio, with prudent and discreet men sitting with us as assessors,[48] and we transmit to you, enclosed[49] under our seal, their statements, having attended to the matter with all the diligence at our command. Concerning the witnesses your discreet self should know, that we know of nothing in them or in

---

[41] 'burgo'.   [42] 'domina'.   [43] 'Aerradum'.   [44] 'me habere ratum et firmum'.
[45] 'cum eo . . . cum dicto procuratore': i.e. between Pere and her proctor.
[46] 'cartulam'.   [47] 'Ananie'.   [48] 'assidentibus nobis'.   [49] 'inclusa'.

any one of them[50] on account of which they could be disqualified from giving testimony. You should know furthermore that, as we have heard from the mouths of many, a whole series of witnesses[51] concerning the marriage of the Count of Comminges and Beatrice of Lomagne would have been available had fear of the same count not prevented it.

Raymond Arnaud de Blannaco said under oath as his testimony that he had seen the lord Count of Comminges have the Lady Beatrice the daughter of Odo of Lomagne – who is now called the wife[52] of Pere of Mota – as his wife.[53] And she had the lord Count of Comminges as husband and called him so. And the same count called and had and treated her in his territory with honour, as his wife.[54] And it is his belief, and common knowledge[55] throughout the land, that he married her. And he says this because this is what he saw and heard and is true. Asked about the time, [he said] that it was fifteen years ago and more. And this the same man saw before the lord count married the Lady Maria, and his wife, the daughter of Guillaume of Montpellier. [Other witness statements follow.]

(Vincke, 'Der Eheprozeß', document no. 22, p. 187)

---

[50] 'eorum aliquo'.   [51] 'plures testes'.
[52] 'dicta uxor': in this context probably not 'the said wife'.
[53] 'tenere per uxorem'.   [54] 'honorifice ut uxorem'.   [55] 'fides sua et publica fama'.

The son of Pere II and Marie, Jaume I continued the Spanish tradition of successive polygamy in the midst of a highly successful military and political career, about which he wrote engagingly in an autobiography. He was a man who fell in love often and ardently, not a mere cynical seducer. Jaume was born in 1207, and succeeded to the throne after his father's death at Muret in 1213. In 1219 – so still very young – he married Lyonor, the daughter of the King of Castile. They were related within the forbidden degrees even as redrawn to a much narrower circle at the Fourth Lateran Council of 1215. It was only in the succeeding pontificate that dispensations became common. There is a phrase that might seem to allude to an earlier dispensation in the document translated below: 'notwithstanding letters contrary to this deed obtained from the apostolic see'. Despite this, it is likely that there had been no such dispensation: the phrase is in fact standard form in papal letters. Rather surprisingly, popes often did not know what relevant past letters they might already have sent, so this phrase or others like it were included routinely to make sure that a current document was not subverted by an earlier one.

Thus Jaume was able to obtain an annulment on solid grounds (**# 1229**). His next wife, Violant, died in 1251. He then seems to have married the much younger Teresa Gil de Vidaure, informally but probably validly, so that he was unable to obtain an annulment of this marriage. This was much later: the pope undiplomatically indicated that at his age he ought to know better (**# 1266**).

Historiographical highlights

Robert I. Burns, 'The Spiritual Life of Jaume the Conqueror of Arago-Catalonia, 1208–1276: Portrait and Self-Portrait', *Catholic Historical Review* 62 (1976), pp. 1–35, gives a lively account of Jaume's relations with women and is relevant also to **# 1266** below (rejection of his attempt to divorce Teresa Gil de Vidaure). Burns evokes Jaume's rollercoaster sentimental life:

Soon estranged from his first wife, Elionor, the daughter of Alfonso VIII of Castile, who had given him a fine son, he divorced her after eight years on the valid but dispensable grounds of consanguinity. Before that deed, he was already deeply involved with one public mistress, the Countess Aurembiaix, and perhaps with the Castilian Lady Elo Álvarez. His second wife, Violant, the daughter of King Andrew of Hungary, gave him nine children; Jaume produced three more from formal mistresses and had besides a fourth woman (Blanca d'Antilló, Berenguera Fernández, Guillema de Cabrera, and one whose name has been lost). [Burns goes on to other relationships to which we will return.] (p. 26)

Burns can say much more than is usually possible about his subject's personal attitudes because Jaume wrote his own chatty autobiography. Burns comments thus on Jaume's relationship to Lyonor:

His references to the first wife during their shared wanderings are tender. Seeing her terrified by hostile captors and 'weeping very loudly', he said, 'I comforted her.' Later he suggested a remedy for the 'harm and shame we are bearing': an elaborate escape through a trapdoor, down to a subterranean passage far below. 'I shall get two ropes, and sit you on a board, and will lower you down from here' to be spirited away by a knight, while James himself effected an escape by a more complicated route. At the end of this long exposition James, the dutiful husband, records her brief reply which ended the scheme: 'Know you, that for nothing in the world will I be lowered down from here on a board with ropes.'

But this teenage marriage, recalled long after, left little mark on his narrative. (pp. 29–30)

Burns thinks that 'his first marriage – at a tender age, by imposition and to guarantee an heir – incorporated strong elements of instability', and suggests that he treated women better than his father, whom Jaume himself criticises as a womaniser (p. 28). Relevant according to Burns is the distinctively Spanish institution of *barragania*: formal concubinage. In accordance with its rules Jaume 'entered into . . . formal and semipermanent written contracts with each successive mistress, providing for her future and for any children resulting. Thus Jaume was never voracious, indiscriminate, or uncommitted like his father' (p. 28).

The translation

The extract is translated from the edition in the École Française de Rome calendar of the register of Gregory IX (details after translation).

1229

To the bishop of Sabina, legate of the apostolic see.

6 February 1229 . . . Since the general council, after revoking the ban on marriage to relatives in the three last degrees, wished it to be observed strictly in the other degrees, and since one should not defer to man, against God, we command you, brother, by apostolic writings, that you should proceed in accordance with the decrees of the aforesaid council to the loosing of the contract of illicit union, which took place after the same council, and concerning which already some time ago our predecessor of happy memory Pope Honorius, sent his letter, between N.[1] the King and[2] the Queen of Aragon, concerning which our predecessor Honorius of happy memory some time ago wrote to you[3] notwithstanding letters contrary to this deed obtained from the apostolic see; however you should take care to ensure that the king makes every effort to make a decent provision for her support, since otherwise it may be feared that a grave scandal will arise from their separation.

> (Lucien Auvray, *Les registres de Grègoire IX: recueil des bulles de ce pape publiées ou analysées d'après les manuscrits . . . du Vatican* (Bibliothèque des Écoles Françaises d'Athènes et de Rome; Paris, 1896), vol. I, no. 267, cols. 159–60, Reg. 14, fol. 98v, ann. II, c. 83)

---

[1] Preceded by double dot.   [2] Preceded by double dot.
[3] 'jam dudum . . . sua scripta direxit'.

9   Sancho of Portugal and Mécia Lopes de Haro ('Mentia Lupi')

Sancho II belongs to the select club of kings deposed by popes in the Middle Ages. His case has been well studied by Edward Peters as an instance of general incompetence as grounds for de-legitimating a king.[1] His replacement as regent, and after his death as king, was his brother Alfonso, the Count of Boulogne, to whom the document below refers. (Alfonso had become count of Boulogne through marriage to the heiress Mathilda: see **# 1263, June 19**.) Alfonso's petition to the pope, which led to the letter translated below, should probably be put in the context of the campaign to unseat Sancho.

Historiographical highlights

For an old account, see Frederico Francisco de la Figanière, *Memorias das Rainhas de Portugal* (Lisbon, 1859), pp. 88–9 and 94. The case and its wider context are well analysed in Edward Peters, *The Shadow King: Rex Inutilis in Medieval Law and Literature 751–1327* (New Haven, CT, 1970), pp. 148–54.

The translation

The document is translated from the edition in the École Française de Rome calendar by Elie Berger (details after translation).

1245, February 12

To the archbishop of Compostella,[2] and the bishop of Astorga.[3] Our beloved son the noble man the Count of Boulogne[4] made it clear to us in

---

[1] E. Peters, *The Shadow King: Rex Inutilis in Medieval Law and Literature, 751–1327* (New Haven, CT, 1970), pp. 148–54.
[2] Preceded by double dot.   [3] Preceded by double dot.
[4] Preceded by double dot.

his supplication that his brother our dearest son in Christ S. the illustrious King of Portugal, contracted a *de facto* marriage, or rather a ménage,
with the noble woman Mécia Lopes, who is related to the same king in
the fourth degree of consanguinity and affinity, imperilling his soul and
scandalising many; we command that after diligent enquiry into the truth
about these things has been made, with anyone summoned who need to
be summoned, if you find the matter to be thus, you should, as justice
dictates,[5] pronounce an annulment of their marriage,[6] afterwards, after
first giving him a warning, compelling the aforesaid king, with appropriate severity, without right of appeal, to set her aside, making sure[7] that
you do not pronounce a sentence of excommunication against the person
of the same king. If both of you are unable, etc., one of you, etc.[8] Given
at Lyons, 2 Ides of February, second year.

> (E. Berger, *Les registres de Innocent IV*, vol. I (Bibliothèque des Écoles
> Françaises d'Athènes et de Rome; Paris, 1884), no. 995, p. 160)

---

[5] 'mediante iustitia'.   [6] 'celebretis divortium . . . inter eos'.
[7] 'attentius provisuri'.
[8] Standard clause allowing one judge delegate to act alone if the other is unable to.

Note on chronology: *Because of post-medieval calendar reform, years in the document do not always correspond to the years in modern chronology. The following analysis gives the key dates in the modern form.*

In 1235 Henry III of England was already in his late twenties, one of the most eligible bachelors in Europe, and it was high time for him to think about getting married. Jeanne of Ponthieu seemed a possible *partie*. Ponthieu was not far from Normandy which Henry's father had lost to France, and was close enough to Paris to make the French king uncomfortable. Henry must have known that he was related to Jeanne within the forbidden degrees of kinship, but he nonetheless arranged to marry her by proxy, to put down a marker as it were, while seeking a dispensation from the pope. Whether he would have got one is another matter: King Louis IX of France could be expected to use influence against it at the papal court, and would probably have opposed the plan on all fronts, as a potential threat of an English comeback. Or Henry may have decided against it anyway. He turned his attention to another young woman, Eleanor of Provence, whose sister had already married King Louis. He instructed his representatives to abandon their attempts to get a dispensation, and married Eleanor. Jeanne, for her part, married the King of Castile.

An attempt the next year to get the 'marriage' to Jeanne formerly annulled seems to have run into the sand. In 1249, however, Henry set about systematically starting an annulment case for his putative marriage with Jeanne. By that time Edward, his son by Eleanor, was almost ten years old. It was in this year that Henry granted him Gascony. It would not be long before the prince could get married, so it was important that his legitimacy should be absolutely above suspicion. A formal papal annulment of the 'marriage' to Jeanne would ensure this, even if it required a lot of trouble. So a lot of trouble was taken by a lot of people to make possible the document translated below.

Henry clearly went to the pope to start the process. The result was the commission in 1249 of the bishop of Hereford and the archbishop of York. In the following year Henry himself appointed a proctor to conduct the case for him: John Capelli. In 1251 the two judges delegate had Henry and his Queen Eleanor of Provence 'summoned' to trial. Of course they did not need to go in person. The proctorial system enabled Capelli to act on their behalf with full legal authority and responsibility. After this the number of judges was halved when the archbishop of York excused himself. This was not a problem, as the original papal commission allowed one judge to act if the other could not. The remaining judge, Peter of Aigueblanche, sent the Cistercian prior of Hautecombe to summon the Queen of Castile to the trial, fixed for the church of St Stephen at Sens, in the following year. She received the prior and his companion benignly and made it clear that she had no intention of coming or sending a proctor. Obviously she had absolutely no reason to want Henry declared her husband, breaking up her own marriage to the Castilian king. In fact this was all a legal formality. The trial could not take place according to due process unless she had formally refused to come. She put her formal refusal in writing. Still in 1251, the Cistercian reported back on his mission.

The scene was set for the trial in 1252. Peter of Aigueblanche appointed assessors to help him. Even though the outcome was obvious from the start, not because the trial was 'fixed' but because anyone close to the circumstances of 1235 knew that the marriage with Jeanne was invalid in canon law, every formality of due process was observed. Thirteen witnesses who had apparently been induced to come to Sens gave their testimony to the genealogies – so the document is a good example of how genealogies were remembered. At the request of the royal proctor, a formal verdict of nullity was pronounced.

The document translated contains all the foregoing but within a later all-encompassing papal letter of 1254. This was the year in which Henry's son the Lord Edward married Eleanor of Castile – the daughter of Jeanne of Ponthieu. That may have been a reason for enclosing all the annulment proceedings in a new bull which additionally removed any possible defect there might be in the original decision.

Historiographical highlights

D. L. d'Avray, 'Authentication of Marital Status: A Thirteenth-Century English Royal Annulment Process and Late Medieval Cases from the Papal Penitentiary', *English Historical Review* 120 (2005), pp. 987–1013, at pp. 991–5, puts the document in context and explains its significance. See also Margaret Howell, *Eleanor of Provence: Queenship in Thirteenth-Century England* (Oxford, 1998), pp. 58–9.

The translation

The translation is from the edition by d'Avray, 'Authentication', pp. 998–1009. The edition is based on British Library, Cotton Cleopatra E.I, fols. 194v–195. This is actually an entire archive on one piece of sheepskin – a large one, measuring 69.5 × 52 cm. It is calendared in Jane Sayer's *Original Papal Documents in England and Wales from the Accession of Pope Innocent III to the Death of Pope Benedict XI (1198–1304)* (Oxford, 1999), no. 453, p. 203. This final 1254 bull of Innocent IV is like a Russian doll, with documents enclosing documents or adding them as appendices. This has been indicated by {} brackets. {{ indicates that a document is an enclosure within an enclosure, or that it has been added to a document that is itself an enclosure.

Readers of the notes will see that some names are 'preceded by double dot'. The double dot '..' before a title is variously interpreted as a sign of reverence and referring to the office-holder rather than the individual; or it may arise from uncertainty about the precise form of the proper name. This divergence is a small problem of which specialists in papal diplomatic are not sufficiently aware.

1254

Innocent, bishop, servant of the servants of God, to his most dear son in Christ Henry, the illustrious King of England, greetings and apostolic blessing. It is fitting for us to grant consent easily to the just desires of petitioners, and to ensure that wishes which do not diverge from the path of reason are translated in consequence into action. Therefore, since the world has grown old in corruption, and many people not only presume the worst in matters of which they are ignorant, but do not even hesitate to misrepresent as evil things which they know without doubt to be good, you, prudently bearing these things in mind, and desiring to make sure that calumny of any jealous men should not in the future become linked to your children, humbly implored us some time ago to take care to provide for your honour and that of your children by our paternal solicitude, regarding the fact that you had sworn to marry our most dear daughter in Christ Jeanne the illustrious Queen of Castile – the daughter of the Count of Ponthieu at that time – who was then single, and decided that the marriage should be contracted[1] with her by proxy so far as it was in your power, and finally, after finding that you were related to her in the fourth degree of consanguinity, when this

---

[1] 'matrimonium duxeras contrahendum'.

marriage had by no means been consummated, you joined to yourself in matrimony in the sight of the Church our most dear daughter in Christ Eleanor, the illustrious Queen of England, daughter of the Count of Provence of famous memory. But when we had entrusted by our letters in mandate form to our venerable brothers the archbishop[2] of York and the bishop[3] of Hereford that they should inquire diligently into the truth of the matter, and make sure to declare by apostolic authority, if this is what they decided was the right verdict, that the first marriage and the oath which you swore to contract this first one do not hold good, and that the second one is valid, restraining by ecclesiastical censure anyone who contradicts them, without the possibility of appeal: in the end, after the archbishop had sent a letter legitimately excusing himself because he was unable to take part in the cognisance of this matter, the same bishop proceeded with this matter alone, as our letter allowed him to do, and, when the parties had been summoned, and the aforesaid Queen of Castile replied that she was related to you in the aforesaid degree of consanguinity, and that she would not send anyone to defend this case, and would not come, nor involve herself in it, and finally neither appeared in person nor through a representative, he [i.e. the bishop of Hereford], in the presence of your proctor, after taking cognisance of the merits of the same case, and observing due process,[4] with the counsel of prudent men, pronounced as his sentence that the marriage between you and the aforesaid Queen of Castile had been null, because of the impediment of your relationship of consanguinity in the fourth degree with her, and that the marriage contracted between you and the aforesaid E. the Queen of England was legitimate, notwithstanding the oath which you swore to contract the first one, [all this] just as is contained more fully in the letter written at the hearing.

Therefore we, after inspecting diligently the proceedings of the aforesaid bishop and the sentence, approving the same proceedings, and making good from our plenitude of power any defect there may have been, and holding the same sentence to be ratified and pleasing: granting your petitions, we confirm by apostolic authority and strengthen by the protection of the present document the sentence together with the aforesaid proceedings. We have had the contents of these proceedings and this sentence set out word for word, and they are as follows.

---

[2] Title preceded by double dot.   [3] Title preceded by double dot.
[4] 'juris ordine'.

{To everyone who will inspect the present letter, Peter by the mercy of God humble servant of the Church of Hereford, greetings in the Lord Jesus Christ. You should know that after letters from the pope had been presented on behalf of the Lord Henry illustrious King of England to the venerable father Walter by the grace of God archbishop of York and to ourselves, as follows:

{{[lines 7–10]

[1249, October 27] Innocent bishop servant of the servants of God to his venerable brothers archbishop[5] of York and bishop[6] of Hereford, greetings and apostolic blessing. On behalf of our dearest son in Christ the illustrious King[7] of England the petition was made that – since he formerly swore that he would marry our dearest daughter in Christ Jeanne the illustrious Queen of Castile, daughter of the nobleman Count[8] of Ponthieu, who was then single, decided that the marriage should be contracted[9] with her by proxy so far as it was in his power, and finally, when it was discovered that he was related to her by the fourth degree of consanguinity, when this marriage had in no way been consummated, he joined to himself in marriage in the eyes of the Church our most beloved daughter in Christ the illustrious Queen[10] of England, daughter of the Count of Provence of famous memory: – we might with paternal solicitude see to it that provision be made for his honour and the honour of his children in this matter, so that it would be not be possible for any stain to be attached to them on this account later on; consequently we command your fraternal selves by apostolic writings that, after diligent enquiry into the truth of this matter, if you find that it is so, you should determine by apostolic authority that the first marriage and the oath that he made to contract the same first marriage do not hold, and that the second one is valid, restraining by ecclesiastical censure anyone who says the contrary, and with no right of appeal;[11] and should you not both be able to take part in carrying this out, one of you may nevertheless do so. Given at Lyon, 6 Kalends of November, seventh year of our pontificate.}}

[line 11]

We both, in obedience to the apostolic order,[12] decided that the aforesaid lord king should be summoned in this form:

---

[5] Title preceded by double dot.   [6] Title preceded by double dot.
[7] Title preceded by double dot.   [8] Title preceded by double dot.
[9] 'matrimonium duxerit contrahendum'.
[10] 'illustrious queen' preceded by double dot.   [11] 'appellatione postposita'.
[12] 'mandato'.

{{[1251 July] Walter, by the grace of God, archbishop of York, primate of England, and Peter by the same grace the bishop of Hereford, judges delegated by the lord pope to the prudent man provost[13] of Beverley sincere greetings in the Lord. We have received an order from the lord pope in these words:

[line 11–12]

{{{[[1249, October 27] Innocent, servant of the servants of God, to his venerable brothers archbishop[14] of York and bishop[15] of Hereford, greetings and apostolic blessing. On behalf of our dearest son in Christ the illustrious King[16] of England the petition was made to us that – since he formerly swore that, etc. Given as above, etc.}}}

[lines 12–13]

By the authority of this order we command you to summon peremptorily, in person or through another, the aforesaid lord King of England and the aforesaid lady Queen of England, the daughter of the noble man the Count of Provence to appear before us, through suitable proctors, if that should seem expedient, at the city of Sens in Burgundy, in St Stephen's church, on the octave of the next Feast of St Gregory, to proceed in the aforesaid matrimonial case, in accordance with the demands of due process and the dictates of rational calculation. We assign this day and appropriate place peremptorily so that we may spare the parties trouble and expense. We have thought good to communicate the citation to the side of the Queen of Castile, and we have summoned her for the same day and place, lest we omit anything relevant.[17] Given in the year of the Lord 1251, in the month of July. Return the letter with your seal on it after our order has been executed.}}

Subsequently the aforesaid lord archbishop, our colleague, excused himself from the aforesaid business in this form:

[lines 13–15]

{{[1251] Walter by the grace of God archbishop of York, judge delegated by the lord pope, to his venerable brother in Christ and dearest friend Peter, by the grace of the same God bishop of Hereford, his colleague, greetings and sincere love in the Lord. Since, prevented by many and arduous matters of business, we cannot devote ourselves in person to taking cognisance of the marriage case[18] which is taking place or hoped to take place between the most illustrious King of England and Jeanne the illustrious Queen of Castile, sometime daughter of the Count

---

[13] Title preceded by double dot.   [14] Title preceded by double dot.
[15] Title preceded by double dot.   [16] Title preceded by double dot.
[17] 'de contingentibus'.   [18] 'cognitioni matrimonii'.

of Ponthieu, delegated to us and to you by the lord pope, we ask you to excuse our absence. Therefore do not expect us to appear in person and have us excused in the aforesaid cognisance, and proceed alone, so far as we are concerned, in the said business. We are communicating this same thing to all the aforesaid parties involved. Given in the year of the Lord 1251.}}

[**line 15**]

Time went by, and, with our aforesaid colleague excused, we had the aforesaid Lady Jeanne, sometime daughter of the Count of Ponthieu, now the illustrious Queen of Castile, summoned through the man of religious J., prior of Hautecombe, of the Cistercian Order, in this form.

[**line 15–18**]

{{Peter by the mercy of God bishop of Hereford to J. prior of Hautecombe of the Cistercian Order, a man of religion and an honest man, greetings in the Lord Jesus Christ. You should know that we together with our venerable father the archbishop of York receive an apostolic order in this form:

{{{Innocent, bishop, servant of the servants of God, to his venerable brothers archbishop[19] of York and bishop[20] of Hereford, greetings and apostolic blessing. On the initiative of our dearest son in Christ the illustrious King[21] of England the petition was made that – since he formerly swore that, etc. Given as above, etc., as above.}}}

Our colleague aforesaid excused himself however through his letters patent, asking us that since he was occupied with matters of business, we should proceed in the said matter[22] and in no way expect him. Consequently we command your discreet self, by the apostolic authority with which we are endowed in this matter, to go to the aforesaid lady Queen of Castile in person and summon her peremptorily to appear before us through a suitable proctor in St Stephen's church on the next Octave of St Gregory, to proceed with the aforesaid matter in the way that the law requires us to proceed. Otherwise we will proceed in this same matter as due process requires.[23] We made this summons in the same form to the party of the lord King of England, lest we omit anything relevant. Return the letter with your seal appended when our order has been carried out, and inform us of the matter as the law requires. Given on the day after the Feast of St Denis, the year of the Lord 1251.}}

---

[19] Title preceded by double dot.   [20] Title preceded by double dot.

[21] Title preceded by double dot.

[22] Matters of business...matter: 'negotiis...negotio'.

[23] 'quantum exegerit ordo juris'.

[**lines 18–21**]

Our aforesaid colleague the prior indeed summoned the aforesaid queen, in the presence of Thomas, monk of Hautecombe, namely in this form.

{{To the venerable father in Christ and Lord Peter by the grace of God bishop of Hereford, judge delegated by the lord pope, John, the prior of Hautecombe of the Cistercian Order, greetings and success in reaching Jerusalem. May you know that, after receiving your order and letter, in which you conveyed to us firmly in your orders[24] that we should, by the lord pope's authority and your own, peremptorily summon Jeanne, now the illustrious Queen of Castile, sometime daughter of the Count of Ponthieu, to appear at Sens in St Stephen's church, in person or through some representative or proctor, on the Octave of St Gregory in the year of the Lord 1251, for the matter of the same queen and of the lord King of England, in the case entrusted by the apostolic see to the venerable father archbishop[25] of York and yourself, we presented ourself in person with Thomas our brother and fellow monk being himself present, and peremptorily summoned the aforesaid queen by apostolic authority and your own to appear in person or through some representative at the aforesaid place and time and for the whole case. The aforesaid queen, however, after receiving the summons benignly, replied that the aforesaid king was her blood relative in the fourth degree, and that she would never send anyone or come to Sens or anywhere else to defend the said case, and that she would not get involved in the said case, or the aforesaid matter, and that she would never look for[26] a verdict in this matter from you or anyone else. In testimony of this thing we have thought fit to put our seal on the present letter. Done in the year of the Lord 1251.}}

[**lines 21–3**]

Indeed, calling together to join us at the aforesaid St Stephen's church, on the aforesaid Octave of St Gregory in the year of the Lord 1251, the venerable father G. by the grace of God the bishop of Auxerre, and the venerable brothers John the Succentor and John, a canon and Official[27] of Auxerre, with the same three sitting together with us, we proceeded in this form. For we received the oath both from the said prior of Hautecombe and from the aforesaid Thomas that they would tell the truth. Both indeed asserted by an oath made with the consent and licence of their

---

[24] 'in mandatis'.   [25] Title preceded by double dot.   [26] 'numquam . . . exspectaret'.
[27] Title preceded by double dot. Normally the two dots mean a new name, but the canon and Official must be the same person or we have four assessors rather than three.

abbot[28] that the said prior summoned the aforesaid Queen Jeanne of Castile just as is contained more fully in the letter in which the said prior speaks; and the queen replied as is contained in the same letter; and that both were present. We established this also through a letter of the same queen, which, sealed with her seal, and enclosed with the same,[29] we saw and diligently inspected in the presence of the said assessors and a number of others. Furthermore we saw and read, in the form set out below, the letter of the said abbot of Hautecombe concerning the licence given to the said monks, that is to the prior of Hautecombe and to brother Thomas his companion, about telling the truth under oath.

{{[lines 23–5]

Brother R. called[30] abbot of Hautecombe of the Cistercian Order, to all those who will inspect the present letter, greetings in the Lord Jesus Christ. We make it clear to you collectively[31] through the present letter that we gave to brother John the cloister prior[32] of Hautecombe and to brother Thomas his companion, the licence to go to the city of Sens and to bear witness, and to swear, in the marriage case that the illustrious man[33] the King of England, and the Queen, are bringing and intend to bring against the illustrious Queen[34] of Castile, before the venerable father the bishop[35] of Hereford, judge delegated by the lord pope, and acting in the place of his colleague both with respect to the summons and of the other things that could pertain to the said case in any way. In witness of this thing we have fortified this letter with the protection of our seal. Given on the Tuesday after Laetare Jerusalem Sunday, 1251 AD.}}

At this, Master John Capelli, presenting himself on behalf of the lord King of England as his proctor, showed to us his commission to act as proctor[36] and the order sealed with the seal of the aforesaid illustrious King H., in this form.

{{[lines 25–8]

To each and every person whom the present letters reach, Henry by the grace of God King of England, Lord of Ireland, Duke of Normandy and Aquitaine and Count of Anjou, greetings. With respect to the marriage that is said to have been contracted *de facto* between ourselves, on one side, and the noble Lady Jeanne Queen of Castile, sometime daughter of

---

[28] Title preceded by double dot.
[29] 'Ibidem': this must mean: in the prior's letter.
[30] 'dictus': probably not 'the said' here, since it is the start of the letter.
[31] 'Universitati vestre'.   [32] 'priori claustrali'.
[33] 'illustrious man' preceded by double dot.   [34] Title preceded by double dot.
[35] Title preceded by double dot.   [36] 'procuratorium suum'.

the noble man the Count[37] of Ponthieu, on the other, since we are related to the same woman in the fourth degree of consanguinity, we made John Capelli, the bearer of the present letter, our proctor for the examination[38] and for setting out of these facts[39] and for each and every other thing pertaining to these or other things to do with the aforesaid[40] which are to be dealt with, announced, or procured in any other way before the lord pope or of any other judges whatsoever: giving to the same John plenary power to execute and procure the aforesaid things and to propose[41] also everything, in whatever way it may be done, that we in our own person, if we were present, might be able to propose or do or expedite in any way, promising with our goods as surety that whatever should be proposed or done by the said proctor in the aforesaid things or any of them we will hold to be ratified for ever and fixed, nor will we at any time, ourselves or through any other person, come against these things or any one of them. In witness of which we have thought it good to put our seal on the present letter. Given at Reading on the 21st February, in the thirty-fourth year of our reign, and the 1249th of the Lord's incarnation.}}

[**lines 28–32**]

Subsequently the said proctor handed over to us and showed us his petition, which we inspected, and we had it sealed with our seal and with the seals of our assessors. Therefore, in view of the contumacy of the aforesaid Jeanne, now Queen of Castile, and that the said Master John, proctor of the King of England, demanded what was just, we – with the counsel of our experts, and together with the aforesaid three assessors, namely the venerable father G., by the grace of God bishop of Auxerre, and the venerable men John the Succentor and John the canon and Official[42] of Auxerre – received in St Stephen's church at Sens the witnesses presented to us by the said proctor of the lord King of England. The aforesaid witnesses – namely, Lord John de Molins, knight, and the others whose names are contained in the depositions[43] sealed with our seal and that of the said assessors – did indeed all swear on the holy gospels of God that they will say[44] the truth concerning the aforesaid matter, and what they know and what they believe, and that they will not for love or money say anything except what they know and believe and strongly hold to be the case.[45] After the oath had been received, they give [*sic*] their depositions privately and one by one, as in their depositions, sealed by our seal and the seals of the assessors, is set out in

---

[37] Title preceded by double dot. [38] Supply 'pro' before 'examinatione'?
[39] 'et pronuntiatione eorundem'. [40] 'ad hec vel aliquea premissorum'.
[41] 'proponendi'. [42] Title preceded by double dot. [43] 'attestationibus'.
[44] 'dicent', in simple future tense. [45] 'extimant vehementer'.

full. After the aforesaid witnesses had been received, and the depositions of each one of them had been taken down in writing, and the same had been inspected carefully, and once, again, and yet again announced,[46] we assigned to the aforesaid Master John the proctor of the aforesaid lord King of England the day of Wednesday before Palm Sunday for the definitive sentence, for the announcement of which he was insistently asking, to be heard concerning the aforesaid matter. Given at Sens on the day after the Octave of St Gregory, in the year of the Lord 1251.

{{{[lines 32–7]

In the year of the Lord 1251, on the Octave of the Feast of St Gregory, before you, O venerable father P., by the grace of God bishop of Hereford, judge delegated by the lord pope, Master John Capelli, proctor of the Lord Henry by the grace of God most illustrious King of England, proposes and asserts that, since the same king had formerly sworn that he would marry Jeanne, then daughter of Count[47] of Ponthieu, now illustrious Queen of Castile, the same king afterwards gave matrimonial consent[48] *de facto* by proxy to the same Lady Jeanne, then unmarried, but they did not however see each other in person, nor were matters taken further between them: finally, when the said king found that he and the said Lady Jeanne were related in the fourth degree of consanguinity, for which reason they were not and could not be married, the marriage being in no way consummated, he adopted a better plan[49] and contracted marriage in the eyes of the Church[50] with Eleanor, then the daughter of Count[51] of Provence, whom he now has by the grace of God as his wife; the said Jeanne however contracted marriage with the King of Castile. So to remove all stain of ill repute, lest there might be anything that could be levelled against the king by way of objection or audaciously imputed, the said proctor asks of you, lord judge, in the name of the said King of England, to receive witnesses to prove the aforesaid consanguinity in the fourth degree, which he offers that he will prove in the exercise of his procuratorial office,[52] especially since the aforesaid Queen of Castile, when summoned peremptorily through the man of religion[53] prior[54] of Hautecombe, of the Cistercian Order, for the Octave of St Gregory, in the church of St Stephen at Sens, for the aforesaid case, replied that she will never appear, and in fact she is not appearing in person or through any proctor. Therefore, since she would seem to be contumacious, as

---

[46] 'publicatis'.   [47] Title preceded by double dot.   [48] 'consensit matrimonialiter'.
[49] 'mutato consilio in melius'.   [50] 'in facie ecclesie'.
[51] Title preceded by double dot.   [52] 'procuratorio nomine'.
[53] 'religiosus' can mean both 'pious' and 'member of a religious order'.
[54] Title preceded by double dot.

disdaining to come after receiving a peremptory summons, the said Master John the proctor of the said King of England earnestly asks that you receive the aforesaid witnesses,[55] and, when they have been received, and when their depositions have been inspected, you may nonetheless proceed to a definitive sentence, by apostolic authority, in accordance with canon law.[56] The said proctor also asks that you may pronounce that – because of the impediment of consanguinity in the fourth degree – that there never was any marriage between the aforesaid King of England and the aforementioned Queen of Castile, sometime daughter of the Count[57] of Ponthieu, and that – notwithstanding the consent or oath which are said to have occurred *de facto* – the marriage contracted between the aforesaid King of England and the Lady Eleanor, sometime daughter of the Count[58] of Provence and now Queen of England, is legitimate; and the said proctor asks that you should do this by apostolic authority, saving the right of adding or taking away, etc.[59]}}} In witness of this matter, we, G. by the grace of God bishop, John the Succentor, and John canon and Official[60] of Auxerre, who were present when this statement of claim[61] was put forward, have thought good to place our seals on the present document. Given in the year and day aforesaid.}}

{{[lines 37–54]

Lord Jean de Molins, a knight said on oath that Louis the Fat the King of France had two sons, King Louis and Pierre de Courtenay. Asked how he knows this, he replied that he heard it from people who were older than him and trustworthy, and that this was and is the common opinion.[62] He also said that the issue of Louis was King Philip and Alaysia the Countess of Ponthieu, who was married to Guillaume Count of Ponthieu, whom he saw many times, as he did King Philip. Again, how he knows. He says that he heard it said by trustworthy elders and that it was the common opinion on the matter and still is. And he said that the whole court of King Philip called the daughter of the aforesaid Alaysia the grandchild of the aforesaid king and the daughter of the said Alaysia the sister of the aforesaid King Philip, and this was the general belief about the matter and common opinion. He said that Marie the Countess of Ponthieu was the issue of the aforesaid Alaysia. Asked how he knew, he said that it was and still is the common opinion, and that he saw her and heard it said by her that she was the daughter of Alaysia and of Guillaume the Count of Ponthieu, and she was the heiress

---

[55] Correcting 'testes productos' (which would be translated: 'the witnesses produced') to 'testes predictos': a probable rather than certain emendation.
[56] 'secundum apostolicas sanctiones'.   [57] Title preceded by double dot.
[58] Title preceded by double dot.
[59] 'salvo jure addendi, minuendi etc': this is a standard formula.
[60] Title preceded by double dot.   [61] 'libelli'.   [62] 'ita fama est et fuit publica'.

of the count and Countess of Ponthieu, and succeeded to the county, and he said that he was frequently in the county with her. Again he said that Jeanne the Queen of Castile as she now is was the issue of Marie. Asked how he knows, he said that this is the common opinion on the matter, and he saw the same Jeanne with Marie her mother, and Marie treated Jeanne as her daughter, and Jeanne Marie as her mother, and he[63] was frequently with her, and Marie married her as her daughter to the King of Castile. He said too that Alaysia the Countess of Angoulême was the direct issue of Pierre de Courtenay and that Isabella Queen of England was the issue of the Countess of Angoulême, and that Henry King of England as he now is was the issue of Isabella. Asked how he knows, he said that he heard it said by people who were older than him and trustworthy, and it both was and used to be and is common opinion. Asked if he saw any of the aforesaid persons, he said yes. He saw the Queen of England, who acted as the mother of that King of England, and was treated as such by the king, and by everybody else. And he saw that King of England, who treated her as a mother. Asked in what degree the King of England and Jeanne the Queen of Castile were related, he said that it was in the fourth degree. Asked how he knows, he said that King Louis and Pierre de Courtenay the sons of Louis the Fat were brothers, and thus in the first degree. Alaysia Countess of Ponthieu the daughter of Louis, and the Countess of Angoulême the daughter of Pierre de Courtenay were first cousins, and thus in the second degree. Marie Countess of Ponthieu daughter of the aforesaid Alaysia, and Isabella the Queen of England, daughter of the said Countess of Angoulême, were blood relations in the third degree, and thus King Henry of England as he now is, the son of the aforesaid Isabella Queen of England, and Jeanne the Queen of Castile, the daughter of Marie the Countess of Ponthieu, are related in the fourth degree. Asked whether, through the things which he had heard and understood or saw, he firmly believes it to be so, he affirmed it on oath. Asked if he was born in the kingdom of France, he said yes. Again he said that he was brought up with and lived a long time among those people of the aforesaid families.[64] Asked how old he is, he said: fifty.

Eudes de Seneschal, under oath, said the same in all respects as the first witness did about Louis the Fat and the brothers Louis and Pierre de Courtenay, sons of the said Louis the Fat, and about Alaysia, daughter of the said Louis, Countess of Ponthieu, and about Alaysia, daughter of Pierre de Courtenay, Countess of Angoulême, except that he does not

---

[63] This more probably refers to the witness, but could also mean 'she', i.e. Jeanne.
[64] 'generibus'.

recall about the names of the said women called Alaysia. Asked about his age, he said: eighty years.

Lord Robert de Gondelez, knight, under oath, said the same in all respects as the Lord Jean de Molins, the first witness, with this addition: he saw Alaysia Countess of Ponthieu, as he believes, and saw Alaysia Countess of Angoulême, and was her vassal, and brought up in her household together with Isabella Queen of England; and except that he did not see Marie Countess of Ponthieu, nor Jeanne Queen of Castile the daughter of the said Marie, nor Henry King of England nor Jeanne Queen of Castile the daughter of the said Marie, nor Henry King of England the son of Isabella Queen of England. On age, he said: eighty.

Lord Étienne de Mongelet, knight, under oath, said the same as Jean de Molins, the first witness, except that he did not see any of the individuals except King Philip and Alaysia Countess of Angoulême and the Queen of England her daughter. Asked how old he was: 'seventy'.

Brother Henri de Brici, Cistercian monk, under oath, ordered by his prior said the same thing in all respects as Lord Jean the first witness, with the addition that he saw Alaysia Countess of Angoulême, and was in her company for six months. Asked how old he was, he said: sixty-six. Again he says that he had spent time together[65] with the relatives[66] of the aforesaid.

Lord Thomas de Capra, knight, under oath, said the same as Lord Jean the first witness, with the addition that he saw King Louis the Fat father of King Philip, and Alaysia of Ponthieu, the daughter of King Louis, and that he had spent time in the household of Marie Countess of Ponthieu. As for his age, he said: eighty years.

Lord Walens, an old knight, under oath, said the same as Lord Jean the first witness, with the addition that he saw Alaysia the Countess of Ponthieu. As for his age: over sixty.[67]

Lord Gilles d'Yseque, under oath, said the same as the said Lord Jean, except that he did not see the Queen of England nor Henry her son, the present King of England.

Lord Nicolas de Vilers, knight, under oath, said the same as the aforesaid Lord Jean, with the addition that he saw Alaysia Countess of Angoulême, and was brought up with her and spent time in her company; but he did not see the present King of England. With respect to his age he said: sixty-four years.

Peter, called the Butler, *bailli* of Auxerre, under oath, said the same as Eudes de Senecchal, except that he knows nothing of Louis the Fat. As for his age he said: sixty years.

---

[65] 'conversatus...'   [66] 'generibus', in the sense of 'extended families'.
[67] 'sexaginta et amplius'.

Syme[68] Tailor,[69] sometime chamberlain of Lord Robert de Courtenay, said the same thing as Lord Jean the first witness, with the addition that he saw A. Countess of Angoulême; but he says nothing of Louis the Fat; nor does he remember the names of the Queen of England and the Countess of Ponthieu, except that he heard it said that Marie was the daughter of Alaysia Countess of Ponthieu. As for his age, he said: seventy years.

Jean de Trocis, sometime servant of Lord Robert de Courtenay, under oath, said the same as the said Lord Jean, with the addition that he saw the Countess of Angoulême, and except for the fact that he was not together with Marie Countess of Ponthieu, nor with Jeanne her daughter, but he saw them both frequently. He does not remember the name of the Queen of England. As for his age he said that he is fifty-five years old.

Master Guillaume de Wisant, canon of Saint-Omer, under oath, said the same as the said Lord Jean, with the addition that he knows the above not only through public repute and witnesses, but through a chronicle that he saw at Saint-Denis. As for his age he said that is fifty-five years old.

Subsequently the depositions were published. Afterwards, however, at the earnest request by Master John the proctor of the lord King of England that we should pronounce the definitive verdict, we assigned the Wednesday before Palm Sunday for pronouncing the definitive verdict in the aforementioned matter. In witness of this thing we, Peter bishop of Hereford, judge delegated by the lord pope, with the venerable father G. by the grace of God bishop of Auxerre, John the Succentor, and John, canon and Official[70] of Auxerre, sitting together with us, with our seal and the seals of the aforesaid assessors, had the present depositions validated. Done in St Stephen's church at Sens on the Octave of St Gregory, the year of the Lord 1251.}}

{{[**lines 54–7**]

In the name of the Father and the Son and the Holy Spirit, Amen. We, Peter by the mercy of God bishop of Hereford, judge delegated by the lord pope, together with our venerable father archbishop[71] of York, in the matter of the marriage which is formerly said to have taken place *de facto* between Lord Henry illustrious King of England and Lady Jeanne, sometime daughter of Count[72] of Ponthieu, now illustrious Queen of Castile, and concerning the consent by proxy with the oath sworn said to have occurred between them, and concerning the fourth degree of consanguinity in which, as it is asserted, they are related, just as these

---

[68] 'Suymus' or 'Synius'.   [69] 'Tallator'.   [70] Title preceded by double dot.
[71] Title preceded by double dot.   [72] Title preceded by double dot.

and other things are contained in fuller form in the apostolic order, after receiving the aforesaid order, and summoning the parties for the Octave of St Gregory in the year of the Lord 1251, to St Stephen's church in Sens, our colleague having excused himself by letter, and with the Queen of Castile failing to appear in person or through any proctor, Master John Capelli, proctor of the lord King of England, with a letter of the same king, as instructed,[73] appeared before us on the day and at the place appointed. Therefore we, sitting on the day and at the place appointed for the tribunal, with the venerable father Lord G. by the grace of God bishop of Auxerre and the venerable men John the Succentor and John the canon and Official of Auxerre joining us as assessors, we received the statement of claim handed over to us by the said proctor of the lord king, which goes as follows:

{{{[**Lines 57–64: same document as quoted lines 32–7**]

In the year of the Lord 1251, on the Octave of the Feast of St Gregory, before you, O venerable father Peter, by the grace of God bishop of Hereford, judge delegated by the lord pope, Master John Capelli, proctor of the Lord Henry by the grace of God most illustrious King of England, proposes and asserts that, since the same king had formally sworn that he would marry Jeanne, then daughter of count[74] of Ponthieu, now illustrious Queen of Castile, the same king afterwards gave matrimonial consent[75] *de facto* by proxy to the same Lady Jeanne, then unmarried, but they did not however see each other in person, nor were matters taken further between them, and finally, when the said king found that he and the said Lady Jeanne were related in the fourth degree of consanguinity, for which reason they were not and could not be married, the marriage being in no way consummated, he adopted a better plan[76] and contracted marriage in the eyes of the Church[77] with Eleanor, then the daughter of the count[78] of Provence, whom he now has by the grace of God as his wife; the said Jeanne however contracted marriage with the King of Castile. So as to remove all stain of ill repute, lest there might be anything that could be levelled against the king by way of objection or audaciously imputed, the said proctor asks of you, Lord Judge, in the name of the said King of England, to receive witnesses to prove the aforesaid consanguinity in the fourth degree, which he offers that he will prove in the exercise of his procuratorial office,[79] especially since the aforesaid Queen of Castile, when summoned peremptorily through the man of

---

[73] 'de mandato': I am not sure if this means 'on the king's instructions' or 'on the instructions of the judge delegate'.

[74] Title preceded by double dot.   [75] 'consensit matrimonialiter'.

[76] 'mutato consilio in melius'.   [77] 'in facie ecclesie'.

[78] Title preceded by double dot.   [79] 'procuratorio nomine'.

religion prior[80] of Hautecombe, for the aforesaid case, replied that she would never appear, and in fact she is not appearing in person or through any proctor. Therefore, since she would seem to be contumacious, as disdaining to come after receiving a peremptory summons, the said Master John the proctor of the said King of England earnestly asks that you receive the aforesaid witnesses, and, when they have been received, and when their depositions have been inspected, you may nonetheless proceed to a definitive sentence, by apostolic authority, in accordance with canon law. The said proctor also asks that you may pronounce that, because of the impediment of consanguinity in the fourth degree, that there never was any marriage between the aforesaid King of England and the aforementioned Queen of Castile, sometime daughter of the Count of Ponthieu, and that notwithstanding the consent or oath which are said to have occurred *de facto*, that the marriage contracted between the aforesaid King of England and the Lady Eleanor, sometime daughter of Count[81] of Provence and now Queen of England, is legitimate; and the said proctor asks that you should do this by apostolic authority, saving the right of adding or taking away, etc.}}}

[**Lines 64–9**]

In view therefore of the contumacy of the aforesaid Queen of Castile, we received the witnesses presented to us by the said proctor of the lord King of England, with the counsel of the aforesaid assessors and of many others, and examined them diligently; the depositions of the same witnesses were faithfully recorded in writing and afterwards solemnly made public; and we thought good to assign the Wednesday before Palm Sunday to the aforesaid proctor of the lord king, who was asking earnestly for sentence to be passed, for the pronouncement of the definitive verdict;[82] on the aforesaid Wednesday, with the said proctor appearing before us and the aforesaid assessors in St Stephen's church at Sens, and requesting that sentence be passed by us, we, noting[83] that the Queen of Castile was contumacious, her contumacy counting for her presence in this matter, our colleague having excused himself by letter, after holding careful discussion with our assessors and other men with expertise,[84] with their counsel, with our eyes on God, passing sentence by apostolic authority, we pronounced the aforesaid Lord Henry King of England and the aforementioned Lady Jeanne, now Queen of Castile, to be related in the fourth degree of consanguinity, and the fourth degree of consanguinity being an impediment, that no marriage between them existed. By the

---

[80] Title preceded by double dot.   [81] Title preceded by double dot.
[82] I now think I should have punctuated this in my edition as a sentence break.
[83] 'attendentes'.   [84] 'viris peritis'.

same authority we also pronounced that, notwithstanding the oath that the said king is said to have sworn to contract marriage with the said Lady Jeanne, now Queen of Castile, and notwithstanding his *de facto* matrimonial consent by proxy, that the marriage afterwards contracted between the aforesaid King of England and the Lady Eleanor Queen of England, sometime daughter of . . . [*sic*] Count of Provence, is legitimate and contracted in accordance with canon law. In witness of this thing both we and the aforesaid assessors have sealed the present sentence with our seals. – We however the aforesaid bishop of Auxerre, John the Succentor, and John canon and Official of Auxerre, assessors of the aforesaid lord the bishop of Hereford, have thought good to put our seals to the present sentence.

[**Line 69**]

Witnesses G. Archdeacon of Lyon, Nicolaus de Abbatia canon of Auxerre, Master Draco canon of Auxerre, and Lord Lambert chaplain of the aforesaid lord bishop of Auxerre. Done at the St Stephen's church, on the Wednesday before Palm Sunday, in the year of the Lord 1251.}}

[**Lines 69–71**]

Therefore no-one is allowed to violate or audaciously attempt to go against this our page in which we grant our confirmation and make good any defects.[85] But if anyone should attempt to do this, let them know that they will incur the indignation of Almighty God and of the blessed Peter and Paul his apostles. Given at Assisi 13 Kalends of June in the eleventh year of our pontificate.

(BL Cotton Cleopatra E., fols. 194v–195r)

---

[85] 'suppletionis'.

11   Plaisance of Cyprus and Balian

The short life of Plaisance was set in the kingdom of Cyprus during the Indian summer of Latin power in the eastern Mediterranean. By her mid-teens she was already a widow of the Lusignan king and mother of the young King of Cyprus. The kingdom was intimately linked in customary feudal law to the kingdom of Acre, the surviving segment of the Latin kingdom of Jerusalem. Control of Plaisance, and thus of her son, might mean control of Acre also, according to an arcane customary law feudal logic. Both kingdoms were dominated by the Ibelin family, which was, however, a house divided against itself. The marriage case is from one point of view an aspect of the power struggle between two Ibelins, John of Jaffa and John of Arsur.

John of Arsur was regent of the Latin kingdom of Acre and apparently in the ascendant when Plaisance married his son Balian. They were related within the forbidden degrees but sent to ask for a dispensation. Presumably the point was to link the two kingdoms tightly together. Afterwards John of Jaffa gained the upper hand. He needed Plaisance and her son and she seems to have been happy to back a winner. She started annulment proceedings against Balian, breaking up with him before the dispensation arrived. This would eventually win her the annulment, since dispensations did not automatically validate a marriage: a new act of mutual assent by the couple was required in logic and law.

The case was started in 1255, when the couple had been married about a year. The excellent modern historian of these events (H. E. Mayer) slipped up by interpreting the papal bull starting the investigation as the actual annulment. That only came three years later, after due process conducted first by successive judges delegate and then in the Roman curia, which had by that time a dossier of the propositions to be tested and the witness testimony. Because the couple had split up before receiving the dispensation, the annulment was finally granted (**# 1258**). A decision on Plaisance's oath to marry Balian was postponed. Balian could bring a case of (in effect) breach of promise if he so wished.

This is the canon law story. There is another story and it is all about Outremer politics. The underage King of Cyprus was in feudal customary law the regent for the underage King of Acre (who was far away in Europe). Via Plaisance, the young King of Cyprus's mother, John of Jaffa hoped to control both kingdoms. For him it was crucial to separate Plaisance from his rival's son. In the end, Balian and his father John of Arsur seem to have been happy with the annulment because the latter managed to get himself made regent of Acre anyway. On the other hand, John of Jaffa persuaded Plaisance to become his mistress. When she died in 1261 she was still in her early twenties. The Lusignans and Ibelins continued to dominate Cyprus, but the Latin kingdom of Acre was overrun in 1291.

Historiographical highlights

Hans Eberhard Mayer, 'Ibelin versus Ibelin: The Struggle for the Regency of Jerusalem 1253–1258', *Proceedings of the American Philosophical Society* 122 (1978), pp. 25–57, is the indispensable background study. It is as erudite as one would expect of a scholar whose heart and (so far as he could manage it) body were never separated from the *Monumenta Germaniae Historica*'s Munich base, even after he took a Chair at the other end of Germany. More unexpected, in view of the high level of scholarship, is its astounding vividness and readability, all the more remarkable from a historian writing in a foreign language.

The translation

The letters are translated from Christopher Schabel, *Bullarium Cyprium*, vol. I: *Papal Letters Concerning Cyprus, 1196–1261* (Nicosia, 2010).

1255, August 28 (a)

Alexander IV appoints the archbishop of Nicosia and the bishop of Famagusta as judges delegate to judge an annulment case brought by Queen Plaisance of Cyprus against Balian of Ibelin.

Schabel, *Bullarium*, vol. I, f-13, pp. 468–70. Schabel lists copies in the Bibliothèque Nationale de France and in Malta as well as the papal register. The Latin words in square brackets are those used in the second, partly identical letter to mark a passage omitted. (Papal registers sensibly try to avoid copying out the same words verbatim in successive letters, and do this by indicating through phrases like 'in the same way . . . up to X', where X is a Latin lemma, that a passage identical to one in the previous letter has been left out. This becomes clearer if the following letter and the one after it are compared.)

To the archbishop of Nicosia, and the bishop of Famagusta.[1] Among the other burdens laid on us by the apostolic office imposed on us, it is especially fitting for us to watch over the salvation of souls in such a way that we may be able to present them as profit to the King of Kings, with the help of his grace, who wished us, unworthy though we are, to exercise authority over them. For that all people, their eyes fixed on God and all their affections focused on him, with the confidence that comes from a pure conscience, should press on step by step to obtain the glory of endless eternal life[2] with him, who comes to meet them lest they delay without end[3] – this is what we are striving for, this is what we embrace with all our desires, it is what we think about all the time, and it is what we strive to bring to fruition so far as our inadequate powers permit.

Indeed, as it was put to us [*coram nobis*] on the part of our most beloved daughter in Christ Plaisance, the illustrious Queen of Cyprus, widow of Henry King of Cyprus of famous memory, she some time ago contracted a *de facto* marriage, or rather, a reprehensible ménage, not without detriment to her own salvation and giving scandal to many, with the noble man Balian, son of the noble man John the lord of Arsur, who is related to the aforesaid king her husband in the third degree of consanguinity. Subsequently, however, seizing an opportune moment, since her conscience was troubling her concerning this crime, anxious about the salvation of her soul, she ceased to live with the aforesaid Balian, leaving him. Nonetheless however the same B., using as his pretext the aforesaid ménage and a certain papal dispensation which had come to the knowledge of the same queen after she had left him and ceased to live with him, covetously keeps her goods and those of our beloved son the noble man Hugh, her son orphaned [of his father],[4] greatly prejudicing and harming her interests and those of the aforesaid orphan. Consequently she has humbly petitioned us to take care with apostolic solicitude to make provision in this matter. Since therefore it pertains to our office that widows be especially cherished,[5] and that we offer appropriate protection to orphans, and assist them in their necessities with the protection and favour[6] when required [*oportuni*], we command you, brothers, with

---

[1] 'archiepiscopo' and 'episcopo' preceded by double dots.
[2] Taking 'sine fine' with 'vite perempnis' rather than with 'gressibus', though 'step-by-step with him' is also possible.
[3] 'absque termino'.   [4] 'nati sui pupilli'.
[5] 'ad nostrum spectet officium viduas maxime devotas esse'.   [6] 'favoris presidio'.

apostolic writings, giving you a strict order, that, *if matters are as stated*,[7] you, or one of you, acting yourselves or through others, altogether condemning by our authority this marriage, or rather ménage, contracted in this way between the same queen and the aforesaid Balian, related[8] to the aforesaid king, her husband, as was stated above, in the third degree of consanguinity, and judging it to be and to have been altogether null, should rule that whatever has followed from it or because of it is null and void [*inane*]. Anyone who contradicts this [standard formula omitted]. Notwithstanding the aforesaid dispensation obtained in relation to this matter, which is said to have by no means come to the notice [*pervenisse*] of the same queen[9] before she left and ceased to live with the aforementioned man, or if a privilege should have been conceded[10] by any persons to the apostolic see that they could not be put under interdict, suspended or excommunicated by apostolic letters not making full and explicit mention of this concession, and [notwithstanding] the general [*generali*] council's constitution 'On two days' journey'. Take care, however, in view of the character of this matter,[11] to execute our command on this matter so speedily and so efficaciously that it may be altogether impossible for you to be reproached for negligence, but, rather, that you may be able to be commended for diligence. Given at Anagni, 28 August, first year [our pontificate].

1255, August 28 (b)

A similar letter to the same recipients, but with an emphasis on the need to force Balian to give up control of the kingdom of Cyprus.

Schabel, *Bullarium* vol. I, f-14, pp. 470–2 (edition listing an eighteenth-century copy in the Bibliothèque nationale de France as well as the papal register). As is usual with papal registers, the copy registered is abridged – see prefatory comments to previous letter. The words 'up to' (*usque*) indicate where the text resumes after an omitted passage. The papal register record was abridged in this way to avoid duplication with the previous letter, sent out at the same time.

In the same way to the same [addressees], up to: 'put to us [*coram nobis*]' – the same lady . . . with the noble man Balian, son of the noble man John

---

[7] My italics.   [8] correcting 'contingentes' to 'contingentem'.
[9] 'ad ipsius regine notitie . . . nullatenus dicitur pervenisse'; for 'notitic' read 'notitiam'.
[10] 'sit indultum'.
[11] 'considerata huiusmodi negotii qualitate': presumably: considering the high status of the people involved.

the lord of Arsur,[12] who is . . . to the aforesaid king her husband in the third degree of consanguinity' – etc., up to 'when required [*oportuni*]' – we have commanded you through other letters that, if matters are as stated – etc., up to 'void [*inane*]'. Notwithstanding the aforesaid dispensation obtained in relation to this matter – etc., up to 'come to the notice [*pervenisse*]'.

Therefore we command you, brothers, with apostolic writings, giving you a strict order, that, after you have proceeded to the condemnation of the aforesaid marriage and the other things set out above, you should take care to publish these proceedings of yours, acting yourself or through another person or persons, in the places where that seems appropriate.

In truth, since the aforementioned Balian, on the pretext of this ménage and dispensation, claiming and pretending that he[13] wishes, as regent[14] of our beloved son the noble man Hugh, the orphan, son of the aforesaid queen, to keep the kingdom of Cyprus on behalf of the same orphan, is said audaciously to hold on to it and occupy it under the pretext[15] of this regency, to the grave and evident prejudice of the same queen and the said orphan: it is our wish, and we strictly command you by the authority of this letter, that you or one of you should require and admonish on our behalf the same Balian, that he should in no way involve himself in the care or regency or custody or governance of the said kingdom from now on, but that leaving it without delay and restoring the income[16] taken from it in the mean time[17] to the same queen and orphan, he should permit the same queen freely to govern, hold and rule the same kingdom, without putting any obstacle in the way of the same queen or her officials or doing them any harm or disturbing them in respect of these things,[18] or causing injury.[19]

And if he should be uncooperative or rebellious in this matter, you should compel him to do it through ecclesiastical censure, without the right of appeal; firmly enjoining all communities of cities and castles,[20] barons and everyone of the aforesaid kingdom that they should humbly obey and look to the said queen as regent of the aforesaid orphan and as looking after and governing the same kingdom, prohibiting them nonetheless most strictly from giving the aforesaid Balian any counsel, aid or favour against the same queen, nor should they presume to answer

---

[12] 'de Arsuro'.   [13] 'pretendens atque fingens se'.
[14] 'balium'. For 'bailli' as regent see Mayer, 'Ibelin versus Ibelin', p. 28.
[15] I conjecturally correct 'spem' to 'speciem'.   [16] 'fructus'.   [17] 'medio tempore'.
[18] 'super hec': if the variant 'super hoc' were adopted, the translation would be: 'in this matter'.
[19] 'vel offensam'.   [20] 'civitatum et castrorum'.

to the said Balian or his bailiffs or officials for any rents,[21] jurisdictions,[22] revenues, sources of income, or any sources of profit and rights of the same kingdom which they have been accustomed to pay to the same lord or his court, since, if they do perchance answer to them for such things, they would not be freed from them[23] so far as the same queen and aforesaid orphan are concerned but would nonetheless remain bound to pay them.

If, however, anyone should presume to oppose this command and your prohibition, you should make sure to put this down with a similar censure,[24] notwithstanding any privilege conceded to the aforesaid Balian or any other persons by the apostolic see that [they may not] be put under interdict – etc., up to 'general [*generali*]';[25] the help of the secular arm having been called in, if necessary, for this purpose, both against the same B. and against communities and barons and the others aforesaid. ['Take care however, after considering the merits of this business, to execute] our command on this matter' – etc., up to the end.

Note the commentary in Mayer, 'Ibelin versus Ibelin', p. 47, note 117.

1258, February 27

The final decision. Schabel, Bullarium, vol. I, f-31, pp. 493–6. Schabel lists a copy in the Bibliothèque nationale de France as well as in the papal register.

This makes it that the 1255 letters three years earlier were not a decision but the start of the process. In fact that could be inferred from the earlier documents. The key phrase is 'if matters are as stated'. Anyone familiar with the Diplomatic of papal documents will know that this means that the claims set out in the letter had to be verified by the delegates on the ground. Due process was followed, the system that we first see clearly in the pontificate of Innocent III, with lists of propositions in contention and witnesses to verify them. In the course of the case a second set of delegates was appointed to take it over. In the end they referred it back to the pope, who appointed the cardinal bishop of Palestrina as the judge at the papal court. The decisive considerations were that Plaisance had already left Balian before a dispensation for forbidden degrees arrived. Such dispensations did not take effect automatically. They required a fresh act of consent. This might be implicit if the couple were living and sleeping together and continued to do so, but not if they had broken up. Furthermore, an oath the queen had sworn to marry Balian was conditional on the consent of a brother, and this had not

---

[21] 'cabellis'.   [22] 'balivis'   [23] Conjecturally correcting 'libertati' to 'liberati'.
[24] 'huiusmodi censura simili compescere procuretis'.
[25] Non obstante si . . . sit indultum, quod interdici etc. usque 'generali'.

been forthcoming. The pope says that if Balian wants to sue the queen to make her fulfil the oath, he must start a separate case, and that after restoring the property and rights of the queen and her son.

As a perpetual memorandum of the matter

When the empire of reason rules[26] in the soul of him who judges, justice sits as a tribunal for the examination of truth, and, like a king on the throne of judgement, rectitude, through whose gaze the judgement of personal wilfulness is brought to nothing,[27] and the privileging of individuals:[28] with the result that small and great, poor and rich, the mighty and the weak, the absent and the present, will be judged with evenly balanced scales.

In truth, after the marriage case between our dearest daughter in Christ Plaisance, the illustrious Queen of Cyprus, and our beloved son the noble man Balian, son of our beloved son the noble man John, lord of Azoto [sic],[29] had been committed by the apostolic see to our venerable brothers the archbishop of Nicosia,[30] and the bishop of Famagusta,[31] the said queen, in their presence, presenting her plaintiff's plea,[32] asked for the marriage which had been contracted between her and the said Balian *de facto*, since it could not be contracted *de iure*, because the King of Cyprus[33] of famous memory, husband of the same queen, was related to the said Balian in the third degree of consanguinity, and everything that had followed from that marriage, or because of it, to be judged invalid and void, concerning which, after the *litis contestatio*[34] had taken place, in accordance with the law,[35] and the oath of calumny[36] had been taken by the parties, and *positiones* and responses to the same[37] had been proposed by both sides, and witness testimony had been taken concerning certain articles,[38] finally our venerable brothers the archbishops of

---

[26] 'Presidente rationis imperio'.

[27] 'cuius dissipatur intuitu proprie voluntatis arbitrium'.   [28] 'acceptio personarum'.

[29] Correct to John of Arsur.   [30] Title preceded by double dot.

[31] Title preceded by double dot.

[32] 'libello'. On the role of the libellus in trials see Linda Fowler-Magerl, *'Ordines iudiciarii' and 'libelli de ordine iudiciorum': From the Middle of the Twelfth to the End of the Fifteenth Century* (Turnhout, 1994), pp. 37–40.

[33] Title preceded by double dot.

[34] On the *litis contestatio*, see Fowler-Magerl, *'Ordines iudiciarii'*, p. 36.   [35] 'legitime'.

[36] On the oath of calumny, see Fowler-Magerl, *'Ordines iudiciarii'*, p. 44.

[37] 'ad easdem': taking this to mean: responses to the *positiones*, with the preceding words, rather than with the words 'receptis testibus' just afterwards.

[38] 'ad easdem et super quibusdam articulis': taking 'ad easdem' to refer to the positions and responses, for if these had been incorporated into the articles, it would be hard to explain why the pope referred only to 'certain articles', as though these had been added – by the judges? – to the claims put forward by either side.

Tyre[39] and Caesarea,[40] to whom we had subsequently committed the same case, sent it to be examined by the same holy see, after a definite final date had been set for the parties by which they should come before the pope[41] with all their documents, legal arguments and evidence[42] relating to this case.

Therefore, with the proctors of the same parties gathered in our presence, and exchanging – before our venerable brother the bishop of Praeneste[43] whom we had appointed as judge[44] in this case – legal arguments at great length about the trial proceedings held before the aforesaid judges,[45] the proctors of the same queen asked in her name before the same judge that he let the case proceed to a definitive sentence in accordance with the plaintiff's plea[46] and the trial proceedings held in the presence of the aforesaid judges, the proctors of the same Balian replying that the requests should not be granted because the aforesaid queen and Balian had sworn an oath that they would marry one another, a dispensation for the relationship of affinity between them having been obtained from the Holy See within the space of a year, before obtaining which dispensation the marriage between them took place, and that at the request of the aforesaid queen and Balian on this matter a dispensation had been granted by Pope Innocent of happy memory, our predecessor, through which this impediment of affinity was removed. But against this it was argued by the queen's proctors that she, before this dispensation had been obtained, had left and ceased to live with the same Balian, and, after the same dispensation came to her notice, that she had several times protested publicly that she did not want to have the same Balian as her husband, and that she did not in any way accept the dispensation. The proctors of the aforesaid queen also added that the said oath was not given without qualification but that it was given subject to a condition, viz., that the same queen would marry the same Balian if it was pleasing to our beloved son the noble man prince of Antioch,[47] brother of the said queen, who never gave his consent to this, but, indeed persisted and persists in unceasing opposition; and that the said dispensation was not

[39] Title preceded by double dot.   [40] Title preceded by double dot.
[41] 'se . . . apostolico conspectui presentarent'.   [42] 'actis, juribus et munimentis'.
[43] Name preceded by double dot.   [44] 'auditorem'.
[45] 'et super processibus coram predictis judicibus habitis, diutius litigantibus'. The comma inserted by the editor gives a misleading impression of the sense, though the same punctuation is in the École Française de Rome edition: C. Bourel de la Roncière, J. de Loye, P. de Cenival and A. Coulon, *Les registres d'Alexandre IV*, vol. II, ed. Joseph de Loye and Pierre de Cenival (Bibliothèque des Écoles Francaises d'Athènes et de Rome; Paris, 1917), no. 2510, pp. 782–3, at 782 col. b.
[46] 'libellum'.   [47] Title preceded by double dot.

obtained in accordance with the content of the oath sworn,[48] and that it did not compel them to remain in the marriage which they had thus contracted *de facto*, but left it to them to decide freely.

Therefore, after the same bishop of Praeneste had diligently related to us and our brothers [the cardinals] these and other things which had been put forward in his presence by the same parties, we, counselled by the said brothers, lay it down as our definitive sentence that this contract made between the aforesaid queen and Balian was not a marriage, or that this marriage is null, and we void or declare to be void whatever followed from it or because of it. And since the aforesaid Balian, taking advantage of the aforesaid contract, took over the kingdom of Cyprus and the other goods of the same queen, we judge that it is right for the aforesaid queen to be restored fully to the same kingdom, in her name and that of our most beloved son in Christ Hugh, the illustrious King of Cyprus, the orphan, her son, and to all her other goods, moveable and immovable, none the less compelling the aforesaid proctors of the same Balian, in his name, and him through them, to restore the aforesaid.

After the often-mentioned queen has been fully and entirely restored to the aforesaid things, however, and is enjoying peaceful possession of them, if the aforesaid Balian wishes to propose that she be compelled to contract marriage with him on the grounds of this oath and wishes to pursue this in court, we will, with God's help, execute justice in this matter. *Nulli nostre sententie et diffinitionis. etc.*[49]

Given at Viterbo, 27 February, fourth year.

---

[48] 'secundum tenorem prestiti juramenti'.
[49] Abridged form of a standard closing formula.

12 Alfonso III of Portugal and Mathilda of Boulogne

Mathilda was the daughter of Count Renaud of Dammartin and Countess Ida of Boulogne, and widow of a son of Philip II Augustus of France and Agnes of Meran (the partner whom Innocent III refused to recognise as Philip's wife because of his marriage to Ingeborg of Denmark). She married the future King Alfonso III of Portugal while he was staying at the French court in 1239. When Alfonso came to the throne in 1248 they still had no children and he divorced her.[1] As the document translated below shows, his subsequent marriage to Beatrice, the daughter of the King of Castile, was not regularised by the pope until after Mathilda's death.

Historiographical highlights

There is a good succinct summary in Peter Linehan, *Spain, 1157–1300: A Partible Inheritance* (Oxford, 2011 edn), p. 109. See also U. Vones-Liebenstein, 'Mathilde', article 5, in R. Auty (ed.), *Lexikon des Mittelalters*, vol. VI (Munich, 1993), cols. 392–3, and Ingo Fleisch, *Sacerdotium – Regnum – Studium: der westiberische Raum und die europäische Universitätskultur im Hochmittelalter: prosopographische und rechtsgeschichtliche Studien* (Berlin, 2006), p. 41.

The translation

The document is translated from the edition in the École Française de Rome calendar by Jean Guiraud (details after translation).

---

[1] U. Vones-Liebenstein, 'Mathilde', article 5, in R. Auty (ed.), *Lexikon des Mittelalters*, vol. VI (Munich, 1993), cols. 392–3.

1263, June 19

To his dearest son in Christ Alfonso, illustrious King of Portugal. He who with omnipotent providence governs heavenly and earthly things together, handing over the keys of the kingdom of heaven to St Peter, as his vicar, and to his successors, conferred the power of binding and loosing to this end: that the supreme pontiff, unconcerned with human ingenuity,[2] but prompted rather by divine inspiration, makes salutary laws and binds men to observe them with a kind of bond of necessity. This bond indeed he sometimes wisely[3] looses through his plenitude of power, when urgent necessity demands it or evident utility, especially public utility,[4] persuades him to do so, with certain people and especially with the Catholic kings and princes of the world in such a way that the others remain nonetheless bound by it, yet without any undue respecting of persons,[5] since one should not deem it to be showing deferential partiality[6] when some concession is granted to some person or persons for a reason, according to place and time, for the sake not of private but of public advantage.[7] In truth, it was put to us by you that, formerly, at the time when you undertook the government of Portugal, because of urgent necessities with which your Sublimity was beset, and to avoid grave and manifest dangers, which pressed in closely on you and your kingdom, and also because of the fear which could fall on a steady man,[8] you contracted a *de facto* marriage with the noble woman Beatrice, the child of our dearest son in Christ A., the illustrious King of Castile, she being then below marriageable age, notwithstanding that she was related to you in the fourth degree of consanguinity,[9] when your wife of famous memory Mathilda, Countess of Boulogne, your legitimate wife, was still alive. But our predecessor Pope Alexander of happy memory, moved by the outraged pleas[10] of the same countess, passed by apostolic authority, with the advice of his brothers, a sentence separating the same countess from you, with respect to the marriage bed and living together and the service which a wife owes a husband by reason of matrimony. And so, not only on your part but on the part of our venerable brothers the archbishop of Braga[11] and of the other bishops and all the chapters and the religious and of all the communities and collectivities[12] of peoples of

---

[2] 'adinventionis'.   [3] 'provide'.   [4] 'evidens utilitas, maxime publica'.
[5] 'acceptione... personarum': i.e. partiality.   [6] 'deferri persone'.   [7] 'commodi'.
[8] To translate thus I have to emend 'statum' to 'constantem', but the former makes no sense, whereas the latter is a stock legal phrase (so, admittedly, the *lectio facilior*).
[9] 'que te nichilominus quarto consanguinitatis gradu contigit'.
[10] 'clamoribus'.   [11] Preceded by double dot.   [12] 'universitatum'.

the same kingdom, though their special letter(s),[13] and also through our venerable brothers the bishops of Coimbra and Lisbon,[14] who came to our presence on this account, the petition was humbly presented to us that – since the aforesaid countess has gone the way of all flesh, and since you would not be able to cease to live with the aforementioned Beatrice without great and certain danger to your person and the said kingdom, and a great slaughter of many people – we might with apostolic solicitude make it our business to provide a solution for this problem,[15] especially since you have already begotten three children with her.[16] We, therefore – in view of the outstanding and devout merits of your ancestors, with which, at various times,[17] they endeared themselves to the apostolic see and made themselves pleasing in the eyes of God, and considering too that the said kingdom pays an annual sum to mark dependence of the Roman Church,[18] because of which we are bound to remove everything through which the peaceful state of the same kingdom might be disturbed, and bearing in mind furthermore that not only the archbishop and bishops and the others aforesaid, but even also our most beloved sons in Christ Louis the illustrious King of the French and Thibaud the illustrious King of Navarre and our beloved son the noble man Charles, Count of Anjou and Provence, have made devout supplications to us on this account, and wishing to make provision for your salvation and that of the aforesaid Beatrice, and also to procure benefits for this kingdom especially[19] in this matter, and to meet the wishes of the kings and the count and the prelates and the others aforementioned in this regard: – yielding to your prayers and those of the same kings, count, prelates and others, grant by apostolic authority to you and the same Beatrice that, these impediments in no way withstanding, you may freely remain in conjugal union,[20] determining by the same authority the offspring that have been or are to be begotten by you to be legitimate, even[21] with respect to the succession of the aforesaid kingdom and any other acts.

[13] 'litteras': since the word for 'letter' is plural in Latin this could grammatically refer either to one or to a number of letters.

[14] Both names preceded by double dot.   [15] 'providere in hac parte'.

[16] See Detlev Schwennicke, *Stammtafeln zur Geschichte der Europäischen Staaten*, vol. II: *Die Ausserdeutschen Staaten: die regierenden Häuser der übrigen Staaten Europas* (Marburg, 1984), Tafel 38, for Alfonso's children and their dates.

[17] 'sub diversitate temporum'.

[18] A free translation of 'est Romane ecclesie censuale'.

[19] 'especially': it is trivially uncertain to which words the 'specialiter' should be attached – 'kingdom' or 'in this matter'.

[20] 'copula'.

[21] One could instead translate 'etiam' as 'also' and and link it with the previous context, which is how the editor took it, to judge from his punctuation.

[Therefore it is forbidden] for any man, etc. [to go against] our concession and constitution. If however anyone, etc. Given at Viterbo 14 Kalends of July, second year.

> (Jean Guiraud, *Les registres d'Urbain IV (1261–1264)*, vol. I: *Registre dit cameral* (Paris, 1899/1900 [1901 on title page], no. 375, cols. 103–4)

13   Jaume I of Aragon and Teresa

Here we see in action the principle that even clandestine marriages were indissoluble. The principle is exemplified again and again at lower social levels, as studies of Church court records show.[1] Understandably, cases at royal level are much rarer, though the marriage of Margaret Tudor to the Earl of Angus (below, **# 1528**), is probably another case in point. Since Jaume's second marriage ended with the death of his wife Violant in 1251, his marriage to Teresa would have been valid in canon law, even without a formal ceremony.

Historiographical highlights

For the Jaume–Teresa case we may return to Burns, 'The Spiritual Life of Jaume the Conqueror', the first part of whose account of Jaume's love life was quoted under **# 1229**. Here is the next part of the story, by which time Jaume would have been about sixty-one – the pope tactlessly draws attention to his advanced years – but clearly not too old to be infatuated:

The king then took to his bed the young Navarrese noblewoman Teresa Gil de Vidaure, and in some murky fashion contrived to lock himself into a common law marriage. After two sons blessed the union, James banished Teresa to Valencia and tried to divorce her on the irrelevant and probably false ground that Teresa had caught leprosy. He was already notorious in Christendom because of his latest and fiercest attachment, the Castilian lady Berenguera Alfonso. (p. 26)

---

[1] In all of the following studies, cases arising in one way or another from clandestine marriage contracts form the bulk of the material: R. H. Helmholz, *Marriage Litigation in Medieval England* (Cambridge, 1974), *passim*; F. Pedersen, *Marriage Disputes in Medieval England* (London, 2000); C. Donahue, *Law, Marriage, and Society in the Later Middle Ages* (Cambridge, 2007).

The translation

The document is translated from E. Martène and U. Durand, *Thesaurus Novus Anecdotorum*, vol. II (Clementis Papae Epistola CCXXX; Paris, 1717).

1266, February 17

Clement IV refuses Jaume I of Aragon's request for a dissolution of his marriage

The greater our sincere affection for you, the more we correct you as one close to you,[2] remembering the saying which shows that a father loves the son whom he corrects in a salutary way, and, conversely, that he who neglects to correct and spares the rod is shown to hate him. In truth, since the Lord endowed you with natural ability to such a degree that you stand out among the other princes of the world who have not received an academic education,[3] and you have learned many things by experience,[4] and have lent a willing ear to the opinions of wise men, and stored them in a retentive memory: we are astonished at the irresponsibility and the motivation[5] that lead you to present a petition contrary to God, abominable to angels, and monstrous to men. For you should not have believed that we would be willing to dissolve a true marriage and become polluted by sharing through consent in an illicit union. We believe indeed that you were aware, previously, that when you espoused the noble woman Teresa through words in the future tense, as is stated in your letter, even though it was not a true marriage, it was however initiated in such a way as[6] to become, once carnal union had followed, a true and consummated marriage. How could the vicar of God put asunder those whom God has joined together? Far be it from us to commit such a crime as to violate the laws of the Lord and, in order to please men, to offend the Creator and Redeemer of men. But, therefore, if the marriage between you and her were invalid, you have chosen the woman with whom it has pleased you to set up a ménage[7] either to be a wife or a mistress; if you wanted to have as a wife a woman whom

---

[2] 'familiarius'.

[3] 'inter alios mundi principes, quos litteralis scientia non instruxit, te Dominus excellenter ingenio naturali dotaverit'. This was true: Jaume was an outstanding writer.

[4] 'multa experientia': taking 'multa' as a plural direct object rather than as an ablative singular adjective going with 'experientia', which is also possible grammatically.

[5] 'miramur . . . qua licentia, quo instinctu'.

[6] 'sic . . . initiatum . . . ut'.   [7] 'superinducere'.

you admit is a bastard,[8] and in no way feared to thus stain your glory,[9] surely you ought not to have believed that we might provide assistance to such a base and ignoble falling off from your high position, by granting a dispensation. If you had opted to keep her for yourself in a state of concubinage,[10] the royal request had neither colour[11] nor taste, since you should not hope that the vicar of Jesus Christ, who detests all filthy things, would become the promoter of filth. If you perhaps ask what you ought to do, since you cannot cohabit with the first woman without bodily danger, there is a perfectly ready answer: endure what the hand of God lays on you.[12] You should not attribute to the guilt of the one who is suffering that which random chance has brought about. Do you believe that, if all the queens there are throughout the whole world[13] became lepers, we would give kings on that account the licence to contract marriage with other women? You know for sure that each and every one of them would suffer a rejection, even if the royal houses were to die out root and branch for want of issue. Therefore, dearest son, keeping the Lord before your eyes, and putting before yourself as an example that most kindly King of France, with whom you have forged a friendship, see how you are getting on in years,[14] see the gifts you have received from the hand of the Most High, see the cross which you have affixed to your shoulders,[15] see the wars and battles[16] into which you threw yourself with great gallantry,[17] and do not add adultery to incest,[18] since from this you may both render the good things which you do sterile so far as you are concerned, and store up the anger of God on the Day of Judgement. Nor should you say that you are incapable of continence. For that complaint long ago received its quietus. For how would a just and righteous Lord have ordained for everybody continence from illicit intercourse, if even one person were able to object that an impossible command did not have to be kept? But it is the custom of all sinners, as St Jerome says, to plead impossibility to excuse their wrongdoing, when unwillingness alone is responsible.[19]

---

[8] 'spuriam'.   [9] 'hanc in tua gloria ponere maculam'.
[10] 'si tibi concubinatum ipsius elegeras'.   [11] In the sense of 'plausibility'.
[12] 'Sustine manum Domini'.   [13] 'mundi climata'.
[14] 'quantum in diebus tuis processeris'.
[15] Presumably a reference to James I's status as a crusader.
[16] 'bellorum discrimina'.   [17] 'multum animose'.
[18] Taken literally this does not quite make sense. 'Incest' does not presumably refer to his marriage with Teresa, as it would in that case be invalid without dispensation. On the other hand, if it applies to the new woman it could not precede adultery. Presumably the meaning is: do not commit a sin combining adultery and incest.
[19] 'ad sui excusationem erroris non posse ponant in causa, cum sit nolle tantum in culpa'. I failed to find this in St Jerome.

Therefore it is just that we, who treat you favourably and kindly when necessity or utility demands, in licit and decent things, do not want in this matter to fulfil your desire, which goes against God. Given at Perugia, 13 Kalends March, second year.

14   Charles IV of France and Blanche: the law of godparenthood

Properly to understand Pope John XXII's legitimation of his decision in the Charles v. Blanche case two kinds of background knowledge are required. One is an understanding of the formal legal rationality of dispensation law and practice. This will be briefly discussed in the next chapter but an analysis of it will be a pivotal part of *Papacy, Monarchy and Marriage*. The other is appreciation of a clarification of godparenthood rules published by Pope Boniface VIII less than a quarter of a century before Charles v. Blanche. The pope tried on the one hand to discourage the practice of multiple godparenthood. On the other hand, however, he explicitly recognised that if the rules were disobeyed and several people together acted as godparents, the same bond was created for all of them as if only one man or woman had done so. This fits the case of Charles IV. His future mother-in-law, Blanche of Burgundy's mother Mahaut, was almost certainly one of many godparents in a chaotic-sounding baptismal ceremony. When this happened, Boniface's ruling was so recent that it might well not yet have filtered down to the laity. Boniface's succinct ruling, published in 1298 in the Sext (his supplement to the decretal compilation of Gregory IX), is important enough to be translated as a preliminary to the documents of the case.

Historiographical highlights

An old but important thesis, Elspeth Jaffé's dissertation 'Die Ehepolitik Bonifazius VIII' (Freiburg i. Breisgau, 1921),[1] stressed the importance of Boniface's declaration of the law on godparenthood. Jaffé traces the history of the rule which was one of the two main grounds for dissolving the marriage: namely, that the child and godchild of the same person could not get married. The rule seems to have been stated by the time

---

[1] The thesis is unpublished but available in libraries of both the Warburg Institute (call number BCB 1650) and the *Monumenta Germaniae Historica* in Munich.

of Innocent III, and Jaffé lists the precedents, but a decision of Boniface VIII refreshed it and gave it emphasis.[2] Jaffé is right to see it as making a difference. Of the precedents she cites, the decretal of Gregory IX covers a somewhat different case, where the baptiser and the child of the baptised are in question (rather than a godparent). As for the decretal of Innocent III, Jean Gaudemet notes that 'the gloss on the text adopts...restrictive interpretation'[3] – so the situation may have been confused. On Boniface VIII's law Jaffé comments that: 'The teaching on the impediment of spiritual relationship became clear-cut law only when Boniface VIII summed it up in an unambiguous formula.'[4] Or again:

Spiritual relationship includes, as *paternitas spiritualis* the godparent, or the baptiser and baptised as also the person confirmed; as *fraternitas* the person baptised and the children of the godparent; as *compaternitas*, it includes the natural parents of the person baptised, and the godparent, or the baptiser as the spiritual father; in a wider extension of the concept, as *affinitas spiritualis*, it includes also the spouse of the godparent. The details of this impediment, and in particular the extension of *compaternitas*, were controversial, until they were codified in a decretal of Boniface VIII.[5]

The translation

I have translated from E. Friedberg, *Corpus Iuris Canonici*, vol. II (Leipzig, 1922 edn), 1068.

---

[2] 'Aber auch schon Innocenz III in c. 7 X 4, 11 [= X.4.11.7] und Gregor IX in c. 8 X 4, 11 [=X.4.11.8] bringen die nachher von Bonifazius übernomennen zweifellose Anerkennung der fraternitas spiritualis zwischen Täufling und Kindern des Paten (aber nicht auch zwischen den Geschwistern des Täuflings und den Kinden des Paten) als impedimentum dirimens und impediens' (Anmerkungen zum I Kapitel, note 5, p. 12). X.4.11.7 seems more directly relevant than the Gregory IX ruling.

[3] J. Gaudemet, *Le mariage en occident: les mœurs et le droit* (Paris, 1987), p. 211.

[4] 'Erst in der eindeutigen, zuammenfassenden Formulierung, wie sie durch Bonifazius gegeben ist, wird die Lehre vom Hindernis der geistlichen Verwandschaft zum klaren Gesetz' (Jaffé, 'Die Ehepolitik', p. 15).

[5] 'Die geistliche Verwandschaft umfasst als paternitas spiritualis Pate, beziehungsweise Täufer und Täufling sowohl als auch Firmling, als fraternitas den Täufling und die Kinder des Paten, als compaternitas, die leiblichen Eltern des Täuflings und den Paten, bzw. Täufer als den geistlichen Vater, in einer weiteren Ausdehnung des Begriffs als affinitas spiritualis auch den angeheirateten Teil des Patenehepaars. Die Einzelheiten dieses Hindernisses, so besonders die Ausdehnung der Compaternitas, waren strittig, bis sie von Bonifazius VIII in einer Decretale normiert wurden' (Jaffé, 'Die Ehepolitik', p. 4).

 # 1298

Sext of Boniface VIII: Multiple godparents and 'spiritual relationship'

Although not several, but one man or one woman ought to go up to receive a baby from baptism according to the institutes of the sacred canons: if nonetheless several people go up to do so, a spiritual relationship is contracted which is an impediment to contracting marriages, and which even dissolves them if they have been contracted. Furthermore, in this respect the same judgement should hold good for confirmation. From the conferral of other sacraments, however, spiritual relationships such as to be an impediment to a marriage or to dissolve one in no way arise.

(Friedberg, VI.4.3.3)

15 Charles IV and Blanche: the annulment process

Charles IV was the last of the Capetians, a royal line stretching from the tenth to the fourteenth century. He was the son of King Philip IV 'the Fair' of France, and two older brothers preceded him as king: Louis X and Philip V. When he and his brothers were young there seemed no reason to doubt that the dynasty's unbroken tradition would continue indefinitely. Philip IV arranged suitable marriages for the boys. In 1305, when only in his mid-teens, Louis married a daughter of the Duke of Burgundy, Marguerite. A dispensation for consanguinity had been obtained. Very shortly after their marriage, still in 1305, they obtained a dispensation to remove an impediment that had been overlooked: he had been engaged to a close relation of Marguerite's. Moreover he had sworn to marry none other than the first girl, while she was alive. This type of impediment was called 'public honesty'. The pope was happy to grant a second dispensation, after which the marriage was watertight, perhaps unfortunately for Marguerite as things turned out.

In 1307 another dispensation was obtained for Charles. It does not specify any particular girl (even though his marriage to Blanche of Burgundy followed not long afterwards). The document allowed the Capetians to fill in the name of the bride, so to speak. To the untutored modern observer the document had a very curious feature: after allowing a marriage to a second cousin it goes on to allow also marriage to remoter relatives, whom one might have thought would be covered already a fortiori. In fact such literal precision was a feature of dispensations by this time. *Mutatis mutandis*, they were like insurance contracts today in their capacity for exactitude.

Louis, Charles and the somewhat more impressive middle brother Philip grew to maturity in a strange time. Pope Boniface VIII was humiliated, died and posthumously almost tried for heresy under pressure of their father and his frighteningly self-righteous minister de Nogaret. The Knights Templar were abolished – the hardest men in Europe broke and confessed anything the royal interrogators wanted. There were also 'leagues to protest various aspects of the royal administration',[1] and, in the same year, a scandal at the heart of the royal family – accusations of adultery against the wives of Louis and Charles. The young men in question were put to death publicly and gruesomely.

Male honour made marital relations between the princes and their wives more than problematic. Both wives were imprisoned, Louis's in such harsh conditions that she died (if she was not actually murdered); Blanche may have been treated more gently. Even after the scandal, it is possible that Charles IV and Blanche had sexual relations when she was in captivity, and that a son resulted (E. A. R. Brown has done important path-breaking work – unfortunately unpublished – on Charles's children). But a son born in such circumstances would not solve the succession problem. The circumstances of his conception and birth would make his legitimacy suspect. Anyway, one male heir was not enough, for even princes died young (as in fact the boy did), and spares were essential. The rapprochement with Blanche (if it did happen) did not mark a resumption of regular marital relations, so further heirs could not be expected from that quarter.

In 1322 Charles started annulment proceedings in the court of the bishop of Paris. The dossier of the proceedings is massive and reveals a rigorously formal procedure of the kind developed first in twelfth-century Italy and then by the papacy from the early thirteenth century onwards. Included are a long list of propositions, which the king's side thought would show the marriage to be null if they could be proved, and a huge dossier of witness depositions designed to prove them. A curious characteristic of the dossier is that some of the points that the king's side laboriously set out to demonstrate were unlikely to impress a pope who knew canon law and precedent. It is in fact a persistent feature of royal annulment proceedings that forlorn-hope arguments are regularly employed.

In the end the bishop of Paris pushed the whole dossier up for the pope to decide. John XXII did that with astonishing rapidity. By that time Charles was King of France. The whole thing looks like a political favour, a put-up job.

The speed was a big favour but it was not a put-up job. John XXII had the data and the canon-legal acumen to analyse it fast. He would have seen straight away that parts of the king's case were useless arguments. The claim that the marriage was invalid because banns had not been read beforehand did no credit to the common sense of the king's

---

[1] E. A. R. Brown's words in a personal communication, correcting my initial characterisation of these as 'revolts'.

advisers. Accepting it would have invalidated a high proportion of marriages in Europe, since clandestine consent was common and reluctantly
recognised by the Church as making a valid marriage. Equally ridiculous
was the argument that the dispensation for Charles to marry Blanche
was invalid because it claimed that Charles could not easily find someone of his own rank to marry. (The king's side argued that there were
some suitable girls around and that no-one would have turned a royal
French prince down.) Whoever came up with this line of reasoning had
no understanding of the conventions of papal dispensation practice. Such
justifications were half rhetorical and could not be considered part of the
'active ingredient' of the dispensation, which was the precise specification
of the impediments dispensed.

John would have seen all this but also that there was quite enough
in the dossier to justify a Persil-clean annulment. The crucial point was
that the dispensation did not cover the impediments blocking a marriage
between Charles and Blanche. This was not by chance. It had not been
custom-built for their marriage. The name of the bride was left blank,
so to speak. If Blanche's family had known their business they would
have asked for a dispensation designed to cover their case. Perhaps they
did not want to rock the boat when a royal marriage was in prospect.
The dispensation they did have was precise enough to make it clear that
such documents were formulated with a high degree of exactitude. It says
Charles can marry a second cousin, and then adds that he can also marry
a second cousin once removed or a third cousin – remoter relationships.
We would expect them to be implicit in the dispensation from closer ties.
But that was not how dispensations worked, as we know from other earlier
evidence. Unfortunately for Blanche, the dispensation, however tightly
worded, was not tightly worded in the right place. It said nothing of
descent from multiple common ancestors. Or perhaps fortunately, when
one thinks of how the analogous problem posed by her sister-in-law to
Louis X had been resolved.

John would also have noticed cumulative factual evidence that
Blanche's mother had been one of the (many) godparents of Charles.
A multiplicity of godparents was normal in the Middle Ages. A fairly
recent decision of Boniface VIII had made it clear that even though large
numbers of godparents were a bad idea, they did establish an impediment. The dispensation was silent on this also. The bull of annulment
mentioned only the multiple common ancestors and the godparenthood.
All the other ingenious yet feeble reasons dropped away.

The key documents translated to illustrate this case are John XXII's
bull of 1322 (printed in the École Française de Rome papal registers series) together with two remarkable documents in the Archives

nationales, J.682.1 and J.682.2,[2] recording the proceedings before the bishop of Paris in 1322. Together these constitute a full set of trial proceedings at this first stage. J.682.2, recording the witness depositions, is not far short of seven metres long. The legally most relevant passages are translated, with a diplomatic edition in Appendices 1 and 2.

Historiographical highlights

The basis of all subsequent understanding of the Charles–Blanche case was laid by M. J. Robert de Chevanne, 'Charles IV le Bel et Blanche de Bourgogne', *Bulletin philologique et historique (jusqu'à 1715) du Comité des travaux historiques et scientifiques, années 1936 et 1937* (Paris, 1938), pp. 313–50. He does not provide an edition or translation, but his full summary of the trial, including witness depositions, must command great respect from anyone who has worked through the same material. Since then, there has been less serious work directly on this famous case than one might have expected – a modest amount compared with the outpouring of writings about the Philip II–Ingeborg case before it or the Louis XII–Jeanne of France case after it, for instance.

Elisabeth Lalou, 'Le souvenir du service de la reine: l'hôtel de Jeanne de Navarre, reine de France, en juin 1294', in J. Paviot and Jacques Verger (eds.), *Guerre, pouvoir et noblesse au Moyen Âge: mélanges en l'honneur de Philippe Contamine* (Cultures et civilisations médiévales XXII; Paris, 2000), pp. 411–26, notes, at pp. 415–16, that a series of very precise questions about the sequence of events was put to the last witness interrogated at Creil (where the baptism of Charles had taken place and where a late set of depositions were taken). She asks whether the questionnaire for this final interrogation represented the condensation of all the previous ones, or if the previous witnesses had also responded to a similar structured questionnaire.[3] She would seem to favour the latter

---

[2] For reasons it would be interesting to know, there are at least a couple of post-medieval, pre-modern transcriptions: Paris, Bibliothèque nationale de France, Lat. 8935 and Paris, Bibliothèque Mazarine, 1986. Though these have no textual authority they are certainly easier to read, especially when the originals are damaged or creased. Though I have worked from the originals in the Archives nationales (microfilm with occasional visits), I have from time to time had recourse to them for ideas about how to transcribe a difficult word or phrase: so my thanks to those anonymous long-dead scholars. My thanks also to Professor Brown for help (which I have tried to acknowledge in each case) with difficult words and above all with proper names. It is to be hoped that she will produce a complete edition of the trial proceedings.

[3] 'À la première lecture du document, on a l'impression que les témoins se souviennent spontanément des événements sur lesquels on les interroge, mais le dernier témoignage recueilli à Creil jette un éclairage curieux sur toutes les réponses précédentes: en effet, des questions très précises sur le déroulement des faits furent posées à Adam Barbier qui

hypothesis, which is indeed plausible, but does not entitle us to discount the testimony. The impression from the large number of witness depositions translated below from Archives nationales, J.682.2 is that the witnesses were not all singing from the same hymnbook.

An unrivalled specialist, E. A. R. Brown, has not yet published her results, which are based on impressive knowledge of the material and the whole context. Olivier Canteaut, 'L'annulation du mariage de Charles IV et de Blanche de Bourgogne: une affaire d'État?', in Emmanuelle Santinelli (ed.), *Répudiation, séparation, divorce dans l'Occident médiéval* (Recherches Valenciennoises XXV; Valenciennes, 2007), pp. 309–27, draws in part on collaboration with Professor Brown; his full and scholarly notes bring together previous scholarship on and around the topic. He is very good on the proctors of Blanche, showing that three of them were probably connected to a Pierre de Mortemart who was close to Charles IV (pp. 322–3). Interestingly, however, 'we know nothing at all' ('nous ignorons tout') of Aymeri Mazerant, the fourth proctor: i.e. there is no evidence that he was in the pocket of the king or his friends. That does not mean there were no such connections: we simply do not know. We should note, though, that he seems to have been playing a poor hand rather well on Blanche's behalf; Canteaut himself remarks on the firmness of his opposition to the royal demand (p. 320).

Nonetheless Canteaut suggests that 'the proceedings as a whole must . . . have been orchestrated by Charles IV and his entourage, to give the appearance of an impartial and equitable trial'[4] and that the royal entourage may have wholly or partly dictated Blanche's defence moves.[5] He argues that:

In any case, and contrary to appearances, when Mazerant invokes the dispensation bull of Clement V, the argument could in no way have surprised the opposing party: from the first effort to obtain a declaration of nullity, in 1318–20, that question of the validity of this bull had already been raised by John XXII, and it was inevitable that it would be invoked again.[6]

---

y répond point par point. Les questions posées lors de ce dernier témoignage étaient-elles le fruit, le condensé de tous les interrogatoires précédents ou bien tous les témoins ont-ils [inc. p. 416] répondu à ces questions si précises? Cela jette sur la lecture que l'on peut faire du document entier un éclairage particulier si c'est le cas' (Lalou, 'Le souvenir', pp. 415–16).

[4] 'L'ensemble de la procédure aurait donc été orchestré par Charles IV et son entourage, afin d'offrir l'image d'un procès impartial et équitable' (Canteaut, 'L'annulation', p. 323).

[5] 'Il est même possible que la défense de Blanche ait été dictée en tout ou en partie par l'entourage royale' (*ibid.*, p. 323).

[6] 'Dans tous les cas, et contrairement aux apparences, lorsque Mazerant invoque la bulle de dispense de Clément V, l'argument ne saurait guère surprendre la partie adverse:

This does not fit easily with the dogged rearguard action in defence of Blanche's marriage by her proctor Aymeri Mazerant. There are several problems with Canteaut's hypothesis. That the king's side were aware of the dispensation as a potential problem does not mean much if one casts one's mind forward to the annulment of Louis XII's marriage with Jeanne of France. In that trial, the king's side must have been well aware of the dispensation for Louis and Jeanne to marry, and yet they tried hard to make a 'forbidden degrees' argument stick. The queen's side stopped this abruptly by producing the dispensation bull. Presumably the king's team hoped she did not have a copy. Probably it was the same with the 1322 case.

In 1322, as it happened, the dispensation did not in the end help Blanche because it did not cover her relationship with Charles, as the keen legal mind of Jean XXII will have immediately understood. Charles IV's legal team do not seem to have been so clear-headed, however, because they seemed to be in disarray when the bull was produced, another fact noted by Canteaut, one which rather tends to undermine his apparent suspicion that the trial was orchestrated by the king's side. Here the reader may see for themselves how the king's side reacted to the dispensation argument (in Appendix 1, third membrane, lines 45–58 for the Latin and **# 1322, J.682.1** paragraph (m) of the translation below). The royal proctor flails around, suggesting that there may never have been a dispensation (in the hope that the queen did not have a copy?) and, no doubt aware that she might have one or be able to obtain one, guessing at a series of different ways in which the dispensation fell short rather than homing in on the relevant legal facts, that it did not cover multiple common ancestors or spiritual affinity, for reasons we have seen. Particularly interesting is the striking evidence of redrafting on the manuscript document itself around this point, suggesting two attempts had to be made to create an acceptable record. The trial was adjourned to allow Blanche's side to produce the dispensation, which of course turned out to be inadequate for their purposes.

Canteaut rightly stresses royal reluctance for the trial to seem like a divorce because of adultery. Charles IV's resentments going back to 1314 and his desperate desire for an heir are indeed obvious motives, but whatever his motivation, it had to be translated into legitimation. For reasons stated, that was possible. The data produced at the trial,

---

lors de la première tentative pour obtenir une déclaration de nullité, en 1318–1320, la question de la validité de cette bulle avait déjà été soulevée par Jean XXII, et il était inéluctable que celle-ci soit de nouveau invoquée' (*ibid.*, p. 323).

coupled with the shortcomings of a too generic, 'fill in the name' form of dispensation, added up to a valid case in canon law for the result the king wanted. Henry VIII would not be so lucky.

The translations

The trial proceedings are translated from the transcription of (substantial) extracts from Archives nationales, J.682.1 and J.682.2 printed as Appendices 1 and 2. I have selected the parts of the proceedings which seem legally decisive. John XXII's bull, which emphasises the same legal issues, is translated from the edition in A. Coulon, *Lettres secrètes et curiales du pape Jean XXII (1316–1334) relatives à la France* (Bibliothèque des Écoles Françaises d'Athènes et de Rome; Paris, 1906), cols. 92–108.

1322, J.682.1

Translation of opening proceedings and of propositions to be put to witnesses.

Note on alphabetical paragraph numbering: the numbering is entirely editorial. It matches the numbering of the Latin, printed as Appendix 1.[7]

(a) In the name of the Lord Amen. Let all people know that in[8] this year of the Lord 1321,[9] on the Thursday before the Feast of St Agatha the Virgin, appeared before ourselves, Stephen, by the permission of God bishop of Paris, in our house at Paris, in the presence of the reverend fathers Lord I. by the provision of God bishop of Beauvais, and Master Geoffrey de Plessy, notary of our lord pope, and the notaries whose names are listed below, and many other honourable men, that man of discretion Master Pierre Gouvanh,[10] cleric, proctor, and with procuratorial commission[11] from the magnificent and most excellent prince the Lord Charles, by the grace of God King of France and Navarre, who had

---

[7] The translation owes a lot to the French précis by de Chevanne (who did not publish the text but who was surely working from a competent transcription) and especially to his conversion of proper names into a modern French form.

[8] 'illo'.

[9] It was 1322 according to modern dating of the start of the year from 1 January (as opposed to the date of Easter), which is probably the dating system used here: Cf. C. R. Cheney and Michael Jones, *A Handbook of Dates for Students of English History* (Cambridge, 2000), p. 5.

[10] Name supplied to me by E. A. R. Brown; de Chevanne, 'Charles IV', p. 320, has 'Gauvain'.

[11] 'nomine procuratorio'.

cited, as he said, for the aforesaid day and place, the noble Lady Blanche
of Burgundy, the daughter of Lady Mahaut the Countess of Artois, and
Aymeri Mazerant, her proctor, by a letter from ourselves sealed with
our seal attached to them,[12] as produced and reproduced[13] below. In
the same place there appeared before us the aforesaid Aymeri Mazerant, proctor, as he said, and with proctorial commission from the said
Lady Blanche; and in the same place the said Master Peter, to authenticate his status as proctor, produced a certain letter of the said lord the
king as being true and authentic and sealed with the true great seal of
the said lord king attached to it,[14] the contents of which follow in these
words:

(b) {¶ Charles by the grace of God King of France and Navarre, to all those
who will inspect the present letter, greetings. You should know that through the
present letter[15] we have made and constituted and still make and constitute as
our proctors and special messengers our beloved and faithful men Master Pierre
Gouvanh[16] and Guillaume Soubut,[17] clerics, and each of them entirely[18] – so
that it should not be the case or happen, at any part of the judgement, that
one cannot complete what another has begun:[19] giving and conceding to our
aforesaid proctors and to each of them entirely full and unlimited[20] power and
a special mandate to act on our behalf, and in our name, in cases which we
have started or which are to be started by us and especially in the case for
the annulment of the marriage once contracted *de facto* between ourselves and
Blanche of Burgundy, and to attack in any way whatsoever the same marriage,
or illicit union looking like a marriage which she and ourselves which formerly
obtained and was contracted,[21] both by reason of the consanguinities and degrees
within which we are related to each other and on any other ground whatsoever,
and also [to attack] whatever should happen to be put up by way of opposition[22] in
defence of the marriage or union, by means of objections, defects, replications[23]
or other rationales[24] of any kind whatsoever pertaining to us or likely to do
so in the future, against the aforesaid or things connected to them; and, with
respect to the aforesaid and things connected to them, to defend us and act on
our behalf before the bishop of Paris and before other judges ordinary, delegate,
commissioners, auditors, and anyone else before whom it may happen that actions

---

[12] 'impendenti'.   [13] 'contentas'.   [14] 'impendenti'.   [15] 'per presentes'.
[16] Or 'Gauvain'.   [17] Or 'Sonbut', as according to de Chevanne, 'Charles IV', p. 320.
[18] 'in solidum'; 'jointly' does not seem to fit the 'each of them' so well.
[19] 'ita quod non sic nec fiat in aliqua parte iudicii melior conditio occupantis' – so
the Roman law rule (Digest 3.3.32) to the contrary did not apply. See Appendix 1,
(b) note 17.
[20] 'liberam'.   [21] 'olim . . . habitam et contractam'.   [22] 'opponi'.
[23] 'replicandi': a replication is 'any response made by one party to the other's argument',
etc. (*Oxford English Dictionary*, s.v.).
[24] 'rationalibus'.

are brought, petitions submitted or objections made,[25] or any other kind of legal proceedings conducted, by us or against us in respect of the above, at any time and at any place, and even before the most Holy Father in the Lord the supreme pontiff, if it should happen that there be legal actions or proceedings before him in any way whatsoever with respect to the same matters, in or outside a judicial framework: both against the said Blanche and against any other person wishing to put up opposition in respect of these things; and to present in our name once or on several occasions a petition or petitions, to accept fully and freely the jurisdiction of any judge whether ordinary or delegate who might not otherwise have cognisance,[26] to swear the oath of calumny[27] and the oath to tell the truth, and swear on my soul[28] any other appropriate or necessary oath, to formulate *positiones*[29] and articles,[30] to produce and receive witnesses, letters and official documents,[31] to make replication, to withdraw formally[32] from and conclude[33] in a trial before a judge ordinary and in a lawsuit,[34] to hear interlocutory[35] and definitive sentences, and, if it should be necessary, to appeal, and to pursue appeals should it happen that they have been made[36] in the matters set out above, to substitute one or several proctors, with the same[37] power once or several times, and of substituting, revoking, and of doing in our name each and every other thing – whatsoever they are[38] and of any sort whatsoever[39] in the aforesaid matters and matters in any way related to them – that we might be able to do were it to happen that we were to intervene personally, even if these might be or will be such things as to require a special mandate: promising nonetheless, by the force of the present document,[40] to all those concerned or who could be concerned in the

---

[25] 'excipi'.

[26] For this sense of 'prorogare' see Adrianus den Bandt, *Specimen Iuridicum Inaugurale De Prorogata Jurisdictione* (Lugduni Batavorum, 1852), p. 2: 'Prorogationem Jurisdictionis igitur putamus eam quae vel voluntate partium, vel legis praecepto, extra terminos suos exercetur.'

[27] 'de calumnia': an oath that the party to the suit was acting in good faith and not out of malice, and would not try to pervert the course of justice.

[28] 'in nostram animam': a technical term implying that the person represented is morally responsible. My thanks to Emily Corran for making this clear to me.

[29] i.e. propositions to be tested.

[30] 'ponendi, articulandi': so I am taking 'ponendi' to refer to the *positiones* formulated by the parties in the canon law procedure, and linking it with 'articulandi', rather than understanding it to refer back to the preceding context as governing 'iuramentum'. On this latter (possible) interpretation the Latin would be punctuated as follows: 'et veritate iurandi et in nostram animam subeundi, quodlibet aliud oportunum . . . iuramentum ponendi, articulandi'.

[31] 'instrumenta'.

[32] 'renuntiandi': see *Oxford English Dictionary*, s.v. 'renounce', under 'Etymology'.

[33] 'concludendi': technical, probably here meaning bringing a case to a close.

[34] 'processui ordinario et in causa renuntiandi et concludendi'.

[35] 'interlocutorias': technical, probably here meaning 'provisional' or 'not final'.

[36] 'si quas interponi contigerit'.   [37] 'consimili'.

[38] 'fuerint' – but English does not use the future perfect in such contexts.

[39] 'cuiuscumque status': taking 'status' in a broad sense.

[40] Taking 'tenore presentium' as the start of the clause after the colon rather than the conclusion of the long passage before it.

future, that we will in the future hold to be ratified and pleasing to us whatever should be done, carried out, raised as an objection,[41] put forward by way of defence,[42] or otherwise done by proxy in our name in the aforesaid matters by these said proctors of ours or one or other of them or by those whom they may in the future appoint to substitute for them, acting together or severally; promising nonetheless on their behalf and on behalf of each one of them security for costs[43] guaranteed by[44] all my goods and relieving each of them from any burden of giving satisfaction.[45] To authenticate[46] and give testimony to these things and to reinforce their validity[47] we have had our seal affixed and appended[48] to the present letter. Given at Paris, 30 January 1321.[49]}

(c) Again, to authenticate the aforesaid citation he produced a certain other letter sent by us and sealed as being true and authentic[50] with our true seal, which is attached to it,[51] the contents of which are known to be as follows:

(d) {¶ Étienne by divine permission bishop of Paris to our beloved Cotard de Moylinis and to all others with the care of souls[52] and to the clerics of our diocese subject to us, greetings. We hereby[53] charge, command and order you, and each one of you who may in the future receive instructions,[54] that you should execute a peremptory summons to appear before us on the Lady Blanche of Burgundy, the daughter of the late Count of Burgundy, or her proctor specially appointed to deal with the matters written below, and through the present letter we nonetheless[55] summons – and peremptorily – her or him to appear either in person, or through a sufficiently instructed[56] proctor, or that the same proctor should appear on her behalf before us, at Paris in our hall on the Wednesday after the Purification of Blessed Mary, unless it should be a holiday, or, if it should be a holiday, on the following day, [to reply][57] to the writ[58] or petition which the proctor of the most excellent and most powerful prince the Lord Charles by the grace of God King of France and Navarre had submitted to us, and nonetheless intends to submit against her on the said day; we have had the contents of his petition or writ inserted in the present summons, so that she may in the meantime give it her full attention, it being worded as follows:

---

[41] 'exceptum'.   [42] 'deffensum'.   [43] 'iudicatum solvi': technical legal term.
[44] 'ypotheca'.   [45] 'a quolibet honere satisdandi': a formulaic legal term.
[46] 'In...fidem'.   [47] 'in...maioris roboris firmitatem'.   [48] 'appendi...apendi'.
[49] i.e. 1322, if the calendar year started at Easter, according to the 'mos gallicanus', the dating system used here. See above, # 1322, J.682.1 note 9.
[50] Taking 'pro vera et autentica' with 'sigillatum', on grounds of word order, rather than with 'citatione'.
[51] 'impendenti'.   [52] 'curatis'.   [53] 'tenore presentium'.   [54] 'fueritis requisiti'.
[55] 'nonetheless' because he is issuing the summons directly, as well as indirectly through his clergy.
[56] 'sufficienter instructum': another technical legal term: see Gaines Post, *Studies in Medieval Legal Thought* (Princeton, NJ, 1964), p. 131.
[57] Omitted in manuscript.   [58] 'libello'.

(e) {{'Before you, reverend father in Christ Lord Étienne by divine provision bishop of Paris, P. Gouvanh, proctor and with procuratorial commission[59] from the renowned and most excellent prince the Lord Charles, by the grace of God King of France and Navarre, asserts and proposes that the aforesaid Lord Charles contracted marriage but only *de facto*, clandestinely, without the banns being read, and in other ways less than legitimately, with the Lady Blanche, daughter of the late Count of Burgundy, she being related to him within the forbidden degrees and with various links of consanguinity, and with respect to several common ancestors, and with both of them being below the age of puberty at that time, for which reasons and others the said Blanche could not legally be joined to him in marriage; nor can the same prince any longer remain in this union which is illicit in this way[60] without detriment to his soul and grave scandal to many. On this account the lord proctor asks that the said marriage be pronounced and declared by a sentence [of the court] to have been and to be null in law, and that a licence may be granted to the said lord king freely to contract marriage with another woman; and he asks for the aforesaid things in whatever permitted way and form that may work best,[61] not binding himself to prove more of the aforesaid things than will suffice for him to achieve his purpose,[62] and he makes the affirmation that he will declare,[63] add and subtract as often as necessary the replies which may be given,[64] and in other respects, furthermore, the proceedings and actions which may duly be undertaken in accordance with reason[65] concerning the matters contained in the aforesaid petition; making it clear to the same lady that whether she comes or not we will nonetheless proceed with respect to all the aforesaid things insofar as it can and should be done in accordance with the law. But you should give a faithful report at the place and day aforesaid of whatever you do in consequence of this. Given at Paris on 26 January 1321.'[66]}}

(f) — asking that before anything else the aforesaid Aymeri should authenticate for us his authority to act as proctor[67] in order that the trial might safely be conducted with the same [Aymeri]; and in the same place[68] the said Aymeri, to authenticate his office as proctor, produced a certain public legal document[69] — as being true and public,[70] produced by the hand of the venerable man Lord Amicus dean of Paris, notary public

---

[59] 'procuratorio nomine'.   [60] 'sic illicita': or perhaps: 'which is so illicit'.
[61] 'omni modo et forma cum quibus melius sibi licet' – technical legal language.
[62] 'non…nisi ad ea dumtaxat probanda que sibi sufficere poterunt de premissis ad propositum consequendum'.
[63] 'protestatur de declarando' (etc.).   [64] 'responsura'.
[65] 'ulterius…debite processura et factura que fuerint rationis'.
[66] i.e. 1322 in modern terms. See above, **# 1322. J.682.1** note 9.
[67] 'de sua procuratione faceret nobis fidem'.
[68] Taking 'ibidem' with the following rather than the preceding clause, though either seems possible.
[69] 'quoddam publicum instrumentum'.
[70] 'pro vero et publico' – another stock legal phrase.

by apostolic authority, as was apparent at first view,[71] and underwritten and co-signed by the discreet man Master Jean de Essartis, also a public notary by the same apostolic authority, as was read at first view – with the following content or tenor:

(g){'In the name of the Lord, amen. Let it be evident to all that in the year of the same Lord 1321, fifth indiction, in the month of January, on the 24th day of the same month, in the sixth year of the pontificate of the most Holy Father and lord, Lord John XXII by divine providence pope, the noble woman the Lady Blanche of Burgundy, being personally in the presence of myself, notary public, and of the witnesses whose names are written below, not tricked,[72] nor deceived by any deceit, fraud or plot on anyone's part, pressured[73] in any way or led astray, but freely, by her own choice,[74] and over her own free will, and after discussing it fully with her friends, as she said, aware that she had a number of times, and from various trustworthy people, heard that marriage [had been] contracted formerly *de facto* only between the most excellent prince Lord Charles, now by the grace of God the illustrious King of France and Navarre, and herself: both[75] because it is commonly said to be and have been null as laid down by law,[76] as a result of the impediments of blood relationship in which they are notoriously related, as he has asserted, and as a result of a number of other obstacles,[77] defects and many other reasons; and because in consequence it would redound to the prejudice of her soul and to the grave scandal of the people if she were to remain any longer in such a reprehensible marriage, or more truly incestuous relationship; and that it is neither expedient nor fitting, because of the fragility of her sex and of what the decency of her status requires, for her to involve herself personally in the twists and turns of the judicial process, especially on a regular basis:[78] she has made, constituted and ordained, [for] whenever she should happen to be away, as her true[79] proctors and special envoys[80] the discreet men Pierre de Culieto,[81] Jocelin de Borderia and Amblard Serem,[82] clerics, and Aymeri Maserant, esquire, and each of them entirely[83] – so that it should and could not be the case that one of them cannot complete what another has begun;[84] giving and conceding to her aforesaid proctors and to each of the same a general, full and free power, and a special mandate to act on her behalf with respect to[85] the annulment of the said marriage, and [to defend] her with respect to the annulment of this marriage,

---

[71] 'prima facie': probably without the modern sense of merely provisionally probative evidence.

[72] 'nec cauta': 'coacta', a tempting emendation, is not possible palaeographically and would be the *lectio facilior*.

[73] 'inducta'.   [74] 'spontanea'.

[75] Taking 'et [both] quod ex' with 'et [and] quod per consequens'.

[76] 'ipso iure' is translated as 'durch Rechtsbestimmung' in A. Sleumer, *Kirchenlateinisches Wörterbuch* (Hildesheim, 2006), s.v. 'ius'.

[77] 'obiectibus' *sic* for 'obiectionibus'?   [78] 'presertim frequenter'.

[79] 'certos'.   [80] 'nuncios'.

[81] Thus in de Chevanne's French paraphrase: but the Latin in J.682.1 seems to read 'de Culreto'.

[82] For the names here I follow de Chevanne's modernisation of the Latin.

[83] 'in solidum'.   [84] 'non sit nec esse possit melior conditio occupantis'.   [85] 'ad'.

whatever the cause or causes on which these proceedings are based,[86] before our venerable father in Christ the lord bishop of Paris, by the grace of God, under whose jurisdiction she falls, as she said,[87] and whose jurisdiction, to put the aforesaid matter on a surer footing, she has expressly accepted on this matter even if he does not have normal cognisance,[88] as she asserted in my presence and that of the witnesses listed below; and before another judge or other judges ordinary, delegate or auditors[89] of any sort, whatever the authority by which they are conducting proceedings;[90] [the proctors have a mandate to act] jointly or separately, in any way whatever, in any place, even before our most Holy Father and lord aforesaid the supreme pontiff, whenever it might come about that there should be dealings, or proceedings of other sorts,[91] in any way whatsoever, with regard to the said marriage or things touching on it essentially[92] or incidentally, before him; and to receive a writ or writs,[93] a summary petition or petitions, to accept, whether tacitly or explicitly, ordinary and delegated jurisdiction that might not otherwise have cognisance,[94] to carry out the *litis contestatio*,[95] to swear the oath that the defence is offered in good faith and the oath to tell the truth, and to swear on the soul of she who is appointing them any other oath,[96] to withdraw formally from a trial before a judge ordinary and take up[97] a summary trial, to state *positiones* and articles, to reply to *positiones* and articles whether by denying or admitting them, to produce witnesses and official documents and to attack the witnesses and official documents that are brought against her, or even to assent to them if when they think fit,[98] to withdraw formally and conclude,[99] to hear interlocutory[100] and definitive sentences, and to appeal from them, or to consent to them tacitly or explicitly, as it seems appropriate to them or any one of them to do, to substitute one or several proctors, with the same[101] power, once or several times, and of revoking the powers of their substitutes,[102] of making use of delays and objections to which they are or will be entitled, and of renouncing the same, and of doing each and everything else whatsoever it might be that she might do and could do if she were present in person, and which in any way, in the matters set out above, or with respect to the these matters, or to any one of them, or to things depending on them,[103] could either depend or arise from the aforementioned[104] or[105] be in any way necessary or even opportune in the

---

[86] 'ex causa seu causis quibuslibet hoc procedit'.

[87] 'suo competenti iudice, ut dicebat'.

[88] 'prorogaverat'. See above, **# 1322. J.682.1** note 29. The sense here would seem to be that Blanche declares that she thinks the bishop of Paris has jurisdiction but that she is prepared to accept his jurisdiction should he not have it already.

[89] 'auditoribus' here = judges – a common term at the papal court.   [90] 'processerint'.

[91] 'alias disceptari'.   [92] 'principaliter'.   [93] 'libellum seu libellos . . . recipiendi'.

[94] 'prorogandi': see above, **# 1322. J.682.1** note 29.

[95] Formal act agreeing to contest the case.

[96] 'in ipsius constituentis animam subeundi quodlibet aliud iuramentum'.

[97] 'assumendi'.   [98] 'si viderint expedire'.   [99] 'renuntiandi et concludendi'.

[100] 'interlocutorias': see **# 1322. J.682.1** note 35 above.   [101] 'consimili'.

[102] 'substitutosque revocandi'.   [103] 'exinde'.

[104] 'dependentia vel dependere seu emergere poterunt'.

[105] Taking 'vel . . . poterunt' and 'vel . . . fuerint' together.

aforementioned matters, and this[106] both in court[107] and outside court, when due process is being observed or when it is set aside,[108] entirely or in part, even if all those things which they do together or separately should be or will be such as require a special order: promising[109] me, the notary whose name is written below, recording this bindingly[110] and receiving it on behalf of each and every person whom it concerns or could concern in the future, that she holds and will in perpetuity hold to be ratified and pleasing to her whatever shall be said, done, conceded, confessed, or otherwise performed or procured in any way whatsoever, together or separately, in the things set out above or in any one of them, by the said proctors or those to be appointed by them or by one of them as substitutes, and also, on their behalf and on behalf of each one of them, security for costs, and, on the guarantee of all her goods, relieving them and each one of them from any burden of giving satisfaction in the aforesaid things and things connected with them; requiring that I, and the notary whose name is written below, keep a record of[111] each and every one of the things set out above and turn them into a legally binding document,[112] one or several, connected or separately,[113] as we are required by her or her proctors.'}

(h) These things were done in the year, indiction, month, day and pontificate set out above, at Chateau Gaillard of the diocese of Rouen, in the presence of the noble and magnificent Lord Robert d'Artois, Count of Beaumont,[114] knight, the noble men the lords Dreux de Roye, Jean de Villeperreuse, Thibaud de Pomolain, knights, Masters Pierrie de Neuville, licentiate of civil law[115] canon of Douai in the diocese of Arras, Jean de Essartis, notary public by the authority of the apostolic see, and certain other men and women of the entourage and household[116] of the said Blanche, witnesses specially summoned and requested for this purpose. And I, Amis d'Orléans,[117] called 'le Ratif', cleric, public notary by apostolic authority, was present and took part in each and every one of the aforesaid things just as they were specified and narrated above, together with the witnesses whose names are given above: I saw them and heard them, and I explained them, set down in a short memo,[118] in her mother tongue,[119] in a comprehensible way, to the said Blanche;[120] and this legally valid public document, which I thereupon[121] prepared

---

[106] 'hoc' – but hec could be read.   [107] 'iudicio'.
[108] 'servato iuris ordine vel obmisso'.
[109] It is Blanche who is making the promise to the notary.   [110] 'stipulanti'.
[111] 'ut . . . reciperemus'.   [112] 'de premissis . . . faceremus publicum instrumentum'.
[113] 'coniunctim vel divisim'.   [114] 'Roberto de Attrebatesio comite Bellimontis'.
[115] 'licentiato in legibus'.   [116] 'domicellis familiaribus'.
[117] 'Amasius de Aurelianis'.   [118] 'notula'.
[119] 'in notula redacta in lingua materna': this probably implies that the 'notula' was in French, though it is conceivable that it was in Latin, and explained orally in French.
[120] 'dicte intelligibiliter exposui Blanche'.   [121] 'inde'.

in my own hand at the request of the said Blanche, I have signed, as requested, with my notarial sign[122] as testimony of the things set out above. And I, Jean des Essartis, cleric of the diocese of Rouen, notary public by apostolic and imperial authority, was present and took part in each and every one of the aforesaid things just as they are specified and narrated above, together with the public notary and the witnesses whose names are written above: I saw them and heard them, and, as requested and required, in testimony to the things set out above, I have confirmed[123] the present public and legally binding document of the aforesaid things – which had been explained in a comprehensible way in a short memo in her mother tongue[124] to the said Blanche by the said notary public – after the document had been drawn up, by my sign manual,[125] together with the sign manual of the same notary public.

(i) After these things had been approved and completed[126] in this way and the appropriate oath administered[127] to each of the aforesaid proctors, the aforementioned proctor of the lord king asked for an urgent reply, as the present day required, by the aforesaid proctor of the said Lady Blanche to the *libellus* which had been handed over on a separate occasion,[128] and which is contained in the aforesaid summons, in the same place asking for this petition again[129] and presenting it, asserting that we were the competent judge of the matters contained in the same *libellus*, both by reason of the residency of the aforesaid Lord Charles and of Blanche and also by reason of the origin of both of them, and again also by the explicit extension of our jurisdiction made in our favour[130] by the oft-mentioned lady, as he asserted to be evident in the public legally valid document prepared by the hand of the aforesaid dean, to be produced below. The proctor of the said lady, indeed, when questioned by us, admitted that the said extension had been made, and nevertheless, beyond what is required, the aforesaid two proctors explicitly agreed to the extension[131] of our jurisdiction, with their certain knowledge[132] and with the power specially given to them with respect to this, as could be made more fully apparent from the contents of the aforesaid procuratorial commissions produced above, and they wished[133] and consented

---

[122] 'signo publico'.   [123] 'communivi'.   [124] See above, note 119.
[125] 'signo et subscriptione'.   [126] 'peractis'.
[127] 'debita data fide': alternatively, but less probably, 'the fiduciary role had been duly transmitted [to the proctors]'.
[128] 'alias': 'elsewhere' is a possible translation.   [129] 'quem libellum . . . repetiit'.
[130] 'ex prorogatione expressa iurisdictionis nostre in nos'.
[131] 'iurisdictionem . . . prorogaverunt'.   [132] 'ex certa scientia'.
[133] 'voluerunt' – here understood as paired with 'consenserunt' after it rather than 'prorogaverunt' before it, though either is possible linguistically.

that we might be able freely to hold hearings, have cognisance of, and give definitive judgements[134] about the things contained in the aforesaid *libellus*, both in our diocese and in some other one, if the consent of the ordinaries[135] of the other places is granted for this, and that in the aforesaid matters, when the nature of the matter[136] demands this, we may be able to proceed summarily, straightforwardly, and without judicial commotion and formalities,[137] entirely or in part, as will seem expedient to us. After this, the aforesaid Master Pierre asked as before that a response might be given as a matter of urgency to his *libellus*, since the opposing party, which had for a long time previously had a copy of the aforesaid summons and *libellus*, had had full opportunity to deliberate, so that it could and should respond with the benefit of due consideration to what had been asked and proposed. He had maintained[138] however that he was not restricting himself to the formal *libellus* and trial procedure[139] except insofar as he is constrained to do so by law.[140] The said Aymeric, questioned about this, admitted that the said lady and he himself had had a copy of the said summons and *libellus* for a suitable period of time[141] and that he had deliberated fully with the said Lady Blanche about the reply that he proposed to give, after which replies we enjoined him to reply to the aforesaid petition or *libellus*; and then the same proctor replied in this way: firstly, he admitted that a marriage had been formerly contracted between the aforementioned Lord Charles and Lady Blanche, and the aforementioned lord king and Blanche were related within forbidden degrees of consanguinities, and that both of the aforesaid persons were below the age of puberty at the time of the said marriage, and that the banns had not been published, since, as he said, it is not customary for these banns to precede marriages of such persons. He denied that all the other things are true, as they are proposed, and said that the things requested should not be granted. And in the same place the said proctors, representing the intentions[142] of those they served,[143] in accordance with legal form,[144] with the power specially given to them in this matter in the aforesaid proxy commissions, swore the oath of calumny,[145] after which they swore the oath in respect of propositions alleged and responses to them,[146] and immediately the aforesaid Master Pierre, whose name was

---

[134] 'audire, cognoscere, et diffinire'.   [135] i.e. the bishops.   [136] 'facti qualitas'.
[137] 'summarie et de plano et sine strepitu iudicii et figura'.   [138] 'Protestatus...fuit'.
[139] 'solempnem libellum vel processum'.
[140] 'de iure artatur'.   [141] 'competenti tempore'.
[142] 'in animas' (with the implication of moral responsibility).
[143] 'dominorum suorum'.   [144] 'secundum formam iuris'.
[145] The oath that a case is being argued in good faith.
[146] 'post quod iuramentum prestiterunt in propositis et responsis'.

given above, wanting, as he said, so far as it was in his power,[147] and it could be well done,[148] the case to proceed with expeditious dispatch,[149] so that the truth might emerge the sooner and so that the aforesaid lord king and Lady Blanche should not remain in an incestuous relationship any longer, he made available and handed over to the aforesaid proctor of the Lady Blanche the *positiones* and articles inserted further on in the proceedings,[150] to which he asked for a response to be given on the [oath] of the proctor of the Lady Blanche. The said proctor replied however that he had not deliberated about the said *positiones* and articles, and that he did not want to take precipitate action with regard to them, asking that he be granted a delay during which the said lady, who knew the truth better, might respond, or he might do so after discussing the matter fully with her. And after a little dispute about this, with the consent of the aforesaid proctors, we assigned 8 February, at Les Andelys, in the place called Gaillard[151] – getting and obtaining the approval and authority[152] of the reverend father in Christ the Lord G. by divine providence the archbishop of Rouen, in whose diocese it is situated, as will be more fully apparent from the letters of the same reverend father to be inserted below – for the oft-mentioned Lady Blanche to reply to the aforesaid *positiones* or articles, and for the proceedings to take their due course in other respects,[153] guided by justice.

(j) ¶ The contents of the aforesaid *positiones* and articles handed over above[154] to the proctor of the said Lady Blanche follows as set out below.[155]

The proctor of the most excellent prince the Lord Charles now by the grace of God King of France and Navarre presents the *positiones* and articles written below against the Lady Blanche of Burgundy, daughter of the late Count of Burgundy, in the annulment case which is at issue between them before the reverend father in Christ the bishop of Paris.

(k)[1] ¶ Firstly he proposes[156] and intends to prove that the Lord Louis of famous memory, formerly King of France, and the Lady Blanche of Spain, were husband and wife and behaved and were held and reputed to be a married couple in their time in the city and diocese of Paris and in the whole kingdom of France and in other places, publicly and generally [deleted words follow].

[2] ¶ Again, the same lord King Louis begat from the same Queen Blanche his wife the Lord St Louis and the first Robert who was Count

---

[147] 'quantum in se erat': one could translate: 'so far he was concerned'.
[148] 'fieri poterit bono modo'.   [149] 'matura celeritate'.   [150] 'processu'.
[151] 'Andeliacum/Audeliacum in loco Gaillardi'.   [152] 'voluntate et potestate'.
[153] 'alias ad procedendum debite'.   [154] 'superius traditorum'.   [155] 'sub hac forma'.
[156] 'ponit': the verb corresponding to the noun 'positio'.

of Artois,[157] and that the same lord King Louis was the father of the same St Louis and the same first Robert, and they, St Louis and the first Robert, were brothers to each other, and the sons of the same Lord Louis and Lady Blanche, and the same parents and sons behaved as and were held and reputed to be such in their times and in the aforesaid places, publicly and generally.

[3] ¶ Again, that the said Lord St Louis, who was afterwards King of France, begat the first Philip, and was father of the same first Philip, and the same Philip was the son of the same St Louis, and they behaved as and were held and reputed to be such in their times and in the aforesaid places, publicly and generally.

[4] ¶ Again, the same lord the first Philip begat the second Lord Philip, who was King of France, and this same first Lord Philip was the father of the same second Lord Philip, and the same second Lord Philip was the son of the same first Lord Philip, and they behaved as and were held and reputed to be such in their times and in the aforesaid places, publicly and generally.

[5] ¶ Again, that the said second Lord Philip, King of France, begat the aforementioned Charles, who is now King of France, by the Lady Jeanne, Queen of Navarre, and the same second lord King Philip was the father of the same Lord Charles. And the same Lord Charles was and is the son of the said second Lord Philip, the late king, and it was as such that they behaved in the time when the same second Lord Philip was alive, and that at the said time they were both held and reputed to be, and the same Lord Charles behaves as, is held and is reputed to be, and in the aforesaid places, publicly and as a matter of common knowledge and generally.

[6] ¶ Again, that the above-mentioned first Lord Robert begat the second Lord Robert, and the same first Lord Robert was the father of the same second Lord Robert, and the same second Lord Robert was the son of the first Lord Robert and first cousin[158] of the said first Lord Philip, and they behaved as and were held and reputed to be such in their times and in the aforesaid places, publicly and generally.

[7] ¶ Again that the same second Lord Robert begat the Lady Mahaut, who is now the Countess of Artois, and the same second Lord Robert was the father of the same Lady Mahaut, and the same Lady Mahaut was and is the daughter of the same second Lord Robert, and they behaved as and were held and reputed to be such in their times and in the aforesaid places, publicly and generally, and the same Lady Mahaut still [so] behaves and is [so] held and reputed.

---

[157] 'attrebatensis', which also means Arras.   [158] 'consanguineus germanus'.

[8] ¶ Again, that the Lady Mahaut gave birth to the Lady Blanche, the daughter of the late Count of Burgundy, husband of the same Lady Mahaut, and the same Lady Mahaut was and is the mother of the same Lady Blanche, and the same Lady Blanche was and is the daughter of the same Lady Mahaut, and they behaved, and were held and reputed as such, and still behave as and are held and reputed to be such in the aforesaid places.

[9] ¶ Again, that the same Lord Charles and Lady Blanche were and are kin[159] in the fourth degree on both sides of the consanguinity relationship recorded and shown above.[160]

[10] ¶ Again, that the aforesaid things were and are publicly said and thought and that the aforesaid are and were public and common knowledge[161] at the aforesaid times and places.

[11] ¶ Again, he proposes, and intends to prove, that the aforesaid first Lord Robert – the son of the aforesaid lord King Louis and the Lady Blanche, who were married – and the Lady Mahaut of Brabant, were a married couple, and behaved as, were held and were reputed to be a married couple in their times, and in the aforesaid places, publicly and generally.

[12] ¶ Again, that the same first Lord Robert begat by the same Lady Mahaut his wife the aforesaid second Lord Robert and the Lady Blanche who was afterwards wife of the King of Navarre, and the same second Lord Robert and aforesaid Lady Blanche were brother and sister to each other and children of the same Lord Robert and Lady Mahaut of Brabant, and the same first Lord Robert was the father of the same second Lord Robert and of the Lady Blanche, and the same parents and children behaved as, and were held and reputed to be such in their times and in the aforesaid places, publicly and generally.

[13] ¶ Again, that the said Lady Blanche, sister of the aforesaid second Lord Robert, gave birth to the Lady Jeanne, late Queen of France, and was the wife of the aforesaid second Lord Philip, the king, and the same Lady Blanche was the mother of the same Lady Jeanne and the same Lady Jeanne was the daughter of the same Lady Blanche, and they behaved as and were held and reputed to be such in their times and in the aforesaid places, publicly and generally.

[14] ¶ Again, that the said Lady Jeanne gave birth to the aforesaid Lord Charles, now King of France, and was the mother of the same Lord Charles, and the same Lord Charles was and is the son of the same Lady Jeanne, and they behaved, and were held and reputed, and the

---

[159] 'se attingerunt et attingunt'.
[160] 'ex utroque latere suprascripte et designate consanguinitatis'.   [161] 'notoria'.

same Charles still behaves, is held and is reputed as such in the said places, publicly and generally.

[15] ¶ Again, that the said second Robert begat the Lady Mahaut, Countess of Artois, and was the father of the same Lady Mahaut, and the said Lady Mahaut was and is the daughter of the said second Lord Robert, and a blood relation and cousin[162] of the aforementioned Lady Jeanne Queen of France, and they behaved as, and were held and reputed to be such, and the said Lady Mahaut behaves, is held and is reputed to be such, in the aforesaid places, publicly and generally.

[16] ¶ Again, he proposes and intends to prove that the aforesaid Lady Mahaut gave birth to the said Lady Blanche and was and is the mother of the said Lady Blanche, and the said Lady Blanche was and is the daughter of the said Lady Mahaut, and they behaved as, and reputed themselves[163] to be, and were held and reputed to be, and behave and repute each other to be and are held and reputed to be such in the aforesaid places publicly and generally.

[17] ¶ Again, that the aforesaid Lord Charles, and Blanche, the daughter of the late aforesaid Count of Burgundy and the aforesaid Lady Mahaut, were and are kin in the third degree on both sides of the consanguinity relationship – going back to the aforesaid first Lord Robert, the common ancestor[164] – shown and recorded above.

[18] ¶ Again, that not only legally, but also in common parlance,[165] people are everywhere reputed to be blood relations and linked in the third degree on both sides when each of them is descended from a common stem through their transverse line in the third degree, so that they are great-grandchildren, that is children of two first cousins; and in the fourth degree on both sides, when each of them is descended through his or her line in the fourth degree from the stem, as great-great-grandchildren are; and in the third and fourth, when one is descended in the third through his or her line, counting from the common stem, and the other is descended in the fourth degree through another line under the same stem, so as to be great-grandchild and great-great-grandchild, and that this is the common and customary way of speaking and understanding 'being linked in the third degree on both sides' or 'in the fourth on both sides' or 'in the third and fourth degree at the same time *tout court*';[166]

---

[162] 'consanguinea et germana'.

[163] Taking 'reputant' with the preceding 'se' rather than as an intransitive verb.

[164] 'a stipite': literally 'stem'.   [165] 'secundum communem modum loquendi'.

[166] 'simpliciter': taking this with the last relationship rather than all the relationships just mentioned: though that is a possible understanding of the text, which might in that case be referring to 'simple' cases without multiple common ancestors.

and this is what is traditional, usual, understood and held to be the case widely, publicly and generally in the whole kingdom of France, and the neighbouring lands and places and even at the Roman curia, and in France with everybody and especially with those of French descent from so long ago and for such a long time that no one remembers anything different.

[19] ¶ Again, that the aforesaid things were publicly said and thought and that the aforesaid were public and common knowledge[167] at the aforesaid places and times.

[20] ¶ Again, that at the time when the same Lord Charles contracted marriage *de facto* with the oft-mentioned Lady Blanche, he had not yet reached the age of thirteen, but was below that age and that this was publicly said and thought at the time of the same marriage, and was subsequently and still is, in the aforesaid places.

[21] ¶ Again, he proposes and intends to prove that the same Lord Charles the king was and had been previously ill-adjusted,[168] simple, helpless, lacking in the discretion required for seeking out a wife near and far and for recognising a woman who was right[169] for him in view of what his status required, and that he was a person absolutely lacking in strength of body or mind,[170] especially in or concerning such matters, and that on these points this was the general opinion and belief of people of the said places, and publicly said and thought in the same places, at the time of the same marriage, and had been previously, and was subsequently, and still is.

[22] ¶ Again, that at the time of the said marriage, and previously from his infancy, and subsequently, many women of high rank,[171] even of royal descent, both in neighbouring and distant parts, were to be found[172] and could easily and without trouble, to any one of whom the said Lord Charles, the present King of France, could have fittingly and without the grant of a dispensation joined to himself in marriage in accordance with the status he had at the time – namely, without land and without a county, and the third-born of the said second Lord Philip the King of France – if he had been old enough to contract marriage; and these women of high rank were to be found and could easily and without trouble be found after the same Lord Charles came to the age of puberty and before that time, and that the same persons of high rank were related to the same said Charles in no prohibited degree of consanguinity or

---

[167] 'notoria'.   [168] 'inhabilis'.   [169] 'condecens'.
[170] 'talis a quo corporis valor vel animi . . . erat penitus alienus'.
[171] 'sublimes'.   [172] 'repperiebantur'.

affinity, but stood to the said Lord Charles and were removed from him beyond every forbidden degree, or if they were related to him, at least not in such close [degrees];[173] and, among other persons of high rank, there were those whose names are written below, namely the sister of the King of Spain, who afterwards married the Duke of Brittany, and who is still his wife; again, the sister of the said duke, who is still alive and not yet married; the Lady Clemence, who was afterwards the wife of King Louis, brother of the said Charles; again, one or other of the daughters of the lord Count of Saint Pol; again, the sister of the King of Bohemia, who is still alive and unmarried, and many others; and that each of the same persons of high rank could have been joined in marriage in accordance with what the status that the same aforesaid Lord Charles had at that time required, and just as appropriately, to the aforesaid Lord Charles as the aforesaid Lady Blanche[174] the daughter of the late Count of Burgundy, even if the same Lord Charles had possessed a dispensation sufficient for contracting marriage with the same Lady Blanche.

[23] ¶ Again, that the aforesaid ladies, with whom, as stated above, he could have contracted marriage, were of a status as great or greater in terms of ancestry[175] and in other regards, as those women have normally been in former times who have normally[176] contracted marriage with sons of the kings of France, especially with last-born sons.

[24] ¶ Again, that the aforesaid things are and were publicly said and thought and that the aforesaid were and are public and common knowledge[177] at the aforesaid places and times.

[25] ¶ Again, he proposes, and intends to prove, that at the time of the marriage contracted between the said Lord Charles, now the King of France, and the aforesaid Lady Blanche, daughter of the late Count of Burgundy, the same Lady Blanche had not yet reached the age of eleven, but was below that age, and that this had been the general opinion and belief of people of the said places, and publicly said and thought, at the time when the same marriage was contracted, and was subsequently, and still is, and the same things were public and common knowledge in the same places.

---

[173] 'in tam proximis'.
[174] 'poterat secundum ipsius domini Karoli predicti status, in quo erat, exigentiam matrimonialiter copulari, et eidem domino Karolo eque decenter sicut surpadicta domina Blancha'.
[175] 'in genere'.
[176] 'normally ... normally' translating 'consueverunt ... consueverunt'.   [177] 'notoria'.

[26] ¶ Again, he proposes, and intends to prove, that both of the aforesaid, namely that the Lord Charles and the Lady Blanche, because they were not old enough and their bodies were too underdeveloped[178] were incapable of sexual intercourse[179] at the time when the said marriage was contracted, and that these things were and had been publicly said and thought, and still are, and the things set out above were common knowledge and public at the said time and in the aforesaid places.

[27] ¶ Again, he proposes, and intends to prove, that the said marriage between the said Lord Charles and Lady Blanche was contracted in a contract where the banns, introduced by law to oppose impediments – which[180] there were to contracting the same marriage – had been omitted; and solemnities that should be and customarily are observed when marriages are to be contracted were omitted; and that the same marriage between the same said Lord Charles and Lady Blanche was contracted clandestinely, and that these things are publicly said and thought.

[28] ¶ Again, he proposes and intends to prove that the said marriage was contracted, though clandestinely, in a place other than the places and parishes from which the aforementioned Lord Charles and Lady Blanche came and in a place other than in the churches of the parishes to which they or one of them belonged, and not through their parish priests[181] or those of one or other of the couple,[182] and even without the permission of the same parish priests; and the aforementioned things are and were common knowledge at the time of the said marriage and afterwards, and these things are and were publicly said and thought in the aforesaid places.

[29] ¶ Again, he proposes, and intends to prove, that when both the same Lord Charles and Blanche had reached the age of puberty they remained, without any other solemnity such as customarily accompanies marriages, and without any other new or explicit consent,[183] in the aforesaid union, which was thus an illicit one, and this is and was the

---

[178] 'propter . . . tenuitatem corporis'.   [179] 'impotentes ad carnis copulam'.

[180] I translate with 'which' rather than 'that' because the sense seems to be that the law about banns had been introduced originally to combat marriages within the forbidden degrees, and this marriage was such a one, not that the law had been introduced to combat the forbidden degrees in this particular marriage.

[181] 'curatores': an unusual sense but clear from context. Cf. 'curé'.

[182] 'alterius eorumdem': from the context, 'alterius' refers to 'one of the couple' rather than 'one of the parish priests'.

[183] 'absque novo alio seu expresso consensu'.

general opinion and publicly said and thought in the aforesaid places and time.

[30] ¶ Again, he proposes and intends to prove that the aforesaid Lady Mahaut, mother of the aforesaid Lady Blanche, was personally present at the baptism of the said Lord Charles, and held him over the baptismal font, and was his godmother, together with certain others, and that in other respects acted with respect to the said baptism and behaved in such a way that spiritual relationship followed and was contracted between the aforesaid Lady Mahaut and the aforesaid Lady Blanche on one side and the parents[184] of the said Lord Charles, and also Lord Charles himself, on the other, such that the same Lord Charles could not contract marriage with the aforesaid Lady Blanche, and these things are and were public and common knowledge, and held to be true, and commonly reputed to be the case, and this is and was the general opinion and publicly said and thought in the aforesaid places on the same matters.

[31] ¶ Again, he proposes that this is the general opinion and publicly said and thought about all the aforesaid things, both taken together and separately, and about each one of them.

(l) And furthermore the aforesaid proctor of the said Lord Charles declares that he could correct and reshape the aforesaid *positiones* and articles, if it should be necessary, and to provide others, and that he does not bind [himself] to prove all the aforesaid except those of the things set out above such as will suffice for him to achieve the objective.[185]

[End of extract]

Resistance by Blanche's legal team

(m) The proctor of the said Lady Blanche, however, said that he wished to put forward his arguments for the defence[186] in accordance with what the present day required, and he put forward and presented his arguments for the defence in these words: Before you, reverend father in Christ, Étienne, by divine providence bishop of Paris, Aymeri Mazerant the proctor of the noble lady the Lady Blanche of Burgundy, and by virtue

---

[184] 'parentes', which can also mean 'blood relatives'.
[185] 'non . . . ad probanda omnia supradicta nisi dumtaxat ad ea que sibi sufficient de premissis ad propositum consequendum': an alternative marginally less likely translation is: 'except what suffices for him to draw the consequence proposed from the premises'.
[186] 'deffensiones'.

of his procuratorial commission puts forward an objection against the
proctor of the most excellent and powerful Prince Charles by the grace
of God King of France and Navarre, saying that – notwithstanding the
consanguinities by which the aforementioned lord king and the aforesaid
Lady Blanche are connected[187] to each other, and[188] the other things
proposed on the part of the proctor of the said lord king, on the basis
of which he requests that the marriage formerly contracted between the
aforesaid lord king and Lady Blanche be pronounced to be and to have
been null, and that permission be given to the said king to contract
marriage with another woman – the said marriage is and was ratified, valid
and canonical, and that it neither can nor should in any way whatsoever
be annulled nor even in any way whatsoever be declared to be null,
since and because a dispensation was granted in respect of the aforesaid
impediments, on the basis of which the aforesaid marriage is asserted to
be null, by the Lord Clement V the supreme pontiff of the most holy and
universal Church, *ex certa scientia*,[189] in accordance with his intention,[190]
and for just reasons which led him to grant this dispensation, in the proper
way and in accordance with canon law, just as he was empowered to do,[191]
as could be made more fully evident from the letter written by the same
supreme pontiff concerning the aforesaid dispensation, on the grounds
of[192] which dispensation the aforesaid lord king and Blanche contracted
marriage and stayed together for a long time, and had children openly
and publicly in good faith, for which reason he said that the said marriage
should not be pronounced to be null, and also no permission should be
given to the lord king to contract marriage with another woman. – He
asked for a response to be given on behalf of the lord king to these things,
and, if they should be denied, that he should be permitted to prove them,
offering to convince them quickly of the aforesaid things. And there and
then[193] the proctor of the said lord king denied that a dispensation was
or had been given by the aforesaid Clement or anyone else with respect
to the aforesaid consanguinities through which it is known that they are
related to each other and to the spiritual relationship through which they
are also connected and to the other impediments through which the
said marriage is *ipso iure*[194] and was from the beginning null, and even

---

[187] 'coniuncti'.   [188] 'nec' – correlating with the 'non' of 'nonobstantibus'.
[189] Technical term, literally 'from certain knowledge', meaning that the document overrode
any other not similarly so described.
[190] 'secundum mentem suum'.
[191] See, however, the transcription of J.682.1, Appendix 1, at paragraph (m) (membrane
3), line 49 for a possible emendation.
[192] 'pretextu'.   [193] 'ibidem'.   [194] 'by the operation of the law'.

if there was some dispensation for some impediments, he says that the said dispensation is and was from the beginning null, as being illicitly obtained,[195] or if it held good, he says that it by no means includes[196] the impediments which invalidate the marriage, as the same proctor offered to propose and explain,[197] once the said dispensation, on the basis of which the opposing party was objecting,[198] had been produced – while the proctor of the said Lady Blanche asserted and protested the contrary.[199] And since the same proctor of the said Lady Blanche did not have proofs prepared and ready at hand with respect to the objections raised above,[200] he asked for a brief adjournment to be granted so that he could prove it[201] [**third membrane, lines 45–54**].

At this point deletions and minute marginal insertions may reflect confusion in the tribunal about how to deal with the dispensation produced by Blanche's side. The context following the palaeographically problematic passage makes it clear that there was a dispute in court and that an adjournment was granted to allow Blanche's proctor a breathing space to prepare the case he wanted to make with respect to the dispensation.

And after the dispute had gone back and forth about the aforesaid points made by each of the two parties, bearing in mind that in the present case the procedure was to be summary and straightforward, and that never-theless each side had multiple grounds for delay,[202] wishing to impose a limit on the matter which would be short, but – as the importance[203] both of the persons involved and of the matter demanded – not premature: with the agreement and assent of the proctors of the aforesaid parties, we ruled as follows, namely that the proctor of the said Lady Blanche should prove whatever he wants to prove concerning the matters set out above on the second Tuesday before the Feast of the Annunciation of the Lord, counting inclusively,[204] and that in the meantime we should send to Creil to have the aforesaid witnesses heard . . . Again, in the year stated above, on the aforesaid day of March, before the Feast of the Annunciation of the Lord, assigned above, the proctors, as listed above, and with the names as above appeared before us, in the presence of the oft-mentioned reverend fathers and notaries: and then the proctor of the

---

[195] 'subreptitia'.   [196] 'quomodolibet non includit'.
[197] 'sicut obtulit idem procurator immediate proponere et docere'.
[198] 'exhibita dicta dispensatione per quam excipiebat pars adversa'.
[199] 'procuratore dicte domine Blanche contrarium asserente et protestante'.
[200] 'Et cum idem procurator dicte domine Blanche non haberet in promptu probationes paratas super superius exceptatis'.
[201] 'petiit ad hoc sibi brevem terminum aliquem assignari ad probandum'.
[202] 'multas dilatationes'.   [203] 'qualitas'.
[204] 'in secunda die martis, que erit ante festum annunciationis divine inclusive'.

aforesaid Lady Blanche, to prove the propositions he had set out by raising an objection,[205] exhibited and produced, as being true and authentic,
a certain papal letter, with a true leaden bull attached to it, on silk, not
damaged or spoiled,[206] to judge from their prima facie appearance, containing the said dispensation. The contents of this are known to be as
follows: 'Clement, bishop . . . '

(Archives nationales, J.682.1; for transcription see Appendix 1)

1322, J.682.2

(a) There follow the depositions of the witnesses produced by the proctor
of the most excellent prince the Lord Charles by the grace of God King
of France and Navarre, against the Lady Blanche of Burgundy and her
proctor, in the case for the annulment of the marriage formerly, as is
said, contracted between them; these witnesses, in the presence of the
parties, swore before us, the bishop of Paris, in the presence and with
the assistance of the reverend fathers the lords the bishop of Beauvais
and Master Geoffrey de Pleyeyo, notary of the lord pope, to give a true
deposition on the articles set out below; and they were examined by
ourselves in the presence of the aforesaid reverend fathers, and of the
notaries whose names are written below; and there made their depositions
as is contained in what follows.

[lines 1–3]

. . .

(b) ¶ Lord Ralph of Mullento, canon of Paris, sixty years of age or
thereabouts, questioned about the first article, deposed in evidence under
oath about hearsay evidence that the things contained in it were just
what the said article contains,[207] and, concerning this, it was what was
commonly said in his time, so he said. And he deposed the same in
evidence concerning the contents of the second article, but added that
he saw the said St Louis and his two brothers, namely the Count of
Anjou and the Count of Poitiers, but he did not however see the said
Lord Robert the first, as he said, but it was commonly said at the said
time that he had been the brother of the aforesaid St Louis and that he had
died at Mansoura, during St Louis's first crusade. Questioned about the
third, fourth, fifth, sixth, seventh, eighth, eleventh, twelfth, thirteenth,

---

[205] 'per viam exceptionis'.   [206] 'non abolitam nec vitiatum'.

[207] 'de auditu dici super contentis in eo prout in dicto articulo continetur'. Alternatively,
one could translate this as: 'what he had heard said with respect to the contents of the
article, as contained in it' – but the otiosity of the 'prout' clause counts against this.

fourteenth, fifteenth, and sixteenth articles, which had been individually explained to him one by one, he said under oath that he had often seen the persons contained and indicated in the aforesaid articles – except in respect of what is said in the eleventh article and in the said twelfth article about the said Robert the first and of the said Lady Mahaut his wife: he does not remember seeing them behaving and acting and being treated publicly and being commonly reputed by everyone who had knowledge of them in their time as being related in the manner and form contained[208] in the aforesaid articles and as they are contained in them, and this he deposed in evidence in turn for each of the aforesaid articles. Again, asked about the eighteenth, he said under oath that great-grandchildren of the common ancestor, when one is descended through one line as far as the third degree counting from the common ancestor, and another through another collateral[209] line in the same third degree, are related in the third degree on both sides, as the aforesaid Lord Charles and Blanche are in that blood relationship in which the first Lord Robert is taken as the main stem; the great-great-grandchildren however, that is the children of the great-grandchildren, are related in the fourth [degree] on each side, as the aforesaid Lord Charles and Blanche are in that blood relationship in which the counting is done from the father of St Louis when he is taken as the main stem, and those who are descended unequally, that is the great-grandson and the great-great-granddaughter, are joined in two degrees, namely in the third and fourth; and this was the way of reckoning and of holding people to be related in the said degrees in the kingdom of France as he made the reckoning in his day and as he heard the reckoning made by others. The same witness, questioned about the thirtieth article, said he did not know for certain, except by hearsay. He said however that it is commonly said to be just as is contained in the aforesaid article, and this he himself heard said by many, as he said. About the other articles, or indeed about these ones, he said nothing else pertinent. He said under oath that he did not make his deposition out of fear, hatred, for profit or for love, but for the sake of telling the truth, as he said.

(c) ¶ Master Aldricus, a man learned in the law, a canon of Metz, originally from Italy, questioned about the eighteenth article, the only one for which he had been called, said under oath that, according to the method and the common and generally known method of reckoning in the regions of Italy, those who are descended from the main stem each through his or her line in the third degree on their side are called and held

---

[208] Taking 'contentas' with 'modum et formam'.   [209] 'transversalem'.

to be related in the third degree on both sides; and those of whom each is descended in the fourth degree through his or her line are called and held to be related in the fourth degree on each side; and those of whom one, on his or her side, is descended in the third degree, and the other, who is descended on the other side, in the fourth, are called and held to be related [in the third and fourth][210] in relation to the same main stem; and this the witness holds to be certain and generally known in the Italian regions, and throughout his life he has seen and heard that the reckoning was made in this way and that it was held to be so, nor has he seen or heard that the reckoning might be made in any other way, as the same witness said.

(d) ¶ Lord Amanuel, a man learned in the law, a canon of St Marcellus, sworn in as a witness and questioned diligently on the eighteenth article, the only one for which he had been called, said under oath that in the regions of Italy from which he came, in reckoning the degrees, to discover in what degree people are related, the third degree on both sides, say,[211] is reckoned when two people in collateral lines each on their line's side are descended from a shared common ancestor[212] in the third degree, and in the fourth degree on both sides when each on their side are descended in the fourth degree, and that people are in the third [and fourth degree][213] when one is descended on one side in the third degree, and the other on the other side in the fourth degree – the same as a [great-] grandson on one side and a great-great-granddaughter on the other side and thus they are called and held to be in the third degree on both sides, or in the fourth degree on both sides, or in the third and the fourth, and this [is] the common method of calculating it[214] and how people commonly speak about it[215] in those parts, as in these[216] parts, and the same witness saw and heard this frequently, as he said, and this is well known among everybody in the aforesaid parts when they reckon how they are related by blood, or how people who want to get married are related by blood, according to whether the degree happens to be equal or unequal. Questioned abut where he came from, he said that he was from the city of Piacenza.

(e) ¶ Guillaume de Piacenza, sworn in as a witness and diligently examined concerning the aforesaid eighteenth article, after it had been explained to him, said that he believed with certainty that the things

---

[210] See emendation of the Latin.   [211] 'gradus videlicet tertius ex utroque latere'.
[212] 'communi stipite'.   [213] See emendation of the Latin.
[214] 'hoc/hec communis computatio'.
[215] 'communis modus loquendi'.   [216] 'illis . . . istis'.

contained in the aforesaid article were true, and that people were held to be related in the third degree on both sides or in the fourth on both sides or in the third and fourth, in accordance with what is contained in the aforesaid article.

(f) ¶ Lady Isabel of Soisy,[217] sworn in as a witness and diligently examined concerning certain articles that follow, concerning which she was asked to submit to examination, and first concerning the twentieth article.

She said under oath that the said Lord Charles was, on the Friday before the Feast of St John the Baptist last, twenty-seven years of age and no more, and she knows this because she suckled him and weaned him from the beginning, and that it was fourteen years ago that he had contracted marriage with the said Lady Blanche between Christmas and the Feast of the Purification back then,[218] and thus at the said time he was less than fourteen years old, and she remembers this perfectly well, as she said, and the said marriage took place at the said time at Hesdin. Questioned about the twenty-first article, she said under oath that the said Lord Charles was simple and ingenuous[219] and thoughtless, especially when it came to seeking a wife for himself as was proper both in respect of his condition and of his age,[220] as she said. On the twenty-second article she said that she believed for certain that both from the women named in the said article and among others he would have been able to find for himself equally easily a wife just as suitable as was the said Lady Blanche, and added that she believed from what she had heard before the time of the aforesaid marriage, at the time when the Lady Jeanne his mother was living, that the said mother would never have allowed him if she had lived to contract marriage with the said Lady Blanche. On the other articles she said nothing else pertinent.

(g) ¶ Master Jean Hellequin, a doctor[221] of medicine, questioned about the twentieth article, said under oath that the said Lord Charles will be

---

[217] E. A. R. Brown identified this witness for me, correcting my transcription from 'Soyriaco' to 'Soyziaco'.

[218] 'xiiii anni fuerunt preteriti inter festum nativitatis Domini et festum Purificationis beate Marie preterita [i.e. the two festa]'. The Latin syntax is awkward and may be a calque of vernacular wording. One might also translate it as 'and fourteen years had passed, by the period between Christmas and the Feast of the Purification of the Blessed Virgin last, from the time when he contracted marriage with the said Lady Blanche', but the 'dicto tempore' speaks against this.

[219] 'sine malitia'.

[220] 'et secundum conditionem suam et secundum etatem': this phrase could refer either to Charles's naivety – due both to character and to youth – or to finding a wife of suitable status and age.

[221] 'Magister'.

twenty-seven or twenty-eight at the most around the time of the next Feast of the Trinity, but he believes twenty-seven to be more likely; and he said that he used to have among his papers a note of[222] the day and the date, which he had written down on the day of the birth,[223] and he remembers this because he was at his place of birth at the said time. Questioned about the twenty-first article, he said under oath that the things contained in the said article were true. Questioned about how he knew, he said that it was because he had taken care of him from his infancy and knows well that he was very simple, without the kind of discretion and savoir faire needed for him to know how or be able to look after himself in this way as his station in life required,[224] or to seek out a suitable wife. Questioned about the twenty-second article, he said that Charles would have been able to find a better or more suitable wife, either one of those named in the aforesaid article or another, since – as the witness said – no woman would have turned him down,[225] as opposed to marrying him eagerly. With respect to the twenty-third article, he said it was true, just as is contained in the article, because Charles could have made an even better match with another of those women than with this one, as he said. Questioned on the twenty-sixth article, he said that for both of the aforesaid pair, Lord Charles and Lady Blanche, he knew both their physical state and their bodily constitutions, since he was the doctor of the king and his children, and that it is his certain judgement, so far as one could see from their age and other indications, that they were not capable of sexual union. On the twenty-eighth and twenty-ninth articles he said under oath that although he was at the aforesaid time a member of the royal household and was in the places where the marriage negotiation took place and where the marriage took place, he heard nothing said about the aforesaid banns, nor that a licence to contract marriage had been requested from their curates or from other bishops, for which reason he believes, as he says, just what is contained in the aforesaid articles. Questioned on the thirtieth article he said under oath that he, the same witness, was staying at that time with the Countess of Dammartin, who had been told to go to the baptism of the said Lord Charles, and the said countess went,

---

[222] Or, if understood to mean that he still had the paper in question: 'and that he had made a written record of the day and the date'.

[223] 'nativitatis': I tentatively understand this to mean 'Charles's birth', but there are two other possililities: Christmas, and Master Hellequin's own birthday. The 'place of birth with 'sue' just afterwards favours the final possibility, but it may be just coincidence.

[224] 'sine tali discretione et notitia quod sciret vel posset secundum statum suum in quo erat sic providere'.

[225] 'dedisset repulsam': literally 'given him a refusal'.

and the same witness, who is speaking, with her, and he was present
when the said Lord Charles was carried to the church, which is in the
castle of Creil, to receive baptism, and he went to the font[226] with the
said Countess of Dammartin, and there, while the aforesaid boy was
being lifted above the font, the aforesaid Lady Mahaut, who was then the
Countess of Burgundy – and still is also the Countess of Artois – as he
said – before the said baptism bustled imperiously[227] to the font, towards
the area where the said witness was,[228] and tugged him back from the said
font, and as she tugged him said to him the following words: 'Sir priest,
what are you doing here? You are certainly not going to be godfather' –
being under the impression that the same witness was a priest, though
he was not. And then the same witness replied to her: 'Lady, priests are
not at all out of place in such matters', and as he spoke these words
the said witness tugged himself back as this countess tugged him, and
she went straight over to the font, and placed herself among those who
were godmothers, among whom no-one that he could remember was
of a status equal to hers, from all of which it is his certain judgement
that the said Lady Mahaut was one of the more important godmothers
and the spiritual parent of the said Lord Charles. He was questioned
whether the said Charles could remain married to the said Lady Blanche
without grave scandal, and he replied that he firmly believed and thought
that the answer was 'no'. Questioned whether he had made his deposition
about anything of the aforesaid out of hatred, for advantage or love, for
the sake of favour or out of fear, he said under oath that the answer was
'no', but that he had done it only for the sake of truth. On the other
articles he was not questioned, and he said nothing else relevant.

(h) ¶ Lord Robert de Brisol, knight, forty-seven years of age – who
stayed for periods of time with Lady Blanche, that is, the mother of Lady
Jeanne the queen the mother of the lord king – on the first, second and
third article gave evidence, under oath, that he had heard said just what is
contained in the said articles. Asked from whom he heard it, he said from
Lady Catherine de Rigny[229] his mother, and from Lord Guy de Roisiere,
otherwise known as 'Quatre Soulz', a knight who was with the aforesaid
first Lord Robert, who is mentioned in the first article, at Mansoura,
where the said Lord Robert died, as he heard from the aforesaid people.
He heard the things set out above also from many others, whose names

---

[226] I translate the plural 'fontes' with the singular 'font' throughout.
[227] 'venit... valde impetuose'.
[228] 'de versus illam partem versus quam erat idem testis'.
[229] 'Rigniaco/Riginaco/Rigmaco/Regmaco' (etc.).

he does not recall at this time. Asked what he believes, he said under oath that it is exactly what is contained in the aforesaid articles, and through the things[230] that he said previously, and that he saw the said first Lord Philip, who acted as the son of the aforesaid St Louis, and so succeeded him as his son, just as was generally held to be the case throughout the whole kingdom of France. Again, questioned on the fourth, fifth, sixth, seventh, eighth, eleventh, twelfth, thirteenth, fifteenth and sixteenth articles, as explained to him individually and in sequence, he said under oath – apart from what is asserted in the fifth and sixth articles of the said Lord Robert, the first one, and in articles eleven and twelve of the same first Lord Robert, and of the Lady Mahaut his wife, about whom he lacks the knowledge to give evidence as the truth,[231] but believes that the said first Lord Robert was the brother of St Louis and the father of the second Lord Robert, and the said Lady Mahaut the mother, since he heard this said often and by many people, as he said – that he often saw all the other people named in the aforesaid articles behaving and acting and being held and reputed to be kinsfolk and relatives, just as is contained in the said article, and because of this he believes, as he said, that they are related with one another just as is contained in the aforesaid articles. Questioned on the ninth article, after it had been explained to him, and after the persons on either side had been counted, he said that it was true, just as is contained in the said articles. Questioned about the reason, he said that it was because he would calculate it thus himself and had heard that reckoning being made in similar cases. Questioned about the tenth article, he said that the aforesaid things that he had deposed in evidence were widely reported. Questioned about the fourteenth article, after it had been set out for him how the people traced their ancestry by each line back to the first Lord Robert, according to the way in which he reckons the degrees and always heard them reckoned, he said that what was contained in the said articles was exactly right. Questioned about the eighteenth article, he deposed in evidence under oath that to judge by what he had heard of how some other people were commonly reckoned or reputed to be related in a degree or degrees, the said article contains the truth according to the mode of reckoning in France, apart from which he does not know, as he said. Questioned about the twentieth, he said under oath that he firmly believes, judging from his own age[232] and the time of

---

[230] 'per ea': i.e. probably 'through the sources'.   [231] 'pro veritate deponere'.

[232] The sense must be that Robert knows how old he was at the time of the marriage, how old he is now, and how old Charles and Blanche are now, so that he can work out how old they were then.

the marriage, that he had not reached the age of thirteen. On the twenty-first article, he does not believe that Charles had sufficient discretion to discern the things that the said article contains, indeed he was extremely naive and undiscriminating, even for his age, and for this reason they called him 'the bear',[233] and he was despised for his naivety even by his mother, according to the witness. Questioned about the twenty-second article, he believes it, apart from that he does not know with certainty. Questioned on the twenty-third article, he believes its contents, since he saw in other cases that sons of kings took some women[234] who were no greater than these, and this he saw in the case of the lord of Valois and others. Questioned on the twenty-fifth article, he believes its contents, apart from that he does not know the truth. On the twenty-seventh and twenty-eighth articles, he said he did not know. On the thirtieth article, he said that this article was true. Asked how he knows, he said he was present at the baptism. Asked where, he said: at Creil, in the church of the canons of St Evremond, the church being inside the castle of the said place. Questioned on what he saw there, he said under oath that he had seen that the said Lady Mahaut took the boy, namely the said Lord Charles, and handed him over, naked, to the lord Count of Valois, over the font, to receive the said baptism. Again, he saw, as he said, that the said Lady Mahaut, like the other godmothers, laid on her hands in the baptism, as is the custom, and held him above the font while he was being baptised, touching him with her hands, and holding [him] together with the others above the font. Questioned on why he had come there, he said that he was staying with Lord Guichard, at that time the abbot of the monastery of Celle near Troyes,[235] the man who was afterwards bishop of Troyes, and he remembers that the abbot was staying – and he with the abbot – in the small town[236] of Montataire near Creil, for a month and more, waiting for the said lady to give birth, since the said Lord Guichard wanted to be at the aforesaid baptism, and finally, after the birth of the said Lord Charles, they went to the said place called Creil, and there saw the aforesaid things, about which he said he remembered perfectly. Questioned about the people present, he said that he remembers that the Count of Flanders was present there, that is Lord Guy, the father of the present count, and he saw that he was holding a sliver of wood with which he was picking his teeth. Again, he saw the Lord Charles Count of Valois, who held the aforesaid boy. He also saw there Guillaume de Saint

---

[233] 'orson' – *sic!*   [234] 'aliquas'.
[235] Montier-la-Celle: see L. H. Cottineau, *Répertoire topo-bibliographique des abbayes et prieurés*, 2 vols. (Macon, 1939), vol. II, col. 1952.
[236] 'villa'.

Marcel and the then lord archbishop of Sens and the then lord bishop of Beauvais,[237] and the Count of Saint Pol, and many others holding their hands out to the boy for the said godparenthood.[238] Questioned about the time, he said that it was around the Feast of St John,[239] and he remembers that he went to Clermont, almost two leagues away, for fish, since in the town of Creil, because of the large number of magnates who were there, there were no fish to be found. Questioned about the other godmothers, he said the Countess of Joigny and the Countess of Dammartin were also there and many others whom he could not really remember. Questioned how many years ago it could be, he said twenty-seven or thereabouts, so far as he could remember. And he said nothing else relevant. And, on oath, [asked] whether he had not deposed anything of the foregoing for love, fear, at someone's instigation, or for any advantage whatsoever, [he said he had not] but only for the sake of truth, as he swore.[240]

(i) ¶ Thomas de Rogueta, provost of Arbilly, in the church of St Aniane of Orleans, an Italian of the diocese of 'Assensis',[241] questioned on the eighteenth article, said under oath that that was the method used in Lombardy for calculating how people are related: in the third degree on both sides, or in the third on one side and the fourth on the other, or in the fourth on both sides, just as the same article says, and he said he knows this because he saw the reckoning being made in this way often and by many people, and it is very well known in those parts, according to him. He was not questioned about the other articles.

(j) Matthew called 'de Moncell.', a Lombard, a merchant of the diocese of V'ren[242] across the Alps, questioned about the said eighteenth article: they call the degrees of consanguinity a joint, as he said, and so he deposed in evidence that those who descend from the main stem through three people, in such a way that this person is the third from the main stem, not counting the same main stem, and another person who is at the same distance down another line of descent, are called and held to be in the third degree or joint on both sides, and those descend through four people, in the fourth on both sides, and when one descends through three people on his side, the other through four, then they are held to be and taken as relatives in the third and fourth, in the regions of Italy, and he had seen it taken to be so and reckoned and held to be so in Italy, publicly and as common knowledge, as he said.

---

[237] 'the then' translating 'qui erant pro tempore', rather than taking this to mean [the archbishop and bishop] 'who were there for the time being'.
[238] Or: 'godfatherhood'.   [239] Probably John the Evangelist, 27 December.
[240] Words seem to be missing from the Latin, probably from carelessness.
[241] Perhaps Assisi?   [242] Verona?

(k) ¶ Ascelanus called 'Taire', a Lombard of the diocese of Asti, questioned on the said eighteenth article, agreed with the previous witness[243] in his deposition evidence concerning the terminology and reckoning method in Italy.

(l) ¶ Jordan de Calochio of the Paris diocese, aged forty years or thereabouts, a Lombard merchant, deposed in evidence to the same effect as the witness immediately preceding him and as Matheus 'de Moncell'.

(m) ¶ Matthew 'Scarempnus', of the diocese of Asti, twenty years of age, a Lombard merchant, sworn in as a witness and interrogated about the said eighteenth article, said that in Italy they call blood relatives in the third degree of consanguinity second consanguines,[244] blood relatives in the fourth degree of consanguinity consobrines, and, when they are in the fourth and the third, one second consanguine and one consobrine, and this was how he saw and heard the reckoning made in those parts. About the remaining contents of the aforesaid article he knows nothing.

(n) Guillaume de Saint-Marcel, a townsman from Provins, sworn in and diligently questioned on the first and second articles, said under oath that he believed the contents of the aforesaid articles to be true. Asked why he believed this, he said that it was because he had heard quite a number of trustworthy people say the same as is stated in the aforesaid two articles, and this was held to be a matter of common knowledge in the time of St Louis, whom the same witness saw, as he said. Questioned on the third and fourth articles, he said under oath that he had seen all the people mentioned in the aforesaid articles behaving and acting and being generally and publicly regarded by others as what the aforesaid articles stated they were, namely St Louis and the first Philip father and son, the first Philip and the second Philip as father and son, and the second Philip and Lord Charles, now King of France, as father and son, and this was regarded as certain and generally known in their times, as he said, and they were commonly said by everybody to be such in their time, and are still said to be. Questioned about the sixth article, he said that he had not seen the first Lord Robert, but he saw the aforesaid second Lord Robert, who was said by everybody to be his son, and who behaved as such, and succeeded him in the county of Artois, as was commonly said, and the same witness also holds this to be true and beyond doubt. And he also saw that the same Lord Robert, the second one, and the first

---

[243] 'testis proximus': the context favours my translation, rather than the alternative probability: 'the next witness'.

[244] 'in tertio gradu vocant consanguineos secundos'. The English terms used in the translation are direct calques of the Latin, sacrificing elegance to precision.

Lord Philip, regarded one another as sons, that is of the two brothers the lords St Louis and the first Robert, related by blood. Questioned on the seventh and eighth articles, he said under oath that he had seen the people mentioned in them descending one from another, and behaving and regarding one another as related in just the ways set out in the aforesaid articles. Again, questioned abut the eleventh article, he said he believed the things contained in it to be true, since he had heard from many people, especially in times now gone by, exactly what the article contained. Questioned about the twelfth article, he said that he knew that the aforesaid Lord Robert, the second one, and the Lady Blanche who was the mother of Lady Jeanne the Queen of France, the mother of the said Lord Charles, regarded one another and were held to be brother and sister, children of the aforesaid Lord Robert and Lady Mahaut of Brabant, and this he saw and heard often, as he said, and in many places, and this was held to be a well-known thing and beyond doubt in their times. And, on the basis of what he had already said, he believes the other things contained in the said article to be true. Questioned about the thirteenth, fourteenth, fifteenth and sixteenth articles, he said under oath that he had very frequently seen all the people mentioned in the said articles behaving and acting and being regarded and held to be related in the ways set out in the aforesaid articles. He believes the other things contained in the said articles to be true, because in their times it was regarded as certain and generally known that this was so. Again, questioned about the thirtieth article, he said under oath that when the birth of the said Lord Charles was imminent, shortly before it he went to Creil with the abbot of the monastery of Celle, the one called Guichard who afterwards became bishop of Troyes, and, since the said queen had not given birth, the aforesaid abbot, and the same witness with him, waited for almost three weeks in a place near Creil for the birth of the said boy, except that in this time the same witness sometimes went to other places and soon came back. Finally, however, after the birth of the said Lord Charles, a certain man named Barber, who was the queen's tailor, came to tell the said abbot about the birth, and the abbot gave him 20 Paris pounds,[245] and took him into his service.[246] And afterwards, on the day of the baptism, he went with the said abbot to the church which is in the castle of Creil, and there he saw that the said boy was carried to the door of the church, and while the rituals at the door customary

---

[245] 'xx.lb. Par'.

[246] 'de raubis' = wearing livery (R. E. Latham, *Revised Medieval Latin Word-List from British and Irish Sources* (London, 1965)). Presumably this refers to Lambert rather than Guillaume.

when a child is to be baptised were being carried out. In the same place he saw, as he said, the Lady Mahaut Countess of Burgundy near to the Lord Charles Count of Valois, who was holding the said child and afterwards entered the church, and in the church saw that after the said child's swaddling clothes had been removed the said Lady Mahaut took him into her hands, and handed him above the font, entirely naked, to the aforesaid Lord Charles, for him to hold at the baptism, and after she had handed him over, as he had just said, he saw her at the font, near the child, and, while he was being baptised, holding her hands out to him over the font like a godmother; and he said that he remembered this because he knew the said countess well, and, wishing to see the king's son baptised, he got the best look he could. Again he said that when the said child had been baptised the said lady took him again, and wrapped him in swaddling clothes with the others, and gave him back to the Lord Charles all wrapped up. Asked about when, he said that it was around the Feast of the Trinity, at the time when the market of Lendi takes place near Saint-Denis, and he remembers this because, while the said abbot was waiting for the birth of the same lord king, the same witness sometimes went to Paris and passed through the aforesaid market which was happening then. Asked how many years ago, he said that it will be twenty-eight years around the Feast of the Trinity, near the Feast of St John the Baptist, as it seems to him for sure. Questioned about the people present, he mentioned the then Count of Flanders[247] and the then archbishop of Narbonne[248] and [the archbishop] of Sens,[249] and the bishop of Soissons,[250] and the aforesaid Lady Mahaut, and others he had mentioned before, and Lord Robert de Brisoles, and many others, and he still remembers, as he said, because[251] a certain small boy had fallen into the water which was in that place, and the mother had dedicated him in a vow, and he had been taken for dead, and he revived miraculously, as she said,[252] and while the Count of Flanders and the aforesaid abbot and many prelates and others were waiting in the aforesaid church for the aforesaid child [i.e. Charles] to be brought forward to be baptised, they desired to see the boy in whose person the miracle had taken place, and they had him come there. Asked whether he had deposed anything in evidence out of hatred or love, for advantage, or for the sake of favour,

---

[247] Guy: see Wilhelm Karl Prinz von Isenburg, *Stammtafeln zur Geschichte der Europäischen Staaten, vol. II: Die außerdeutschen Staaten* (2nd edn, Marburg, 1953), Tafel 10.

[248] Gilles Aycelin. See Pius Bonifacius Gams, *Series Episcoporum Ecclesiae Catholicae* (Graz, 1957 reprint), p. 583.

[249] Étienne Béguart de Penous (*ibid.*, p. 630).

[250] Gerard de Montcornet (*ibid.*, p. 633).   [251] Almost certainly thus rather than 'that'.

[252] It is not certain that the subject is the mother.

or out of fear, he said he had not, but because that was the truth, as he said.

(o) ¶ Lord Ralph de Paredo, seventy-two years old, the chanter of Meaux, formerly master of the children's hospital of the Lord Philip and Lady Jeanne the queen, parents of the lord king, both of the current lord king and of his brothers, deposed in evidence with respect to the first and second articles concerning what he had heard and what he believed, and that the said Louis had died at Montpensier, and he had heard said what the said articles contain, and [concerning] the Lady Marguerite, the widow of St Louis, to whose retinue he belonged[253] for fifteen years.

Again, questioned about all the articles bearing on consanguinities, both the consanguinity descending from the aforesaid Lord Louis father of St Louis, in which the said Lord Charles and the said Lady Blanche are claimed to be in the fourth degree on both sides, and in the other consanguinity descending from the aforesaid Lord Robert the first brother of St Louis, he deposed in evidence under oath so far as that was concerned that the persons mentioned in the said articles act and are thought to be just as is set out in the article, apart from the said Lord Robert, the first one, whom he did not see – but he heard concerning him what the aforesaid article contains from a number of trustworthy people; but all the others he saw, and he knew and saw that they were generally regarded and commonly held to be, and behaved towards each other, exactly as the said article states. Again, on the eighteenth article, he deposed in evidence, in respect of the mode of reckoning, that he hears and has often heard exactly what is contained in the article, as he said.[254] Questioned on the twenty-second article he deposed in evidence under oath just what the article says. Asked about the reason, he said that he heard it said that Charles could have had the sister of the Duke of Brittany – mention is made of her in the said article – with the county of La Perche, which would have been given to him with a value of 10,000 in revenue and 50,000 in coin, and therefore, etc. – for he did not believe that any woman would have refused him, as he said. Questioned on the thirtieth article, he said under oath that he did not know the truth, since he was not present. He did not depose anything else relevant on the aforesaid articles about which he had been questioned. [Questioned] whether out of hatred, etc.

---

[253] 'cum qua moratus fuit'.

[254] 'deposuit, quantum est de modo computandi, prout in articulo continetur sic audit et audivit sepius, sicut dixit'. The 'prout' and 'sic' might or might not correlate syntactically. The content is not much affected.

(p) Lord Guy de Jouy, a knight, sworn in as a witness and interrogated on the said twentieth article, deposed in evidence that at the time of the said baptism he was in the household of the lady queen, and that the Countess of Burgundy was in the town of Creil, but the witness himself was not at the said baptism, as he said, since he stayed in the chamber of the said lady queen, but after the baptism he feels sure that the said Countess Mahaut of Burgundy brought the child back to the chamber, and said to the aforesaid lady Queen Jeanne that she was the godmother, and, on his conscience, if he were to maintain under oath that Mahaut was a godmother his[255] conscience would be clear, and in the meantime he also heard it said by many people that she had held the said Lord Charles over the font, and he believes, under oath, this to be true – that she held him; and he did not depose anything else relevant in evidence. Asked if he had given his deposition, or said anything that he had deposed in evidence and said, out of hatred, fear, for advantage or love, he said, on his oath, that he had not, but for the sake of telling the truth.

(q) Richard 'le Poissonnier', townsman of Creil, sixty years of age, produced and sworn in, in respect of the said thirtieth article said, on his oath, that he saw the Lady Mahaut by the font when the same Lord Charles was being baptised, by the child himself, and she was the greatest lady who was there, as it seems to him, but he was not able to tell whether she stretched out her hands to hold him, but he believes as a matter of certainty that she was a godmother, and he would swear this more readily than the alternative,[256] and he saw at the said baptism the Count of Burgundy her husband. Asked about the people standing around, he mentioned the Lord Charles of Valois, the Count of Flanders, the Countess of Joigny, and many others whom he does not recall, and when questioned in connection with the aforesaid Count of Burgundy and the Countess whether he believes that she held the said Charles over the font, he said 'yes', because he saw her among the godmothers, as he said, and in his judgement she was a greater lady than the others. And he did not say anything else relevant.

(r) Colard Heitie, fifty-three years of age, sworn in as a witness and carefully questioned about the said thirtieth article, said under oath that he was present at the church of St Evremond of Creil when the said lord king was baptised, and there saw the said Lady Mahaut Countess of Burgundy near the Lord Charles Count of Valois, who was holding the said child above the font. Questioned whether he saw that the said Lady

---

[255] 'his . . . he . . . his'. This must refer to the witness rather than Mahaut, though the Latin could be masculine or feminine.
[256] 'citius quam aliud': or: 'without the slightest hesitation'?

Mahaut held the said Lord Charles above the font, he said he does not remember very well, since he was in a crowd of people and he could not properly see everything that was happening. Asked what he thought, he said that he believes as a matter of certainty that she was the godmother of the said Lord Charles, from the things he had already mentioned, and because at the time he heard this said by the lady Countess of Iogny, for whom he worked as a pelterer, and from a certain lady-in-waiting, Amabilete by name, of the lady Queen Jeanne, the mother of the said lord king – this Amabilete carried the secret sign[257] of the said queen, as he[258] said – and from many others at the said time, more than forty in the aforesaid town of Creil and in the household[259] of the said lady queen. Asked for what purpose he had come there when he saw the aforesaid things, he said that it was because he lived and still lives in the said town of Creil, and he wanted to see the baptism of the king's son. Asked about what was commonly reported, he said under oath that the common report was and is in the said town and in the queen's household that the said Lady Mahaut was fellow parent of the said lady queen through spiritual kinship and godmother[260] of the said Lord Charles. And he did not say anything else relevant. Asked whether he had deposed any of the aforesaid things in evidence out of hatred, love, for the sake of favour, or profit, or fear, he said under oath that he had not, but that it was the truth. On the other articles he was not asked to answer questions.

(s) The nobleman and magnate Gaucher de Châtillon, the Constable of France, sworn in as a witness and carefully questioned on the first, second, third, fourth, fifth, sixth, seventh, eighth, eleventh, twelfth, thirteenth, fourteenth, fifteenth, and sixteenth articles, these being set out for him in turn, replied that he did not know how to give evidence as the truth[261] with respect to namely to the parents of St Louis, who were mentioned in the first and second articles, nor with respect to the first Lord Robert and Lady Mahaut of Brabant either, since he had not seen the aforesaid, as he said, but he had heard the contents of the aforesaid articles said often and by many trustworthy people, with respect to the things that the articles say are true of the aforesaid persons, and so he believes, as the same witness asserts. He said however that he saw the other persons mentioned in the aforesaid articles, and that one descended from another just as is stated in the aforesaid articles, in sequence, namely: from St Louis, whom he saw, the first Philip; from the first Philip, the second Philip; from the second Philip, the Lord Charles who

---

[257] Some sort of seal?
[258] Linguistically, this could also mean 'as she [Amabilete] said'.   [259] 'domo'.
[260] 'commater dicte domine regine et matrina [Karoli]'.   [261] 'de veritate deponere'.

is now king. Again, from the second Lord Robert, whom he saw, the Lady Mahaut, and from the said Lady Mahaut, the said Lady Blanche. Again, from the Lady Blanche the wife of the King of Navarre, who was the sister of the second Lord Robert, descends the Lady Jeanne the Queen of France, the mother of the said King Charles, and from the said Lady Jeanne descends the aforesaid lord king, and he saw that the said Lord Robert, the second one, and the first Lord Philip regarded each other as first cousins, sons of two brothers, namely of St Louis and the first Robert, and that the lady Queen of Navarre and the aforesaid Lady Mahaut regarded each other as first cousins, that is, daughters of brother and sister, namely of the aforesaid second Lord Robert and Lady Blanche the Queen of Navarre; and the foregoing was regarded and among those who know about the times still is regarded as certain and beyond doubt. Questioned about the thirtieth article, he deposed in evidence under oath that he remembered that the Lady Jeanne, the mother of the said lord king, was at Creil at the time of the birth of the same lord king, and King Philip was coming there, and the witness himself who speaks, and many others with him, and it was indicated to lord the lord[262] King Philip by the aforesaid Malengrene, a *valet de chambre*, that the said Lady Jeanne his wife, the queen, had given birth, and then the said lord King Philip changed his itinerary and went to Saint Christopher in Halatte at Senlis,[263] and told the same witness to go to the baptism of the said Lord Charles, and he went there and saw that the Lord Charles Count of Valois held the same Lord Charles, the present king, above the baptismal font, and in the same place he saw the Countess of Burgundy, namely the said Lady Mahaut, and many other people, and the said witness was one of the godparents of the said Lord Charles, and linked by spiritual kinship[264] with his parents. And the aforesaid Lady Mahaut was one of the godmothers at the said baptism of the same Lord Charles, and linked by spiritual kinship[265] with his parents. Asked about how he knows, he said: because he saw and heard it to be so. For he saw, as he said, that the aforesaid Lady Mahaut held – together with the Lord Valois, who was the primary person holding the boy, and the witness himself and the other godfathers and godmothers there present – the said Lord Charles, who is now the king, over the baptismal font, while he was being baptised. Asked about the place, he said that it was in the church of St Evremond at Creil. Asked about the people present, he mentioned the aforesaid Lord Valois and the Lady Mahaut. And he feels certain, as he said, that the Count of Burgundy, husband of the same Lady Mahaut and father of the said Blanche was there, and the Count of Flanders and many other

---

[262] 'domino domino'.   [263] 'Silvan'.   [264] 'compater'.   [265] 'commater'.

nobles and prelates. Asked whether he had deposed in evidence any of the foregoing out of hatred, love, for the sake of favour, for advantage, or out of fear, he said no, under oath, but only for the sake of the truth which he had sworn he would tell.

(t) The great and magnificent prince the Lord Charles Count of Valois and Anjou, sworn in as a witness and carefully questioned about the thirtieth article, said under oath that he had held the said lord King Charles at the baptism of the said lord king, and that he remembered clearly that the said Lady Mahaut, then Countess of Burgundy, and now of Artois, was there present in the church of Creil, at the baptismal font of the said church – which is now within the castle of the said place – while the aforesaid Lord Charles was baptised; but he does not very well remember if she held him, but there were a number of people[266] who held out their hands to the said lord king at the said baptism, but he does not very well remember who. Asked what he believes: – whether or not he believes that she held her hands [out to the baby Charles] and was a godmother – he said under oath that he believes that she was a godmother and that she held out her hands to him at the baptism, and, on his oath, he believes this more than the alternative.[267] Asked about the time, he said that it was around the Feast of John the Baptist about twenty-eight years ago. And he said nothing else relevant about the contents of the aforesaid article. But, concerning the age of the aforesaid Lord Charles and Blanche at the time of the marriage contracted between them, he said that the said Lord Charles was less than fourteen, indeed he had five months or thereabouts to go before turning fourteen. Again, that the said Lady Blanche was not yet twelve; and he knew this because he had stood godfather to both of them, as he had said before.[268] And he also remembers the time of the marriage, since it was fourteen years ago around the Feast of the Purification of Blessed Mary last. He was not questioned on the other things, and said nothing else relevant.

(u) Lord P. called 'd'Argent', chanter of the church of Melun, questioned on the thirtieth article, the only one for which he had been produced, deposed on evidence under oath that he was present when the said Lord Charles was carried to the church of St Evremond at Creil to be baptised, and there he saw and heard that Brother Jean de Granches, the almoner of Queen Jeanne the mother of the said Lord Charles, who, while the boy was being prepared for handing over for baptism, read a certain list on which were written the names of the men and women who were to be godfathers and godmothers, and among others was named the

[266] 'plures'.   [267] 'et hoc per iuramentum suum magis quam aliud'.
[268] Though his godparenthood of Blanche was not mentioned in this statement.

said Lady Mahaut Countess of Burgundy, who was present there. And it seems to him that hers was the first or the second name on the list, and he saw immediately, as he said, that the aforesaid Lady Mahaut took the said Lord Charles from the lap of Lady Jeanne the midwife, and carried him between her hands, naked, to over the baptismal font, and there handed him to Lord Charles Count of Valois, who was the principal godfather, and the said Lady Mahaut was by the font all the time while the child was being baptised, as he said. Such was the crowd – so he deposed in evidence – that he was not able to see the laying-on of hands by the fellow godparents who were holding him, but it was commonly said in the royal household after the said baptism that she was a godmother. Asked why he was there, he said that it was because he was the chaplain of the said lady queen and was staying with her and had come with her to the said town of Creil, and had then come to the said church to see the said Lord Charles baptised. Asked if he saw that the said Lady Mahaut laid her hands[269] on the said child to hold him after she had handed him to the said Lord Valois, he said that he did not remember, not with respect to her nor with respect to the others, apart from the said Lord Charles Count of Valois, because there was a crowd, and he could not get near enough to get a good look at it. Asked what was commonly believed about it, he said: that the said Lady Mahaut Countess of Burgundy was a godmother, as he had deposed in evidence above. And he did not say anything else relevant. And he did not depose in evidence out of hatred, love, for advantage or out of fear, but for the sake of the truth, as he said.

(v) Lord Ger. de Saponhia, a priest, a canon of Roya, sworn in as a witness and carefully questioned about the said thirtieth article, the only one for which he had been produced, deposed in evidence under oath that he saw and heard that the said Lady Mahaut was named, among the others who were to be godmothers, by the almoner of the said Lady Jeanne Queen of France in the church of Creil where the same Lord Charles was baptised. He also saw that the said Lady Mahaut, then Countess of Burgundy, took the said child naked into her hands and handed him, over the font, to the said Lord Charles Count of Valois, and he saw that she was near the said Lord Charles at the baptismal font while the said child was being baptised. Asked if he saw that she held him above the font, he said under oath that he did not, since he could not see this because of the crowd of people there, but he firmly believes that she was a godmother on the basis of the things that he deposed in evidence. Asked if it was subsequently said that she had been a godmother, he said

---

[269] 'apponeret manus'.

that he could not remember. Asked where he saw the aforesaid things, he said that it was in the church of Creil where the same Lord Charles King of France was baptised, as he had said before. Asked why he had come there, he said that it was because he was a cleric in the chapel of the said Lady Jeanne the queen, and he had come to that town with her, and he went to the church, like the rest, to see the said baptism. And he had not given his deposition out of hatred or love, etc.

(w) Lord Nicolas de Fara, priest, canon of Roya, sworn in as a witness and carefully questioned on the thirtieth article, the only one for which he had been produced, said, under oath, that he saw that the said Lady Mahaut, at the entrance of the church of Creil, in which the said child was baptised, took the said child and carried him to the vicinity of the font. And afterwards he saw that the said Lady Mahaut handed over the child, entirely naked after his swaddling clothes had been removed, above the font to Lord Charles Count of Valois. And he also saw, as he said, that the aforesaid Lady Mahaut held the said child over the aforesaid font by one of the same child's feet while he was being baptised. Asked about what was commonly believed, he said under oath that on that day it was commonly said in the aforesaid town of Creil and especially in the queen's household that the said Lady Mahaut had been a fellow godmother, and she was held to be such. Asked why he was there, he said that it was because he was a cleric of the chapel of the lady queen, and he had come to the church to see the said baptism. Again, he added that the said Mahaut had been told by the said lady queen, through Michael le Flamenc, who had been sent to her, to come to the baptism of the said Lord Charles. And he did not say anything else relevant. And he deposed the aforesaid things in evidence for the sake of the truth, which was just as he said, and not out of hatred or love, for advantage or out of fear.

(Archives nationales, J.682.2; for transcription see Appendix 2)

[Depositions continue]

1322, May 19

Pope John XXII's definitive sentence

As noted above, I have translated from the École Française de Rome edition by Coulon (for details see end of translation). Because the bull is so long, I have indicated the page breaks in the edition, with the incipit of the new page, to help users match the translation with the

original, and I have added alphabetical paragraph numbering, which
has no status except as an aid to reference.

(a) As a perpetual record of the matter.[270]

To this the conscientious fulfilment of the authoritative office we have
undertaken directs us, for this the salvation of souls calls, and of this
public utility convinces us, that we should make every effort, taking the
time that is appropriate,[271] to dissolve the union of those who are joined
together contrary to the statutes of the canons, and willingly to grant
to them the freedom to go their separate ways. These things indeed
should be observed more strictly and carried through more promptly
with persons of high status, wrongdoing on whose part could[272] offend
the divine majesty more gravely, and graver dangers could follow from
them,[273] and graver scandals be caused by them.

(b) In truth, our beloved sons the noble men Louis Count of Clare-
mont and Milo, Lord of Noeris, and Master Étienne de Mornay, dean
of the church of St Martin of Tours, and Pierre de 'Mortuomari', the
cantor of the church of Bourges, gathered[274] in our presence and that
of our brothers[275] as ambassadors of our most beloved son in Christ
Charles, King of France and Navarre – with Pierre 'Galvandi' and Aymer
Mazerant, proctors of the said king and of our beloved daughter in Christ
Blanche of Burgundy respectively, being also present – carefully communicated to us in the king's name that some while ago a *de facto* marriage
had been celebrated between the aforesaid king and Blanche, when they
were below the age for marriage,[276] by their parents on their behalf,[277]
and that they remained in this for many years up to and after the age of
marriage, producing both masculine and feminine offspring from the said
marriage. With the passage of time, however, because a credible report
had been brought to the same king's attention that various impediments
deriving from both consanguinity [**col. 93: | -tate quam**] and spiritual
relationship stood against the said marriage, in such a way that it was not

---

[270] 'Ad perpetuam rei memoriam': from the pontificate of Alexander IV the standard
opening of the type of papal letter called 'Litterae solemnes': see P. Rabikauskas,
Diplomatica Pontificia (Praelectionum lineamenta), 6th edn (Rome, 1998), pp. 54–5.
[271] 'adhibita maturitate debita'.
[272] 'excessus . . . posset': the 'posset' indicates that 'excessus' is in the singular, but sense
and context suggest the plural. Though Coulon, *Lettres*, has transcribed 'posset' correctly from the original papal register, I would be inclined to emend it to 'possent' and
take 'excessus' as the plural. See next note.
[273] 'excessus . . . posset . . . ex eis pericula possent': rather than take 'eis' to refer to the
high-status persons, I understand 'excessus' as plural, and take the 'posset' to be
scribal carelessness (see previous note).
[274] 'constituti'.   [275] i.e. the cardinals.
[276] 'tunc infra annos nubiles'.   [277] 'parentibus ipsorum procurantibus'.

valid *de jure*, and that they could not remain in it without offence to God, the same king, wishing to become better informed about these things by taking counsel from experts, held careful discussions with a number of masters of theology and doctors of canon law and professors of civil law;[278] the consensus they came to was that the marriage was undoubtedly invalid and that those who had contracted it could not licitly remain in it.

(c) Because of this, the same king, desiring to be a father, and to have plenty of legitimate offspring for the service of God, and governance of his kingdoms, and the security of all the faithful, and for the Church's judgement to declare whether the said marriage was valid or not, took care to come to our venerable brother Étienne, the bishop of Paris, his and Blanche's ordinary,[279] through his proctor legally appointed for this purpose; and the said bishop, when the matter had been explained to him, conscientiously considering the importance[280] of the matter[281] and the high position[282] of the said persons, in order that he might proceed in it with greater solemnity and riper reflection and greater seriousness, in such a way as to exclude all suspicion, had our brother the bishop of Beauvais[283] and our beloved son Master Geoffrey de Plessy,[284] notary, join him to assist him in the same matter, having join him in their capacity as notaries public in this case [our] beloved son Master Amisius, called 'le Ratif', from Orleans, the dean of the church of Paris, and Master Guillaume de Morcento, canon of the church of Laon, notaries public by apostolic authority, men learned in law and experts in the facts of the case,[285] and had the said Blanche summoned peremptorily for a specified day, inserted in the petition of summons,[286] on which day she would need to respond to this document[287] in person or through a proctor, and to proceed in this case as justice should recommend.

(d) On that day the proctor appointed to represent the case of the said Blanche appeared as the law demanded, the jurisdiction of the said

---

[278] 'masters . . . doctors . . . professors': this is stylistic variation: the Latin words do all indicate the same academic status.

[279] 'ordinarium': i.e. their local bishop.   [280] 'qualitatem'.

[281] 'ipsius': in context, clearly refering to 'negotium', rather than to Charles.

[282] 'excellentiam'.

[283] Preceded by a double dot: see Archivio Segreta Vaticana, Registra Vaticana, 111, fo. 29rb, line 28. As noted elsewhere, before the name of an office the double dot seems to indicate reverence, or perhaps uncertainty about the form of the proper name. This is misleadingly transcribed as a triple dot, indicating an omission, by Coulon, *Lettres*, col. 93.

[284] 'Plexeyo' in the papal register. E. A. R. Brown informed me of the correct French version of his name.

[285] 'expertos in facto'.   [286] 'citatorio . . . libello'.   [287] 'libello'.

bishop was extended[288] as a precaution, and the case started by the said *libellus* went to trial in accordance with the law,[289] the oath both concerning good faith and to tell the truth[290] was administered on the one side and on the other, the *positiones* on the side of the same king were stated[291] and presented, the replies to them on the side of the said Blanche followed, the articles[292] were handed over, witnesses were produced on the side of the said king in relation to them, the same witnesses put themselves under oath [**col. 94: |-mento recepto**] in the presence of the proctors of the same parties, they were examined, and their depositions set out in writing, but before these were made public the proctor of the said Blanche, raising an objection,[293] put before the aforesaid bishop the proposition that the impediments brought up previously as arguments against the marriage did not put any obstacle whatsoever in its way, viz., because an apostolic dispensation for the king and the woman with whom he would contract marriage had been granted and antedated the aforesaid marriage, and this removed all the aforesaid impediments: for which reason he asserted that the marriage had been contracted in accordance with the law.

(e) On the side of the said king however the proposition was put forward by way of reply that the said dispensation in no way refuted the aforesaid king,[294] and neither could nor should provide support for the said marriage, because of the impediments of multiple consanguinities and affinities deriving from different prohibited degrees,[295] and again because of the spiritual kinship contracted as a result of the fact that the aforesaid Charles had been raised from the baptismal font by the mother of the said Blanche together with certain other people, and concerning these things sufficient mention was not made in the said dispensation, and the said dispensation did not by any means extend to them, and also since many things had been implied[296] in the same dispensation which certainly did not correspond with the truth, on account

---

[288] 'prorogata'. The sense seems to be that the parties agreed to accept the bishop's jurisdiction even if there was a question of whether it extended to this case.

[289] 'liteque super dicto libello legitime contestata'.

[290] 'tam de calumnia quam de veritate dicenda'.

[291] 'factisque positionibus . . . pro parte regis ejusdem'.

[292] The articles 'stated the points that [a plaintiff] expected each witness to prove'. Brundage, *Medieval Origins of the Legal Profession*, p. 158.

[293] 'excipiendo': 'exceptiones', a technical term of Romano-canonical procedure, were objections of various sorts.

[294] 'regi predicto nullatenus obsistebat'.

[295] 'tum propter impedimenta multiplicium consanguinitatum et affinitatum ex diversis prohibitis gradibus provenientium'.

[296] 'suggesta'.

of which it seemed that it should be judged to be obtained under false pretences.[297]

(f) After this the aforesaid bishop, conscientiously considering that with respect to the said apostolic dispensation many things were rendered doubtful by the arguments put forward on one side and on the other,[298] and in view of the fact that it pertained to the supreme pontiff to clarify the words of his and his predecessors' dispensations and the doubts raised in respect of them, thought it would be more expedient for the aforesaid matter to be referred, set out in orderly form, to us.[299] To this referral the aforesaid king consented though not unreservedly,[300] and the proctor of the said Blanche without reservation. After this the said bishop of Paris ruled that the referral to us of this whole business as it had been conducted before him should be carried through, in such a way however that if it should by any chance happen that the aforesaid business should not be decided by ourselves, this would not be prejudicial to his being able to take it up again and even decide it.

(g) For this reason both the ambassadors and the aforesaid proctors on behalf of the aforesaid king and Blanche have humbly petitioned that we might deign to accept the said business, and decide it quickly, as the nature[301] of the matter required, one where delay would carry danger [**col. 95: | -periculum**] with it; they showed us the letter of the same bishop concerning the said referral, and their proctorial commissions,[302] and the trial proceedings held before him; and the aforesaid proctor of the aforesaid Blanche showed to us the sealed letters of our dearest Jeanne illustrious Queen of France and Navarre, and our beloved daughters in Christ Mahaut Countess of Artois and of the aforesaid Blanche,[303] and indeed to this letter of referral and to the proceedings the seals of the aforesaid bishops of Paris and Beauvais and of the aforesaid Geoffrey the notary were appended.

(h) Therefore, after the letter of the said referral had been opened and read, and after the proctorial commissions of the aforesaid proctors had also been read, we, who are bound by the duty of our pastoral office to devote ourselves conscientiously to removing the dangers that threaten our children and to taking care to make salutary provision[304] for them against those dangers, took on the aforesaid business, intending if God

---

[297] 'subreptitia'.

[298] 'super dicta dispensatione apostolica multa resultare dubia ex propositis hinc et inde'.

[299] 'quod ad nos prefatum negotium remittteretur instructum'.

[300] 'sub certo modo'.   [301] 'qualitas'.

[302] 'sua procuratoria': taking this as the plural of 'procurarorium', and to refer to the letters by Charles and Blanche appointing their proctors.

[303] 'clausas . . . ac Blance litteras supradicte'.   [304] 'salubriter providere'.

grants it to bring it to an suitable end, and desiring and announcing expressly that, if it should happen that the said matter were by no means brought to a conclusion by ourselves, the right in respect of cognisance over it would remain with the bishop of Paris, if and insofar as it pertained to him before this referral, in all respects untouched.[305]

(i) Determined therefore to take proceedings in the aforesaid matter forward, in the presence of our venerable brothers Berengar, cardinal bishop of Tusculum, and Raynaud, cardinal bishop of Ostia, and of our beloved sons Peter, cardinal priest of the church of Santa Susanna, Gaucelmus, cardinal priest of the church of Saints Marcellinus and Peter, and Simon, cardinal priest of the church of St Prisca, Bertrand, cardinal deacon of Santa Maria in Aquiro, and Arnaud, cardinal deacon of St Eustace, in the episcopal hall at Avignon,[306] where it has been the custom for some time[307] for the consistory to be held, with the aforesaid ambassadors[308] and proctors also being present, and with the same proctors mutually acknowledging[309] the seal of the same king attached to the procuratorial commission from him and the signs and signatures[310] written at the foot of the procuratorial commission from the aforesaid Blanche, and also the seals appended to the records[311] of the said trial proceedings[312] as they had been recorded[313] in a form to be made public[314] and also those appended to the written record[315] of the depositions[316] not yet made public, and with the seals of the letters close of the aforesaid queen, countess, and Blanche, also being accorded recognition by the aforesaid proctors,[317] and on their urging and making supplication to us to do so, we opened and made public the aforesaid depositions.[318] After this we had the aforesaid depositions and trial proceedings viewed and examined and the same depositions [**col. 96: |-tiones easdem**] rubricated carefully,[319] and then we had a thorough discussion with our brothers about the said depositions and trial proceedings.

(j) And although the aforesaid ambassadors and proctors petitioned us urgently that an end might be put to the said matter and that we

---

[305] 'ante remissionem hujusmodi'.
[306] On John XXII's residence in and refurbishment of the episcopal palace at Avignon see M. Faucon, 'Les arts à la cour d'Avignon sous Clément V et Jean XXII (1307–1334)', *Mélanges d'archéologie et d'histoire* 2 (1882), pp. 36–83, at pp. 43–5.
[307] 'dudum'.   [308] 'nuntiis'.   [309] 'recognitis'.   [310] 'subscriptiones'.
[311] 'actis'.   [312] This must be Archives nationales, J.682.1.   [313] 'redactis'.
[314] 'in publicam formam'.   [315] 'scriptura': this must be Archives nationales, J.682.2.
[316] 'in scriptura attestationum'.
[317] Note that the punctuation in the edition seems misleading here.
[318] 'attestationes aperuimus et publicavimus supradictas'.
[319] 'attestationes et processum predictos videri et examinari ac rubricari attesta|tiones easdem fecimus diligenter'.

should proceed to giving our verdict, we however – in view of the various dangers that might follow from any mistake if perchance one were to be made in these matters, and desiring to prevent such dangers and to make salutary provision for so difficult a matter, decided, without departing from the trial proceedings that were held or took place before the said bishop of Paris, nor intending to depart from it in any way – decided that it was expedient that we should, acting by virtue of our office,[320] inform ourselves, straightforwardly, and without judicial commotion and formalities,[321] both about the trial proceedings in the presence of the said bishop of Paris and about the principal matter.

(k) Therefore for information about this,[322] proceeding by virtue of our office, we had produced in our presence there the procuratorial commissions shown and produced in the presence of the [said][323] bishop of Paris by the proctors of the aforesaid parties; and after acknowledging[324] the seal attached to the procuratorial commission of the same king and the signatures[325] of the notaries who had signed the procuratorial commission from the said Blanche, with the said proctors acknowledging the supplication presented in the presence of the aforesaid bishop on the said king's side and the subsequent response to this by the proctor of the said Blanche in her name, viz., [the proctors] of the said king acknowledging that he submitted the aforesaid supplication, and [the proctors] of the said Blanche that she made the response as written above, we questioned them on whether they held to what was contained in the aforesaid supplication and response. To this indeed, with the proctor of the said king replying in the affirmative,[326] the proctor of the said Blanche replied that the said Blanche had said to him after the aforesaid response that she had had and still had a heavily burdened conscience on account of this marriage since, as she had understood, the apostolic dispensation by no means extended to all the impediments in the way of the aforesaid marriage, for which reason she was not able to persist in the aforesaid response with a clear conscience.

(l) Afterwards[327] however we had read out in the same place[328] the *positiones* and articles most especially relevant to the said business,[329] and

---

[320] 'ex officio'.   [321] 'de plano absque strepitu iudicii et figura'.

[322] 'Ad informationem . . . hujusmodi'.

[323] The square brackets are in Coulon's, *Lettres*, col. 96.   [324] 'recognitis'.

[325] 'subscriptiones'.   [326] 'sic respondente procuratore dicti regis'.

[327] The two stages seem to be: (1) John questions the proctors about the original supplication and Blanche's response to it, then (2) John questions the proctors about the propositions and articles and Blanche's response to them.

[328] 'ibidem' presumably referring to the reading rather than the original responses.

[329] 'ad dictum negotium principalius pertinentes': the 'principalius' from its position and from sense probably an adverb going with 'pertinentes' rather than an adjective going with 'negotium'.

the responses made to the same, asking the aforesaid proctors whether the aforesaid *positiones* and articles had been produced by the proctor of the said king before the said bishop of Paris, and whether [**col. 97:** | **in illis persisteret**] he persisted in them now,[330] and also the proctor of the said Blanche, whether the said Blanche had replied to the *positiones* and articles as had been read above, and whether she wished to stand by those responses at present. With them replying that the aforesaid had been produced, done and replied as set out above, and that they wished to persist in them, and with both of them put under the oath of calumny[331] and the oath to tell the truth,[332] they persisted in what had been proposed and in the responses given.[333]

(m) Afterwards, with the aforesaid ambassadors and proctors present in the same place, we had some of our brothers the cardinals of the holy Roman Church and not a few other witnesses to whom no possible exception could be made,[334] after they had been put under oath in the presence of the said proctors, [we had] them also examined[335] diligently, by the aforesaid Raynaud, cardinal bishop of Ostia, and P[eter], cardinal priest of the church of Santa Susanna, and [B]ertrand, cardinal deacon of Santa Maria in Aquiro, specially about the various consanguinities and the spiritual relationship through which the said king and Blanche were said to be linked within the forbidden degrees; we committed to them the power to call[336] and examine other witnesses also about the aforesaid, after those in the case of whom it seemed expedient to them[337] had been put under oath.[338] These men [i.e. the cardinals commissioned to collect more evidence] had the words[339] of the aforesaid witnesses who had been called by us and of not a few others who had been called by themselves faithfully[340] set down in writing by notaries assigned to this task, and they presented to us these depositions,[341] our venerable brothers the cardinal

---

[330] 'in presenti'.   [331] 'calumpnia'.

[332] The Latin could be translated as if this were one single oath, but in fact we know that these were two distinct oaths.

[333] 'in propositis et responsis'.   [334] 'omni exceptione majores'.

[335] There is an infelicitous extra pronoun in the Latin: 'quosdam...ipsos...examinari fecimus'. My insertion in square brackets tries to bring this out.

[336] 'recipere'.   [337] i.e. to the cardinals conducting this supplementary investigation.

[338] 'super predictis...de quibus eis expediens videretur': I take 'de quibus' to refer to the extra witnesses, not to the 'supradictis' about which they are being examined, in which case one would translate: 'we committed to them the power to call and examine other witnesses also, after they had been put under oath, about the aforesaid, where it seemed useful to do so'. The passage could be taken either way.

[339] 'dicta'.

[340] 'fideliter': grammar and the word order enable this to refer to the actions of the cardinals, but sense suggests that it refers to the accuracy of the record.

[341] 'nobis attestationes hujusmodi' is repeated: it is both before and after the list of cardinals.

bishop of Tusculum and the cardinal bishop of Ostia, [P]eter, cardinal priest of the church of Santa Susanna, Gaucelmus, cardinal priest of the church of Sts Marcellinus and Peter, and Simon, cardinal priest of the church of St Prisca, Bertrand, cardinal deacon of Santa Maria in Aquiro, and Arnaud, cardinal deacon of St Eustace, being present and assisting us; and, at the instance and in response to the supplication of the aforesaid proctors, we decided to publish them.[342]

(n) Afterwards, when the aforesaid proctors had been asked if they wished to propose, produce or prove[343] anything on or relating to[344] the aforesaid matter or relating to the trial proceedings[345] held before us or before the said bishop, the proctor of the aforesaid Blanche produced before us the papal bull[346] which had been issued[347] in respect of the said dispensation, which he had also produced in the trial proceedings held in the presence of the bishop of Paris, while the proctor of the said king put forward before us in the same place[348] the objections[349] or replications[350] put forward by him elsewhere against the aforesaid dispensation [**col. 98: |propositas supradictam**] and produced in the trial before the aforesaid bishop of Paris, the aforesaid proctors asserting that they did not wish to make any other propositions, objections, replications, statements, allegations nor to produce anything,[351] but that they were prepared to make renunciation[352] and to make an end in the afore-mentioned case in respect of both trials. And when they were insistent that we should give them permission for these things,[353] we decided to assent to their petitions. Therefore, with the aforesaid proctors making renunciation and an end with respect to the aforesaid trials and each of them individually,[354] we also held them both to be concluded.[355]

(o) Finally, then, after seeing, examining and carefully reviewing both the other documents[356] and the depositions occasioned and produced[357] in this case, both before us and before the archbishop of Paris, and after first discussing them carefully with our brothers, holding a solemn consistory[358] this day with our brothers at the accustomed hour, with very

---

[342] i.e. the depositions.   [343] 'propnere, producere vel probare'.   [344] 'in vel super'.
[345] 'processu'.   [346] 'litteras apostolicas'.   [347] 'confectas'.
[348] 'ibidem': taking this to mean at the same hearing before the pope: but it could be taken to refer to the same hearing before the bishop of Paris.
[349] 'exceptiones'.   [350] 'replicationes'.
[351] 'se nolle ulterius aliquid proponere, excipere, replicare, dicere, allegare vel producere'.
[352] 'renunciare'.
[353] 'ut ad hec ipsos admittere deberemus': a more obvious meaning would be that they pressed him to let them attend the session at which he was going to pronounce his final judgement – but that would make less sense in context.
[354] 'et quemlibet eorumdem'.
[355] Literally: 'that it was at an end with respect to both of them'.   [356] 'actis'.
[357] 'habitis atque factis'.   [358] 'consistorium celebrantes'.

many prelates and also auditors of our palace[359] and other chaplains of ours being specially summoned to it, and with various other persons both clerical and lay being present there, and with the aforesaid ambassadors and proctors also appearing at the said consistory in our presence, a humble and urgent petition was made on the part of the said ambassadors and proctors that we might deign to bring to a close this case and matter in harmony with God and justice by a definitive sentence, notwithstanding the fact that perchance the said day, by reason of the rogations or litanies that were done then, might be held by some to be a holiday – which holidays, if they were such, we might deign to suspend[360] in respect of this matter, and to make good from the plenitude of our apostolic power any defect, if such there might be, in the aforesaid trial proceedings.

(p) We therefore, bearing in mind how much danger delay in the previously mentioned matter might bring with it, and wishing to prevent it[361] by expediting the matter in a timely manner,[362] assenting to their petitions, gave our judgement[363] with the counsel of our brothers; – determining that the things that are done and will be done today in or with respect to the aforementioned matter, notwithstanding that it might be a holiday, should be as valid and should have the full force and strength[364] as if the said day were not a holiday, granting a dispensation on this matter from the plenitude of apostolic power, with the counsel of the same brothers dispensing no less with respect to [**col. 99: | defectibus, si qui**] any defects that might perhaps present themselves in the aforesaid trial proceedings, and making them good so far as we are able, also from the plenitude of our apostolic power. Therefore, after the name of God had been invoked, and the aforesaid trial proceedings and the said bishop of Paris's letter of referral[365] had been repeated in summary form, as also the *libellus* presented before the said bishop of Paris in the said case, and the procuratorial commissions through which the aforesaid proctors had been appointed to pursue this matter in our presence, also the supplications to us from the said proctors, and also the papal bull[366] issued concerning the said dispensation, with in addition, the letters of the aforesaid queen, countess and Blanche, through which indeed they humbly petitioned us to deign to accept the said referral and to bring this matter to a swift conclusion in a just way, being read aloud[367] in the same

---

[359] 'auditores palatii nostri': presumably the judges of the Rota.   [360] 'amovere'.

[361] Taking 'illique' to refer to 'danger'.   [362] 'per maturam expeditionem negotii'.

[363] 'ordinavimus'.   [364] 'roburque plenum obtineant firmitatis'.

[365] 'littera remissionis'.   [366] 'littera apostolica'.

[367] 'perlectis': because of the word order in the Latin, I tentatively understood this as going with just the letters of the three ladies, so that the preceding nouns go with the preceding 'recitatis'.

place: – we proceeded to pass a definitive sentence in the aforesaid case – with the counsel of the same brothers, after first conducting a careful discussion with them – in the following way.

{(q) Since, through what has been proposed and proved, first before the said bishop of Paris and subsequently before ourselves, it is evidently and clearly apparent that the aforesaid king and Blanche are related[368] in the fourth degree of consanguinity on both sides in respect of one stem, and in the third similarly on both sides in respect of another stem, and it is established also that the aforesaid Mahaut, Countess of Artois, is[369] the mother of the aforesaid Blanche and that the same countess together with several[370] others raised the said king from the sacred font, and that thus the countess herself was made the godmother[371] and the aforesaid Blanche spiritual sister of the said king, each, indeed, of which aforesaid consanguinities and this spiritual relationship contracted between the same king and Blanche, is enough[372] not only to be an impediment to marriage being contracted between the same king and Blanche, but also to render the contract invalid, unless the aforesaid impediments were removed[373] by the authority of the apostolic see through the privilege[374] of a sufficient dispensation, and it is furthermore established clearly from the form of the aforesaid dispensation, produced both before the aforesaid bishop of Paris and before ourselves by the aforesaid Blanche's side, and from other things proposed and proved, that it in no way includes[375] all the impediments specified[376] above, nor can it by any means be extended to them all: – we, wishing to free the same king and Blanche from the bond by which on account of the said marriage [**col. 100: |-monii mutuo**] they were held bound[377] to one another, and to grant to each of them leave to go away to wherever they wish so far as this marriage is concerned, passing a sentence of *divortium* between them, pronounce and declare as our sentence that the said marriage is null and that it never existed *de jure*, and we grant to them together and individually[378] permission to contract another marriage,[379] the aforesaid marriage notwithstanding.}

(r) The said *libellus* presented in this case reads as follows:[380]

{Before you, reverend father in Christ Lord Étienne by divine permission bishop of Paris, Pierre Gouvanh, proctor and with procuratorial commission[381] from the renowned and most excellent prince the Lord Charles, by the grace of God

---

[368] 'conjunctos'.   [369] 'fore' in ms.: literally 'will be'.

[370] 'pluribus'.   [371] 'matrina'.   [372] 'sufficit' in the singular.

[373] 'sint sublata' in the subjunctive (which translates awkwardly into English here).

[374] 'beneficium'.   [375] 'comprehendit'.   [376] 'expressata'.

[377] 'tenebantur astricti' rather than 'tenebatur esse astricti', which would more easily fit the tempting translation: 'by which they were held to be bound'.

[378] 'ipsis et eorum cuilibet'.   [379] 'ad vota alia transeundi'.

[380] There are one or two very minor differences between the text printed from the register by Coulon, *Lettres*, col. 100, and the text printed from Archives nationales, J.682.1 (my paragraph (e)) in this volume: e.g. Coulon has 'permissione divina' while J.682.1 has 'provisione divina'. The Register/Coulon version is also slightly truncated.

[381] 'procuratorio nomine'.

King of France and Navarre, has asserted and proposes that the aforesaid Lord Charles contracted marriage but only *de facto*, clandestinely, without the banns being read, and in other ways less than legitimately, with the Lady Blanche, daughter of the late Count of Burgundy, she being related to him within the forbidden degrees and with various links of consanguinity, and with respect to several common ancestors, and with both of them being below the age of puberty at that time, for which reasons and others[382] the said Blanche could not legally be joined to him in marriage; nor can the same prince any longer remain in this union which is illicit in this way[383] without detriment to his soul and grave scandal to many. On this account the lord proctor asks that the said marriage be pronounced and declared by a sentence [of the court] to have been and to be null in law, and that a licence may be granted to the said lord king freely to contract marriage with another woman; and he asks for the aforesaid things in whatever permitted way and form that may work best,[384] not binding himself to prove more of the aforesaid things than will suffice for him to achieve his purpose,[385] and he makes the affirmation that he will declare,[386] add and subtract as often as necessary.}

(s) Again, the aforesaid papal bull of dispensation reads as follows:[387]

{Clement, bishop, servant of the servants of God, to his beloved son the noble man Charles, son of our most dearest son in Christ Philip, illustrious King of France, greetings and apostolic blessing. The Roman pontiff exercises the plenitude of power granted to him from above in the bestowal of the keys not only towards more lowly persons, but also to those who are endowed with high authority however great, [**col. 101: | exercet relaxando**] by sometimes relaxing the rigour of the sacred canons, and by benign grace granting as an indulgence what their severity forbids, as he sees it to be expedient and salutary in God.[388] Therefore since your royal line has been enlarged together with[389] persons of high rank both near and far almost to the point where you can scarcely find any women among them to whom you can decently be joined in matrimony in accordance with what your rank requires, without the grace of a marriage dispensation, we, yielding to your petitions, by apostolic authority grant to you a dispensation that you may licitly contract marriage with some woman[390] who is related to you in the third degree of consanguinity or affinity on both sides or in the third and the fourth or even in the fourth only on both sides, notwithstanding the impediment that arises from the aforesaid consanguinity and affinity and from the justice of public honesty, and to the woman with whom you wish in the future[391] to contract marriage that she may freely contract marriage with you, announcing

---

[382] 'alias'.   [383] 'sic illicita': or perhaps: 'which is so illicit'.

[384] 'omni modo et forma cum quibus melius sibi licet' – technical legal language.

[385] 'non...nisi ad ea dumtaxat probanda que sibi sufficere poterunt de premissis ad propositum consequendum'.

[386] 'protestatur de declarando' (etc.).

[387] Coulon, *Lettres*, compared it with the original in Archives nationales, J.436.21: see col. 108, notes 4 and 5.

[388] 'prout in Deo conspicit salubriter expedire'.   [389] 'cum'.

[390] 'aliqua'.   [391] 'volueris': future perfect.

out of the plenitude of apostolic power that the children that you should have from this marriage will be legitimate. Therefore let no-one [*Nulli ergo*] – But if anyone [*Si quis autem*]. Given at Poitiers 8 Kal. June, in the second year of our pontificate [= 24 May 1307].}

(t) Again, the procuratorial commission of the said king reads as follows:

{Charles, by the grace of God King of France and Navarre, to all those who will inspect the present letter, greetings. You should know that, since between ourselves or our proctor on one side, and Blanche of Burgundy or her proctor on the other, a certain case concerning the annulment of the marriage formerly contracted *de facto* between ourselves and the aforesaid Blanche had for some time been going on[392] before the bishop of Paris, and proceedings had been taken forward in the aforesaid case both for and against us, without however going as far as the publication of the witnesses, in his presence, and finally the whole matter has been in a certain manner[393] referred by the aforesaid bishop of Paris to the cognisance, ruling,[394] and decision of our most Holy Father in Christ John by divine providence supreme pontiff of the most holy Roman and universal Church: we, regarding, with our certain knowledge,[395] all and everything that has been done up until now through our proctors before the bishop of Paris in the aforesaid, whether at the same time or separately, as ratified and pleasing to us, create and constitute, as our special proctor for taking the aforesaid matter forward in the presence of the same most Holy Father, our beloved Master Pierre Galvani, cleric, giving and conceding [**col. 102: ||eidem| plenam**] [to him][396] full and free powers to act on our behalf and in our name in the presence of the aforesaid most Holy Father with regard to the nullity of the said marriage, and of swearing the oath of calumny and submitting to any other oath on my soul,[397] and of proceeding in respect of things done or things that need to be done absolutely from the beginning[398] concerning the [nullity][399] of the said marriage, and of continuing the aforesaid trial proceedings, and making renunciation and an end in respect of it, and of consenting that from the said trial proceedings sentence be pronounced by the aforesaid most Holy Father, even if perchance there might possibly be some defect with respect to the said trial proceedings, and of hearing the said sentence and of substituting one or more proctors, whenever he wishes, in his place with the same[400] power as he has, and of doing all and every single thing that we might be able to do, were it to happen for us to be present, whatever they might be and whatever their nature,[401] even if they should be things such as demand a special command, promising to all those whom it concerns or will concern in the future, by the force of this document, that we will hold as ratified and pleasing[402] in perpetuity whatever is done, carried out or otherwise in any way procured by our aforesaid proctor or by someone to be chosen by him as a

---

[392] 'ventilata'.   [393] 'certo modo'.   [394] 'ordinationem'.
[395] 'ex certa scientia': standard formula showing that the ruler was aware of what was going out under his name.
[396] 'eidem' supplied in square brackets by Coulon, *Lettres*.   [397] 'in nostram animam'.
[398] 'noviter'.   [399] Supplied in square brackets by Coulon, *Lettres*.   [400] 'consimili'.
[401] 'cuiuscunque status'.   [402] 'ratum et gratum … habituros'.

substitute in the aforesaid matters and things touching on them, and [promising] also the 'security for costs'[403] with its clauses[404] guaranteed by all our goods,[405] relieving him and any persons to be appointed by him as substitutes from any burden of giving satisfaction,[406] not intending from this to revoke in any way other power given to him or to the others appointed by us to take this matter forward.[407] In witness of these things we have had the present letter sealed by our seal. Given in the royal abbey by Pontoise[408] on the 14th day of the month of April, in the year of the Lord 1322.}

(u) Again, the procuratorial commission of the same Blanche reads as follows:

{In the name of the Lord, amen. Through this the present public document[409] let it be clearly evident to all that, in the year of the same Lord 1321,[410] indiction 5, in the month of April, on the sixth day of the same month, in the sixth year of the pontificate of our most Holy Father and Lord John XXII by divine providence pope, in my[411] presence and that of the prudent man Master Guillaume de Murcento, notaries public, and of the witnesses whose names are written below, the discreet man Aymeri Mazerant, proctor of the noble woman Lady Blanche of Burgundy, explained to the same Blanche, in whose service he is,[412] in her presence, how [col. 103: venerabilis vir] the venerable man Master Pierre Gouvanh, the proctor of the lord king, on one side, and he, Aymeri, proctor of and with a proctorial commission from[413] the same Lady Blanche, on the other, thought fit[414] to proceed from the time when she responded to the *positiones* put forward for the aforesaid proctor of the aforesaid most excellent prince the Lord Charles, King of France and Navarre, in the case brought by the proctor of the said king against the oft-mentioned Blanche, before the reverend father the lord bishop of Paris, for the annulment of the marriage between the aforesaid lord king and the aforesaid Lady Blanche – recounting to her in order clearly and in her mother tongue, in order:

– that the proctor of the lord king in the said case had produced many witnesses (and these had been named in the presence of the said lady), who had been sworn in in the presence of the same proctor, and been examined by the aforesaid lord bishop of Paris together with the revered fathers in Christ Lord John, by divine

---

403 'judicatum solvi'.   404 'cum suis clausulis'.

405 'sub nostrorum bonorum omnium ypotheca'.   406 'a quolibet onere satisdandi'.

407 'ad prosecutionem huiusmodi negotii'.   408 'Pontisara'.   409 'instrumentum'.

410 The year 1322 by modern reckoning. Blanche was presumably using the 'mos galli-canus' reckoning introduced into the royal chancery by Philip Augustus: see Cheney and Jones, *A Handbook of Dates for Students of English History*, p. 13. In 1321 the date of Easter was 19 April and in 1322 it was 11 April (*ibid.*, p. 158), which places a document which is dated 6 April in 1322 – as does the dating by the year of John's pontificate, since he was crowned on 5 September 1316 (*ibid.*, p. 38).

411 This is not Blanche but the notary writing the document, Amisius 'le Ratif' (see end of document, and Coulon, *Lettres*, no. 1419, col. 105).

412 'domine sue'.   413 'procurator et procuratorio nomine'.

414 'duxerat': singular, though both proctors seem to be the subject, suggesting emendation to 'duxerant'.

providence bishop of Beauvais, and Lord Geoffrey de Plessis, notary of the lord pope, and that the same Aymeri had put forward an objection at the end aiming to show[415] that the said marriage was not null, from a dispensation,[416] which excused the making of the marriage,[417] and with respect to this dispensation he gave convincing evidence among the documents of the trial;[418]

— and that many replications[419] had been made against the said dispensation by the other side, and many witnesses had been heard concerning the articles of the said case, in which the substance[420] of the said replications was contained, as he said;

— and that in respect of these things a ruling had been made by the said bishop at the request of the two sides;[421]

— and how, because of the importance[422] of the case and of the persons involved and by reason of the said, oft-mentioned apostolic dispensation, and for other reasons contained in the account[423] and the referral, the lord bishop of Paris had decided[424] that the aforesaid case and all its proceedings should be remitted to our lord the supreme pontiff and his holiness, and he had decided that it should be assigned to the aforesaid lord king and his proctor and to the same Lady Blanche and to the same Aymeri, as her proctor and by virtue of the procuratorial commission from the oft-mentioned lady, to appear before our lord pope, without postponement being permitted,[425] on the 8th of May,[426] or earlier[427] if it was conveniently possible, to present themselves and the said trial proceedings and to proceed further in the matter, to which referral[428] and assignation the same proctor had consented, as the same Aymeri said, by virtue of his procuratorial commission from the same [**col. 104: | -dem domine**] lady, and voluntarily, and that the said lady should consider[429] carefully what she would like to be done about these things.

This aforesaid Lady Blanche, by her certain knowledge[430] and without any deception whatsoever, as she said,[431] but making a considered decision[432] after

---

[415] 'ad finem'.   [416] 'de dispensatione'.

[417] 'pretextu cuius dictum matrimonium fuit factum': more naturally: 'which provided a pretext for the making of the marriage' – but the implication that this was a mere pretext does not fit the context, a document from Blanche's side.

[418] 'de predicta dispensatione fidem fecerat inter acta'.

[419] 'replicationes': replies embodying an objection. Note *Oxford English Dictionary* definition of 'replication' (5a): In traditional English pleadings: 'a claimant's answer to a defendant's plea'.

[420] 'factum': literally: 'fact'.

[421] 'fuerat per predictum dominum episcopum de voluntate partium ordinatum'.

[422] 'statum'.   [423] 'relatione'.   [424] 'duxeras': *sic* for 'duxerat'.   [425] 'peremptorie'.

[426] 'octava[m] die[m]' in edition. If Coulon's plausible emendation is adopted, the translation should read: 'and he had decided that the eighth day of May, or earlier if it was conveniently possible, should be assigned to the aforesaid lord king and his proctor and to the same Blanche and to the same Aymeri... to present themselves... [etc.]'.

[427] 'interim'.   [428] 'remissioni'.   [429] 'deliberaret'.

[430] 'ex certa scientia'.   [431] 'ut dicebat'.

[432] 'consulta': probably a nominative qualifying 'Blanca' rather than an ablative going with 'deliberatione'.

giving the matter careful consideration, as she said,[433] replied that she held to be ratified and pleasing to her all and everything of the aforesaid and the entire trial proceedings of the said case and each and all and everything done and dealt with in connection with it, and that she, so far as they affected her, approved and promised that she would hold them all to be ratified in perpetuity;[434] she also gave and granted to the same Aymeri general power and a special order[435] to appear on her behalf before the lord our pope, and to take forward[436] the same matter and to defend her at the Roman curia, and of consenting to the pronouncing of sentence in the aforesaid Roman curia on the basis of the trial proceedings held or to be held, solemn and informal,[437] and to do everything else there which she herself might be able to do in any way whatsoever were she present in the curia [in person],[438] whatever they might be and whatever their importance or nature might be,[439] whether by acting, or by defending, or doing anything else you like in respect of the aforesaid matter, even if they should be such things as might require a special order. And, nonetheless, she wished the power otherwise given by herself to the same man, and the rest of the proctors, also[440] in connection with ensuring that the said matter be taken forward before our lord the supreme pontiff, to be securely based[441] in all things and whatever happens, giving also to the same man the power of substituting in his place one or several men endowed with a power just like[442] his whenever he wishes, and promising to treat as[443] ratified and pleasing to her, in perpetuity, whatever is done, carried out or otherwise in any way whatsoever procured by her proctors or by someone to be appointed by the same Aymeri as a substitute,[444] and [promising] security for costs[445] with all her goods as guarantee.[446]

And she asked us, the notaries public listed below, to make for the same Aymeri a public document about these things. These things took place[447] in the aforesaid year, indiction, month and day and pontificate, at Chateau Gaillard, in the diocese of Rouen, in the presence of the following prudent men: Lord Jean Chevelli, beneficed priest of the church of Paris, Master Pierre de Neuville,[448] doctor[449] of civil law, canon of the church of Douai in the diocese of Arras, Pierre de Thoulis, Pierre called 'la Vache', squires, Jean de Noa, cleric, Egidia de Pormort, widow of the late Guillaume de Villaribus, and Jeanne [**col. 105: | de Blaincourt**] de Blaincourt, members of the said Blanche's household.

And I, Amisius, called 'le Ratif', of Orleans, cleric, notary public by the authority of the holy Roman Church, was present at and participated in all and everything set out previously, just as these things are detailed above and narrated, together with the notary public and witnesses whose names are written above and below: I saw those things and heard them and faithfully wrote them down

---

[433] 'ut dixit'.   [434] 'se ea omnia rata in perpetuum habiturum'.
[435] 'generale potestatem et speciale mandatum'.   [436] 'prosequendi'.
[437] 'non solenni'.   [438] 'personaliter' supplied in square brackets by Coulon, *Lettres*.
[439] 'cuiuscumque status seu conditionis existant'.   [440] 'etiam': even?
[441] 'firmitatem . . . obtinere'.   [442] 'consimili'.   [443] 'habituram'.
[444] 'vel substituendum ab eodem Aymerico'.   [445] 'iudicatum solvi'.
[446] 'sub suorum bonorum omnium hypotheca'.   [447] 'sunt . . . acta'.
[448] 'Novavilla'.   [449] 'licentiatus'.

in a publicly available form,[450] and I have signed my name to the present public instrument made from it[451] in witness to the things set out above, and at the urging of the said Blanche I have signed the instrument with my [customary][452] sign as asked.

And I Guillaume de Mortento, cleric of the diocese of Paris, public notary by apostolic authority, was present at and participated in all and everything set out previously, just as these things are detailed above and narrated, together with the notary public and witnesses whose names are written above, I saw those things and heard them and faithfully had them written down in a publicly available form, and I have signed my name to the present public instrument made from it in witness of the things set out above, and at the urging of the said Blanche I have signed the instrument with my [customary][453] sign as asked.}

(v) Again the supplication presented to us by the proctor of the said king reads as follows:

{P[ierre] Gouvanh, proctor of and by virtue of his procuratorial commission from the most excellent prince Lord Charles, illustrious King of France and Navarre, signifies to your holiness that – since formerly, between the aforesaid lord king and the noble woman the Lady Blanche of Burgundy, related to him by spiritual relationship and also by several consanguinities proceeding from different main stems and in several of them and in different degrees, each of them being then within the age of childhood which is not capable of matrimony,[454] clandestinely and otherwise contrary to the law, with many other impediments also existing at the same time between them, they contracted a marriage,[455] *de facto* only, illicit and reprehensible,[456] although the aforesaid couple making the contract were at that time unaware of the aforesaid impediments: – finally however, when these impediments became known to the same king with certainty and beyond doubt, the same lord king, with his conscience much weighed down by these things, had the said Lady Blanche or her proctor solemnly summoned before their reverend father in Christ Lord Étienne, bishop of Paris, the judge with jurisdiction,[457] in respect of the nullity of the same marriage, and he presented a *libellus* against her; and after the suit had been contested on the side of the aforesaid lady in accordance with the law before the aforesaid bishop of Paris, [**col. 106: |episcopo lite**] and the oath of calumny[458] [sworn] on both

---

[450] 'in formam publicam'.
[451] 'inde' – implying that the document in which this statement is made is an official and notarised copy of the original notarial record.
[452] 'solito' supplied in square brackets by Coulon, *Lettres*.
[453] 'solito' supplied in square brackets, *ibid.*
[454] 'infra pupillarem etatem matrimonii non capacem'.
[455] 'cum ... inter ... regem ... et ... Blancam ... matrimonium contraxerunt': *sic*! The syntax of the passage beginning 'cum ... inter' really requires some such phrase as 'matrimonium contractum fuit', but Gouvanh probably lost the grammatical thread – not too unlikely with these lengthy and complicated sentences.
[456] 'de facto duntaxat illicitum et dampnatum': taking 'duntaxat' with the preceding rather than the following phrase.
[457] 'judice competenti'.   [458] Some such word as 'prestito' has been omitted.

sides, certain *positiones* and articles put together[459] with responses by the aforesaid lady following, a number[460] of witnesses of high public repute[461] and unstained reputation,[462] beyond all reproach,[463] produced and examined on the side of the lord king, and their depositions[464] set down in writing and written up[465] by faithful and expert notaries, and also a certain dispensation put forward by way of defence on the side of the said Lady Blanche, and cogent[466] reasons against it given by way of replication, and the proceedings had been conducted in other respects [too] in accordance with the law, with formal procedure, and with the canons,[467] short of[468] the publication of the deposition of the aforesaid witnesses, in the presence of the aforesaid bishop of Paris, in the presence of the reverend fathers the lords Jean, bishop of Beauvais, and Geoffrey de Plessis, your notary, who at the request of the same bishop were present continually at all and everything that was done, [after all the foregoing] the same bishop for certain reasons saw fit, with the consent of both the aforesaid parties, in accordance with canon law,[469] in a certain way[470] to refer to your holiness the aforesaid case and its trial proceedings and also the depositions of the aforesaid witnesses, which had definitely not yet been published, enclosed under his seal and those of the aforesaid reverend fathers the lord bishop and the Lord Geoffrey, in order that the said case be brought to a salutary end by the same holiness – as is contained in greater detail[471] – these things and other things[472] – in the trial proceedings of the case itself and in the account given to us[473] [*read:* 'to you'?] by the oft-mentioned bishop. Therefore he petitions that, – although the benignity of your blessedness graciously, in giving his favourable reception to the aforesaid trial proceeding, depositions,[474] and account, thought fit to make provision regarding the safeguarding[475] of the jurisdiction of the oft-mentioned

---

[459] 'factis' should probably be taken with 'positionibus', etc. (Cf., for a parallel, Decretals of Gregory IX, X.1.6.54: 'praestito... iuramento de veritate dicenda, et factis positionibus et responsionibus hinc inde' (E. Friedberg, *Corpus Iuris Canonici*, vol. II, col. 94). Despite their role in the decretal just cited, in this document and even more so in the one from Blanche which follows with similar phraseology, 'hinc et inde' seem to go better with 'iuramento': 'the oath of calumny being sworn on both sides'. The parallelism of the rest of the clauses even raises the unattractive possibility that, after all, the plural 'factis' might go with the singular 'iuramento': 'oath(s) of calumny being made on both sides'.

[460] 'pluribus'.   [461] 'clare fame'.   [462] 'opinionis integre'.

[463] 'omni exceptione majoribus'.   [464] 'depositionibus'.

[465] 'in scriptis positis et redactis': probably the distinction between the record made on the spot and the fair copy.

[466] 'efficacibus'.   [467] 'alias processo legitime solemniter et canonice'.

[468] 'usque'. Without the following context, 'not yet been published', one would translate this as 'up to the point of'.

[469] canonice'.

[470] 'certo modo': implying not absolutely and without qualification: this may refer to the condition that the case could still come back to the bishop if the pope did not deal with it.

[471] 'plenius'.   [472] 'sicut hec et alia... continetur'.

[473] 'relatione... nobis facta': for 'nobis' read 'vobis'?   [474] 'atestationum'.

[475] 'reservatione': John had said that if he were not to bring the case to a close, the bishop of Paris could resume whatever jurisdiction over it to which he had been entitled before referring it to the pope.

bishop of Paris, insofar as his competence is involved[476] in respect of the aforesaid things – your same holiness may deign to bring to completion swiftly whatever seems to remain to be done to bring the said trial proceedings to a conclusion, and, if he should find any shortcoming in the aforesaid, that he may also deign benignly to make it good from the plenitude of his power, and also through his definitive sentence, in accordance with the form of the said *libellus*, to bring the same case to a swift and salutary end,[477] without judicial commotion and formalities,[478] since the status[479] of the people involved and of the matter in question requires this, and the consensus of the aforesaid sides has been and is given to this already.}

(w) Again, the supplication presented to us by the proctor of the said Blanche reads as follows [**col. 107: | Sanctitati Vestre**].

{Aymeri Mazerant, proctor of and in virtue of proctorial authority from the noble Lady Blanche of Burgundy, petitions your holiness that – since, in respect of the nullity of the marriage formerly contracted between the excellent prince the Lord Charles, illustrious King of France and Navarre, and the same Lady Blanche, the same lord king, or his proctor in his name, had the same Lady Blanche summoned to judgement before the reverend father in Christ the lord bishop of Paris, and, after the *libellus* had been presented by the proctor of the said lord king, and the case about it contested[480] according to the law, the oath of calumny [sworn] on both sides, certain *positiones* and articles put together on the king's side[481] with responses by the aforesaid lady following, [and] a number[482] of witnesses produced in respect of the said articles – the same Aymeri, after consultation with the oft-mentioned lady and her friends and counsellors, proposed arguments for the defence[483] that had been rightly applicable[484] to the said lady in regard to the aforesaid case, and he did what he could to give convincing evidence with respect to them,[485] and – certain replications being put forward against the same [arguments for the defence], and proceedings being in other respects continued[486] before the said bishop between the aforesaid parties, short of the publication of the depositions of the aforesaid witnesses – the same bishop, for certain reasons, with the consent of both the aforesaid parties, referred the aforesaid case and its trial proceedings and also the depositions of the said witnesses, which had definitely not yet been published, to your holiness – as is contained in greater detail in the aforesaid trial proceedings and in the account given by the oft-mentioned bishop to you[487] concerning these things – which, the trial proceedings and the

---

[476] 'quatenus . . . competere sibi potest'.

[477] 'necnon et per suam diffinitivam sententiam juxta formam dicti libelli eiusdem cause . . . dare finem'. I take 'eiusdem cause' with 'dare finem' rather than with 'dicti libelli'. If taken with the latter the translation would read: 'in accordance with the form of the said *libellus*'.

[478] 'absque strepitu judicii et figura'.

[479] 'qualitas': I regularly translate this as 'nature', but 'status' fits better in this context.

[480] 'lite . . . contestata'.   [481] See above, **# 1322, May 19** note 459.   [482] 'pluribus'.

[483] 'defensiones'.   [484] 'competere poterant et debebant'.

[485] 'fidem quam potuit fecerit de eisdem'.   [486] 'alias processo'.

[487] 'vobis': 'nobis' in the king's proctor's version as printed here.

account, together with the aforesaid depositions, the same proctor in the presence of the other party, in accordance with the order given to him by the same bishop concerning this, presented to your holiness last Wednesday – in order that it might please your holiness to proceed further in the aforesaid case summarily and without judicial commotion and formalities,[488] and, if anything should have been done in the aforesaid that falls short of canon law requirements,[489] that your holiness might deign to make it good from the plenitude of your power, and, in harmony with the will of God and with justice,[490] bring the case to a close by your definitive sentence.}

(x) Let no one therefore. – Given at Avignon, Kal. 14 [sic] June, sixth year.

> (A. Coulon, *Lettres secrètes et curiales du pape Jean XXII (1316–1334) relatives à la France* (Bibliothèque des Écoles Françaises d'Athènes et de Rome; Paris, 1906), vol. II, no. 1419, cols. 92–108)

---

[488] 'summarie et de plano absque strepitu iudicii et figura'.
[489] 'si quid minus canonice factum fuerit in predictis'.
[490] 'secundum Deum et iustitiam'.

16 Maximilian I, Anne of Brittany and Charles VIII of France

Maximilian I as much as anyone made the Habsburg dynasty the force it became in European history. He was a rising star of European politics in the last decades of the fifteenth century but his Breton marriage turned out to be a major setback. Maximilian had interests both to the east and to the west of his core domains in Austria. To the east, he was a contender for the Hungarian throne and on the receiving end of attack from Hungary. To the west, he confronted the resurgent kingdom of France. When the duchy of Burgundy fell apart in 1477, Maximilian obtained Flanders through his marriage to the duke's daughter, while the King of France got most of the rest. In 1490, the Duke of Brittany died, leaving as heir his daughter, Anne. Maximilian hoped to get the better of the young King Charles VIII of France by marrying her. On his eastern front things seemed peaceful enough to allow a bold move to the west.

As the son of his father Louis XI, Charles was not going to allow that. He and his successor Louis XII made the annexation of Brittany a top priority, far above the interests of the women involved. Coastal Brittany was a potential point of entry for English or other invaders. Even before the marriage, France faced an alliance of English and Spanish forces with troops supplied by Maximilian. And no doubt the sea coast of Brittany seemed like a 'natural frontier' for France.

Charles VIII was in the dark about the marriage until it was a fait accompli. Maximilian did not go to Brittany in person. He sent proxies empowered to contract the marriage for him. One of them famously touched Anne with his naked knee in a marriage bed in front of the whole court. This is usually assumed to be a clear symbol of present consent to marriage, if not of a kind of theoretical consummation, but that could be open to question. Henry VII of England's daughter Mary Tudor went through a solemn proxy ceremony with the future Emperor Charles V,[1] the wording suggesting actual marriage rather than engagement, but he

[1] Thomas Rymer, *Foedera*, vol. V, part 3 (The Hague, 1741), p. 265.

was well below puberty at the time and the arrangement was simply broken off later as the political situation changed. Thus, solemn wording may not mean all it seems to say. The same Mary went through another proxy ceremony with a representative of Louis XII of France (13 August 1514). It was very reminiscent of the proxy union of Maximilian and Anne of Brittany, in that it included the leg-touching in bed. But Mary subsequently sent her own proctor to go through a complementary proxy ceremony – this time her proxy marrying Louis on her behalf – in Paris.[2] If the ceremony was so definitive, why repeat it? Despite long-established conceptual clarity on the canon law side, it looks as if there was still something of a no-man's-land between betrothal and definitive marriage.

Later the validity of the marriage of Maximilian and Anne would be challenged by the French side on the grounds that there were formal defects in the proxy document. This has been taken quite seriously in recent work,[3] and it is certainly true that proxy documents of the later Middle Ages are excruciatingly precise, presumably because they had to be: but Charles VIII appears not to have tried his luck at making this point in a papal trial. Anyway action came before legitimation.

French armies invaded Brittany. The timing could not have been worse for Maximilian, who had to fight unexpected fires in southern Germany and Hungary. He could not help his Breton bride. Neither could his Spanish allies, who were engaged in a final push against the Islamic kingdom of Granada. The English were not prepared to go it alone. Anne had no chance of holding off France, though she dragged out the defeat.

What she could have done is to escape and join Maximilian. That option remained open for some time. The problem was that it would mean abandoning her duchy. She reconsidered. Charles VIII offered her several noble French partis. If she was going to give up King Maximilian, however, it would not be for anything less than a king. She and Charles got married, to the astonishment of Europe.

What made it worse was that Charles had been solemnly engaged – to Maximilian's daughter, Marguerite! They even appear to have been fond of each other. She was still only a child, but there was an emotional ruthlessness about his treatment of her.

The engagement between Charles VIII and Marguerite did not affect the validity of his marriage to Anne, but Anne's proxy marriage to

[2] Mary Anne Everett Green, *Lives of the Princesses of England from the Norman Conquest*, vol. V (London, 1854), pp. 30–1, and Rymer, *Foedera*, vol. VI, part 1, pp. 72–3 and 76–7.

[3] Yvonne Labande-Mailfert, *Charles VIII et son milieu (1470-1498): la jeunesse au pouvoir* (Paris, 1975), p. 103.

Maximilian was a more serious problem. So far as the evidence allows us to see, Charles dealt with it by ignoring it, helped by Maximilian's decision to cut his losses and do the same. There is no evidence of an annulment process. All we have is the rather problematic document translated below, granting a dispensation for quite different impediments to the marriage of Charles and Anne of Brittany: their blood relationship, and the fact that Charles had been betrothed to a woman (Marguerite) related to Anne – a recondite impediment known as 'public honesty'. This bull furthermore appears to have been backdated (see below under 'Historiographical highlights'), so there is a question mark over its own validity. The dispensation is under the name of Innocent VIII, who died in July 1492.

If none of the parties involved brought a case about the Anne–Maximilian match, the pope was not going to do so. That had never been the practice. If Henry III had not chosen to bring a case about his own early de facto proxy marriage, there would have been no proceedings. Instead of trying to get Anne back, Maximilian restored his honour by a campaign in which he managed to recuperate some more of the territories formerly united under the dukes of Burgundy.

Historiographical highlights

Francis Rapp, *Maximilien d'Autriche: souverain du saint empire romain germanique, bâtisseur de la maison d'Autriche, 1459–1519* (Paris, 2007), is a popularisation by a good historian, but, still, without footnotes. On Anne, Yvonne Labande-Mailfert, *Charles VIII et son milieu (1470–1498): la jeunesse au pouvoir* (Paris, 1975), has some scholarly apparatus, but is short on references where one wants them to support statements about dispensations. On Maximilian, Manfred Holleger, *Maximilian I. (1459–1519): Herrscher und Mensch einer Zeitenwende* (Stuttgart, 2005), p. 77, could leave a misleading impression: he writes that a papal dispensation 'for the time being related only to the dissolution of the betrothal between Charles VIII and Marguerite'[4] – as if a papal dissolution of the union of Maximilian and Anne followed, which so far as we know it never did. Georges-Gustave Toudouze, *Anne de Bretagne: duchesse et reine* (Paris, 1938), and Georges Minois, *Anne de Bretagne* (Paris, 1999), are popularisations without footnotes. Henri Pigaillem, *Anne de Bretagne: épouse*

---

[4] 'heiratete Anna am 6. Dezember 1491 unter gleichzeitiger Dispensierung ihrer Ehe mit Maximilian durch den französischen Hofklerus Karl VIII. von Frankreich... Obwohl die päpstliche Dispens sich noch fast ein Jahr lang verzögerte und vorerst nur die Auflösung des Verlöbnisses zwischen Karl VIII. und Margarethe betraf, war am Faktum der französisch-bretonischen Heirat nicht zu rütteln' (Holleger, *Maximilian*, p. 77).

de Charles VIII et de Louis XII (Paris, 2008), has a few. See also Georges Bischoff, 'Maximilien 1er, roi des Romains, duc de Bourgogne et de Bretagne', in Jean Kerhervé and Tanguy Daniel (eds.), *1491: la Bretagne, terre d'Europe.* International conference, Brest, 2–4 October 1991 (Brest, 1992), pp. 457–71. The best account by far is, in my view, that of Hermann Wiesflecker, *Kaiser Maximilian I: Das Reich, Österreich und Europa an der Wende zur Neuzeit,* vol. I: *Jugend, burgundisches Erbe und Römisches Königtum bis zur Alleinherrschaft 1459–1493* (Vienna, 1971), ch. IX.

Wiesflecker develops a bold hypothesis about the dispensation issued. Firstly, he implies that Maximilian had agreed to its wording – which does not even refer to a possible antecedent marriage between himself and Charles VIII's new bride. Wiesecker plausibly surmises that Maximilian had cut his losses. He implies that the pope who actually granted the dispensation was not Innocent VIII, whose name is on it, but his successor Alexander VI.[5] According to Wiesflecker, furthermore, the bull was backdated not to the date of the marriage between Charles VIII and Anne of Brittany, 6 December 1491, but to slightly later, so that a fine could be imposed.[6]

Now, this hypothesis cannot stand, as formulated by Wiesflecker, in its maximalist form, i.e. including the theory that Alexander VI issued a bull under the name of Innocent VIII. The leading specialist on the later medieval papal chancery informs me that it would have been impossible to publish a bull under the name of a dead predecessor.[7] Two possibilities remain.

The first one is extreme: that the bull was a forgery put out by the French court. There are precedents. A forged dispensation enabled Casimir of Poland to marry his new preference Jadwiga (in 1365) when the pope had urged him to return to his living first wife Adelheid of Hesse.[8] A dispensation for Sancho IV of Castile was forged in the thirteenth century, possible under the aegis of the archbishop of Toledo.[9]

---

[5] Wiesflecker, *Jugend,* p. 333: 'Unrest und Cuspinian wissen zu berichten, daß erst Alexander VI. dem König von Frankreich entgegenkam', and, p. 334: 'ist es höchstwahrscheinlich, daß diese Dispens auch erst im Spätherbst 1492 . . . ausgestellt . . . wurde'. Late autumn presumable means after Alexander VI had taken over – he was crowned on 26 August 1492. See also Wiesflecker's full notes, *ibid.,* p. 521.

[6] *Ibid.,* p. 334.

[7] 'Es ist unmöglich, eine Urkunde unter dem Namen eines bereits verstorbenen Papstes auszustellen. Beim Tode des Papstes wird der Namensstempel für die Bleibulle zerstört; das Siegel an einer solchen "rückdatierten" Urkunde könnte also nur betrügerisch von einer anderen Urkunde umgehängt worden sein' (Thomas Frenz, personal communication).

[8] Knoll, *The Rise of the Polish Monarchy,* pp. 221–2.

[9] Linehan, *Spain, 1157–1300,* p. 211; for Boniface VIII's reaction: Georges Alfred Laurent Digard *et al.* (eds.), *Les registres de Boniface VIII,* 4 vols. (Paris: 1884–1939), 2nd series, vol. IV.1, no. 2335, pp. 921–5.

Was the French court incapable of *Realpolitik* on this scale? One cannot rule it out, but the risk of exposure would have been considerable. On balance, it seems a far-fetched theory. The second possibility is that the dispensation had indeed been backdated, but by Innocent VIII.[10] This has the advantage of being a less drastic hypothesis, but one which takes care of the fact that even in April 1492 (a few months before Innocent's death) Maximilian's ambassadors in Rome had been able to tell him that the King of France had not received any dispensation from the pope.[11] Perhaps this is the more likely guess, but uncertainty remains. The salient fact is that Maximilian, Anne and Charles VIII presented a united front, at least insofar as they refrained from bringing the matter of the proxy marriage to the pope's attention. There seems to have been a systematic effort to remove all traces of it from written records.[12]

The translation

There is no modern edition of the bull but at least two very old ones – cf. Wiesflecker, *Jugend*, p. 521, note 49 – of which I have used that of Lobineau, working in the scholarly Maurist tradition at the start of the eighteenth century: Gui Alexis Lobineau, *Histoire de Bretagne*, 2 vols. (Paris, 1707); that of J. J. Du Mont, *Corps universel diplomatique du droit de gens*, vol. III, Part II (Amsterdam, 1726), p. 275, appears to be a copy of Lobineau's edition, which is cited at the end of it.

1491 or 1492

The dispensation for Anne of Brittany to marry Charles VIII of France

Innocent, bishop, servant of the servants of God, to his dearest son in Christ Charles, illustrious King of the French, and his dearest daughter in Christ the noble woman Anne Duchess of Brittany, greetings and apostolic blessing. The tenor of the supplication recently presented to us on your part is that you, without being unaware that you were related in the fourth degree of consanguinity, and that a betrothal in words in the future tense had been contracted between you, dearest son in Christ

---

[10] 'Bei hochpolitischen Angelegenheiten kann der Papst natürlich Ausnahmeregelungen anordnen, auch die Rückdatierung von Urkunden, aber niemals über den eigenen Pontifikat hinaus' (Thomas Frenz, personal communication).

[11] Wiesflecker, *Jugend*, p. 333.

[12] *Ibid.*, p. 326: 'Alle anderen Urkunden und Zeugnisse wurden später wohl im Interesse beider Parteien sorgfältig weggeräumt, damit nichts an diese tragikomische Geschichte errinnern solle'.

King Charles, and our beloved daughter in Christ the noble woman Marguerite, who is the child of our dearest son in Christ Maximilian illustrious King of the Romans, and also related to you, beloved daughter in Christ Duchess Anne, in the fourth degree of consanguinity, sometime[13] previously, she being an infant at that time: in order to put an end to the wars which had for some time been going on[14] between you in the duchy of Brittany – in which wars the countryside was being depopulated,[15] fortified and other places captured,[16] goods taken as booty, men taken into captivity, massacres and the mutilation of limbs and the very many other evils which usually happen in wars had been committed and were being committed on a daily basis – persuaded by the leading men of the aforesaid kingdom and duchy – contracted marriage with each other and consummated it with carnal union; – since however – as the same supplication went on to say – you are not able to remain in this marriage thus contracted by you, with the impediment of consanguinity, and the impediment of justice of public honesty arising from the aforesaid betrothal, standing in the way; and [since] if your marriage were to be dissolved,[17] it is likely that grave scandals could arise from this, and that you, Duchess Anne, would be deprived of your good name forever: on this account a humble petition was laid before us on your part that we might with apostolic benignity deign to make provision for you in this matter by conferring absolution from the sentence of excommunication that you[18] have incurred because of these things, and with the grace of an appropriate[19] dispensation. Therefore we, who feel an intense desire for peace and concord to flourish among all Christ's faithful people, especially kings, dukes and princes who are very devoted to this holy see: for the reasons set out above and certain others that have been explained to us, by apostolic authority, through this document, grant you a dispensation from the sentence of excommunication which you are known to have incurred because of the aforesaid things, and that you may be able freely and licitly to remain in this marriage that you have thus contracted, notwithstanding the impediment that derives from consanguinity and the aforesaid betrothal, so long as you, our beloved daughter in Christ Anne, were not abducted for this purpose; and we announce that offspring that has been conceived (if such there is[20]) and is to be conceived from this

---

[13] 'dudum'.   [14] 'viguerant'.

[15] 'agrorum depopulationes'. 'commissa fuerant', further down, provides a main verb after the list of the evils of war.

[16] 'castrorum et aliorum locorum eversiones'.   [17] 'si divortium fieret inter vos'.

[18] plural.   [19] 'oportune': 'timely' would also be a possible translation.

[20] 'si qua sit'.

marriage to be legitimate, and order you by giving strict instructions,[21] by virtue of holy obedience, that you should not be guilty of similar things in the future, nor give aid, counsel or favour to those that commit them, and that, with a salutary penance to fit the crime,[22] you should, for the marriage of poor girls to be chosen by yourselves, make sure that you pay[23] the sum of a thousand gold écus[24] of France for their dowries within the next six months. It is therefore forbidden to any man to infringe this document conferring our absolution, dispensation, announcement and order, or to make a rash attempt to go against it. But if someone should presume to attempt this, they should know that they will incur the anger of Almighty God and of the blessed Peter and Paul his apostles. Given at Rome in the year of the Lord's incarnation 1491, 18th Kal. January [15 December], eighth year of our pontificate.

(Gui Alexis Lobineau, *Histoire de Bretagne*, 2 vols. (Paris, 1707), vol. II, cols. 1546–7)

---

[21] 'precipiendo mandantes': on the principle of never using one word when two will do.
[22] 'pro modo culpe penitentia salutari'.   [23] 'cum effectu exponatis'.   [24] 'scutorum'.

17 Louis XII and Jeanne of France

Louis XII married Jeanne of France in 1476. She was the sister of his predecessor as King of France and daughter of the king before that, Louis XI (1483), the embodiment of *Realpolitik*. Jeanne and the future Louis XII were closely related but they obtained the necessary dispensation.

The annulment of the marriage must be understood against the background of the French monarchy's sustained attempt to get control of Brittany. Until his death in 1488, Francis II of Brittany had tried to keep the duchy autonomous by alliances with England, Burgundy (another even greater independent duchy, on the verge of becoming a state to rival France) and the Emperor Maximilian of Habsburg.

We have seen how Maximilian had (more or less) married Anne of Brittany by proxy and might have hoped to add the principality to his domain, but had been frustrated in his plans by Charles VIII of France (1483–98). Charles VIII's plans were nonetheless frustrated in their turn as he died without male heirs. With him ended the Valois dynasty.

He was succeeded by Louis XII who aimed to hold on to Brittany by marrying Anne in his turn. To do so he tried to get his marriage to Jeanne annulled; this was in the year of his succession, 1498. Judges delegate were appointed, propositions stated by both sides, and witnesses heard – mostly on the king's side. The queen's legal team was forced to accept the case, though they then took it seriously. As the documents translated show, arguments about the forbidden degrees of kinship and godparenthood fell apart when the queen's side produced a valid dispensation. The royal side had to depend on the argument – embarrassing for all concerned to put it mildly – that this daughter and wife of kings was physically incapable of consummation. This makes it a painful set of proceedings to read. It is hard not to share the distress of the queen, an appealing personality. One also respects her lawyers. They developed an ingenious argument. The king had originally claimed that she could not consummate the marriage because she had been bewitched. If the problem was magic, the lawyers argued, then it was not physical – so the king could not claim a physical impediment without contradicting

190

his earlier statement. The king's team parried this, and the documents translated show how the case against the marriage was built. There was a letter written before the marriage by Louis XI, hinting that their children would not cost anything to bring up. This seems to be a veiled and rather sinister way of saying that they would not be having any children. There was Jeanne's strong reluctance to undergo the physical examination (by women) commanded by the judges – in the end it never happened. Two of the king's doctors swore that he had told them how he and Jeanne had sex all right, but that he could not penetrate her and spilled his semen. The king took an extra oath in the most solemn circumstances to back up his version.

Historiographical highlights

M. de Maulde (ed.), *Procédures politiques du règne de Louis XII* (Collection de Documents inédits sur l'histoire de France, 1st series: Histoire; Paris, 1885), pp. 787–1132, is the key contribution. The introduction (pp. 789–805) is excellent. Michel Lhospice, *Divorce et dynastie* (Paris, 1960), argues for a development towards ecclesiastical pragmatism: willingness to sacrifice indissolubility to preserve a royal dynasty. Early medieval popes are hardliners in the Lothar, Robert and Philip I cases. The new pattern emerges with Louis VII and Eleanor, to whose 'divorce' Eugenius turns a blind eye. Innocent III makes it clear that monarchs cannot go too far, by refusing to endorse Philip II's discarding of Ingeborg. After that, though, there is flexibility: Lhospice makes it clear that he does not really believe the grounds alleged for annulling the marriages of Louis XII and Jeanne, Henri IV and Marguerite, or Napoleon and Josephine (this last one despite, rather than through, the pope, by the way). What the Church obtained in return was acceptance of its authority over such cases. I take a different view: that the combination of Jeanne's successful reluctance to undergo a physical examination and the solemn oath of the king would have made it hard for the judges to reach a verdict other than annulment, on the evidence before them. That comes out of the passages translated below, and an alternative to Lhospice's general interpretation will be presented in *Papacy, Monarchy and Marriage*.

Eugène Vouters, *Essai juridique et historique sur un procès en annulation de mariage au XVème siècle: Louis XII et Jeanne de France* (Lille, 1931), approaching the problem in what appears to be a legalistic spirit, thinks that the verdict was wrong. Eccentrically, he ends his book with a very long quotation from the address delivered a century (1599) later by the eminent jurist La Guesle before Henri IV, during another dissolution crisis. The aim of La Guesle's confident and detailed but highly inaccurate rhetorical history of royal divorces is to persuade Henri IV to change wives. In the case of Louis XII, his argument is that the marriage was valid but that it was right to dissolve it because Jeanne was sterile. This curious climax quotation, and his comment that La Guesle's authority is such as to make further argument otiose ('l'opinion de cet éminent juriste clôt toute discussion et tout controverse', p. 255), do not say a lot for Vouters's judgement.

Vouters seems to think that the marriage of Louis and Jeanne had been consummated (p. 219), without necessarily understanding that to mean penetration, since (he says) we will never know if Jeanne was really impotent or not.[1] She did not actually formally refuse to be examined, says Vouters; had she refused outright, she could have been compelled by 'measures such as excommunication'; she presented arguments against a physical examination which the tribunal chose to reject, but in the end it never actually took place.[2] In his lawyerly style, Vouters says that he does not think much of her first argument against undergoing an examination (that it would be beneath her royal dignity) but approves of her second. This was the ingenious argument that if she was impotent through magic as the king's side had claimed, then she could not be impotent physically. Vouters likes this argument on which he elaborates for several pages (pp. 232–4). Conversely, he is unimpressed by Louis's solemn oath: firstly because there were no 'oath-helpers' (co-swearers);[3] and, secondly, he could instead have insisted on a physical examination, since Jeanne had never refused that outright but only objected to it.[4]

The facts that impress Vouters could be read rather differently. Louis XII for all his ruthlessness may have preferred to avoid forcing Jeanne to undergo an inspection which she clearly found repugnant. The 'impotence magic' argument would have been a way to prove his point – had she been willing to cooperate, as he may have initially hoped she would; and his solemn oath was another way. We should bear in mind that there was additional evidence for impotence, not all of it available to Vouters.

---

[1] 'Jeanne était-elle arcta ou viripotens? Telle était un point obscur qui n'était connu que d'elle-même, de son mari et de dieu' (Vouters, *Essai juridique*, pp. 251–2).

[2] 'Par son opposition, ainsi que par les exceptions soulevées, Jeanne avait réussi à y échapper... précisons que Jeanne n'a jamais refusé formellement l'expertise; il ne faudrait pas conclure que si celle-ci n'eut pas lieu, c'est parce que Jeanne n'a pas voulu exécuter l'arrêt du Tribunal et que dès lors cette opposition démontrerait l'impuissance. Jeanne n'a jamais refusé de se soumettre à une décision de la justice, qui aurait d'ailleurs pu l'y contraindre par des mesures telles que l'excommunication; elle a simplement présenté des conclusions que le Tribunal n'a pas cru devoir retenir' (*ibid.*, p. 231).

[3] 'd'abord en raison de l'absence des cojurantes' (*ibid.*, p. 245).

[4] 'Jeanne n'ayant jamais refusé de se soumettre aux ordres de la justice, mais ayant simplement présenté des objections' (*ibid.*, p. 245).

Evidence from Louis's doctors was presented by Abel Destefanis, *Louis XII et Jeanne de France: étude historique et juridique sur une cause en nullité de mariage à la fin du XVe siècle (1498)* (Avignon, 1975), whose overall assessment of the case and the final judgement can probably be considered a response to that of Vouters. Destefanis quotes doctors: Jean Bourgeois, whom Louis told about his vain efforts to penetrate Jeanne.[5] Another doctor, Salomon de Bombelles, is quoted to the same effect.[6] Destefanis also attaches more weight to the king's solemn oath – even from a technical legal point of view. He argues that the oath of a king had a special legal status, so that oath-helpers and the principle that one could not give evidence in one's own case did not apply.[7]

Destefanis has sympathy for all concerned, and blames Louis XI for the circumstances which had put Jeanne in this horrible situation.[8] Louis XI's role in this regard has been discussed by Philippe Contamine, 'Un aspect de la "tyrannie" de Louis XI: variations sur le thème du "roi marieur"', in Michel Rouche and Jean Heuclin (eds.), *La femme au Moyen Age: Actes*

---

[5] 'Jean Bourgeois, docteur en médecine, fit également part d'un entretien avec le duc Louis, entretien dans lequel celui-ci disait combien il lui était impossible, malgré tous les efforts tentés, de connaître sa femme' (Destefanis, *Louis XII et Jeanne de France*, p. 161). He quotes his source (*ibid.*, p. 3: 'Audivit dici ab ipso Rege moderno, tunc duce Aureliense [*sic* de Maulde], quod multum laborabat ad cognoscendum eam et quod non spargebat in agro naturae, sed post multum laborem et magnam agitacionem spargebat semen inter coxas, ut ipse Rex credebat et sibi retulit', with a reference to de Maulde, *Procédures politiques*, p. 1033, and to his manuscript source for the trial he (Destefanis) also used.

[6] 'Cui respondit quod nesciret et quando volebat cum ea cohire, inveniebat quod . . . in orificio vulve . . . virga ejus non poterat ingredi sed caleficiendo se emitebat semen inter seu supra crura istius domine Johanne, et iste actus tantum sibi displicebat quod voluisset desponsasse pauperiorem nobiliorem hujus regni' (Destefanis, *Louis XII et Jeanne de France*, p. 162, note 1, citing de Maulde, *Procédures politiques*, p. 1081).

[7] 'Que penser de ce serment qui décide ainsi cette cause en nullité de mariage? . . . en matière de dissolution de mariage, le droit commun sur l'utilisation du serment n'était pas applicable, ou plutôt, il s'appliquait différemment. Le serment était seulement déféré à une personne qui affirmait le mariage, selon l'adage: "L'aveu en faveur du mariage lui profite, le désaveu ne saurait lui nuire" . . . En principe, le *juramentum* n'aurait donc pas dû être déféré au roi puisqu'il niait le mariage. Mais il s'agit ici précisément d'un souverain et cela change tout le problème. Au point de vue canonique la parole d'un roi jouit d'un poids exceptionnel. Nous voyons, en effet, que le droit canon reconnaît une valeur décisive à la parole du pape, et, par extension, à la parole de l'empereur et tout autre [inc. p. 170] prince qui n'a pas de supérieur, lorsqu'ils déposent à leur propre sujet, "de proprio facto". Ainsi donc, il est fait dérogation au principe: "Nullus idoneus in re sua", et le "vox unius, vox nullius" ne joue pas non plus. Il était d'ailleurs prévu, dans certains cas, que le témoignage d'un seul suffisait à compléter une demi-preuve et à clore, par le fait même, un litige. Le serment de Louis XII doit donc être considéré à la lumière de ces principes juridiques. Le roi avait qualité pour déposer "in re propria" et il l'a fait avec le consentement de son épouse, complétant ainsi les demi-preuves déjà établies . . . Tout fut régulier et légal' (Destefanis, *Louis XII et Jeanne de France*, pp. 169–70). (I have not retained paragraph breaks.)

[8] 'Dans ce procès l'humble et douce Jeanne apparaît peut-être comme une victime, en tout cas, elle ne le fut ni de son mari, ni des juges mais uniquement des circonstances voulues par son père Louis XI' (*ibid.*, p. 177).

du colloque de Maubeuge (1988) (Ville de Maubeuge, 1990), pp. 431–42: at pp. 433–5, on the marriage of Louis XII and Jeanne. (The article puts Louis XI's intervention in context. He exercised heavy-handed influence over noble marriages in a manner reminiscent of the English Angevin monarchy before Magna Carta. Other French kings also fixed marriages, but less brutally. Contamine broadens out his discussion to the general issue of consent in upper-class marriages in the later Middle Ages.) The events around this dissolution are also discussed in more general studies such as Frederic J. Baumgartner, *Louis XII* (Stroud, 1994), pp. 72–8.

For an able popular presentation of the ruthless marriage policies of Charles VIII and Louis XII, see Franck Collard, 'Les scandaleux divorces des rois de France', *L'Histoire* 189 (1995), pp. 56–61.[9] For general background, Pauline Matarasso, *Queen's Mate: Three Women of Power in France on the Eve of the Renaissance* (Aldershot, 2001), has a 'popular history' style but a scholarly approach to footnoting untypical of the genre.

In a personal communication – in anticipation of her forthcoming book on medieval French queens – Dr Murielle Gaude-Ferragu notes that a clause of the marriage contract between Anne of Brittany and Charles VIII specified that in the event of Charles's death she would marry his successor as King of France. See her *La reine de France au Moyen Âge* (Paris, 2014) pp. 31–2. So there is a long back history behind Louis's determination to marry her after freeing himself from Jeanne.

The translation

Translated from 'Procès de divorce de Louis XII', in de Maulde, *Procédures politiques du règne de Louis XII*, and, for passages omitted in the edition, from British Library, Add. 20917, an original notarised record of the trial. These passages are printed in bold type in the translation, and on the basis of the transcriptions printed in Appendix 3. Though short, the passages are important. Note that de Maulde omitted passages relating to the circumstances of the king's solemn oath that he had not penetrated Jeanne, and to his doctors' testimony to the same effect.

For proper names in general I follow de Maulde.

1476

The dispensation for the marriage of the future Louis XII and Jeanne of France, granted by Cardinal Julian della Rovere, on the strength of delegated papal powers (de Maulde, *Procédures politiques*, no. 53,

---

[9] My thanks to Alexander Murray for drawing my attention to this.

pp. 926–9). In the trial proceedings this is recorded as being copied from a notarised copy made in 1485 from the original at Saint-Germain l'Auxerrois, Paris.[10]

There follow now the contents of the said transcript or copy of the alleged dispensation.

In the name of the Lord, amen. Let each and every person know that this is the true transcript and copy, reproduced and extracted by us, the aforementioned public notaries.[11]

Julian, by divine mercy cardinal priest of St Peter in Chains of the church of Rome, legate *de latere* of the apostolic see in the kingdom of France, and all the parts of Gaul, and the province of Provence, and also in the city of Avignon and county of Venaissin and the provinces, cities and places adjacent to them,[12] to the most reverend fathers in Christ the archbishop of Bourges and the bishops of Orleans and Évreux, greetings in the Lord.

It was explained in the petition submitted to us on behalf of our beloved in Christ the most illustrious Lord Louis, Duke of Orleans, and our beloved in Christ the most illustrious Lady Jeanne of France, daughter of the most serene prince the Lord Louis, the most Christian King of the French, that they earlier – without being ignorant of the fact that they are related in the third and fourth degrees of consanguinity, and that the said lord king raised the same duke from the sacred font, but nonetheless considering that the said duke, among the princes who descend from the royal line[13] of the kings of the French, is the nearest to her,[14] and, for the sake of preserving and maintaining the faith[15] and love between them and their relatives and on other rational grounds, desiring, as they still desire, to be joined to each other in marriage, with their parents involved and arranging it – became betrothed[16] through words in the future tense, but by no means having carnal intercourse afterwards. Since however they are unable to fulfil this desire of theirs, because of the impediments of the said consanguinity and – as follows from what was stated above – of spiritual relationship, without a dispensation from the pope to cover it, a petition was submitted to us on the part of the same duke and Jeanne that we might, by the power of the faculty granted to us from above,

---

[10] de Maulde, *Procédures politiques*, p. 929.

[11] According to de Maulde, *ibid.*, p. 926, note 1, there follows a description of the original document and affirmation that its marks of authenticity are genuine.

[12] 'illis adjacentibus provinciis': probably thus rather than 'those adjacent provinces'.

[13] 'stirpe'.

[14] 'proximiorem illi': I take the pronoun to refer to Jeanne and the sense to be that Louis of Orleans (the future Louis XII) is the nearest to her in status among the French princes and thus the most appropriate *parti* for the daughter of the King of France.

[15] 'fidere' for 'fide' in edition.   [16] 'sponsalia . . . contraxerunt'.

deign to make provision for them in this matter through the grace of a suitable[17] dispensation. Therefore we, on these[18] aforesaid grounds and others that have been explained to us, yielding to the petitions, with the apostolic authority granted to us by the letters whose contents are set out below,[19] through these writings commission and command you, as a man whose judgement we trust in the Lord in this and other matters[20] that you, or two, or one of you, should, if matters are as stated, and if the said Jeanne has not been taken for this purpose against her will,[21] grant a dispensation by the aforesaid authority to the same duke and Jeanne that, notwithstanding these impediments, they may be able to contract marriage with each other, and, after it has been contracted, remain in it freely and licitly; and we declare that the children that should issue from the same marriage to be legitimate.

The tenor of the said letter follows and is this:

{Sixtus, bishop, servant of the servants of God, to his beloved son Julian, cardinal priest of St Peter in Chains, legate of the apostolic see to the kingdom of France and all the parts of the Gallic regions[22] and to the province of Provence and also our cities of Avignon and the county of the Venaissin and the provinces, cities and places adjacent to them, greetings and apostolic blessing. Since, with the counsel of our brothers the cardinals of the holy Roman Church, we are sending you, now in our presence,[23] to the kingdom of France, and all the parts of the regions of Gaul, and to the province of Provence, and also to our city of Avignon, and the county of the Venaissin, and the provinces, cities and places adjacent to them, as legate *de latere*, for the sake of various arduous and great matters of business of ours and of the Roman Church, we – wishing to honour your person, in order that, through the honour shown to you in this office of this legation, you may be able to carry [it] out the more usefully in that you are equipped by us with greater authority – through this present letter, by apostolic authority, concede to you as a man of judgement[24] for this period of time, as long as[25] your legation lasts, the full and free power of granting dispensations by our authority,[26] as you think fit, to any persons of either sex who are within the boundaries to which your legatine commission extends who are joined in the third or fourth degrees of consanguinity of affinity or these in combination,[27]

---

[17] 'opportune' – 'timely' is also a possible translation.

[18] 'huiusmodi', which could alternatively be taken to apply only to 'aliis nobis . . . causis', in which case the translation would read 'and other causes of this kind'.

[19] 'infrascripti tenoris'.

[20] 'circumspectioni vestre, de qua in hiis et aliis in Domino fiduciam obtinemus'.

[21] 'propter hoc rapta non fuerit'.   [22] 'universas Galliarum partes'.

[23] 'presencialiter'.   [24] 'Circumspectioni tue'.   [25] 'dumtaxat'.

[26] The letter has 'auctoritate nostra' near the start of the long sentence and 'auctoritate appostolica' near the end of it. This may be just an oversight, or the sense may be that the letter is granted by apostolic authority and that the legate will dispense by apostolic authority. My word order reflects the latter understanding.

[27] 'consanguinitatis vel affinitatis gradibus seu illis mixtim'.

or however they may be related to each other,[28] and, should they be of royal, ducal or comital blood, in any degree, even the second degree, or who are joined or bound together in another way by any spiritual relationship or relationship of justice of public honesty, and persons who have polluted each other through adultery and desire to be joined in marriage when there are special grounds for considering that,[29] or persons who, whether or not they knew that they would be joined in these degrees or in another way, contracted and consummated marriages with each other, even if they had offspring – those persons namely who want to get married[30] – that, notwithstanding such an impediment deriving from consanguinity or affinity or spiritual relationship or justice of public honesty, they may be able to contract marriage with each other, in the case of those who acted in ignorance however to remain in the marriage contracted – but of absolving those who knowingly entered into the contract from the sentence of excommunication that they incurred because of the aforesaid things, and of granting to them – after, however, they have been separated from each other for a period of time to be left to your discretion – [of granting dispensations] to contract marriage anew and to remain in it freely and licitly[31] after it has been contracted – [all this] so long as these women have not been taken for this purpose against their will; and of determining that the offspring that have or should issue from these unions are legitimate. We desire however that those persons to whom you grant a dispensation to contract marriage in the said second or third degrees of this sort or a combination of these,[32] and those persons who knew that they were in any of the said degrees whatsoever when they contracted and consummated marriage, should be bound, in proportion to their resources, to pay and actually hand over to you[33] a certain amount of money for the help of the faithful against the Turks, the details being left to your discretion.[34]

Given at Rome, at St Peters, in the year of the Lord's incarnation 20 February 1475,[35] in the fifth year of our pontificate.}

As guarantee of and testimony to each and every one of the aforesaid we have written this letter and ordered it to be authenticated by appending to it our episcopal seal. Given at Avignon, in the apostolic palace, in the year of the Lord's incarnation, 6 August 1476, in the fifth year of the said most holy lord, the lord Pope Sixtus IV.

(de Maulde, *Procédures politiques*, pp. 926–9)

---

[28] 'aut qualitercumque se invicem actingentes'.   [29] 'certis suadentibus causis'.

[30] The meaning is that such people are not married and may go their separate ways, but could with a dispensation now contract a proper valid marriage.

[31] 'freely and licitly' might also be taken to apply to the whole set of cases covered in this long passage.

[32] 'talibus mixtim'.   [33] 'realiter consignare'.   [34] 'iuxta tue discrecionis arbitrium'.

[35] Assuming that the Roman curia dated the start of the year from the Annunciation, 25 March (see Cheney and Jones, *A Handbook of Dates*, p. 13), this should in fact be dated to 1476.

1498, July 29

Bull of Alexander VI, setting up the tribunal

Alexander, bishop, servant of the servants of God, to his venerable brothers Louis bishop of Albi and Fernand bishop of Ceuta, greetings and apostolic blessing. We willingly grant the humble desires of petitioners, especially those who are endowed with royal dignity, and attend to them with appropriate favours. Recently indeed our dearest son in Christ Louis XII, illustrious King of the French, had it explained to us that formerly – when he was Duke of Orleans and twelve years old or thereabouts, and after he had lost his father – Louis of famous memory, at that time King Louis XI of the French, compelled Marie of Cleves, the mother of the same Louis the present king, by means of threats and intimidation, to make the same Louis the present king contract a marriage with the noble woman Jeanne of France, the daughter of the same King Louis XI, who was related to the same Louis the present king in the fourth degree of consanguinity, and who was, as she still is, impotent to conceive offspring, and then – this marriage being contracted by the same Louis, currently king, to whom the said King Louis XI, while still alive, had stood godfather, with the same Jeanne, without any dispensation making good for them the impediment of the fourth degree of consanguinity and the impediment of spiritual kinship that derives from the godparenthood in question, invalidly and *de facto* and being null, and the same King Louis XI commanding the aforesaid Louis the present king, once he had reached puberty, to contract marriage anew with the aforesaid Jeanne – the same Louis the present king, compelled by the threats and intimidation brought to bear on him by the same King Louis XI and his people – by threats of death, by panic and in other ways by force and fear such as could take hold of a steady man – contracted marriage anew with the same Jeanne, although, also, as stated above, the apostolic see had not granted them a dispensation for those impediments; and when in the mean time the said King Louis XI of famous memory had died, but was survived by Charles, King of the French when he was alive, the brother of the said Jeanne, after the said Louis, the current king, had betaken himself to Brittany and been captured in hostilities and imprisoned for three years or thereabouts, and had finally been released from this imprisonment – he, who had lived together for twenty-five or twenty-six years or thereabouts with the same Jeanne, while the aforesaid force and fear lasted, and who had never given consent to the same Jeanne in mind and will, after the said King Charles had died, and the aforesaid force and fear had ceased, immediately brought suit against this marriage.

Consequently, on behalf[36] of the said Louis the present king, supplication was humbly made to us that we might deign out of apostolic beneficence to order that this marriage be annulled, and to make suitable provision for the aforesaid Louis the current king and for his status in the aforesaid matters. Therefore we, who do not have certain knowledge of the aforesaid things, yielding to these supplications, by apostolic writings command you, our brothers, whom in these and other things we especially trust in the Lord, that, acting together, in person, wherever you may be, you may by our authority inform yourself carefully about each and every one of the aforesaid matters, after summoning the said Jeanne and any others who need to be summoned; and, if through what you have thus learned you should legally establish that the said Louis the current king and Jeanne were joined in the said fourth degree, or that the said King Louis XI stood godparent to the said Louis the present king, and that no dispensation followed, or that the aforesaid Louis the present king contracted the said marriage with the said Jeanne in consequence of the aforesaid force and fear such as could take hold of a steady man, and that this force and fear continued right up to the death of the aforesaid King Charles, the brother of the said Jeanne, and the predecessor of the aforesaid Louis the present king, or that the aforesaid Louis the present king lived together with the said Jeanne for the time laid down by law, in the meantime made genuine efforts and attempts to have carnal intercourse, and that the said Jeanne has fallen victim to magic[37] and is impotent to such an extent the same Louis the present king could not and cannot by any means have carnal knowledge of her in the meantime within the bars of modesty, or any other legal impediment on account of which it was and is impossible for a marriage between the said Louis the present king and Jeanne to stand in canon law, you should, by the said authority, declare this marriage to have been and to be null, just as the law requires you to do, using ecclesiastical censure to make that which you have declared strictly observed;[38] and nonetheless, if it should happen that this declaration be made by you, by the authority of the present letter, as is stated above, you may by the said authority grant to the same Louis the present king the licence to contract a different[39] marriage in proper form[40] with another woman whom he

---

[36] 'ex parte' translated thus here and below.   [37] 'maleficiata'.

[38] My translation presupposes changing the punctuation of the edition, 'prout de jure fuerit faciendum facientes, quod declaraveritis per censuram ecclesiasticam firmiter observari', which makes 'facientes' the end of the clause beginning with 'prout', to 'prout de jure fuerit faciendum, facientes quod declaveritis per censuram ecclesiasticam firmiter observari', with 'facientes' as the start of the clause ending with 'observari'.

[39] 'alias'.   [40] 'rite'.

may legally take as his wife: notwithstanding constitutions and apostolic ordinances – of our predecessor Boniface VIII,[41] by which it is forbidden for anyone to be summoned to judgement outside his city and diocese except in certain exceptional cases, and in those not more than one day's journey from the boundary of his diocese, or for judges deputed by the aforesaid see to presume to initiate proceedings against anyone or permit another person or persons to do so on their behalf outside the city and diocese in which they were deputed to act, and, promulgated by the general council, concerning two days' journey,[42] and any others whatsoever – to the contrary; and notwithstanding any indult by the same see to the said Jeanne or any other persons, collectively or severally, that they are not to be put under interdict, suspended or excommunicated, or brought to judgement outside or beyond certain places, by apostolic letters not making full and explicit verbatim mention of this indult. Given at Rome, at St Peters, 1498 AD, 3 Kal. August, in the sixth year of our pontificate. Thus signed, above the plica: A. de Comitibus.

(Printed in de Maulde, *Procédures politiques*, pp. 812–15)

1498, August 10

The opening of the trial

Let everyone present and future know that, since, recently, Louis, the present King of the French, presented or had presented to us, Louis d'Amboise and Fernand d'Almeïda, bishops, judges delegated by our most Holy Father in Christ, and lord, Lord Alexander VI, by divine providence pope, apostolic letters from the same lord our pope, sealed in the manner of the Roman curia, with the seal hanging from a hemp cord, and asked that we proceed to execute them and the things they contain: we, Louis d'Amboise and Fernand d'Almeïda, the aforesaid bishops and judges delegate, in the year of the Lord 1498, first indiction, and tenth day of the month of August, in the seventh year of the pontificate of the aforesaid lord our pope, decided on and dispatched our letters of citation,[43] and then had them handed over to be executed.[44] And, since the day assigned in this citation[45] was a holiday because of the Feast of the Beheading of John the Baptist, we adjourned it to the Thursday

---

[41] Sext 2.2 according to de Maulde: VI 2.2.1 (Friedberg, *Corpus Iuris Canonici*, cols. 996–7) seems to come closest to fitting the bill. It is a decretal of Innocent IV, but the Sext as a collection was known to have been put together by Boniface VIII.

[42] X.1.3.28.   [43] 'litteras ... citatorias'.

[44] 'execucioni demandari fecimus'.   [45] 'assignacionis citacionis'.

which was the next day following it,[46] that is, the penultimate day of the same month of August. When this Thursday came round, after Vespers had been sung in the church at Tours, appearing before us in the church at Tours and, moving from there, in the house in the cathedral close of the dean of the same church, with Master Antoine de Lestang, doctor of both laws, proctor of the same Louis, King of the French, authorised[47] specially and in writing, and who was bringing the case in that same king's name,[48] on the one side, and the most illustrious lady the Lady Jeanne of France, as defendant, on her own behalf and in person, on the other side, appearing there before us; with the most venerable and learned men Pierre de Bellessor, the Official of Paris, Guillaume Feydelli, the dean of Gassecourt, and Robert La Longue, the Official of the lord archdeacon of Paris, giving their assistance in the same place, and being co-opted as our assessors in the same case by ourselves the aforesaid judges; and, assigned to give counsel to the same Lady Jeanne of France, the venerable and also learned men Masters Marco Travers, the Official of Tours, Robert Salomon, professor of theology, of the order of the Brothers of Blessed Mary of Mount Carmel, and Pierre Borelli, advocate in the ecclesiastical court of Tours, who, though they made many excuses and put off taking on this burden, we nevertheless compelled and constrained them[49] by apostolic and also royal authority to look after the interests of the same Lady Jeanne; we also gave and compelled, in the same manner, the venerable man Master Pierre Duban as adjunct notary on the side of the said lady, with the scribes taken on by us in this case, and indeed this man Duban will be enabled to provide assistance,[50] both in this town of Tours and in other places to which we will move for the sake of clearing up the present matter; and since he nevertheless failed to present himself,[51] the record and minutes[52] of the case will be written up and looked after[53] by the said scribes of the same case. The said lord proctor of the same lord our king, after first disclaiming any intention of impugning in any way the good character and honour of the said lady by the things he needed to say and propose, produced the apostolic letter or rescript in question,[54] the citation with the execution set out on its

---

[46] 'ad diem Jovis crastinam et inde sequentem'.
[47] 'fundato'.   [48] 'eodem nomine'.
[49] This mirrors the linguistic awkwardness of the Latin original here.
[50] 'quidquidem Duban...assistere poterit'] here 'poterit' is probably a future perfect rather than a perfect subjunctive: in a final clause one would expect the imperfect subjunctive.
[51] 'nichilominus eo minime comparente': could also be translated as 'despite his failure to present himself', but the Latin syntax would be awkward with that reading.
[52] 'registra et acta'.   [53] 'conficientur et expedientur'.   [54] 'huiusmodi'.

dorse,[55] and the procuratorial commission of the aforesaid lord our king, which he handed over to serve as a basis for judgement[56] and left in the hands of the notaries or scribes of the case set out in writing below. Then, after the said proctor of the same lord our king had presented and outlined his petition, and explained the various kinds of impediments on account of which he said the marriage between the same lord our king and the same Lady Jeanne, contracted *de facto*, was and is null, and to be without force,[57] he concluded in the manner and form contained in his petition, which was given to be copied[58] by the said scribes; the content of which is inserted below. To which the same Lady Jeanne, both in her own person and through her aforesaid counsellors, replied in effect that, together with the said counsellors who had been assigned to her, she wished also to have other counsellors also outside the town, and she asked for a duplicate of the procuratorial commission, the petition, and the other actions taken by[59] the aforesaid lord our king, and for a date for providing her with counsellors and for coming and replying to the propositions set out above. After all this had been done, we the aforesaid judges, obeying the petition and request of the same Lady Jeanne, offered to let her receive as many and whatever kind of counsellors she wanted to take at Tours and elsewhere, whom we will compel by apostolic and also by royal authority to accept this burden; asserting and declaring to her that we had not permitted[60] the said proctor of the lord our king to take counsel[61] until and up to the point when the said Lady Jeanne has furnished herself with counsel. And furthermore, after we had decided on a record of the actions taken,[62] we assigned to the same Lady Jeanne, at her request, a date a week hence[63] and the place and hour aforementioned to come and to answer in reply with whatever she wished to say and propose on the aforesaid matters.

The content of the apostolic letter, of the commission to the procurator, and the petition in question follow in order.

(de Maulde, *Procédures politiques*, pp. 807–12)

---

[55] 'citacionem cum execucione in dorso ejus descripta'. Cf. above, notes 43 and 44: the phrases 'litteras . . . citatorias' and 'execucioni demandari fecimus' (de Maulde, *Procédures politiques*, p. 809).

[56] 'pro fundactione judicii'.

[57] 'viribus non subsistere': taking 'viribus' as an ablative rather than a dative indirect object.

[58] 'scripto . . . data': i.e. it looks as though they were copying a written text rather than committing an oral presentation to writing.

[59] 'explectorum'.

[60] 'permiseramus': error for 'permiserimus' ('will not permit') in future perfect?

[61] 'concilium assumere': is the sense that he may not add advisers to his team until she does?

[62] 'decreta per nos copia explectorum'.   [63] 'diem octavam proxime futuram'.

1498, September 13

Tours. Interrogation of Jeanne of France

And first that, unless her reply gave the truth, and at least insofar as she knows it, she could and would incur the penalty of perjury, and that it would be better for her to lose all her temporal goods than to knowingly deny the truth, with the oath she had just sworn being shown to her again and explained. – Replying to the *positio*, the lady defendant gave an affirmative.

(de Maulde, *Procédures politiques*, p. 830)

Again ... the same Lady Jeanne of France, from her birth or by nature, was lastingly and [is] at present, deformed,[64] and imperfect beyond what is normal[65] with other women. She replies that she knows well that she is not so beautiful or attractive in body as other women frequently are.

Again, and not fitted for a man. – She believes the contrary.

Again, that she was not and is not capable of conceiving. – She believes the contrary.

Again, nor of receiving the semen of a man in the way that is naturally fitting.[66] – She believes that the contrary is the case.[67]

Again, nor of being known by a man naturally within the gates of modesty. – She believes the contrary.

Again, and [this] just as could be judged and known through examination of her body. – She believes the contrary.

Again, and, if she believes the contrary with respect to the aforesaid impediments, she should be asked what she believes with respect to all of them and each of them or any one of them individually,[68] since she ought to be sure about her body and limbs. – She replies that she does not know of any impediment in herself.[69]

Again, and so that the judgement should be secure and that the Church should not be deceived, whether she might wish to make herself available for an examination and inspection[70] by honest women, who are expert in such matters. She replies first that she wanted to think carefully about that.[71] And, when she was further asked by the lords [judges] when she would give a reply on this matter, she says that she wanted to do what she was bound to do according to the ordinances of the Church.

(de Maulde, *Procédures politiques*, pp. 833–4)

---

[64] 'fuit continue et de presenti corpore vitiata' – so, not taking 'presenti' with 'corpore'.
[65] 'preter solitum modum'.   [66] 'secundum congruenciam nature'.
[67] 'credit quod ymo est'.   [68] 'eorum altero'.   [69] 'in ea'.   [70] 'visitacioni'.
[71] 'quod bene super hoc volebat cogitare'.

1498, October 14

*Amboise. Jeanne of France asks to be exempt from
the physical examination*

In the year of the Lord 1498, on Sunday 14 October, the prudent man
Master Francis Behoulat, legal representative[72] of the Lady Jeanne of
France, and on her behalf and in her name, produced and presented
not a few arguments or writings, with the content and in the form set
out below, before us, Philip, cardinal priest, of Le Mans, Louis of Albi
and Fernand of Ceuta,[73] judges delegate here[74] in the annulment case,
initiated and pending, between the most Christian King of the French
our Lord Louis, the plaintiff, on one side, and the same Lady Jeanne of
France, the defendant, on the other, the parties to the case, which had
been brought and was pending:

{That it may be declared by you, very reverend father and lord Philip, by the
divine mercy cardinal with the title[75] of St Peter and Marcellinus, bishop of Le
Mans, and reverend fathers and lords, and Louis, bishop of Albi, and Ferdinand,
bishop of Ceuta, presented[76] as judges, by apostolic authority delegated for the
case, and the parties whose names are written below: that the most illustrious
lady, Lady Jeanne of France, the legitimate wife of the most serene prince and
lord, Lord Louis XII the present King of the French, and in consequence Queen
of France, the defendant, at the hearing which [you held] on the Friday after
the Feast of St Denis,[77] the present date,[78] at least at this stage[79] of the trial or
process, be declared to be free from the obligation of an examination or of her
body being examined, indeed furthermore that the said defendant be set free
by the same hearing, at least[80] [until] a verdict be given in favour of the said
defendant and against the said plaintiff, in accordance with law and reason, in
short order.[81]

   Therefore, to continue, the aforesaid most illustrious defendant presupposes
the trial or tribunal, in the matter – currently before you,[82] of divorce and dissolution of the marriage between the said parties, namely the plaintiff and defendant –
at issue,[83] and its assignment[84] pending for next Monday, reporting,[85] on behalf

---

[72] 'sollicitator'.   [73] 'Septensi'.   [74] 'in hac parte'.

[75] 'tituli'.   [76] 'pretensos'.

[77] 9 October: is this a reference to an earlier hearing or does it refer to the current one,
which on that hypothesis would have taken place four days later than expected?

[78] 'in instancia quam die veneris post festum sancti Dionisii datis presentium'.

[79] 'instantia'.

[80] 'saltem': though there cannot be a serious suggestion that she would be examined if and
after she had won. The whole sentence seems carelessly drafted.

[81] 'compendiose'. 'Summarily' is another possibility.   [82] 'coram vobis pendenti'.

[83] 'presupponit dicta rea processum seu instanciam, in materia divorcii et separacionis
matrimonii inter dictas partes, actorem videlicet et ream, coram vobis pendenti, in
discussionem'.

[84] 'assignacionem'.   [85] 'ad refferendum'.

of the said plaintiff, the statements and depositions, the witness testimony,[86] produced and examined in the context of this tribunal on behalf of the said plaintiff against the said defendant, with no other fixing or assignment of a date granted to the parties in the meantime.

These things being presupposed,[87] therefore, the aforesaid most illustrious defendant proposes that, aware that a rescript delegating authority to you by the pope has been obtained,[88] directed to you, the lords of Albi and Ceuta, through whose contents, obtained through the most serene lord,[89] which[90] must prevail against the advantage of the one who obtains it,[91] the same plaintiff expressed the view that this defendant had been bewitched; but, according to the law, this bewitchment or defect never affects a person who is impotent (impotence proceeding from a bodily defect such as narrowness, on account of which this inspection of the body appears to have been requested), but was and is a non-intrinsic defect.[92] This bewitchment, indeed, just as it is caused by the art of the devil, so too it is only cured by the art of God, namely through exorcisms, fasts, prayers and the like, and thus, by the presumption of the law, this alleged impediment is not deemed to proceed from a bodily defect:[93] consequently, the defendant is deemed to be capable of consummating and not blocked by any bodily impediment. And anyone who says that his wife is bewitched, confesses, by the presumption of the law, that by nature she is capable of intercourse, without defect of body, but is bound by the subsequent intervention of the devil or his servants, which can only be cured by the art of God, and thus it should rightly be deemed absurd – as she is described as bewitched in the rescript – to allege that the said defendant is impotent through narrowness,[94] and to dispute about narrowness.

Besides, it still remains, on behalf of the said most illustrious lady the defendant, to put forward the decisive facts on her side,[95] among which she intends to put it that she was carnally known by the aforesaid most serene lord, and this among the articles of *positiones* which she intends to have the said lord the plaintiff respond to personally[96] and, with God's help, confessed by the said lord the plaintiff, as she knows for certain that the said lord the plaintiff knows for certain: from which confession the contrary objection will fall away; and the said defendant is prepared to make known her objections[97] and propositions without delay, expediting and shortening the aforesaid trial. It follows therefore that it is pointless to enter into a dispute about the said inspection.

Furthermore, the said most illustrious lady the defendant was and is descended from the royal line through her father, grandparents, great-grandparents and

---

[86] 'dicta deposicionesque, actestaciones testium'.   [87] 'his presuppositis'.

[88] 'actenta impetracione rescripti delegacionis vestre apostolice'.

[89] This probably refers to the king, rather than the pope, as the case was being heard at the king's request, and as usual with papal bulls the 'narratio' would probably reflect the wording of his petition.

[90] Taking 'cui' to refer to 'tenor' rather than 'dominum'.

[91] 'cui standum est in prejudicium impetrantis'.   [92] 'vicium accidentis'.

[93] 'a vicio corporis progressum'.   [94] 'arctam'.

[95] 'proponere sua facta peremptoria'.   [96] 'quibus . . . responsurum . . . ponere'.

[97] Or, to stay close to the Latin technical term, 'exceptions'.

great-great-grandparents, and so it is not for the sake of putting off the discussion of the matter at issue, but because, in law, deference is due to such a bloodline, so as not to offend[98] the modesty of the said most illustrious lady the defendant and to therefore[99] exhibit the private parts[100] of the said defendant, unless the witness statements to be produced on both sides have first been seen; from the inspection of which parts, furthermore, by the presumption of the law, a misleading judgement follows;[101] on account of which there should be no publication[102] at the present time, but it should be omitted at the time of the publication[103] of the witnesses from both sides to be produced and examined; that being also, as set out above, incompatible with things asserted in the rescript from which your jurisdiction derives, it would seem that it would be very well advised to omit it, in deference also to the appalling distress and misery [this would mean] for such a great bloodline. The same defendant concluding as above, and to the ends[104] set out above.}

Given in the year 1498, Sunday 14 October.

(de Maulde, *Procédures politiques*, no. 32, pp. 859–62)

1498, October 15

The reply of the king's proctor concerning the physical examination

In the year of the Lord 1498, Monday, 15 October, the learned[105] Master Antoine de Stagno, proctor of our lord king, in the case before ...[106] put forward many arguments or written statements[107] and presented them in the following form.

{That, notwithstanding certain frivolous written statements, in no way supported by laws or arguments, put forward on behalf of the most illustrious Lady Jeanne of France, the defendant, in the annulment case before ... a certain alleged marriage contracted *de facto*, feignedly and in fear, with the said Lady Jeanne ... to be declared null ... in reply indeed to these written statements, the honourable Lord Antoine de Stagno, doctor of both laws, proctor of the said lord King Louis, says and proposes, with the reasons and arguments set out below, that, through you, lord judges, and your interlocutory sentence, the said lady, the defendant, should and ought to be inspected[108] and to undergo inspection, and that she should

---

[98] 'actemptare'.   [99] The awkward placing of 'therefore' follows the Latin.
[100] 'loca nature puribunda [*sic*] ... exhibere'.
[101] 'ex quorum etiam inspectione sequitur presumpcione juris judicium fallax'. I tentatively take this to refer to an inspection of Jeanne rather than of the depositions, but am not certain how to interpret it.
[102] Presumably, publication of the results of an examination of the queen. Note that 'publicatio' was a semi-technical term.
[103] 'in tempore publicacionis ... supersedendum'.
[104] 'ad fines' – unless this means 'by the dates set'.   [105] 'scientificus'.
[106] Here and below the omission marks are transcribed as in the edition.
[107] 'scripturas'.   [108] 'fore et esse visitandum'.

and ought not to be permitted to proceed to the presentation of contrary facts, if the said inspection has not first taken place; and, through the evidence to be produced[109] before you on behalf of the said lord the plaintiff, that the said case and cases, which are to be finished, decided and brought to an end by deciding on a sentence,[110] ought to be finished, decided and brought to an end, presupposing that the standing of the case for the nullity of the asserted marriage will have been ascertained;[111] in which case, indeed, it remains for testimonies or depositions, concerning impediments of consanguinity, spiritual relationship, and of force and fear, of witnesses produced on the side of the aforesaid lord the plaintiff [to be introduced][112] by the same lord proctor;[113] it also remains for a statement to be made this coming Monday by you, lords, concerning the inspection requested by the said proctor of the body and members of the said lady through honest, sensible, experienced and expert women.}

With all this laid out for your consideration, the aforesaid proctor, replying briefly and clearly, furnished with reasons and arguments, quite secure in his position,[114] to the legal considerations put forward on behalf of the said lady, the defendant, to prevent the said inspection from taking place, says that, according to what the *ius commune* requires and the rules[115] of ecclesiastical courts of this kingdom of France, while and when [there is a case][116] before ecclesiastical judges concerning narrowness, bodily inability to have intercourse, and a woman's unsuitability [for intercourse],[117] at the husband's insistence and when he requires it because of the said inability to have intercourse with her and to mingle with her carnally, even[118] at the start of the trial, by the authority of the said ecclesiastical judges, she comes to be inspected and to undergo an inspection, and you too, my lords the judges, with all respect, ought to have had it done and so ruled;[119] for once the said impediment has been found, nothing seems to be left to do except for the marriage between the man and woman to be annulled;[120] the said visitation cannot be postponed by you any longer without a very public injury being inflicted on the aforesaid lord king.

Again, nor do the inferences in the second article of the said statements have any force,[121] the article beginning 'These things being presupposed'

---

[109] 'producta . . . facienda'.
[110] 'sentencie calculo finiendas fore, decidendas, terminandas'.
[111] 'primo presupposito statu cause nullitatis matrimonii asserti habito'.
[112] A word appears to be missing from the Latin.
[113] 'restat testium, pro parte prefati domini actoris productorum, actestaciones seu deposiciones super impedimentis consanguinitatis, cognacionis spiritualis ac vis et metus factas per eundem dominum procuratorem [introduci]' (I supply 'introduci').
[114] 'rationibus munitus, sufficienter fulcitus'.   [115] 'stilum'.
[116] Words apparently omitted in Latin.   [117] 'indisposicione'.
[118] 'et'.   [119] 'ita fieri et declarari debuissetis'.
[120] 'nil restare videture nisi divorcium inter virum et mulierem celebrari'.
[121] 'Nec militant . . . deducta'.

through which the said lady tries to assert that according to the contents of the rescript delegating the case to you my lords the judges,[122] no power or warrant[123] has been conceded by the holy apostolic see to inspect her or declare that she should be inspected, on the grounds that, in the letter of the said rescript, the aforesaid lord the plaintiff says and puts it that the said lady, the defendant, will have been and is[124] bewitched, and thus seems to admit that she will have been and is capable [of intercourse] in her body and members; and that bewitchment is caused and can be caused only by the art of the devil, and also can be ended and removed through prayers and other intercessions by the power of God: with all respects to the lord scribe, [the proctor maintains] that her shaky[125] argument is based on something torn out of its original context, which goes against the laws. For in the said rescript it is not specified that the said lady was simply bewitched, but that she was impotent, with a bodily impotence, so and in such a way that the aforesaid lord the plaintiff, although he tried, was nonetheless unable to know her carnally within the bars of modesty; nor can you, lords judges, establish anything about the said bodily impotence, specified both in the rescript and in the petition,[126] in any other way than through the deposition of trustworthy and experienced persons, deputed through you and by your authority to conduct the said inspection; nor is required by what the law ordains, according to which, in the petition of a man asking for his marriage to be dissolved, to specify the cause of the impediment to consummating a marriage it suffices to say that[127] the woman would be incapable of returning the marital embraces[128] of a husband, as is stipulated in [the] c[hapter] *Fraternitatis*,[129] at the beginning, *On the frigid and the bewitched*, and from then on,[130] and the learned commentaries on that place.[131] And there is another reason why the aforesaid argument alleged on behalf of the said lady the queen has no force. For the law is absolutely clear that[132] the petition of the plaintiff is to be interpreted as broadly as possible according to the material that it covers,[133] as in *Si quis intencioni, De judi.* ff.,[134] for since the dispute today is about impotence in intercourse, and

---

[122] Dative agreeing with 'you', not vocative.
[123] 'facultatem'.   [124] 'fore et esse'.
[125] 'trementis [read trementem?] a textu truncato suam fulciri racionem': accusative and infinitive: her argument ['suam . . . rationem'] is based ['fulciri'] on something torn out ['truncato'] from its original context ['a textu'].
[126] 'libello'.
[127] Revising the edition's punctuation as follows: 'requiritur ex disposicione juris, qua, in libello viri divorcium celebrari petentis, causam [causa in edition] impedimenti consummacionis matrimonii specificare, sufficit dicere mulierem impotentem fore ad amplexus', etc.
[128] 'amplexus viriles et mentales', correcting 'mentales' to 'maritales'.   [129] X.4.15.6.
[130] 'in antea'.   [131] 'et ibi per doctores'.   [132] 'Juris . . . enucleatissimi existit'.
[133] 'materiam subjectam'.   [134] Justinian, Digest 5.1.66.

his not being able to mingle carnally with the said lady the defendant,[135] it is clearer than light that by virtue of the said rescript the warrant and power to have her inspected will have been and is granted.

Again, the aforesaid lady the defendant is late in coming to put forward the said dilatory objection,[136] which ought to have been put forward before the trial stage of the action,[137] as stated in [the] c[hapter] *Pastoralis*, *De excep.*[138]

Again, nor, similarly, can the points made in the third article, beginning, 'Besides', help the same lady the defendant: asserting that she wants to put forward opposing facts,[139] and extract *positiones*[140] from them, in which, among other things, she intends to infer[141] that the said lord the plaintiff had known her carnally, and there was no need for someone who revealed the truth[142] to have the said lady the defendant inspected;[143] – since, as was stated and claimed on behalf of the said lord the plaintiff in the preamble, the said lady ought to have put forward her opposing facts at the same time as the said lord the plaintiff (since the case which is being discussed and examined is a matrimonial question, and ought to be treated summarily and plainly, without [the] clamour [of lawyers] and judicial formality,[144] as in Cle[mentine Constitution], *Dispendiosam*,[145] *De judi.*, and *Cle. Sepe, De verbo. signif.*[146] with the things noted there[147]), and therefore [the proctor argues that] the said lady the defendant ought by no means, unless an inspection has been conducted first, to be admitted before you, the judges, to put forward opposing facts, from the things inferred on behalf of the said lady the defendant, who is striving to drag out the said business and trying not to reveal the truth of her aforementioned impediment. Nor is it likely – even if your answer is 'no',[148] if the said lady the defendant were to be admitted by you to put forward the said opposing facts – in view of the fact that the aforementioned lord the defendant, who, or the said lord his proctor in his name and instructed by him, swore that the case he was sustaining is good and just and that the positions put forward through the said proctor in the name of the said lord the plaintiff will have been true and contain the truth,

---

[135] 'in presenciarum certetur de impotencia coeundi et cum dicta domina rea carnaliter commisceri non valenti' – removing the editor's comma after 'cum'.
[136] Or 'exception', to stay close to the Latin technical legal term.
[137] 'litiscontestatio': cf. Brundage, *Medieval Origins of the Legal Profession*, p. 432.
[138] X.2.25.4.   [139] 'facta contraria'.   [140] 'positiones' – see Appendix 5, s.v.
[141] 'deducere'.
[142] 'fatendo' – presumably, by originally claiming that the problem was witchcraft and thus revealing that it was not a physical impediment.
[143] 'ream visitari faciendi'.
[144] Cf. Brundage, *Medieval Origins*, p. 449.   [145] Clem. 2.1.2.   [146] Clem. 5.11.2.
[147] 'cum ibi notatis' – a reference also to commentaries on the chapter?
[148] 'etiam si pro non'.

and among other things that he had by no means known the said lady the defendant carnally – that he would wish to take on himself in the great and grave danger that perjury brings with it.

Again, when it is added[149] finally and in the final article that the said lady the defendant, out of reverence for the royal line from which she is known to be descended, ought not to be subjected to inspection – this reason ought not to make any impression on you or move you at all, since no respect of persons is recognised in judgements, in the administration of justice to opposing parties and in the discovery of the truth, as is laid down in [the] c[hapter] *Novit, De iudi.*[150]

Now therefore that these things that have been put forward by the said lady the defendant have been cut away and are unsupported by reason, the aforesaid proctor, concluding as above and to the ends as above,[151] it should be done as you, reverend fathers, think best.

1498, Monday 15 October.

> (de Maulde, *Procédures politiques*, no. 33, pp. 862–5)

1498, October 16

Amboise. Interim judgement on the inspection

In view of the contents of the apostolic rescript sent to us on this matter, and by which we are commanded to inform ourselves diligently about each and every point contained in it, as a request has been put forward by the king's proctor, and an interim response has been made to it, with written evidence[152] and reasons being offered on both sides, and in view of the other things that needed to be scrutinised and considered, we, after taking the advice of experts, say that the lady defendant should and is to be inspected by honest and expert persons, and, as is fitting, should present herself in person[153] in this town of Amboise by a date to be chosen and fixed by us.

> (de Maulde, *Procédures politiques*, no. 35, p. 869)

1498, October 26

Evidence produced by Jeanne

From de Maulde, *Procédures politiques*, no. 41, pp. 871–84, 'Contrary facts and defences of the lady Jeanne'.

---

[149] 'subjungendo'.   [150] X.2.1.13.   [151] 'ad fines quos supra'.
[152] 'scripturis'.   [153] 'personaliterque . . . se . . . exhibere'.

The dispensation

Again, since . . . it was said and reported by a number of people that there was consanguinity in the prohibited degree between the said parties and also a spiritual relationship, from the fact that the said lord the late King Louis XI is said to have raised the aforesaid lord the plaintiff from the sacred font of baptism and christened him; consequently, a mandate to dispense from these impediments was obtained from the most reverend father and lord in Christ, Lord Julian, cardinal priest of St Peter in Chains of the Roman Church, legate *de latere* in the kingdom of France, in the territory of Avignon and other provinces, with the explicit power of being able to dispense from the aforesaid impediments,[154] that indeed the mandate to dispense was sent to the archbishop of Bourges and to the reverend fathers and lords in Christ the lords bishops of Orleans and Évreux, with the tag[155] 'That[156] you or two or [one of] you', etc.[157]

Again, that the aforesaid mandate to dispense was presented to the reverend father and lord in Christ, Lord Francis, then and now bishop of Orleans,[158] and indeed this bishop of Orleans, as judge commissioned and delegated in this matter, with the aforesaid parties, who had then reached the age of puberty, and who were present in the chapel of the castle of Montrichard, which was consecrated to God many years ago, a place, indeed, enjoying immunity, such that every kind of man was, had been, used to be, and is free to enjoy the liberty of immunity, after satisfying himself[159] concerning the things asserted in the said mandate, gave a legally correct dispensation to the aforesaid plaintiff and defendant, carrying out the aforesaid rescript, in respect of the aforesaid alleged impediments of consanguinity and spiritual relationship,[160] namely in such a manner that they might be able to be joined together in marriage, and from that moment, in the presence of a notary and of trustworthy witnesses, he declared that any children that should issue from the same marriage to be legitimate, in accordance with the form and contents of the aforesaid dispensation, omitting nothing of what it contained.

(de Maulde, *Procédures politiques*, pp. 873–4)

Significantly, the replies made (de Maulde, *Procédures politiques*, no. 42, pp. 884–91) to the various claims made by Jeanne do not include any

---

[154] 'de super predictis impedimentis posse dispensare'.
[155] 'cedula'.   [156] 'Qualis': read 'Quatenus'?
[157] Common formula of letters commissioning judges delegate, enabling two or one to conduct the trial if not all three judges nominated are able to.
[158] 'François de Brilhac', according to de Maulde, *Procédures politiques*, p. 874, note 1.
[159] 'constito sibi'.
[160] The edition is misleadingly punctuated in the immediately preceding passage.

answer on the matter of the dispensation. The inference follows that the king's side abandoned that line of argument.

Conjugal relations?

Again, that the same plaintiff, every year, twice or thrice, used to come to the same place of Lignières to see the same defendant, his wife, and remained there for ten or twelve days or longer, and spent the night with her, alone with one another, naked man with naked woman, paying the marriage debt through conjugal union, smiling, kissing, embracing and openly showing other signs suggesting desire for the experience of sexual conjugal union,[161] indeed furthermore of true sexual union, as is right between man and wife,[162] as the aforesaid plaintiff showed;[163] and this had been and was at that time true, public, notorious and manifest.

Again, that the same plaintiff, when he rose from the marriage bed, quite a number of times said and boasted in front of quite a number of people that he needed to drink something and restore himself with breakfast,[164] because he had known the same defendant carnally three or four times saying, in French, 'I have earned a drink because I rode my wife three or four times in the night' – speaking of the defendant.

(de Maulde, Procédures politiques, pp. 875–6)

1498, October 27

Replies from the king's proctor (de Maulde, *Procédures politiques*, no. 42, pp. 884–91).

The nature of the alleged conjugal relations

Again, insofar as the same lady defendant, as her shield, so many times over and over again, alleges carnal union and that she was carnally known by the same lord king, that this will not be found to be true; it is replied that, if any attempt at carnal union was made, or if they were together alone with each other, naked man with naked woman, that was not as a true proof[165] of marriage, but as a pretence, and because he had been compelled to act in this way, though without carnal union taking place,[166] because otherwise he would lose his goods and even the pension that he

---

[161] 'appetitiva experiencie copule conjugalis'.
[162] This clause would seem to go with 'sexual union' rather than 'openly showing'.
[163] 'showing . . . showed': the repetition seems to be in the original Latin.
[164] 'bibere et gentari'.   [165] 'pro vera approbacione'.
[166] 'cessante tamen copula carnali'.

regularly received from the aforesaid kings, which supported his way of life, which he would not have been able to do in any other way;[167] and, so long as the aforesaid kings Louis and Charles lived, he had to put up a pretence, but he never wanted nor gave true consent to contracting marriage with the aforesaid lady defendant.

(de Maulde, *Procédures politiques*, p. 891)

1498, October 29

Interrogation of Louis XII (de Maulde, *Procédures politiques*, no. 46, pp. 896–912).

Solemn oath to tell the truth, and awareness of the consequences of perjury

... in the presence of ourselves, [names] ... judges delegated by the holy apostolic see, and with the expert assistance of Masters Pierre de Bellessor, the Official of Paris, Guillaume Feidelli, the dean of Gassicourt[168] and Robert La Longue, the Official of the archdeacon of Paris, brought in as assessors in this matter,[169] the most Christian King of the French Louis XII, appearing as plaintiff, in the presence of Charles de Preux, the proctor of Jeanne the lady of France,[170] the defendant, and, touching the most holy gospels and giving his word as king, swore to tell the truth, by saying 'he believes it to be so' or 'He does not believe it to be the case', in response to the propositions[171] written below ...

It is proposed that a person who knowingly commits a mortal sin, is liable to the penalty of perpetual damnation. – The aforesaid King Louis believes it to be the case.

It is proposed that a person who knowingly commits perjury, sins mortally, incurs the wrath of God, and deserves eternal damnation. – The same king believes it to be the case.

(de Maulde, *Procédures politiques*, p. 897)

The alleged conjugal relations

(15) It is proposed: and that they consummated the marriage by subsequent carnal union. – He does not believe it to be the case that he had

---

[167] 'quod alias non potuisset facere': preferable, because of the position in the sentence, to 'because he could not do otherwise [than pretend]'.
[168] 'Gassicuria'   [169] 'in hac parte'.
[170] Following the Latin word order: 'Johanne domine de francia'.   [171] 'positiones'.

intercourse with her, neither with mindset of a married man nor in reality at all, although he tried . . .

(17) It is proposed that, when the said lady defendant was at Lignières, the same lord the plaintiff every year, twice or thrice, used to come to the same place of Lignières . . .

It is proposed [that he was] spending the night with the said lady. – He believes that he spent the night, being compelled to do so,[172] as stated above – otherwise he would have been killed.[173]

It is proposed [that he was] paying the conjugal debt. – He replies as above, when he spoke of carnal union.

It is proposed [that he was] also knowing her carnally. – He replies as above.

It is proposed that the said lord the defendant, when he rose from the marriage bed, quite a number of times said and boasted in front of quite a number of people that he needed to drink something and restore himself with breakfast. He replies as above, and does not believe what is contained in the proposition.

It is proposed that he knew carnally the said defendant, his wife, three or four times. – He does not believe it to be the case.

It is proposed [that he was] saying. in French: 'I have earned a drink because I rode my wife three or four times in the night.' – He does not believe it to be the case, nor is it true.

(de Maulde, *Procédures politiques*, pp. 900–1)

1498, November 7

From the enquiry at Blois conducted by the Official of Paris. Deposition of Salomon de Bombelles, doctor of medicine and of arts, the king's doctor. Passages supplied from British Library, Add. 20917, fol. 203v, in bold.

He said besides that, when our lord king was in the tower of Bourges, and the aforesaid Lady Jeanne came to him, and stayed with him there for some days, and since he seemed to be losing weight every day beyond what was normal,[174] several of the king's Scottish archer bodyguard said or complained to the speaker, because he was the king's doctor, that the same lord our king was having too much sex with the said Lady Jeanne; after hearing which, on a certain day after that, confidentially and privately, the same speaker said to the same lord our king that the

---

[172] 'Credit pernoctasse coactus' – ungrammatical, as he must mean 'Credid [se] coactu[m] prenoctasse', rather than 'Coactus credit'.
[173] 'aultrement il eust esté affolé'.   [174] 'magis solito'.

aforesaid archers of the guard had said to him that the same lord king was getting thin from having too much sexual intercourse with the said lady; to which the same lord our king replied to the speaker in these words: 'The devil I do:[175] I have never in my life mounted her naturally like another woman.' And, when the speaker replied that the same lord our king ought to have a talk with her with a view to obtaining his freedom,[176] he replied to this[177] that he did not know and, when he wanted to have intercourse with her, he found [178]**a certain twistedness**[179] at the orifice of the vulva, such that his penis could not enter, but as he aroused himself[180] **he ejaculated the semen between or over the legs of the same Lady Jeanne**, and this act displeased him so much that he would have wished to have married one of the poorer noblewomen[181] of this kingdom and endowed her with ten thousand pounds of revenue;[182] and, though the same speaker several times advised the same lord our king to have a talk with the said Lady Jeanne, especially at the time when he was imprisoned, with a view to obtaining his freedom, he never discovered, from any reply of his, that he loved her or wanted to treat her with marital affection, even in the face of any amount of fear.

(de Maulde, *Procédures politiques*, p. 1081)

1498, November 20

Louis XI's letter written prior to the marriage is produced as evidence on the king's side

I have planned to make a marriage between my little daughter Jeanne and the little Duke of Orleans, since it seems to me that the children they will have together will not cost them anything at all to support, advising you that I hope to make the said marriage or otherwise those who oppose it will never be out of mortal danger in my kingdom.

(Evidence for the authenticity of the letter follows.)

(de Maulde, *Procédures politiques*, no. 49, pp. 915–16)

---

[175] 'Je fays le grant dyable.'

[176] 'interteneret eam ad ejus liberacionem': a risky translation among several possible meanings. I have understood the implicit connection between Louis's captivity and the couple's sexual problems to be that they made it harder for him to get her help in arranging his release, rather than taking the 'liberation' to mean the overcoming of a sexual problem on Jeanne's part.

[177] 'cui respondit'.

[178] 'a certain . . . Lady Jeanne' supplied from British Library, Add. 20917, fol. 203v.

[179] 'tortuositatem'.   [180] 'calificiendo se'.   [181] 'pauperiorem nobiliorem'.

[182] 'constitisset sibi decem mille libras redditus'.

1498, December 4 and 5

Solemn supplementary interrogation and oath of Louis XII

For the whole context see de Maulde, *Procédures politiques*, no. 55, pp. 931–8. The passages in bold type in the extract printed below are omitted by de Maulde and supplied from British Library Add. 20917.

Preliminaries to the oath

In the year of the Lord **1498, second indiction,** Tuesday 4 December **in the seventh year of the pontificate of our most Holy Father in Christ and lord, the Lord Alexander VI pope by divine providence, we, Philip by divine mercy cardinal priest of the church of saints Peter and Marcellinus of the holy Roman Church, of Luxembourg, bishop of Le Mans; Louis bishop of Albi and Fernando bishop of Ceuta, judges delegated by the holy apostolic see,** in accordance with the appointment made by us on the preceding Monday **in the annulment suit pending and carried on**[183] **between the most Christian King of the French Louis, the plaintiff, the party on one side, and the most illustrious Lady Jeanne of France, the defendant, the party on the other,** we – **together with the learned men**[184] **Masters**[185] **Pierre de Bellessor, the Official**[186] **of Paris, and Robert Lalongue, the Official of the archdeacon of Paris, our assessors appointed for this case** – moved from the village of Amboise to the fortified settlement[187] or town of Fau, of the diocese of Tours, in order to[188] receive the[189] oath of truth to settle the fact in dispute[190] from same lord our king with respect to certain articles set out[191] in the same case by the same defendant. In this fortified settlement or town, however, because of the flooding that occurred all around the fortified settlement on the night of the same day,[192] or because of the bad weather,[193] or because of danger to his person, or for some other reason, King Louis himself did not come at all. And, for this reason, on the following Wednesday, 5 December, assigned by us to the same parties to witness[194] the said oath being taken, we, the judges, with the aforementioned assessors,[195] moved to the village of Ligueil, of the same diocese of Tours, subject in

---

[183] 'mota'.   [184] 'scientificis viris' could also be translated simply as 'experts'.
[185] 'scientificis viris magistris'.   [186] Bishop's deputy. See Appendix 5, s.v.
[187] 'castrum'.   [188] 'et (*sic*)' de Maulde: 'ut' British Library, Add. 20917.
[189] 'delatum'.   [190] 'juramentum…delatum'.   [191] 'quotatis'.
[192] 'illa nocte ejusdem diei'.   [193] 'indispositio temporis'.
[194] 'videndum'.   [195] 'accessoribus' in de Maulde.

temporal matters to the dean of the [church of the] most holy Martin of Tours; in which village, and in the house of the same dean, coming into the presence of the same lord King Louis, and to the same King Louis who was there and whom we had found there,[196] fortified with the counsel of learned men – of Masters Antoine de Stagno, doctor of both laws, counsellor and proctor of the same lord our king, of Charles de Haut-Bois, his counsellor and president of his *Chambre d'Enquêtes* of the Parlement of Paris, and Philip Baudot, also a counsellor of the said lord our king in the said court of the Parlement of Paris and in his great council, we, through our spokesman,[197] Cardinal Philip, remonstrated that the matter at stake between the same parties was a great one, in view of the status of the people involved, and also considering the issue, which was of the nullity of an alleged marriage, and that it was the business of a true king, such as the same plaintiff is and continues to be,[198] to fear God and tell the truth, following in the steps of the same Jesus, our creator, who is truth itself; and, if he were to tell the truth, he would prosper in God, and obtain inestimable treasure, namely paradise; but by doing the opposite he would be setting himself on the way for hell.[199] After these considerations and many authorities of holy scripture had been brought to his attention, and he had been admonished about his salvation and the danger to his soul, we Philip, Louis and Fernando, bishops, the aforesaid judges, sitting in tribunal, **in the presence of the nobleman Charles de Preux, proctor of the said Lady Jeanne, authorised by a letter,[200] expressly consenting to the taking of the oath of truth in the same village of Ligeuil – with a representation of Jesus Christ, it should be said,[201] being first placed in front of him and shown to him – with his head reverently bared, we had him take the oath, put to and received[202] by the same lord king, on the holy gospels and on his word as king, to tell the truth about the same articles set out by the same defendant, which he took, after the aforementioned things had been done as is set out above, with him asking[203] and requiring that these articles be read to him, asserting that he would not want to swear rashly[204] for anything in the world, and that he would tell the truth about the said articles. After this oath had been taken in this way, obeying the request of the said lord our king, we, the aforesaid judges, had the said articles read**

---

[196] 'ad personam ejusdem Ludovici Regis accedentes, eidem Regi Ludovico inibi existenti et reperto'.
[197] 'organo nostri'. [198] 'est et existit'. [199] 'edificaret ad gehannam'.
[200] 'literatorie fundatus'. [201] 'tamen'.
[202] 'iuramentum . . . delatum et per . . . regem susceptum'.
[203] 'quod . . . prestitit petendo'. [204] 'deierare'.

and expounded to the same King Louis in full[205] and in French
by the said Master Pierre de Bellessor, the Official of Paris, one
of the assessors. When they had been read and expounded, we
questioned the same lord King Louis on each and every article
that the same Lady Jeanne of France had set out, the aforesaid Charles de Preux the proctor of the said Lady Jeanne being
present. King Louis then indeed asked these articles to be made
available to him so that he could take a closer look at some of
them[206] and be able to give a response with regard to them with
greater certainty and more truthfully. Granting his request, we
judges, with the assessors and the others withdrew to another
place, and after we returned after an interval of an hour or
thereabouts to the same Louis the king, and were in session as
a tribunal, the aforesaid King Louis, in the presence of the said
Charles the proctor of the said Lady Jeanne, gave an individual
response to each of the articles, and this [response], set down
in writing, he had read aloud, and after that, signing off on it,
he handed it over just as and in the manner that is set out and
to be found[207] at the end of each article. And there follows first
the contents of the fifteenth article and the reply in respect of
it . . . [seventeenth article]. Again, that the same plaintiff, every
year, twice or thrice, used to come to the same place of Lignières
to see the same defendant, his wife, and remained there for ten or
twelve days or longer, and spent the night with her, alone with one
another, naked man with naked woman, paying the marriage debt
through carnal union, smiling, kissing, embracing and openly
showing other signs suggesting desire for the experience of sexual conjugal union,[208] indeed furthermore of true sexual union,
as is right between man and wife,[209] as the aforesaid plaintiff
showed;[210] and this had been and was at that time true, public,
notorious and manifest.[211]

    — With respect to this seventeenth article he replies that he was at
Lignières, but that each and every time that he had been at the said place
of Lignières, this had been at the command and express order of the late
King Louis, the father of the said defendant, and out of fear for him, and

---

[205] 'de longo ad longum'.   [206] 'ut ad partem peramplius videret'.
[207] 'continetur et habetur'.   [208] 'appetitiva experiencie copule conjugalis'.
[209] This clause would seem to go with 'sexual union' rather than 'openly showing'.
[210] 'showing . . . showed': the repetition seems to be in the original Latin.
[211] The article is omitted by de Maulde here, but is as in articles of Jeanne which he prints
    earlier, pp. 875–6.

because he was forced to do this,[212] making as little of it as possible.[213] Notwithstanding this [i.e. the visits], he was never at the said place with her as if with his wife, nor did he make any attempt to have marital intercourse with her;[214] and did not in fact have intercourse with her,[215] and, what is more, did not ever sleep with her when they were both nude.

Again, that the same plaintiff, when he rose from the marriage bed, quite a number of times said and boasted in front of quite a number of people that he needed to drink something and restore himself with breakfast,[216] because he had known the same defendant carnally three or four times, saying, in French, 'I have earned a drink because I rode my wife three or four times in the night' – speaking of the defendant.[217]

– With respect to the eighteenth article he affirms on oath that it is not true.

> (de Maulde, *Procédures politiques*, pp. 931–3 and British Library, Add. 20917, fol. 77v–80r and 203v)

---

[212] 'force luy estoit de ainsi le faire'.
[213] 'en faisant aussi mauvaise chere qu'on sauroit faire'.
[214] 'ne ne s'efforça icelle congnoistre par affection maritalle'.
[215] 'et si ne la congnut realement'.   [216] 'bibere et gentari'.
[217] Omitted here by de Maulde, but as in articles of Jeanne printed earlier, p. 876.

18   Margaret of Scotland and Archibald Douglas, the Earl of Angus

Margaret's annulment was of a second marriage.[1] She had married James IV of Scotland in 1502. James IV aimed to fit the mould of the Renaissance sovereign monarch. He wore a type of crown new for Scotland, one that symbolised sovereignty, the monarch as emperor in his own domain, and he tried to round off the boundaries of royal power – notably, he suppressed the Lordship of the Isles. He also tightened control on the Scottish Church. He was ambitious enough to take on England too, though married to King Henry VIII's sister, but in 1513 he was killed at the battle of Flodden fighting the forces of his brother-in-law. His son with Margaret had been born only the year before, and she was pregnant. The following year (1514) Margaret married Archibald Douglas, Earl of Angus. Theirs was a stormy relationship. They lived apart for a long period. Before their marriage was dissolved both had other partners, Henry Stuart for Margaret, Lady Jane of Traquair for Angus. Jane and Angus had earlier been in a relationship which was almost certainly a marriage in canon law, though Margaret had probably not known that. When the marriage was eventually annulled, the grounds appear to have been 'pre-contract' – that he had been previously married clandestinely to Jane.[2] We need to remember that simple words of consent to marry in the present tense were enough to make a valid marriage in medieval canon law, and also that an engaged couple could turn betrothal into marriage by sleeping together: the courts would normally take intercourse in those circumstances as indicating present consent. Untypically, in this

---

[1] This section is heavily indebted to Dr Ken Emond, Dr Lucy Wooding and Professor Jane Dawson.

[2] Here I may gratefully quote from a personal communication kindly sent to me by Professor Jane Dawson: 'this is a slightly odd royal marriage in that Margaret went ahead in a secret ceremony probably on 14 August 1514 and did not tell her brother Henry VIII until 1 Sept! Given that context there were no officials doing any checks or "tidying up" on past status. Pre-nuptial contracts were common among the Scottish nobility in this period and in many ways it would be a surprise if Angus didn't have one! . . . During that time Angus had spent some time living with his former fiancée Lady Jane Stewart [of Traquair – near Peebles] so the reasons for the dissolution "make sense".'

case it was the queen who started the annulment proceedings. The Earl of Angus for a long time resisted. He needed the marriage to survive to keep control of the young King James V.

It took a long time for the annulment to come through. It was pronounced on 11 March 1527. The trial proceedings are not known to have survived. We do have a document produced by the cardinal of Ancona in 1528 attesting to the annulment and attempting to make arrangements for the property settlement.

Historiographical highlights

Compared with the preceding case of Louis XII and the following case of Henry VIII, good scholarship on the Angus–Margaret annulment appears to be scarce. There are some references to the annulment in Richard Glen Eaves, *Henry VIII and James V's Regency, 1524–1528: A Study in Anglo-Scottish Diplomacy* (Lanham, MD, 1987), pp. 94, 133, 134, 150. Eaves probably underestimates the difficulty of getting an annulment without legal grounds. He draws attention to a discussion of how much to give the judge after his verdict: 'large rewards (bribes)?' (p. 150). This raises a general issue. Such payments would not be acceptable in the modern British civil service, but if paid after the verdict, if there was no prior arrangement to fix the verdict, and, crucially, if a payment might be expected from whichever side won, is it not misleading to call it a bribe? It could not influence the outcome without reverse causality.

The most scholarly assessment of the case is in the important thesis of K. Emond, 'The Minority of King James V, 1513–1528' (PhD thesis, University of St Andrews, 1988), p. 534 at notes 62 and 63 and p. 563, notes. The *Oxford Dictionary of National Biography* has entries on both Margaret and Angus. On the latter, Marcus Merriman writes that 'Angus lost interest in Margaret during her absence and took a mistress, Lady Jane Stewart of Traquair (to whom he had earlier been briefly betrothed). The queen responded by beginning divorce proceedings shortly afterwards.'[3] On Margaret, Richard Glen Eaves, apparently on the basis of research or reflection subsequent to his book, writes:

An attempt by the third Earl of Lennox to free King James from Angus's custody had been defeated at Linlithgow on 4 September 1526. Lennox was killed, and Angus and the Douglases were left without a rival. Margaret had continued to urge Albany to use his influence at Rome to help her obtain a divorce from

---

[3] Marcus Merriman, 'Douglas, Archibald, Sixth Earl of Angus (c. 1489–1557)', *Oxford Dictionary of National Biography*, online version.

Angus, since she was determined never to be reconciled with him but to marry Henry Stewart instead. She had originally attempted to justify the separation on the specious grounds that James IV had not been killed at Flodden, but was still alive when she married Angus; however, when Clement VII finally annulled the marriage, on 11 March 1527, it was by reference to Angus's pre-contract to Lady Jane Stewart.[4]

This fits the suggestion above that the dissolution fits the 'pre-contract' model. Other recent historians tell the same story: 'It was to the great credit of the pope and the Roman curia that when Clement VII finally granted her divorce . . . the decree was on the grounds of Angus's pre-contract with Lady Jane of Traquair'[5] – as opposed to the tale about the survival of James V. 'The final decree was based, as it frequently was in those days, on an already existing contract; in this case, Angus's betrothal to Lady Jane Stewart of Traquair.'[6] (Buchanan adds that Margaret had been reluctant to use this argument before because she did not want her daughter's legitimacy taken away – but in the event the daughter was legitimised.[7]) Or again 'Pope Clement VII granted her desired divorce on the grounds of Angus's pre-contract with Lady Jane Stewart.'[8] Agnes Strickland, *Lives of the Queens of Scotland and English Princesses Connected with The Regal Succession of Great Britain*, vol. I (Edinburgh, 1850), p. 230, gives a circumstantial account of a hearing before the Consistorial Court of St Andrews in which the queen alleged and Angus confessed the pre-contract; according to her the papal decision followed this. The source, *Mackenzie's Lives*,[9] vol. II, p. 572, is late. Another late but not quite so late source tells a similar story.[10] The decisive evidence,

---

[4] Richard Glen Eaves, 'Margaret (1489–1541)', *Oxford Dictionary of National Biography*, online version.

[5] Maria Perry, *Sisters to the King* (London, 2002), p. 231.

[6] Patricia Hill Buchanan, *Margaret Tudor Queen of Scots* (Edinburgh, 1985), pp. 229–30. Buchanan may not have realised that betrothal to Lady Jane would only have invalidated the marriage to Margaret if Jane and Angus had slept together or if the contract had been in words of the present tense, but essentially she is giving the same version as other historians.

[7] *Ibid.*, p. 230.

[8] Rosalind K. Marshall, *Scottish Queens, 1034–1714* (East Linton, East Lothian, 2003), p. 96.

[9] This must be George Mackenzie, *The Lives and Characters of the Most Eminent Writers of the Scots Nation*, vol. II (Edinburgh, 1711).

[10] Ioannes Leslaeus, *De Origine, Moribus et Rebus Gestis Scotorum Libri Decem* (Rome, 1578), lib. IX, pp. 399–400: 'Aliquanto post Regina Angusium in jus vocari curat, coram Archiepiscopo Sanctandreapolitano sistendum,ut illa de divortio controversia, inter illos verbis privatim saepius disceptata, ad juris judicii formam, ac praescriptum juste tandem dirimeretur. Ad diem sistit Angusius, Regina illum fidem primariae foeminae ante nuptias secum initas astrinxisse acerrime contendit. Archiepiscopus Sanctandreapolitanus divortii sententiam tulit, ea tamen lege, ut proles ex eo matrimonio suscepta, propter parentis, saltem Reginae [inc. p. 400] ignorantiam, nihil inde damni pateretur. Idque

however, was presented and correctly analysed by A. E. Anton in his article on '"Handfasting" in Scotland', *Scottish Historical Review* 37 (1958), pp. 89–102, at p. 99, where he provides references to fairly conclusive evidence for a prior contract between the Earl of Angus and Jane of Traquair – evidence apparently arising out of an inheritance suit brought by Angus's daughter Margaret, Countess of Lennox in 1563, after both her parents had been dead for some time.[11]

The translation

The translation is from an attested copy of the verdict dated 1528 (the verdict was in the previous year). It survives in at least two copies in the National Archives and is printed without a reference number in *State Papers Published Under the Authority of His Majesty's Commission: King Henry VIII*, 11 vols. 1830–52 (British Library, Call Number RB.31.b.121), vol. IV, *King Henry VIII Part 4: Correspondence Relative to Scotland and the Borders, 1513–1534* (London, 1836),[12] pp. 490–1, note 1 (corresponding to National Archives ref: SP 49/3, dated 2 April 1528, though the reference is not given in the edition). It is also possible to find the document in the electronic database 'State Papers Online' by searching under at 'St.P.iv 490'. I have added numbers in square brackets to the dispositive part of the document (the part in which the legally binding decision is stated), which is indented, in order to assist readers to follow the extremely complex syntax of the document, as only the most experienced Latinists could do from the original.

1528

The sentence

We, Peter, by divine mercy, bishop of Sabina, cardinal of the Roman Church, called 'of Ancona', formally record[13] and bear witness to each and every person who will examine this letter of ours of how we, at another time,[14] as judge and representative of the most Holy Father our

---

eo libentius, & quod res videbatur nulla dubitatione implicita, & quod reginae mens in eam partem propendere videbatur. Regina, pronunciata divortii sententia, paulo post nupserat Henrico Stuarto'.

[11] *Calendar of the State Papers Relating to Scotland and Mary, Queen of Scots 1547–1603*, ed. Joseph Bain, vol. I: *A.D. 1547–1563* (Edinburgh, 1898), no. 1175, p. 690, and no. 1179, p. 694.

[12] I give these full bibliographical details because the volume is often so counter-intuitively catalogued, notably by the British Library, as to seem virtually unfindable.

[13] 'fidem facimus'.   [14] 'alias'.

pope in the Roman curia, specially delegated to deal with the case and cases between, on the one side,[15] the most serene lady, the lady Queen Margaret, wife of the late Lord James IV, most serene King of the Scots, of famous memory, and, on the other,[16] the illustrious lord, the Lord Archibald Douglas, Earl of Angus, about and concerning the invalidity of the alleged marriage contracted and consummated between them, and other things set out in the records[17] of this case and cases, and prompted by them,[18] promulgated, as justice urged us, our definitive sentence, at Rome on the 11th March 1528[19] AD; the contents of this sentence follows, and it is this:

After invoking the name of Christ, with the counsel of the lords the legal experts,[20] we, through this our definitive sentence, which, sitting in judgement,[21] and having God alone before our eyes, in the case and cases which have been and are being contested before us as court of first instance[22] between, on the one side, the plaintiff her most serene majesty and lady the lady Queen Margaret, the wife of the late most serene Lord James IV King of the Scots, of famous memory, and, on the other side, the illustrious lord the Lord Archibald Count of Angus, her opponent, about and concerning the nullity and invalidity of the alleged marriage contracted and consummated – as it is said – between them, and the other things set out more fully in the records of this case and cases, and prompted by them, we pronounce in this document,[23] we give sentence, we announce, we determine, and we declare: [1] that the alleged marriage contracted and consummated by the union of the flesh between the aforesaid Lady Margaret and Archibald Douglas was and is null and invalid, and that it went ahead *de facto*,[24] and consequently, it should be dissolved, just as it went ahead, *de facto*, and the said Lady Margaret and Archibald should be made to separate in perpetuity[25] – and accordingly[26] we dissolve it and make them [separate]; – [2] and that the said Lord Archibald should be condemned, obliged, compelled and constrained to give back each and every

---

[15] 'ex una . . . partibus [ex altera]' is the odd structure of this sentence.

[16] 'ex altera' belongs here in the translation though it comes further down in the Latin original.

[17] 'actis'.

[18] 'occasione illorum': grammatically, because of the masculine gender, this must refer to the 'actis'.

[19] 'millesimi quingentesimi vigesimi septimi': but he was probably following the system by which the year began on 25 March after Christmas, so this would fall in 1528 in modern terms.

[20] 'Dominorum Jurisperitorum'.   [21] 'pro tribunali sedentes'.

[22] 'In prima versae fuerunt et vertuntur instanter' in the edition, whose editor probably did not understand the construction of the Latin, since 'In prima' should not be the start of a new sentence, but belongs with the previous context, as in the translation, and since 'instanter' is either a transcription or scribal error for 'instantia'.

[23] 'ferimus in his scriptis'.   [24] i.e. as opposed to *de jure*.

[25] 'perpetuum divortium . . . faciendum esse'.   [26] 'prout' – literally 'just as'.

one of the movable[27] and immovable[28] and self-moving[29] goods of any kind whatsoever, acquired and received from the aforesaid Lady Margaret as[30] dowry – and
we condemn, oblige, compel and constrain him to release, restore and hand them
over;[31] [3] also that moves made and instigated against the same Lady Margaret by
the aforesaid lord Earl Archibald, in the matters set out above and any one of them
and in any way with respect to them, to oppose and contradict and
refuse and put up obstacles of any kind,[32] were and are audacious, unwarranted
and iniquitous, and presumed to be *de facto*, and that *de jure* it was and is in no
way licit for the same lord Earl Archibald to have done or to do them; [4] and
that perpetual silence should be imposed on the same lord Earl Archibald about
and concerning them and this alleged marriage and the other aforesaid things;
[5] and that the same lord Earl Archibald should be held liable[33] both for the
profits[34] made from the alleged dowry and the aforesaid goods from the time
when the aforesaid case began,[35] and for the expenses legitimately incurred in
this case before us on the part of[36] the aforesaid Lady Margaret – and we do hold
him liable, and reserve the assessment of these expenses[37] to ourselves for a later
date.

Thus I, Peter, cardinal of Sabina, have pronounced, and that the said sentence,
which has not been held up by any appeal,[38] should now be treated as a thing
ajudged.[39]

And we, because of our absence from the said curia, were not able to
order letters of execution.[40] Consequently we urge each and every one
of you aforesaid in the Lord to give unreserved credence,[41] and have
others give it, to this our present testimony guaranteeing the truth,[42]
in judgement and in the Church. As a guarantee and testimony of these

---

[27] i.e. real property.   [28] i.e. inanimate chattels.
[29] i.e. animals and, presumably, also dependent peasants.   [30] 'occacione' [*sic*].
[31] 'Archibaldum ad restitutionem . . . bonorum . . . a . . . Margarita . . . receptorum, relax-
ationem, restitutionem et dimissionem condemnandum, cogendum, compellendum,
et constringendum, condemnamusque, cogimus, compellimus, et constingimus'. Since
'restitutionem' is repeated (and in view of the writer's preference for artificial word
order), I have taken the first occurrence with the gerunds and the second (where it is
among synonyms) with the third-person plural 'condemnamusque', etc.
[32] 'oppositiones . . . et contradictiones et recusationes et impedimenta quaecumque per . . .
Archibaldum . . . eidem . . . Margaritae . . . factas et praestitas, factaque et prestita', the
feminine plural accusative participles agreeing with 'contradictiones et recusationes',
and the neuter plural accusative participles agreeing with 'impedimenta'. Adjectives are
repeated for the same reason in the context that follows, though the repetition makes
no sense in English.
[33] 'contemnandum'.   [34] 'fructibus'.
[35] 'de tempore motae litis praedictae citra perceptis'.
[36] 'pro parte' – would normally be translated as 'on behalf of', which fits less well here.
[37] 'quarum', agreeing with 'expensae' but not with the masculine 'fructuum'.
[38] 'nulla provocatione suspensa'.
[39] 'in rem transivit judicatam': i.e. further litigation is precluded.
[40] 'litteras executoriales'.   [41] 'fidem indubiam adhibeatis'.
[42] 'nostrae fidei veritatisque attestationis'.

things we have undersigned this letter in our own hand, and have ordered that it be confirmed by the application of our seal. Given at Ancona, in the episcopal palace, 2 April 1528, in the fifth year of the pontificate of our most Holy Father and lord in Christ the Lord Clement VII, pope by divine providence.

19   Henry VIII and Catherine of Aragon

This is perhaps the most famous divorce in history. Familiar though it is, however, the case is not widely understood. One still meets with the idea that everything turned on whether or not Catherine of Aragon came to Henry VIII as a virgin, or, alternatively, had consummated her marriage with his deceased brother Arthur.[1] It is important to realise that this was irrelevant to the process as it played out in and was viewed from Rome, even if it was important to Henry and to Catherine (for different reasons).

The consummation question did have some relevance to an ingenious technical argument considered by Cardinal Wolsey: namely, that the dispensation obtained for Catherine to marry Henry presupposed that she had consummated her marriage with Arthur. (This 'path not taken' was first intellectually explored by J. J. Scarisbrick, *Henry VIII* (London, 1968, 1997): see 'Historiographical highlights' below.) Wolsey wanted Henry to argue that his marriage to Catherine was based on the wrong kind of dispensation. If her marriage to his brother had been consummated, the dispensation would have been for 'affinity'. And in fact it was for 'affinity'. If the marriage had not been consummated, it should have been for 'public honesty'. Wolsey saw a way out for Henry: argue that it was the wrong kind of dispensation. The dispensation assumed consummation with Arthur, Catherine had never had intercourse with Arthur, so the dispensation was invalid and Henry was free to marry Anne Boleyn. Catherine's insistence that the marriage had not been consummated could potentially have holed her case below the waterline – had Henry agreed to take this legal line.

In the event, Henry did not take this route, as explained below. Consequently, it made no difference to the papal court whether or not Catherine had been a virgin when she married Henry. It mattered to Henry because of his biblical argument, but its premises were alien to the rationality of

---

[1] E.g. Giles Tremlett, *Catherine of Aragon: Henry's Spanish Queen* (London, 2010), pp. 336–8.

papal canon law. Why did Catherine herself make such an issue of her virginity when she married Henry? Probably because Henry was asserting the contrary in such a way as to make it seem crucial, and because she knew his assertion to be untrue (as seems highly likely). Her insistence has sown confusion in accounts of the case, and may betray some confusion on her part.

Henry VIII disregarded Cardinal Wolsey's advice and instead based his case for annulment on the claim that a papal dispensation could not override the Bible (Leviticus). That line had little chance of success before papal judges. It was a given for the medieval Church establishment that not all Old Testament rules remained in force. Furthermore, dispensation practice since at least the thirteenth century was based on the assumption that it was ultimately for the pope to decide the limits of his own dispensing power. But Henry liked the Leviticus line, which did indeed fit with 'Bible-first' beliefs widely current at the time. If he had taken a different line and admitted that Catherine of Aragon had been a virgin when he married her as his brother's widow, he might have had a fighting chance of showing that the dispensation to marry her was formally faulty. Since the likelihood is that she was indeed a virgin when she married Henry, this would have had the added advantage of being true. But this strategy would have been a gamble, since a last-minute intervention by Catherine's mother had altered the dispensation in such a way that it might be valid after all – unless it was deemed internally contradictory.

These were Henry's options: on the one hand, an arguable but risky canon law case, based on the claim that Catherine had not slept with Arthur and that her dispensation to marry him was consequently faulty. It might just have worked, but there was no fall-back plan. Henry would have burned his boats. On the other hand, he could opt for the argument that no papal dispensation could override biblical prohibition and enable Catherine to marry her deceased husband's brother, an option likely to fail at the papal court, but with an exciting and attractive fall-back plan: to do what he actually did and rally around him the anti-papist 'Bible-alone' sentiment that was in the air in the first flush of the Reformation. Investigation showed, however, that he could only do this if he claimed that Catherine had not consummated her marriage with his brother. All his potential Bible-Christian supporters, and even a rabbi he consulted, thought that the Leviticus argument did not work otherwise. Henry himself seems to have thought that, according to Leviticus, his marriage to Catherine was invalid irrespective of whether she had slept with Arthur before the latter's death. Since his marriage was invalid – he may have reasoned – a white lie about Catherine's virginity or lack of it to get him clear of a sinful union was not too terrible, especially since he avoided supporting it with an oath.

It is still possible to make some unfamiliar documents on this case known, or at least more widely known than through the massive scholarly study by Edward Surtz, *Henry VIII's Great Matter in Italy: An Introduction to Representative Italians in the King's Divorce, Mainly 1527–1535*, 2 vols. (Ann Arbor, University Microfilms, 1975, 1982). This was published in an unusual and low-diffusion format: the microfilm series usually associated with US doctoral dissertations. Even Surtz had space only to paraphrase in his impressive opus magnum, not to transcribe or translate. The manuscript British Library, Add. 37154 is an eighteenth-century transcript of the trial proceedings in the Roman curia. Its accuracy is 'attested by Joseph Spalletti, Vaticanae Bibliothecae Graecus Scholiastes, on the Ides of June 1778' (*ibid.*, vol. II, p. 976). Surtz comments that 'There is no clue as to who desired this copy or why. Amazingly, little or no use has been made of this important transcript.' His own summary goes a long way to filling the gap, but still the proceedings have never been translated or even edited – which is indeed amazing in view of the celebrity of the case.

The documents translated below are mostly from this manuscript. They include an extract from the statement of her case by Catherine and illustrations of the 'positiones' she proposed to prove, in accordance with the medieval Church's 'due process' for settling marriage cases.

Historiographical highlights

My own analysis above is essentially a condensed version of the findings of Henry Ansgar Kelly, *The Matrimonial Trials of Henry VIII* (Stanford, CA, 1976), an outstanding study of the whole subject. Surtz's findings, however, could not be fully exploited in Kelly's admirable work because he only obtained a xerograph of Surtz's volumes 'just as [his book] was being given to the printer'[2] – though he did manage to make some use of Surtz's work.[3] Reading Arthur J. Slavin, 'Defining the Divorce: A Review Article', *Sixteenth Century Journal* 20 (1989), pp. 105–111, one might take away the impression that Kelly's findings have been radically revised by Edward Surtz and Virginia Murphy, *The Divorce Tracts of Henry VIII* (Angers, 1988). Though Virginia Murphy's work on the divorce tracts greatly advanced the field and correct an emphasis in Kelly (cf. Murphy in Surtz and Murphy, *Divorce Tracts*, p. xvii, with Kelly, *Matrimonial*

---

[2] Kelly, *Matrimonial Trials*, p. 77, note 2 from p. 76.
[3] See *ibid.*, p. 299, index entries under Additional 37154.

Trials, p. 66), their overall interpretations are not in fact very far apart. Both emphasise the centrality of the biblical argument in Henry's mind. On attitudes to the Bible which would have influenced Henry, Lucy Wooding, *Henry VIII* (Abingdon, 2009), pp. 131–7, has good insights. As already noted, it was Scarisbrick who drew attention to the possibly valid canon law case which Henry might have argued (*Henry VIII*, ch. 7, 'The Canon Law of the Divorce', *passim*). Scarisbrick would have made a good canon lawyer. He probably underestimates the risk that following Wolsey's 'wrong dispensation' advice would have entailed. One can see why it appealed to Wolsey: a fighting legal chance, which his gifts would have maximised, instead of the nuclear option which would blow up a world in which he ultimately believed.

Scarisbrick helps make sense of a piece of evidence that has thrown popularisers off the scent by making the issue of consummation seem more important than it was ('wrong kind of dispensation' arguments aside). Catherine's father King Ferdinand said that the 'wretched' English told Rome that consummation had occurred.[4] On the face of it this is hard to interpret. Scarisbrick's explanation (itself over-compressed) is that the English thought they were playing safe by getting a dispensation for affinity, which presupposed consummation, since that was a greater impediment requiring a greater concession on the pope's part. They were so fixated on this that they did not think to get a dispensation for the lesser impediment of 'public honesty' (assuming the first marriage had not been consummated) as well. They obtained braces but not a belt. Actually, as already explained, it was all totally irrelevant to the trial so far as the curia was concerned.

For the reactions of intellectuals to the divorce see Guy Bedouelle and Patrick Le Gal, *Le 'divorce' du roi Henry VIII: études et documents* (Geneva, 1987).

The translation

Appendix 3 contains the extracts, translated from British Library, Add. 37154, on which nearly all the translations below are based. The hard work was done by Surtz, whose detailed analysis provides folio numbers: in effect a detailed and accurate map of the manuscript. (In addition, I also translate a short passage translated from a published collection of documents: see notes 39 and 40.) In translating the two papal dispensations, wording more or less common to both is italicised.

---

[4] Scarisbrick, *Henry VIII* (1997 edn), p. 192.

1529, May 10

Catherine of Aragon summarises her case before appointing proctors

The following extract is (to quote Surtz) from 'Queen Catherine's des-
ignation of the Cardinal Croce ... and the imperial ambassador ... as
her proctors under date of May 10, 1529'. He provided a precis of the
interesting introduction:

> she confesses that Arthur lay with her for several nights but without
> sexual intercourse ... inserts verbatim Julius II's dispensation of
> December 26, 1503, for her marriage with Henry [in both the forms in
> which it was sent] ... According to Catherine, very many are zealous
> for the divorce and, in order to achieve it more easily by Apostolic
> authority, suggest to the Supreme Pontiff that she desires the divorce
> and for that reason promises to enter religion, together with many
> other fictions and lies, against all of which she protests vehemently.
> (Surtz, *Henry VIII's Great Matter*, vol. II, pp. 978–9)

[**fol. 8r**]: The contents, however, of the official documents giving a mandate to act as proctor and to appoint substitute proctors,[5] of which mention is made above, follow, and are as follows:

Queen Catherine:

To all the Christians to whom the present letter or this present
document, appointing proctors, protesting, denying[6] and dissenting
should reach, Catherine by the grace of God Queen of England and
consort, wife and legitimate spouse of the most invincible Prince Henry,
the eighth of that name since the Conquest, current King of England and
France, greetings in Christ and his mercy.[7]

I draw it to your attention, and wish it to be drawn to your attention by
this letter, that Arthur, may God have mercy on his soul, commended [to
him],[8] as a young man married me when a young woman,[9] and lay for
some nights with me, without however sexual intercourse taking place;
after his death and burial the aforesaid most illustrious King Henry VIII,
the biological[10] brother of the same Arthur, when he was scarcely twelve
years old, became betrothed to me,[11] and afterwards our parents obtained
papal dispensations to allow us to contract marriage in the present tense

---

[5] 'procurationis ac substitutionis publicorum instrumentorum'.
[6] 'reclamationis'.
[7] 'in visceribus Ihesu Christi': a free translations, as 'bowels' sounds too literal in modern
English.
[8] 'cuius anime [eo?] commisse (commisso ms.?) Deus condonet'.
[9] 'pubes me puberem duxit in uxorem'.   [10] 'naturalis'.
[11] 'mecum sponsalia contraxit'.

notwithstanding the impediment of affinity; the contents of these follow, and is this, verbatim:

{Julius, bishop, servant of the servants of God, to our beloved son Henry, son of our most illustrious beloved son in Christ Henry illustrious King of England, and to our illustrious beloved daughter in Christ Catherine, child of our dearest son in Christ King Ferdinand, and of our most dear daughter in Christ Isabella, Queen, of the Spanish lands[12] and of Sicily, the Catholic [monarchs], greetings and apostolic blessing. *The pre-eminent authority of the Roman pontiff, uses the power granted to him from above as he sees it to be fitting in the Lord, taking into account the nature of the persons, matters and the times.*[13] *The purport of the petition presented to us recently on your behalf was that, although*[14] *at another time*[15] *you, our daughter Catherine, and Arthur, being alive at that time, the first born of our dearest son in Christ Henry the illustrious King of England, in order to preserve the ties and bonds of peace and friendship* between our dearest son in Christ Ferdinand and our dearest daughter in Christ Isabella, the Catholic [monarchs] of Spain and Sicily, and the aforesaid King and Queen of England, *contracted a legitimate marriage through words in the present tense, and perhaps consummated it through carnal union, the said Arthur passed away, without any offspring resulting from this marriage,* but since, however, as the same petition went on to say, to the end that this bond of peace and friendship should last longer, you want *to contract with one another a legitimate marriage through words of the present tense,* you have had a petition presented to me that we *might deign out of apostolic benignity to make provision for you in the aforesaid matters with the* opportune *grace of a dispensation. Therefore we, who desire with intense longings for the delightful condition of peace and harmony to flourish among each and every Christian, and especially Catholic kings and princes,* and absolving, and deeming to be absolved, to take effect that is by virtue of the purport of the present letter,[16] you and each of you individually from any ecclesiastical sentences, censures and penalties[17] of excommunication, suspension and interdict, and any others laid on them by the law or by man for any reason or cause,[18] if you are bound by these in any way whatsoever, *yielding to these petitions,*[19] – we, *by apostolic authority,* through the contents of the *present letter,* by a gift of special grace, *grant a dispensation to you that you may be able to contract marriage legitimately by words in the present tense, and to remain in it licitly after it has been contracted even if you have already perhaps before now contracted it de facto publicly or clandestinely, and consummated it by the union of the flesh, notwithstanding in any way the impediment of this affinity deriving from the facts set out above* and papal and other contrary constitutions and ordinances,[20] and, if you contracted as stated above, *by the same authority we absolve you and each of you individually from this transgression and the sentence of excommunication that you have incurred in consequence; deeming the children which have been or perhaps will*

---

[12] 'Hispaniarum'.   [13] 'temporum qualitate'.   [14] 'cum'.   [15] 'alias'.
[16] 'ad effectum presentium dumtaxat consequendum harum serie'.   [17] 'penis'.
[18] 'quibuscumque excumminicationis, suspensionis et interdicti aliisque ecclesiasticis sententiis, censuris et penis a iure vel ab homine quavis occasione vel causa latis'.
[19] 'huiusmodi supplicationibus inclinati'.
[20] 'constitutionibus et ordinationibus apostolicis ceterisque contrariis'.

be begotten from this marriage, whether it has been contracted or is to be contracted, to be legitimate, provided that you, our daughter Catherine, were not abducted[21] on account of this. *We wish however that, if you have contracted this marriage de facto, a confessor to be chosen by you and each one of you individually, should enjoin on you a salutary penance on this account, which you should be bound to fulfil.* Therefore it is permitted to no man whatsoever to infringe this document containing our absolution, dispensation and will, or to make some audacious effort to contravene it. If anyone however should presume to attempt this, let him know that he will incur the wrath of Almighty God and of his blessed apostles Peter and Paul. Given at Rome, at St Peter's in the year of the Lord's incarnation 1503,[22] on the kalends of January in the first year of our pontificate. Sigismund signed it.}

{Beloved son and beloved daughter, greetings and apostolic blessing. *The preeminent authority of the Roman pontiff uses the power granted to him from above as he sees it to be fitting in the Lord, taking into account the nature of the persons, matters and the times. The purport of the petition presented to us recently on your behalf was that, although*[23] *at another time*[24] *you, our daughter Catherine, and Arthur, being alive at that time, the first born of our dearest son in Christ Henry the illustrious King of England in order to preserve the ties and bonds of peace and friendship between the aforesaid [King] of England and our dearest son in Christ Ferdinand, King, and our dearest daughter in Christ the Queen, the Catholic [monarchs] of the Spanish lands,*[25] *and Sicily, contracted a legitimate marriage through words in the present tense, and consummated it through carnal union, since however Arthur passed away, without any offspring resulting from this marriage, and* this bond of peace and entente[26] between the aforesaid kings and queen would probably not hold so firmly unless it was also strengthened and confirmed by some bond of affinity, for these and certain other reasons you desire *to contract a legitimate marriage with each other through words in the present tense,* but since you are not able to fulfil your desire in the aforesaid matters without an apostolic dispensation covering them[27] being obtained, you have humbly had us petitioned that we *might deign out of apostolic beneficence to make provision for you in the aforesaid matters with the grace of a dispensation and apostolic benignity. Therefore we, who desire with intense longings for the delightful condition of peace and harmony to flourish among each and every Christian, and especially Catholic kings and princes, – we – our mind being moved by these and other reasons, after being swayed by these petitions,*[28] *– by apostolic authority, grant a dispensation to you by the present letter that you may be able to contract marriage between you, and to remain in it after it has been contracted,* licitly and freely, and insofar as *you may perhaps have contracted a de facto marriage between yourselves publicly or clandestinely and consummated it by the union of the flesh, by the same authority we absolve you and each of you individually from this transgression [and] the sentence of excommunication that you have incurred in consequence*; and we also similarly grant a dispensation to you that you may be able freely and licitly [to remain] in

---

21 'rapta'.   22 'millesimo quinquagentesimo tertio septimo' ms, in error.
23 'cum'.   24 'alias'.   25 'Hispaniarum'.   26 'connexitatis'.
27 'desuper': an alternative translation would be 'from above', i.e. 'from higher authority'.
28 'huiusmodi supplicationibus inclinati'.

the marriage thus contracted *de facto* or to contract it between yourselves anew; *deeming the children which have been or perhaps will be begotten from this marriage, whether it has been contracted or is to be contracted, to be legitimate. We wish however that, if you have contracted this marriage de facto, a confessor, to be chosen by you and each one of you individually, should enjoin on you a penance on this account, which you should be bound to fulfil.* Given at Rome, at St Peter's, sealed with the Ring of the Fisherman, on 26 December 1503, in the first year of our pontificate. Sigismund.

The superscription is as follows: 'To our beloved son Henry, illustrious child of our dearest son in Christ Henry, illustrious King of England, and to our beloved daughter in Christ Catherine, illustrious child of our dearest son also in Christ Ferdinand, king and our dearest daughter in Christ Isabella, Catholic [monarchs].'" And[29] between in the margin affixed the ring of the Fisherman.'}

On the strength of these in the meantime he became betrothed to me[30] when he was about eighteen, and we remained in this state for four years; finally the aforesaid most illustrious King Henry VIII wanted me[31] to marry him; our wedding was solemnised, in the customary way, publicly, after the dispensation had first been read out;[32] we lived together as a married couple[33] for eighteen years, just as we do at present,[34] we begat and had children, of whom one, a daughter, remains alive. Recently however, and this I find hard to bear, the validity of that marriage between us, contracted and consummated as stated above, has been called into question by many, and to the point that, allegedly, the most illustrious King Henry VIII, my most beloved husband, has an unquiet[35] conscience on account of this marriage. There are many who want our marriage to be dissolved,[36] and to achieve this more easily by apostolic authority, they suggest to the supreme pontiff that I desire for the marriage between myself and the aforesaid most illustrious King Henry VIII to be dissolved, and that I consent to this happening, and that for this reason I promise to become a nun; and they relate and explain in my name many other things equally fictitious and false, when in truth I have never given my assent to such a dissolution being brought about,[37] nor have I determined to enter the religious life for that or any other reason, nor have I given, conveyed,[38] or conceded to anyone a mandate for proctors, or any power, to suggest

---

[29] 'inter immargine/inmargine'.   [30] 'mecum sponsalia contraxit'.

[31] 'sollicitavit me'.

[32] 'interim perlecta dispensatione': 'read through' is also possible, and would change the sense.

[33] 'ut vir et uxor . . . viximus et cohabitavimus'.

[34] 'prout in presenti vivimus et cohabitamus'.   [35] 'lesam'.

[36] 'divortium inter nos fieri': but 'get divorced' would be a misleading translation, since at this time 'divortium' mainly stood for annulment or legal separation, when the couple were baptised and the marriage had been consumated.

[37] 'divortium celebrandum'.   [38] 'feci'.

this to the supreme pontiff – indeed I dissented from each and every one of the deeds and words through which this dissolution could be brought about and procured, and I counter-claimed as soon as any such thing came to my notice, just as I now by the contents of the present letter dissent, and counterclaim, protesting, as I protest[39] openly, publicly, and for all to see through these writings of mine, that I will never agree to this divorce taking place.

Catherine then proceeds (fols. 11v–14r) formally to appoint her proctors. This part of the document is very similar in its content and technicality to **# 1322, J.682.1 (b)** and **(g)**. The queen's proctors are allowed to appoint substitute proctors.

1529, July 16

On this day the imperial ambassador in Rome, in the name of Queen Catherine, applied to have the case transferred to the curia in Rome, and in doing so invoked the theological underpinnings of the indissolubility doctrine.[40] From the 'Application to have the matter transferred to the curia, made and justified in detail in the name of Queen Catherine by the imperial ambassador in Rome, and then signed by [Pope] Clement'.[41]

Most merciful father. It is not believed to have been or to be your holiness's intention, – in a matrimonial case and where the sacrament of marriage is in question, a sacrament that is more noble than the rest of the sacraments by reason of the place where it was instituted, since it was instituted and ordained in the earthly paradise and the state of innocence, and because marriage by consent or professions, after it has been consummated, cannot be dissolved – to wish to prevent defence motions and objections, legitimate appeals, which have been introduced by the law of nature, and nature herself teaches that all living souls are entitled to a defence and that this is not to be taken away from them.[42]

---

[39] 'protestando prout protestor'.

[40] 'Antrag auf Avokation der Sache an die Kurie, vorgelegt und näher begründet im Namen der Königin Katharina durch die kaiserlichen Gesandten in Rom, dann von Clemens VII. unterzeichnet' (S. Ehses, *Römische Dokumente zur Geschichte der Ehescheidung Heinrichs VIII. von England 1527–1534* (Quellen und Forschungen aus dem Gebiete der Geschichte II; Paderborn, 1893), no. 61, pp. 122–5, at p. 122).

[41] *Ibid.*

[42] 'Clementissime Pater! Non creditur de mente Sanctitatis Vestre fuisse aut esse, in causa matrimoniali et ubi agitur de sacramento matrimonii, quod ceteris sacramentis ratione loci institutionis nobilius existit, quia in paradiso terrestri et in statu inocentiae institutum et ordinatum fuit, et quod coniugum consensu aut confessionibus postquam consumatum est, dissolvi non possit, velle tollere defensiones recusationesque, appellationes legitimas, quae iure [**p. 123**] naturae inductae fuerunt, ipsaque natura docet, omnibus animantibus defensionem deberi et non tolli' (Ehses, *Römische Dokumente,*

1529, July 25

The queen's articles

The established canon law procedure allowed both sides to make a list of the propositions they wished to prove. (Normally the two lists would be consolidated before being put before witnesses, but Henry VIII never turned up or sent a proctor to the trial, so there was no formal list of 'articuli' or 'positiones' on his side – though, as we shall see, an unofficial non-proctorial representative later turned up with articles to explain why Henry could neither appear nor send a proctor). A finalised version of the queen's articles was handed over on 25 January 1531.[43]

The following articles are of particular interest. Number XVI shows that according to the queen's side the dispensation covered both public honesty and affinity. Numbers XVII–XIX stress that the dispensation was well known to Henry and Catherine before they got married.

[**fol. 45v**]: XVI. Again, that the aforesaid Pope Julius II of happy memory, in view of the importance of maintaining peace, alliance,[44] and friendship between the said kings of Spain and England, and to counteract the scandals, disagreements and discords between the same kings, if there was a plausible fear that such would arise,[45] and for other reasons, and with regard to these, gave a dispensation, to be on the safe side,[46] [that] Henry VIII and the most serene Catherine, the aforesaid king and queen,[47] notwithstanding the impediments of public honesty and affinity, if these had perchance been contracted, might be able to contract marriage with each other and remain in it, as is set out more fully in the apostolic letters issued on the matter,[48] which the aforesaid proctor gives here in the place of *positiones* and articles, insofar as they support or may be seen[49] to support his case and that of his party aforementioned, and tell against the opposing side,[50] and not otherwise nor in any other way, and concerning this he makes an explicit declaration.

no. 61, pp. 122–5, at pp. 122–3). coniugum] coniugium British Library, Add. 37154, fol. 18r. The British Library manuscript's reading seems to make better sense. If one reads 'coniugum', then the meaning becomes 'consummated by consent' of the *coniuges*, which goes against the disjunction between consent and consummation that had been standard in canon law since at least the thirteenth century.

[43] Surtz, *Henry VIII's Great Matter*, vol. II, p. 984.   [44] 'federis'.

[45] 'si que verisimiliter oriri formidabantur'.   [46] 'potiori pro cathela'.   [47] 'reges'.

[48] 'prout in litteris apostolicis desuper confectis'. 'Litterae' can be singular but in this case there were two dispensations.

[49] 'videantur': not translated as 'seem' because that implies that the reality is otherwise.

[50] 'quatenus pro se dictaque parte sua et contra partem adversam faciant aut facere videantur'.

XVII. Again, he asserts[51] that the dispensation, as set out above, granted, as set out above, by Pope Julius II of happy memory to the aforesaid king and queen[52] Henry VIII and the most serene Catherine, was public and common knowledge in the kingdom of England,[53] and, at the time when the aforesaid king and queen Henry and Catherine contracted marriage publicly in the eyes of the Church,[54] was there read, and published, and fully understood, just as the witnesses who were present will be able to state and depose in testimony, and do say and depose in testimony, openly and publicly, and this was and is the truth.[55]

XVIII. Again, that the most illustrious Henry VIII and the most serene Catherine, King and Queen of England, before and at the time of the marriage contracted and confirmed between them, knew and were aware of[56] this dispensation granted to them by the apostolic see to contract marriage with one another, and had full knowledge of it, over a period of time,[57] publicly and openly, and this was and is the truth.

XIX. Again, that the aforesaid most illustrious Henry VIII and the most serene Catherine, King and Queen of England, after the said dispensation which had been granted before that[58] had been read publicly and published in their presence, being of a legal age for contracting marriage, contracted ... through words in the present tense, publicly and in the eyes of[59] holy mother Church, with a multitude of the people and the magnates and prelates of the kingdom of England present.

(British Library, Add. 37154, fols. 46r−v)

1531, January 31

Henry VIII's explanation of why he cannot appear

Even as late as 1531 Henry VIII did not want to burn his boats and simply reject the proceedings in Rome. He sent Edward Carne, doctor of laws, to explain to the court why he could not come or send a proctor.[60]

---

[51] 'ponit'.   [52] 'regibus'.   [53] 'publica et notoria'.   [54] 'in facie ecclesie'.
[55] 'et sic fuit et est verum'.   [56] 'sciverunt et sciebant'.
[57] 'plenam noticiam habuerunt et habebant'.
[58] 'previa dicta dispensatione'.   [59] 'in facie'.
[60] Surtz, *Henry VIII's Great Matter*, vol. II, pp. 987–8. The option of sending a proctor to act for him had naturally been available, as the citation of Henry makes clear: 'quos nos etiam et eorum quemlibet [**fol. 21v**] [in margin: 'terminus comparitionis'] tenore presentium sic citamus quatenus sexagesima die post citationem vestram huiusmodi per vos vel alterum vestrum eis facta immediate sequente [sequen'] si dies ipsa sexagesima iuridica fuerit, alioquin proxima die iuridica immediate sequente [sequen'], qua nos seu alterum forsan interim loco nostri surrogandum auditorem Rome vel alibi ubi tunc

> Carne presented his arguments in a form similar to official articles or *positiones*, though they had no legal standing as part of the trial. The following extracts encapsulate this position, in bombastic and repetitive legalese.

Again, similarly he says it is established, and establishes,[61] that for the aforesaid causes and reasons it is against the same lord King Henry's interest[62] and that it is important and expedient for him as the person with the best and most knowledge and information, if and where the same case is in question, to take part in it, to assist, to inform those who need to be informed and tell those who need to be told, himself and in person, but not through a proctor, as indeed was and is clear in law, and as was and is true, public, common knowledge, and manifest...
[**fol. 61v**]... Again, that the truth was and is that, in past times, when kings and princes left their kingdoms and principalities [**fol. 62r**] and betook themselves to remote places and absented themselves – especially kings of England – because of their withdrawal and absence, in the said kingdoms and principalities, and especially in the kingdom of England, revolts, disturbances, scandals, disputes, conflicts and dissensions arose, which led to complete ruin[63] and grave loss[64] and enormous damage, both to the said kingdoms and principalities and to their kings and princes and the inhabitants of the kingdoms and those who dwelt in them, and this was public, manifest, and common knowledge.

(British Library, Add. 37154, fols. 61r–v)

---

dominus noster papa cum sua Romana curia residebit in palatio causarum apostolico, mane, hora audientie causarum consueta ad iura reddendum et causas audiendum pro tribunali sedere contigerit, compareant in iudicio legittime coram nobis seu surrogando auditore prefato, per se vel procuratorem seu procuratores suos ydoneum vel ydoneos ad causam et causas huiusmodi sufficienter instructos' (British Library Add. 37154, fols. 21r–v). 'vos vel alterum vestrum' seems to refer to the person or persons required to serve the summons. For the citation see Surtz, *Henry VIII's Great Matter*, vol. II, p. 979.

[61] 'constare dicit et constat'.   [62] 'minus interest'.
[63] Emending 'exilium' to 'exitium'.   [64] Emending 'factura' to 'iactura'.

The attempted Reformation in France is the background to the marriage of Henri of Navarre (1553–1610), who became Henri IV of France, and Marguerite of Valois. Marguerite belonged to the Catholic royal house: she was the daughter of Henri II and the sister of his three successors as king. Henri of Navarre had been brought up a Calvinist by his mother, who publicly professed her Protestant faith in 1560, when he was still a small boy. Hers was a conversion of conviction. These were years when Calvinism was too strong to be crushed but too weak to win outright. Henri's marriage to Marguerite was a failed attempt to end the bloody stalemate. The royal family were not on the extreme wing of the Catholic party, and were threatened by its leaders, the Guise family.

Henri was still eighteen when they married in 1572, the year in which his mother died and when he became King of Navarre. He was still a Protestant. A papal dispensation was expected but delayed, and in the end they did not wait for it. A few days after the lavish wedding party, violence engulfed Paris. An attempted assassination of the Protestant Admiral Coligny provoked fears of Protestant retaliation, against the background of a possibly genuine if probably unfounded fear by the king of a Calvinist coup. A pre-emptive strike was launched – the notorious massacre of St Bartholomew's Eve. Many of the Protestants around Henri himself were massacred, and he was more or less forced into an external conversion to Catholicism, which took place not long after the massacre and was quickly abandoned. Probably after the massacre, but still in 1572, the dispensation finally arrived. There is evidence that Henri did not show any interest in it and that it was not approved by the bishop of Paris as new rules laid down by the Council of Trent required. Nonetheless the couple would remain married for more than two decades. Henri and Marguerite seem to have spent some happy times together, but she may have had other partners and he certainly did. They also spent a great deal of time apart. Henri quickly reverted to Protestantism and led Huguenot resistance to the crown. Marguerite helped keep a line of communication open with the French royal family, as it tried to steer a path between Protestantism and the hard-line Catholic Guise party.

In 1589 Henri inherited the French crown as Henri IV, and in 1593 he converted to Catholicism, this time permanently – who knows whether sincerely? He was absolved by the pope in 1595, and in 1598 he published the Edict of Nantes, granting a measure of toleration to Protestants. An end to religious war seemed in sight, but he still had no heir, leaving the future after his death unclear. If only he could marry again and have a son, contemporaries reasoned, the equilibrium could continue. The death in childbirth of Henri's mistress Gabrielle d'Estrées, whom he might have married if he were free, but who was deemed inappropriate as a consort by people who mattered, removed a reason for leaving his marriage alone. This is the immediate context for the annulment.

The pressure for it in high places was immense, notably from Gallican Catholics like the top lawyer La Guesle, who hinted heavily that the canon law way might not be the only way to achieve the essential aim. Furthermore, the example of what had happened in England under Henry VIII in a not dissimilar case hardly needed spelling out. There was plenty of pressure on the pope. Marguerite was prepared to cooperate if she was well looked after financially. There is no doubt about the motivation of all concerned. The documents translated below concentrate on the legitimation, which has received less attention.

The key issue was whether the marriage was covered by a dispensation. As noted above, it had arrived late, and new rules laid down by the Council of Trent had apparently been ignored. This provided valid grounds for annulment, fortunately for all concerned. A papal commission annulled the marriage in 1599, and Henri married Marie de Medici in the following year. The translated extracts show that a genuinely thorough search was conducted to see if the dispensation for the marriage of Henri and Marguerite had been sent to the bishop: the Council of Trent had made this a *sine qua non* for the validity of marriage dispensations.

Historiographical highlights

Henri IV and 'la reine Marguerite' enjoy name recognition far beyond the world of academic research. In France at least they must be almost in the class of Eleanor of Aquitaine. Understandably, there are innumerable books about them, in that their lives had the kind of interest that attracts tabloid newspapers in our own time. Amidst this great pile of paper there is one old but first-rate study which remains the best starting point:

P. Feret, 'Nullité du mariage de Henri IV avec Marguerite de Valois', *Revue des Questions historiques* 11ième année, 39e livraison (1876), pp. 77–114. Vincent J. Pitts, *Henri IV of France: His Reign and Age* (Baltimore, MD, 2009), is one way into the complicated background of religious conflict and dynastic uncertainty. For the background to La Guesle and Gallicanism, see Nancy Lyman Roelker, *One King, One Faith: The Parlement of Paris and the Religious Reformations of the Sixteenth Century* (Berkeley, 1996).

The translation

I translate from the edition in [le sieur] Aubery, *L'histoire du Cardinal Duc de Ioyeuse, a la fin de laquelle sont plusieurs Memoires, Lettres, Dépéches, Instructions, Ambassades, Relations, & autres pieces non encore imprimées* (Paris, 1654), British Library, call no. 205.a.10, pp. 369–73, checked against the original documents in Archives nationales, J.934.1/27 and J.934.1/29).[1]

The original of the first part of the dossier translated below is Archives nationales, J.934.1/27, which is a paper booklet of four folios, probably two bifolia, though the outer two are reinforced so it is hard to tell if they were originally one sheet. Height 34 cm × width 21 cm. Large blank inner margin. The last 3⅓ pages are blank. The '27' at the foot of the first page is not a page or folio number but the number of the document in the dossier.

The divergences from the manuscript are mostly too trivial to be worth recording: e.g. omission of 'christianissimum' before 'Henricum' in the printed version, doubtless by oversight; 'dilligens' for 'diligens'; omission of 'exhiberet', again doubtless by oversight. Once or twice the edition seems to correct or improve the manuscript: 'coperturam habens... 340 folia continens' in the edition as opposed to '... habens... habens' in the manuscript (between 'Tertius liber minutarum' and 'Sabbati 13.'). There is, however, one quite serious mistake in the edition, which by eyeskip misses out the words 'se nullos alios libros, seu registra, expeditiones et acta Curiae episcopalis <Parisiensis continentia in suo graphariatu habere, nulla tamen alia predictorum annorum expeditiones> continentia quam supradicto duo quae nobis superius exhibuit volumina' (see note 39 below).

---

[1] My thanks to Bernard Barbiche for directing me to the original dossier in the Archives nationales.

1599

The search in the archives

Report of the search for the said dispensation.[2]

On 7 December, we, Georges Loüet, priest, commendatory abbot of the monastery of All Saints of the diocese of Anjou, canon and major archdeacon of the church of Anjou, and clerical counsellor of the supreme Senate of Paris,[3] and Christophe Rossignol, public notary of the holy apostolic see and the episcopal court of Paris, commissioned and sub-delegated in this matter by the most illustrious Lord François, cardinal priest of St Peter ad Vincula of the holy Roman Church, called 'de Joyeuse', and the most reverend Lord Horace archbishop of Arles, and Gaspar bishop of Modena, nuncio of our holy lord the pope and of the apostolic see in the kingdom of France, judges delegated by his holiness in the case for the annulment and dissolution of the marriage between Henri IV most Christian[4] King of the French and of Navarre on one side, and the most serene Queen Marguerite of France, Duchess of Valois[5] on the other,[6] the respective parties in the case,[7] as communicated to us in legal form[8] through their letter of subdelegation dated 3 December of the aforesaid year, betook ourselves around one o'clock[9] to the close[10] of Notre Dame[11] of this city, at the chapter bar[12] as it is popularly called, following an appointment[13] given, at the instance of the noble and distinguished Lord Charles Faye abbot in commendam of the monastery of Saint Fuscien[14] au Bois[15] of the diocese of Amiens, canon of the church of Paris, and clerical counsellor in the supreme Parlement of Paris, promoter in the said case for annulment and dissolution of the marriage, to Master Jean Baudouyn, secretary of the reverend lord bishop of Paris. And when the aforesaid lord promoter and the said Baudouyn had arrived there, the request was made by the aforesaid lord promoter that the said Badouyn

---

[2] In French: the report itself is in Latin.   [3] i.e. the Parlement.

[4] Christianissimum] J.934.1/27, omitted in edition.   [5] 'Valesiae Ducem'.

[6] 'ex una . . . partibus ex altera'.

[7] 'respective actores', so literally: 'respectively, the parties'.

[8] 'ut nobis . . . legitime constitit'.   [9] 'horam primam post meridiem'.

[10] On the cathedral close ('cloître') of Notre Dame, see L. Tanon, *Histoire des justices des anciennes églises et communautés monastiques de Paris* (Paris, 1883), pp. 129–30.

[11] 'claustrum D. Mariae'.

[12] 'apud barram capituli': the 'bar of the chapter'/'Barre du chapitre' was a tribunal, 'qui se tient au cloître Notre Dame', through which the chapter of Notre Dame exercised its extensive rights of temporal justice in Paris: Robert Gane and Claudine Billot, *Le chapitre de Notre-Dame de Paris au XIVe siècle: étude sociale d'un groupe canonial* (Saint-Étienne, 1999), p. 84. Cf. also Tanon, *Histoire*, p. 137.

[13] 'assignationem'.   [14] 'Fusciani'.   [15] Cottineau, *Répertoire*, vol. II, col. 2683.

should produce[16] the books, which they call the registers, of grants,[17] correspondence,[18] papal letters, and other acts[19] of the said secretariat, from August 1572 to September 1575, so that in these books or registers a diligent and rigorous search could be made for the dispensation granted by the supreme pontiff Gregory XIII concerning the third degree of consanguinity by which the said most Christian King Henry IV of the French and of Navarre and the most serene Queen Marguerite were joined. With respect to these[20] we ordered the said Badouyn to make available to us the aforesaid books or registers of the said secretariat and of the grants, papal letters, correspondence and other acts[21] from 1572 to 1576. This Badouyn did indeed say he was entirely ready to obey our commands. And in order that the said registers or books might more easily be made available to us, we went to the house of the secretary Baudouyn situated in the said close of Notre Dame, and the said Baudouyn made available to us volumes of many registers, and after the said Baudouyn had taken the oath that is customarily sworn in such cases, he asserted that no other volumes of any kind of correspondence existed or were held for the aforesaid years in the said premises of the secretariat, and that he had not seen any other of the aforesaid books of the said correspondence during the time of his knowledge of the secretariat, and that the late Master Hatton, who exercised the office of secretary for thirty years, and who had been the said Baudouyn's superior for a long period of time, had not had any others. From these registers we took and handled[22] two, in the presence of the said lord promoter, and found them to be entire, not cancelled, torn, or damaged in any part, the first of which – bound in vellum[23] – beginning in the first page with these words: 'die 9. Septembris ann. 1572. visa certa supplicatione',[24] and in the blank folio preceding 'Registrum inceptum anno Dom. 1572';[25] and ending on the last page with the words: 'praesentibus magistro Nicolao Forguex Presbytero in dicta Ecclesia Parisiensi habituato, et Nicolao Ellain Doctore Medico Parisiensi testibus',[26] on the cover of which book the letter T is written, with the addition of 'year 72. 8 September'; the second volume, however,

---

[16] exhiberet] omitted in J.934.1/27, supplied in edition.   [17] 'collationum'.
[18] 'expeditionum'.
[19] 'actuum' – elsewhere translated 'records', which fits less well here.
[20] 'super quibus'.   [21] 'actuum'.   [22] 'prae manibus habuimus'.
[23] 'pergameno'.   [24] '9 September 1572, after seeing a certain supplication'.
[25] 'Register begun in 1572'.
[26] 'in the presence of Master Nicholas Forguex Priest, domiciled at the said Church of Paris [I take this to refer to Paris itself as in 'canon of the Church of Paris' above, rather than to a particular church within Paris, though the point is immaterial here], and Nicholas Ellain, medical doctor at Paris, witnesses'.

also bound in vellum, with these words written[27] on it: 'for the years 74, first of April, 75, 76, 77, 78, 79, 30, month of July', beginning on the first page of writing with these words: 'Registrum collationum, et aliarum expeditionum sub sigillo Rever. in Christo Patris et Dom. Dom. Petri de Gondy Parisiensis Episcopi expeditarum',[28] and ending on the final page with these words: 'facta est magistro Lino de Glatini Presbytero dioecesis Lexoviensis sufficiente et idoneo, dictoque Rever. Dom. Parisiensi Episcopo litteratorie praesentato praesentibus testibus'.[29] We went through these two volumes from the first page to the page for January 1576, containing these words,[30] and we read them word by word, and we found nothing whatsoever about the said dispensation, nor did we find any mention of it, of any kind, in these two registers, although the contents of dispensations, rescripts, and bulls obtained from the supreme pontiff Gregory XIII is recounted in many places; concerning which things we gave and submitted a documentary record[31] to the said promoter at his request, and we left the said registers or volumes in the hands of the said Baudouyn.

When the ninth day of the aforesaid month and year came, however, we betook ourselves to the said close of Notre Dame, at around 9 a.m.,[32] to the said chapter bar,[33] and there the aforesaid lord promoter, and Master Adrien Thinot, notary and scribe of the apostolic see and the episcopal court of Paris, or the registrar[34] of the said court, appeared. To this scribe or registrar, at the urging of the said lord promoter, and by virtue of the command we had received,[35] the day and hour had been named,[36] for him to make available and show to us the registers or volumes of the said registry[37] from 1572 to 1576. The said lord promoter asked and required that these registers be made available in order that a diligent and rigorous search be made to find and seek out the said dispensation or documents making mention of it. And indeed this Thinot said that in obedience to our command he had brought with him the said registers or volumes, and that he was more than ready to make these available to us and the said lord promoter. With respect to these we commanded[38] and ordered the aforesaid Thinot to show to us the aforesaid registers or volumes containing correspondence from the aforesaid years. And when he had shown us

---

[27] 'hiisque verbis notato'.

[28] 'Register of grants, and other correspondence dispatched, under the seal of the reverend[/most reverend] father in Christ and Lord the Lord Pierre de Gondy bishop of Paris'.

[29] Translation unclear [and immaterial here] with only a fragment of the sentence.

[30] 'haec verba facientem': presumably, the words quoted above.   [31] 'actum'.

[32] 'circiter horam nonam ante meridiem'.   [33] 'Barram Capituli'.

[34] 'Grapharius'.   [35] 'nostrae ordinationis'.   [36] 'dies dicta erat ad hanc horam'.

[37] 'graphariatus'.   [38] 'statuimus'.

two registers and volumes, after the said Thinot had taken the oath that is customarily sworn in such cases, he asserted that he had in his registry no other books or registers, containing correspondence and records of the episcopal court, nor yet any others containing correspondence of the aforesaid years apart from the aforesaid two volumes that he showed us above,[39] had come to his notice, and that he had not had such in his possession nor seen them,[40] and that he knew for certain that the late Master Louis Ioisel, his predecessor as registrar, who had continued to hold and exercise the office of registrar[41] from 1566 to 1582, had not had any others, apart from the ones Thinot has, and could not have done so, since in the said registers all correspondence for every single day from the year 1568 up to the year 1579 may be found. We took these two registers and found and recognised them as being entire, undamaged, and not suspect in any part; and the first of them [was] bound in vellum containing forty-four written folios, and beginning on folio 1 with these words: 'Veneris 21 Maii ann. Dom. 1568. de Magistro Petro Breaule Presbytero actore contra Magistrum Philippum reum etiam Presbyterum',[42] the last folio ending with these words: 'Cum partibus actore secum Gilbert, et reo secum dicto patre, et Pecuin[43] eius Procuratore 13. Decembris ann. Dom. 1572';[44] and these words are read as a title of the book:[45] 'Tertius liber Minutarum';[46] the second, however, having the same vellum binding, containing 340 folios, with the first of these folios beginning with these words: 'Sabbati 13. Ianuarii anno 1573. de Iacobo Picquet actore in caussa matrimoniali, seu sponsalium contra Georgetam Delle',[47] and ending on the last folio[48] with these words: 'Die Mercurii 21. Octobris

---

[39] 'se nullos alios libros, seu registra, expeditiones et acta Curiae episcopalis <Parisiensis continentia in suo graphariatu habere, nulla tamen alia predictorum annorum expeditiones> continentia quam supradicto duo quae nobis superius exhibuit volumina' *ms.*, the words in angle brackets omitted in edition by eyeskip from 'continentia' to 'continentia'.

[40] The syntax does not quite work: 'se nullos alios libros . . . ad sui notitiam pervenisse nec unquam habuisse nec vidisse asseveravit'. The 'se' goes with 'habuisse' and 'vidisse' but not with 'pervenisse'.

[41] 'in graphariatus officio et exercitio . . . remansit'.

[42] 'Friday 21 May 1568, concerning Master Pierre Breaule, priest, plaintiff, v. Master Philippe, defendant, also a priest'.

[43] Reading proposed to me by Professor Marc Smith of the École des Chartes, who suggests that Loüet and Rossignol may have had difficulty deciphering the name in the book: 'per eum', the reading in the edition, makes no sense.

[44] Translation unclear with only a fragment of the sentence.

[45] 'et in cuius inscriptione haec verba leguntur'.   [46] 'Third book of minutes'.

[47] 'Saturday 13 January, 1573, concerning Jacques Picquet, plaintiff, in a matrimonial, or betrothal case against Georgette Delle'.

[48] 'horum foliorum 1. per haec verba incipiente . . . et finiente folio ultimo per haec verba' is not strictly grammatical, though the sense is clear.

ann. Dom. 1579. electis domiciliis in domibus Procuratorum partium';[49] and the book is entitled thus:[50] 'Fourth Book of Minutes 1573. 74. 75. 76. 77. 78. et 79'.[51] After reading these two books or registers from the first folio to the last with appropriate diligence and fidelity, we found and discovered nothing whatsoever concerning the aforesaid dispensation. And we gave and submitted a documentary record of the aforementioned things to the said lord promoter as he requested, and restored the two books to the aforesaid Thinot. Given at Paris, on the aforesaid day and year, Loüet, Rossignol.

1599

The promoter's case

In the following document, the 'promoter' of the case for annulment argues that the dispensation never took effect because it was not registered with the bishop as the Council of Trent required. The various imaginative grounds for annulment in play originally have dropped away. Instead, a cast-iron formally rational reason has been found.

The document is translated from Aubery, L'histoire, checked against Paris, AN J.934.1/29.[52] The differences between the manuscript document and the seventeenth-century edition are insignificant. Thus the edition corrects 'facto' to 'factam' (at the words in the translation 'search conducted'); it eliminates the repetition of 'coram vobis' at 'before you by the most illustrious lord the cardinal de Gondi' (the manuscript puts it both before and after his name), but omits the 'Dominum' found before 'Cardinalem' in the manuscript; at one point it changes the manuscript's 'ac' to 'et'; in the last sentence the manuscript's 'reginae' is omitted after 'Margaretae'.

Description of J.934.1/29: A paper bifolium, written on the first page only apart from the summary of the contents which I have used as a heading below. This summary is written, upside-down in relation to the text on the front, on the back of the folded sheets (Aubery's edition simply has 'Conclusions du Promoteur' as a heading): 'Conclusions of the promoter in the case for the annulment[53] of the marriage between the most Christian Henri IV King of France and Navarre, on one side, and the most serene Queen Margaret of France, Duchess de Valois,[54] on the other' ('Conclusiones Promotoris in causa dissolutionis matrimonii

---

[49] Translation unclear with only a fragment of the sentence.
[50] 'cui libro haec verba inscripta sunt'.   [51] 'Liber quartus Minutarum 1573' (etc.).
[52] Thanks to Michael Crawford for suggesting the translation of 'producendum' and 'productionibus' by 'stating' and 'statements'.
[53] 'in Causa dissolutionis'.   [54] 'a Francia, Valesiae Ducem'.

inter Christianissimum Henricum quartum Franciae et Navarrae regem ex una et serenissimam reginam Margaretam a Francia Valesiae ducem ex altera partibus'). Height *c.* 36 cm × width 23 cm. Large blank left-hand margin. Different script from J.934.1/27.

I, Charles Faye, abbot 'in commendam' of S. Fuscien in the forest of the diocese of Amiens, royal counsellor in the supreme court of the Parlement of Paris, and promoter deputed by you in the case for the dissolution of the marriage between the most Christian King Henri IV of France[55] and Navarre, and the most serene Queen Marguerite of France, Duchess[56] of Anjou which is pending before you, most illustrious Lord Francis cardinal de Joyeuse and the most reverend lords Horace, archbishop of Arles, and Gaspar, bishop of Modena and nuncio of the most holy lord our pope and of the apostolic see in this kingdom of France, deputed by you to be promoter, in view of:[57]

- the bulls or apostolic letters of our aforesaid most holy lord, by divine providence Pope Clement VIII, containing the delegation of this case which had been assigned to you to arrange and judge, issued in Rome, at St Mark's on 24 September 1599, the records[58] of the case, both with respect to the presentation made to you of the said bulls and of the officiators,[59] the interlocutory sentence[60] on 29 October, the writings[61] or *positiones*, the questions to[62] and responses of the parties, the *ex officio* questioning[63] or examination of witnesses by you, most illustrious and most reverend judges, conducted at my request,[64] the records[65] both of the reception of the said enquiry or inquest,[66] and for the stating and hearing of the legal case,[67] the letter patent[68] of the most Christian King Henri II of the French,[69] containing the marriage treaty between the most serene Prince Antoine de Bourbon, Duke of Vendôme[70] and the most serene Lady Jeanne, daughter of King Henri of Navarre and Marguerite de France, issued in October AD 1548, and exemplar or

---

[55] 'Franc.' in edition, but 'Franciae' in Archives nationales, J.934.1/29.   [56] 'Ducem'.
[57] 'visis' – agreeing as ablative absolute with all the kinds of evidence he goes on to list: so the syntactic structure of the sentence is: 'the bulls, etc., having been seen by me, Charles etc., I require that the marriage be declared null'.
[58] 'actis'.
[59] 'officariorum': see Sleumer, *Kirchenlateinisches Wörterbuch*, p. 563: 'officiarius... Offiziator, der diensthabende Geistliche'.
[60] 'sententia interlocutoria' = interim judgement.   [61] 'scripturis'
[62] 'interrogationibus'.   [63] 'inquisitione'.   [64] 'ad meam instantiam'.   [65] 'actis'.
[66] 'inquisitionis seu inquestae'.   [67] 'quam ad producendum et audiendum ius'.
[68] 'litteris patentibus': which could be either singular or plural.
[69] 'Franc.' in edition, 'Francorum' in Archives nationales, J.934.1/29.
[70] 'Vindocinorum'.

copy of the dispensation or absolution regarding the third degree of consanguinity of the said parties, issued in Rome, at St Peter's in Rome on 27 October 1572, the official record[71] of the search conducted, in my presence and at my request, in the registers both of the episcopal court and of the secretariat of the bishop of Paris by the Lord George Loüet, counsellor of the said Parlement, and clerk[72] to this case, and Master Christopher Rossignol, apostolic notary, in which registers – in accordance with the declaration and deposition made before you by the most illustrious lord the cardinal de Gondi – nothing concerning the aforesaid dispensation, and its presentation and ratification[73] was found, [and] the statements made[74] by the said parties, after they had relinquished the right of raising objections against each other's.[75]

- [in view of all this] I require that the aforesaid marriage contracted and celebrated between the aforementioned most Christian King Henri IV and Queen Margaret of France, Duchess of Valois, be declared to be null and invalid, and that for the future it should be permitted both to the said lord king to marry another woman, and to the aforesaid Lady Margaret to marry another man, in the Lord.

[Signature follows, more or less illegibly: the printed edition transcribes as 'Signed, C. Faye'.]

---

[71] 'processu verbali'.   [72] 'scribam'.
[73] 'homologationem'.   [74] 'productionibus'.
[75] 'productionibus partium dictarum, postquam contradictis adversus illas proponendis renunciarunt'.

Appendix 1   Paris, Archives nationales, J.682.1

Physical description

J.682.1 is a roll about 43 cm in width and about 240.5 cm in length: 1st membrane: 69.5 cm; 2nd membrane 51 cm; 3rd membrane: 77 cm; 4th membrane: 43 cm long + plica 6–7 cm. Four parchment membranes glued and also tied together with string. Two separate notarial signs over the joins as evidence of authenticity.[1]

Notes: (i) in the *apparatus criticus*, '*ms.*' = Paris, Archives nationales, J.682.1. (ii) The paragraph numbering is editorial and aims to help readers match the Latin with the English translation.

(a) In nomine Domini Amen. [2]Noverint universi quod anno Domini illo trecentesimo vicesimo primo die Iovis ante festum beate Agathe virginis comparuit coram nobis, Stephano divina permissione [3]Par*isiensi* episcopo, in domo nostra [4]Par*isius*, presentibus reverendis patribus domino [5]I. [6]divina provisione episcopo /1// Belvacensi et magistro Gauffrido de Plesseyo domini nostri pape notario, et [7]notariis infrascriptis et pluribus aliis probis viris, discretus vir magister Petrus [8]Gouvanh clericus, procurator et nomine procuratorio [9]magnifici et excellentissimi principis domini [10]Karoli dei gratia Francie et Navarre /2// Regis, qui citari fecerat sicut dixit ad predictos diem et locum nobilem mulierem dominam [11]Blancham de Burgundia filiam domine Matildis Comitisse Attrebatensis, et Aymericum Mazerant procuratorem suum, per litteras nostras nostro sigillo inpendenti sigillatas, productas inferius et contentas. Comparuit /3// ibidem coram nobis predictus Aymericus Mazerant procurator, ut dixit, et procuratorio nomine predicte domine Blanche; et ibidem dictus magister Petrus ad faciendum fidem de sua procuratione

---

[1] E. A. R. Brown has done a fuller description, which it is hoped she will publish.
[2] Noverint] *preceded by double dot.*   [3] Parisiensi] Par' *ms.*   [4] Par*isius*] Par' *ms.*
[5] I.] *preceded by double dot.*   [6] divina] *preceded by double dot.*
[7] notariis infrascriptis] 'notar' infrascript' *ms.*
[8] Name supplied by E. A. R. Brown.   [9] magnifici] magnific' *ms.*
[10] Karoli] *preceded by double dot.*   [11] Blancham] *preceded by double dot.*

produxit quamdam litteram eiusdem domini [12]regis pro vera et autentica et vero sigillo magno dicti domini [13]regis impendenti /4// sigillatam, cuius tenor sequitur sub hiis verbis:

(b) ¶ Karolus dei gratia rex [14]Francie et Navarre [15]Universis presentes litteras inspecturis, salutem. Noveritis nos fecisse et constituisse et adhuc facimus et constituimus per presentes procuratores nostros et nuntios speciales dilectos et fideles nostros /5// magistrum Petrum Galvani et Guillelmum [16]Soubuti clericos, et eorum quemlibet in solidum, ita quod non sit nec fiat in aliqua parte iudicii melior conditio occupantis, [17]dantes et concedentes predictis procuratoribus nostris et cuilibet eorumdem [18]in solidum plenam et liberam potestatem et speciale mandatum agendi pro nobis /6// et nostro nomine in causis nostris motis et movendis et specialiter in causa nullitatis matrimonii inter nos et Blancham de Burgundia de facto quondam contracti et ipsum matrimonium, seu illicitam coniunctionem sub matrimoniii specie olim inter nos et ipsam habitam et contractam, tam ratione consanguinita- /7// - tum et graduum in quibus ad invicem attinemus quam alia qualibet ratione, necnon et quicquid opponi contigerit ad defensionem matrimonii seu [19]coniunctio[nis . . . qu]ibuslibet [20]obiectibus, deffectibus, replicationibus seu [21]aliis [22]rationalibus quibuscumque nobis competentibus seu competituris contra premissa vel ea tangentia /8// quomodolibet impugnandi; – nosque super premissis et ea tangentibus coram [23]Episcopo Parisiensi et coram aliis iudicibus ordinariis, delegatis, commissariis, auditoribus, et ceteris omnibus coram quibus agi, supplicari, excipi, seu quomodolibet disceptari, per nos vel contra nos, contigerit de premissis quandocumque et ubicumque et etiam coram /9// sanctissimo patre in Domino summo pontifice, si coram ipso agi vel disceptari quomodolibet contigerit de eisdem, in iudicio et extra iudicium deffendendi et pro nobis agendi, tam contra dictam Blancham quam [24]contra quemlibet alium super hiis opponere se volentem, et petitionem seu

---

[12] regis] *preceded by double dot.*   [13] regis] *preceded by double dot.*

[14] Francie] *thus, in full, not* Francorum: *so I have extended* Franc' *as* Francie *throughout.*

[15] Universis] *preceded by double dot.*   [16] Soubuti] *or* Sonbuti.

[17] Cf. Digest 3.3.32, the Roman law rule that when proctors had been appointed 'et eorum quemlibet in solidum', any business started by a given proctor had to be completed by the same proctor. Charles's proctor is saying that this rule does not apply here. Cf. P. Chaplais, *Medieval Diplomatic Practice*, part I, vol. I (London, Public Record Office, 1975), p. 471.

[18] in] *with abbreviation mark deleted?*

[19] coniunctio[nis? . . . qu]ibuslibet] *physical damage in ms.*

[20] obiectibus] *sic for* obiectionibus?   [21] aliis] al *without abbreviation ms.?*

[22] rationalibus] rati'abus *ms.; perhaps read* rationibus, *but this would be the* facilior lectio.

[23] Episcopo] *preceded by double dot.*   [24] contra quemlibet] *unclear on microfilm.*

petitiones semel vel pluries nostro /10// nomine [25]porrigendi, iurisdictionem cuiuslibet iudicis tam ordinarii quam delegati plene et libere prorogandi de calumpnia et veritate dicenda iurandi et in nostram animam subeundi quodlibet aliud oportunum vel necessarium iuramentum, ponendi, articulandi, testes, litteras et instrumenta producendi, recipiendi, repli- /11// -candi, processui ordinario et in causa renuntiandi et concludendi, [26]sententias interlocutorias et diffinitivas audiendi, et ab ipsis si necesse fuerit apellandi et apellationes si quas interponi contigerit in premissis prosequendi, substituendi unum vel plures procuratores semel vel pluries sub consimili potestate /12// et [27]substituendi, revocandi, et cetera omnia et singula – quecumque fuerint et cuiuscumque status in premissis et ea quomodolibet tangentibus – nostro nomine faciendi que possemus facere si personaliter nos contingeret interesse, etiam si talia sint vel fuerint que mandatum exigant speciale: tenore presentium nichilominus promittentes omnibus quorum /13// interest vel interesse poterit in futurum nos ratum et gratum habituros quicquid per dictos procuratores nostros vel alterum eorumdem vel per substituendos ab eis insimul vel divisim actum, gestum, exceptum, deffensum seu alias procuratum nostro nomine fuerit in premissis, promittentes nichilominus pro ipsis et [28]quolibet /14// eorumdem iudicatum solvi sub meorum bonorum omnium ypotheca ipsos et ipsorum quemlibet relevantes a quolibet honere satisdandi. In quorum fidem et testimonium et maioris roboris firmitatem sigillum nostrum presentibus litteris apponi fecimus et apendi. Datum Parisius xxixª die Ianuarii anno domini millesimo /15// CCCᵒ vicesimo [29]primo.

(c) Item ad faciendum fidem de predicta citatione produxit quandam aliam litteram a nobis emanatam et vero sigillo nostro impendenti sigillatam pro vera et autentica, cuius [30]tenor noscitur esse talis.

(d) ¶ Stephanus permissione divina Parisiensis episcopus dilecto nostro Cotardo de Moylinis et omnibus aliis curatis /16// et clericis nostre diocesis [31]subditis nostris salutem. Vobis et vestrum cuilibet qui de sequentibus fueritis requisiti tenore presentium, committimus, precipimus et mandamus quatinus citetis peremptorie coram nobis dominam Blancham de Burgundia filiam quondam Comitis Burgundie vel procuratorem suum ad infrascripta specialiter constitutum /17// quam seu quem nichilominus nos citamus et peremptorie per presentes ut Parisius in aula nostra die Mercurii post Purificationem beate Marie

---

[25] porrigendi] *unclear on microfilm.*
[26] sententias . . . diffinitivas] sentent' interlocutor' et diffinitivas *ms.*
[27] substituendi] *unclear on microfilm.*   [28] quolibet] *from sense: microfilm unclear.*
[29] primo] *followed by a sign like a reverse* L *with two points before and parallel to the ascender.*
[30] tenor] *between lines.*   [31] subditis] *unclear:* sb'd' *ms.?*

nisi ³²[fuerit feriata, vel sequenti die si fuerit feriata, per se, vel] per procuratorem sufficienter instructum, vel idem procurator pro ipsa compareat coram nobis [³³responsura] libello seu /18// petitioni, quem seu quam procurator excellentissimi et potentissimi principis domini ³⁴Karoli dei gratia Francie et Navarre regis nobis tradidit, et nichilominus dicta die intendit tradere contra eam, cuius petitionis seu libelli, ut interim plene deliberare valeat super eo, tenorem in presenti citatorio /19// fecimus inseri sub hiis verbis:

(e) Coram vobis reverendo in Christo patre domino Stephano provisione divina episcopo ³⁵Parisiensi asserit et proponit ³⁶P. ³⁷Galvani procurator et procuratorio nomine incliti et excellentissimi principis domini ³⁸Karoli dei gratia Francie et Navarre regis quod predictus dominus ³⁹Karolus de facto /20// dumtaxat clandestine bannis omissis et alias minus legittime contraxit matrimonium cum domina Blancha quondam Comitis Burgundie filia sibi in gradibus prohibitis et diversis consanguinitatibus et respectu diversorum stipitum attinente et utroque ipsorum infra tempora pubertatis tunc temporis ⁴⁰existente /21// ex quibus causis et ⁴¹aliis de iure sibi non potuit dicta Blancha matrimonialiter copulare; nec potest ulterius idem princeps in predicto coniunctione sic illicita absque sue anime detrimento et multorum gravi scandalo remanere. Quare petit dictus procurator pronuntiari et per sententiam declarari de iure dictum matri- /22// -monium nullum fuisse et esse et eidem domino ⁴²regi licentiam impertiri cum altera libere contrahendi; et predicta petit omni modo et forma cum quibus melius sibi licet, non astringens se nisi ad ea dumtaxat probanda que sibi sufficere poterunt de premissis ad propositum consequendum, et protestatur de declarando, addendo et /23// minuendo quoties opus erit responsura et alias ulterius super contentis in predicta petitione debite processura et factura que fuerint rationis, significantes eidem quod sive venerit sive non nichilominus super predictis omnibus procedemus quantum de iure fieri poterit et debebit. Quidquid autem inde feceritis, nobis predictis loco et /24// die fideliter refferatis. Datum Parisius xxvᵐᵃ die ianuarii, anno Domini MᵒCCCᵒ vicesimo ⁴³primo.

(f) Petens quod ante omnia predictus Aymericus de sua procuratione faceret nobis fidem ut in tuto processus fieret cum eodem, et ibidem

³² fuerit feriata... per se, vel] *illegible because of crease in ms. (J 682.1): supplied* faute de mieux *from Bibliothèque nationale de France, Lat. 8935, fol. 28v.*

³³ responsura] *conjecturally supplied.*   ³⁴ Karoli] *preceded by double dot.*

³⁵ Parisiensi] Par' *ms.*   ³⁶ P.] *preceded by double dot.*

³⁷ Galvani] Malvani *ms.? Preceded by double dot.*

³⁸ Karoli] *preceded by double dot.*   ³⁹ Karoli] *preceded by double dot.*

⁴⁰ existente] existent' *ms. Present participle in ablative absolute phrase.*

⁴¹ aliis] al' *ms.*   ⁴² regi] *preceded by double dot.*

⁴³ primo] *followed by a sign like a closing square bracket (date unclear).*

dictus Aymericus ad faciendum fidem de procuratione sua produxit quoddam publicum in- /25// -strumentum, pro vero et publico – confectum per manum venerabilis viri domini Amici decani [44]Parisiensis publici auctoritate apostolica notarii, ut prima facie apparebat, et subscriptum et consignatum per discretum virum magistrum Iohannem de [45]Essartis publicum etiam eadem apostolica auctoritate notarium, ut prima facie legebatur /26// – sequentis continentie seu tenoris.

(g) In nomine Domini, amen. Per presens publicum [46]instrumentum pateat universis quod anno eiusdem Domini millesimo trecentesimo vicesimo primo [47]indictione quinta mense ianuarii eiusdem mensis die xxiiii^{a} pontificatus sanctissimi patris et domini domini Iohannis divina /27// providentia pape vicesimi secundi anno sexto, in presentia mei notarii publici et infrascriptorum testium personaliter constituta nobilis mulier domina Blancha de Burgundia non cauta nec dolo fraude vel machinatione cuiuslibet circonventa, inducta quomodolibet vel seducta, sed gratis /28// spontanea et sua libera voluntate et cum amicis suis plena deliberatione prehabita, ut dicebat, attendens se pluries et a fidedignis pluribus [48]audivisse matrimonium olim inter [49]exellentissimum principem dominum [50]Karolum nunc dei gratia Francie et Navarre regem illustrem et ipsam de facto dumtaxat /29// contractum [[51]fuisse]: et quod ex consanguinitatum impedimentis quibus ad invicem sunt notorie, sicut asseruit, coniuncti, et ex aliis pluribus obiectibus, defectibus, et multis aliis rationibus ipso iure communiter nullum esse dicitur et fuisse; et quod per consequens in anime sue preiudicium et populi grave scandalum redundaret si ulterius in /30// tali matrimonio, immo verius incestu, tam dampnabili remaneret; quodque non expedit, neque decet, propter fragilitatem sexus et decentiam sui status, se presertim frequenter iudicialibus anfractibus personaliter inmiscere, fecit, constituit, et ordinavit quotiens ipsam abesse contigerit, suos certos procuratores et nuntios /31// [52]speciales discretos viros Petrum de Culreto, Jocelinum de Borderia, Amblardum Serem clericos, et Aymericum Maserant domicellum et ipsorum quemlibet in solidum ita quod non sit nec esse possit melior conditio occupantis; – dans et concedens suis procuratoribus supradictis et cuilibet eorumdem generalem plenam et liberam potestatem /32// et [53]speciale mandatum agendi pro ipsa ad dicti [54]matrimonii nullitatem,

---

[44] Parisiensis] Par' *ms., so* Parisius *is possible.* [45] Essartis] Essart' *ms.*
[46] instrumentum] instumentum *ms.?*
[47] indictione] *inditione ms.; E. A. R. Brown informs me that this scribe frequently omits the* 'c'.
[48] audivisse] *preceded by deleted letters, possibly* se. [49] exellentissimum] *sic ms.*
[50] Karolum] *preceded by double dot.* [51] fuisse] *om. ms.*
[52] speciales] *rather than* spirituales *given the context.*
[53] speciale] *rather than* spirituale *given the context.*
[54] matrimonii] *followed by* two minims, *deleted.*

ipsamque super ipsius matrimonii nullitate, ex causa seu causis quibuslibet hoc procedit, coram venerabili in Christo patre domino dei gratia
Parisiensi episcopo suo competenti iudice, ut dicebat, et cuius iurisdictionem expresse pro maiori firmitate negotii /33// supradicti super
hoc prorogaverat, prout asseruit coram me et testibus infrascriptis; et
coram alio seu aliis iudice seu iudicibus ordinariis, delegatis, vel auditoribus quibuscumque quacumque auctoritate processerint, coniunctim
vel divisim, [55]quovismodo, ubicumque, etiam coram sanctissimo patre
et domino predicto nostro [56]summo pon- /34// -tifice, quandocumque
super dicto matrimonio vel incidentibus circa illud principaliter vel inci-
denter pertractari aut alias disceptari quomodolibet contigerit coram
ipso, [[57]defendendi] et libellum seu libellos, petitionem summariam seu
petitiones recipiendi, iurisdictionem ordinariam [58]et delegatam prorogandi tam tacite quam expresse, litem contestandi, /35// de calumpnia
et de veritate dicenda iurandi, et in ipsius constituentis animam subeundi quodlibet aliud iuramentum, processui ordinario renuntiandi et
processum summarium assumendi, ponendi et articulandi, positionibus
et articulis respondendi tam negando quam confitendo, testes et instrumenta producendi et contra se /36// producendos impugnandi et etiam
consentiendi si viderint expedire, renuntiandi et concludendi, sententias interlocutorias et diffinitivas audiendi, et ab eis appellandi vel ipsis
consentiendi tacite vel expresse, prout ipsis vel ipsorum alteri videbitur
faciendum, procuratores unum vel plures semel vel pluries substi- /37//
-tuendi sub consimili potestate, substitutosque revocandi, dilationibus et
exceptionibus sibi competentibus et competituris utendi et ipsis renuntiandi et cetera omnia et singula quecumque fuerint faciendi que ipsa
faceret et facere posset si personaliter presens esset, et que quomodolibet
in premissis vel circa premissa vel ipsorum quodlibet vel /38// exinde
dependentia vel dependere seu emergere poterunt de premissis vel in
premissis quoquo modo necessaria fuerint vel etiam oportuna, et [59]hoc
tam in iudicio quam extra iudicium, servato iuris ordine vel obmisso,
totaliter vel pro parte, etiam si ea omnia que fecerint insimul vel divisim
talia sint vel fuerint que mandatum /39// exigant speciale, promittens
michi notario infrascripto stipulanti et recipienti pro omnibus et singulis quorum interest vel interesse poterit in futurum se ratum et gratum habere et in perpetuum habituram quicquid per dictos procuratores
suos vel substituendos ab eis vel ipsorum altero insimul vel divisim dictum /40// factum concessum confessatum aut alias quomodolibet gestum
seu procuratum fuerit in premissis vel aliquo premissorum, necnon pro
ipsis et quolibet eorumdem iudicatum solvi, et sub suorum omnium

---

[55] quovismodo] *two superscript lines above* m *in ms.*   [56] Summo] *preceded by double dot.*
[57] defendendi] *om. ms.*   [58] et] *or* vel *(ms. is unclear).*   [59] hoc] *or* hec.

bonorum ypotheca ipsos et eorum quemlibet in predictis et ea tangentibus, relevando a quolibet genere satisdandi, requirens me et infrascrip-
tum notarium /41// ut de premissis omnibus et singulis reciperemus et faceremus publicum instrumentum, unum vel plura, coniunctim vel divisim, prout ab ipsa vel suis procuratoribus fuerimus
requisiti.

(h) [60]Acta sunt hec anno, inditione, mense, die et pontificatu premissis apud Castrum Gaillardi Rothomagensis diocesis, presentibus nobili et
magnifico viro /42// domino [61]Roberto de Attrebatesio Comite Bellimontis milite, nobilibus viris dominis Drocone de Roya, Iohanne de Villa
Petrosa, Theobaldo de Pomolun, militibus, magistris Petro de Novilla,
licentiato in legibus, canonico [62]Duacen' Attrebatensis diocesis, Iohanne
de Essartis, auctoritate sedis /43// apostolice notario publico, et quibusdam aliis viris et mulieribus domicellis familiaribus dicte Blanche,
testibus ad hoc vocatis specialiter et rogatis. Et ego Amisius de Aurelianis,
dictus 'le Ratif', clericus, auctoritate apostolica notarius publicus, premissis omnibus et singulis prout specificata sunt /44// superius et narrata
[63]una cum suprascriptis testibus presens interfui, ea vidi et audivi, et ea
in notula redacta in lingua materna dicte intelligibiliter exposui Blanche,
ac presens publicum instrumentum, quod inde ad rogatum dicte Blanche
manu propria confeci, in testimonium premissorum signo publico [64]meo
signavi rogatus. /45// Et ego Iohannes de Essartis, clericus Rothomagensis diocesis apostolica et imperiali auctoritate notarius publicus premissis
omnibus et singulis prout specificata sunt et narrata superius, una cum
notario publico et testibus suprascriptis, presens interfui, ea vidi et audivi,
ac presens [65]puplicum instrumentum de /46// predictis in notula in lingua
materna dicte Blanche per prefatum notarium publicum suprascriptum
intelligibiliter expositis, confectum signo et subscriptione meis una cum
signo et subscriptione ipsius notarii publici communivi, requisitus et
rogatus in testimonium premissorum.

(i) Quibus sic aprobatis /47// et peractis et utrique procuratorum predictorum debita data fide, procurator prefatus dicti domini regis petiit
libello alias a se nobis tradito, et in predicto citatorio contento, per procuratorem predictum prefate domine Blanche, sicut presens dies exigebat –
quem libellum ibidem repetiit et porrexit – cum instantia responderi,
asserens nos /48// esse super contentis in eodem iudicem competentem,
tum ratione domicilii predictorum domini [66]Karoli et Blanche tum etiam
ratione originis eorumdem, tum etiam ex prorogatione expressa iurisdictionis nostre in nos facta per dominam sepedictam sicut in instrumento

---

[60] Acta] *preceded by double dot.*   [61] Roberto] *preceded by double dot.*
[62] Duacen'] *probably* Duacensi *but possibly* Duaceno.   [63] una] *between lines.*
[64] meo] *between lines.*   [65] puplicum] *sic ms.*   [66] Karoli] *preceded by double dot.*

publico per manum predicti decani confecto inferius producendo asseruit
apparere. /49// Procurator autem dicte domine Blanche, a nobis interrogatus, confessus fuit dictam prorogationem fuisse factam, et nichilominus
ex habundanti predicti duo procuratores iurisdictionem nostram ex certa
scientia et ex potestate super hoc specialiter sibi data, sicut ex tenore predictorum [67]procuratoriorum superius productorum plenius /50// poterat
apparere, expresse prorogaverunt et voluerunt et consenserunt quod nos
de contentis in predicto libello et omnibus ad ea pertinentibus et pertinere
valentibus audire, cognoscere, et diffinire libere valeamus, tam in nostra diocesi quam in alia, si consensus ordinariorum locorum aliorum ad
hoc accedat, et quod in predictis, cum facti qua- /51// -litas hoc requirat,
summarie et de plano et sine strepitu iudicii et figura procedere valeamus
in totum vel in partem sicut nobis videbitur expedire. Post que predictus
magister Petrus libello suo cum instantia sicut prius petiit responderi,
cum pars adversa, que habuerat diu ante copiam predictorum citatorii
/52// et libelli plene deliberare potuisset, ut consulte posset et deberet
petitis et propositis respondere. Protestatus autem fuit quod ad sollemp-
nem libellum vel processum nisi quatenus de iure artatur se nullatenus
astringebat. Dictus autem Aymericus, super hoc interrogatus, confessus
fuit predictam dominam et se ipsum copiam dictorum /53// citatorii et
libelli competenti tempore habuisse et super responsione quam facere
proponebat cum predicta domina Blancha plene deliberasse, quibus
responsis iniunximus eidem quod petitioni seu libello predicto responderet; et tunc idem procurator respondit in hunc modum: In primis
confessus fuit matrimonium olim /54// fuisse contractum inter prefatos
dominum [68]Karolum et dominam Blancham, et quod prefatus dominus
Rex et Blancha se in consanguinitatum prohibitis gradibus attinebant,
quodque uterque predictorum tempore dicti matrimonii erant infra tempora pubertatis, et quod banna non fuerunt emissa, cum sicut dixit, non
[69]sit moris in talium /55// personarum matrimoniis quod banna huiusmodi premittantur. Cetera omnia, ut proponuntur, negavit esse vera,
dicens petita fieri non debere. Et ibidem dicti procuratores, in animas
dominorum suorum, secundum formam iuris, ex potestate in predictis
[70]procuratoriis specialiter super hoc sibi data prestiterunt de calumpnia
iuramentum, post [71]quod iuramentum presti- /56// -terunt in propositis et responsis, et statim prefatus magister Petrus quo supra nomine,
volens, ut dixit, quantum in se erat, et fieri poterat bono modo, cum

---

[67] procurator'] *ms.: but* procuratorum *is less likely because of the* productorum *which follows.*
[68] Karolum] *preceded by double dot.*   [69] sit] sic *ms.?*
[70] procurator'] *ms.: but* 'procuratoribus' *is less likely in context.*
[71] quod] *otiose strokes in ms.?*

celeritate matura causam procedere, ut brevius veritas elucescat et ut
prefati domini rex et Blancha non remaneant diutius in incestu, exibuit
et tradidit prefato procuratori domine /57// Blanche positiones et articulos insertos inferius in processu, quibus per [72]prestitum procuratoris
domine Blanche petiit responderi. Dictus autem procurator respondit
se super dictis positionibus et articulis non deliberasse et quod super
illis nolebat precipitare, petens quod daretur sibi dilatio in qua predicta
domina, que melius veritatem noverat, /58// responderet, vel ipse plena
deliberatione super hoc habita cum eadem. Et aliquantulum super hoc
[73]altercato, de consensu procuratorum predictorum, nos assignavimus
octavam diem [74]februarii apud Andeliacum in loco Gaillardi – voluntate
et potestate a reverendo in Christo patre domino G. divina providentia Rothomagensi [75]archiepiscopo /59// in cuius est diocesi, habitis super
hoc et obtentis, sicut per ipsius reverendi patris litteras inferius inserendas
plenius apparebat – ad respondendum predictis positionibus seu articulis
per dominam Blancham sepedictam, et alias ad procedendum debite, ut
iustitia suadabit.

(j) ¶ Tenor autem [76]predictarum positionum et articulorum pro-/60//-
curatori dicte domine Blanche superius traditorum sequitur sub hac
forma.

[77]Positiones et articulos infrascriptos dat procurator excellentissimi
principis domini [78]Karoli nunc dei gratia Francie et Navarre regis contra
dominam Blancham de Burgundia filiam quondam Comitis Burgundie
/61// in causa nullitatis matrimonii que vertitur inter ipsos coram reverendo in Christo patre domino Parisiensi episcopo.

(k) [1] ¶ In primis ponit et probare intendit quod inclite recordationis dominus Ludovicus quondam rex Francie, et domina Blancha de
Yspania, fuerunt coniuges et pro coniugibus se gesserunt et habiti et reputati /62// fuerunt temporibus suis in civitate et diocesi Parisiensi et in
toto regno Francie et aliis locis publice et [79]communiter.

[2] ¶ Item quod idem dominus Ludovicus rex ex ipsa domina Blancha
uxore sua genuit dominum Ludovicum sanctum et Robertum primum
qui fuit Comes Attrebatensis, quodque ipse dominus /63// Ludovicus rex
fuit pater ipsorum Ludovici sancti et Roberti primi et ipsi, Ludovicus
sanctus et Robertus primus, fuerunt inter se fratres ac filii eorumdem
domini Ludovici et domine Blanche et pro talibus ipsi parentes et filii se

---

[72] prestitum] *read* prestitum iuramentum.   [73] altercato] *from sense:* altercat' *ms.*
[74] februarii] februr' *ms.?*   [75] archiepiscopo] *preceded by double dot.*
[76] predictarum ... traditorum] *the difference in gender is stylistic awkwardness not scribal error.*
[77] Positiones] *preceded by double dot.*   [78] Karoli] *preceded by double dot.*
[79] communiter] *followed by* credit articulum esse verum *deleted.*

gesserunt et habiti et reputati fuerunt temporibus suis et locis predictis publice et communiter.

[3] ¶ Item quod dictus dominus /64// Ludovicus sanctus, qui postmodum fuit rex Francie, genuit Philippum primum et fuit pater ipsius Philippi primi et ipse Philippus fuit filius [80]eiusdem Ludovici sancti et pro talibus se gesserunt et habiti et reputati fuerunt temporibus suis et locis predictis publice et communiter.

[4] ¶ Item quod idem dominus Philippus primus genuit dominum /65// Philippum secundum qui fuit Rex Francie, et ipse dominus Philippus primus fuit pater eiusdem domini Philippi secundi, et idem dominus Philippus secundus fuit filius ipsius domini Philippi primi, et pro talibus se gesserunt et habiti et reputati fuerunt temporibus suis et locis predictis publice et communiter.

[5] ¶ Item quod dictus dominus Philippus secundus rex Francie genuit /66// supradictum [81]Karolum nunc regem Francie ex domina Iohanna [82]regina Navarre, et ipse dominus Philippus secundus rex fuit pater eiusdem domini [83]Karoli. Et idem dominus [84]Karolus fuit et est filius dicti domini Philippi secundi, quondam regis, et pro talibus se gesserunt tempore quo vivebat idem dominus Philippus secundus et dicto tempore et habiti et reputati /67// fuerunt, et se gerit, habetur et reputatur idem dominus Karolus et in locis predictis publice et notorie et communiter.

[6] ¶ Item quod supradictus dominus Robertus primus genuit dominum Robertum secundum, et ipse dominus Robertus primus fuit pater eiusdem domini Roberti secundi, et idem dominus Robertus secundus fuit filius domini Roberti primi et consanguineus germanus /68// dicti domini Philippi primi, et pro talibus se gesserunt et habiti et reputati fuerunt temporibus suis et locis predictis publice et communiter.

[7] ¶ Item quod idem dominus Robertus secundus genuit dominam Matildim nunc Comitissam Attrabatensem, et idem dominus Robertus secundus fuit pater ipsius domine Matildis, et ipsa domina Matildis fuit filia et est /69// eiusdem domini Roberti secundi, et pro talibus se gesserunt et habiti et reputati fuerunt temporibus suis et locis predictis publice et communiter, et adhuc se gerit et habetur et reputatur eadem domina Mathildis.

[8] ¶ Item quod domina Matildis peperit dominam Blancham filiam quondam Comitis Burgundie, mariti ipsius domine Matildis, et ipsa domina Matildis /70// fuit et est mater eiusdem domine Blanche et ipsa

---

[80] eiusdem Ludovici] *supplied from sense – physical damage in ms.*
[81] Karolum] *preceded by double dot.*   [82] regina] reg' *ms., probably inserted after correction.*
[83] Karoli] *preceded by double dot.*   [84] Karolus] *preceded by double dot.*

domina Blancha fuit et est filia eiusdem domine Matildis, et pro talibus se gesserunt at habite et reputate fuerunt, et adhuc se gerunt, et habentur, et reputantur in predictis locis.

[9] ¶ Item quod ipsi dominus Karolus et domina Blancha in quarto gradu ex utroque latere /71// ⁸⁵suprascripte et designate consanguinitatis se attigerunt et attingunt.

[10] ¶ Item quod de predictis est et fuit publica vox et fama et predicta sunt et fuerunt publica et notoria temporibus et locis predictis.

[11] ¶ Item ponit et probare intendit quod supradictus dominus Robertus primus, filius supradictorum domini Ludovici regis et /72// domine Blanche coniugum, et domina Matildis de Brebantia fuerunt coniuges et pro coniugibus se gesserunt et habiti et reputati fuerunt temporibus suis, et supradictis locis, publice et communiter.

[12] ¶ Item quod idem dominus Robertus primus ex ipsa domina Matildi uxore sua genuit supradictum dominum Robertum secundum et dominam /73// Blancham que postea fuit uxor Regis Navarre, et ipsi dominus Robertus secundus et domina Blancha predicta fuerunt inter se frater et soror ac filii eorumdem domini Roberti et domine Matildis de Brebantia, et ipse dominus Robertus primus fuit pater ipsorum domini Roberti secundi et domine Blanche et pro talibus ipsi /74// parentes et filii se gesserunt et habiti et reputati fuerunt temporibus suis et locis predictis publice et communiter.

[13] ¶ Item quod dicta domina Blancha soror predicti domini Roberti secundi peperit dominam Iohannam quondam Reginam Francie, et fuit uxor supradicti domini Philippi secundi regis, et ipsa domina Blancha fuit mater ipsius /75// domine Iohanne et eadem domina Iohanna fuit filia ipsius domine Blanche, et pro talibus se gesserunt et habite et reputate fuerunt temporibus suis et locis predictis publice et communiter.

[14] ¶ Item quod dicta domina Iohanna peperit supradictum dominum Karolum nunc regem Francie, et fuit mater eiusdem domini Karoli /76// et ipse dominus Karolus fuit et est filius eiusdem domine Iohanne, et pro talibus se gesserunt, et habiti et reputati fuerunt et ⁸⁶adhuc se gerit, habetur, et reputatur idem dominus Karolus rex in dictis locis publice et communiter.

[15] ¶ Item quod dictus Robertus secundus genuit dominam Matildim Comitissam Attrebatensem et /77// fuit pater eiusdem domine Matildis et predicta domina Matildis fuit et est filia dicti domini Roberti secundi et consanguinea et germana prefate domine Iohanne Regine Francie, et pro talibus se gesserunt et habiti et reputati fuerunt et se gerit, habetur et

⁸⁵ suprascripte et designate] suprascript' et designat'.   ⁸⁶ adhuc] *between lines.*

reputatur dicta domina Matildis locis predictis publice et communiter. /78//

[16] ¶ Item ponit et probare intendit quod predicta domina Matildis peperit dictam dominam Blancham et fuit et est mater ipsius domine Blanche et dicta domina Blancha fuit et est filia dicte domine Matildis et pro talibus se gesserunt et reputaverunt et habite et reputate fuerunt et se gerunt et reputant et habentur et reputantur in /79// dictis locis publice et communiter.

[17] ¶ Item, quod supradicti dominus Karolus et Blancha, filia quondam predicti Comitis Burgundie et supradicte domine Matildis, in tertio gradu ex utroque latere suprascripte et designate consanguinitatis a stipite supradicto domino Roberto primo se attigerunt et attingunt.

[18] ¶ Item quod [87]nedum de iure /80// sed etiam secundum communem modum loquendi ubique illi reputantur esse consanguinei et coniuncti in tertio gradu ex utroque latere quando uterque descendit a communi stipite per suam lineam transversalem in gradu tertio ut sunt pronepotes, scilicet filii duorum consanguineorum germanorum, et illi in quarto ex utroque /81// latere, quorum quilibet descendit per suam lineam in quarto gradu a stipite, sicut [88]apnepotes; et illi in tertio et quarto quorum unus a communi stipite computando descendit in tertio per suam lineam, et alter per alteram lineam sub eodem stipite descendit in quarto gradu, ut sunt pronepos et abneptis, et quod iste /82// est communis et usitatus modus loquendi et intelligendi coniunctos esse in tertio gradu ex utroque latere, vel in quarto ex utroque latere, vel in tertio et quarto gradu simul simpliciter; et ita est servatum, usitatum, intellectum et reputatum notorie, publice et communiter in toto regno Francie, et terris et locis convicinis et etiam /83// in curia romana et in Francia inter omnes et specialiter inter illos de genere [89]Francorum a tantis temporibus et per tanta tempora de quibus hominum memoria in contrarium non existit.

[19] ¶ Item quod de predictis est publica vox et fama et eadem fuerunt et sunt publica et notoria, locis et temporibus supradictis.

[20] ¶ Item quod tempore quo /84// contraxit idem dominus Karolus de facto cum sepedicta domina Blancha nondum attigerat [90]tredicimum etatis sue annum, sed infra ipsum annum existebat quodque de hoc, tempore eiusdem matrimonii, erat, et postea fuit, et est, publica vox et fama in locis supradictis.

[21] ¶ Item ponit et probare intendit quod idem dominus Karolus rex /85// erat et ante fuerat inhabilis, simplex, et [91]inbecillis, discretione

---

[87] nedum] nondum *or* necdum *ms.*   [88] apnepotes] *i.e.* abnepotes.
[89] Francorum] Franc' *ms.*   [90] tredecimum] xiii^cim *ms.?*   [91] inbecillis] *in full with* n.

carens pro [92]querenda uxore in locis proximis et remotis et pro discernendo que erat sibi condecens secundum exigentiam sui status, et talis a quo corporis valor vel animi, presertim in talibus vel circa talia, erat penitus alienus, quodque de hiis, tempore /86// ipsius matrimonii erat, et ante fuerat, et postea fuit et est communis opinio et credulitas hominum dictorum locorum ac publica vox et fama in locis eisdem.

[22] ¶ Item quod tempore dicti matrimoniii, et ante ab infantia sua et post, multe mulieres sublimes, etiam de regali progenie descendentes, tam in partibus proximis quam remotis, /87// repperiebantur et repperiri poterant faciliter et commode, quarum quamlibet dictus dominus Karolus, nunc rex Francie, secundum exigentiam sui status in quo tunc erat – scilicet sine terra et sine comitatu, et tertio genitus dicti domini Philippi secundi Francie regis – sibi poterat decenter absque dispensationis gratia matrimonialiter copulare /88// si etatem ad matrimonium contrahendum aptam habuisset; et huiusmodi sublimes mulieres repperiebantur et repperiri poterant faciliter et commode postquam ipse dominus Karolus ad annos pervenit pubertatis et ante, et quod eedem sublimes persone in nullo gradu prohibito consanguinitatis vel affinitatis attin-/89//-gebant eundem dominum Karolum, sed extra omnem gradum prohibitum ab eodem domino Karolo existebant, et erant remote, vel si attinebant, saltem non in tam proximis; et inter alias personas sublimes erant infrascripte, videlicet soror regis Yspanie, que contraxit postmodum cum duce Britannie, et adhuc est eius uxor; /90// item soror dicti ducis, adhuc superstes et nondum coniugatus; item domina Clementia, que fuit postmodum uxor regis Ludovici fratris dicti Karoli; item aliqua de filiabus domini Comitis Sancti Pauli; item soror regis Boemie, adhuc superstes et non coniugata, et multe alie; quodque quelibet personarum earumdem sublimium /91// poterat secundum ipsius domini Karoli predicti status, in quo tunc erat, exigentiam matrimonialiter copulari, et eidem domino Karolo eque decenter sicut supradicta domina Blancha filia quondam comitis Burgundie, etiam si ipse dominus Karolus ad contrahendum matrimonium cum ipsa domina Blancha [93]sufficientem /92// dispensationem habuisset.

[23] ¶ Item quod predicte domine cum quibus ut prefertur contrahere potuisset erant tanti status vel maioris in genere et alias quanti consueverunt esse ille que olim cum filiis regum [94]Francie contrahere consueverunt, presertim cum ultimo genitis.

[24] ¶ Item quod de predictis est et fuit publica vox /93// et fama, et eadem fuerunt et sunt publica et notoria locis et temporibus supradictis.

---

[92] querenda uxore] *sic, though* querendo uxorem *might have been expected.*
[93] sufficienter] sufficient' *ms.*   [94] Francie] *followed by* regum, *deleted.*

[**25**] ¶ Item ponit et probare intendit quod tempore contracti matrimonii inter ⁹⁵dictos dominum Karolum nunc regem Francie et predictam
dominam Blancham filiam quondam comitis Burgundie eadem domina
Blancha xi. annum etatis sue /94// nondum attigerat, sed infra ipsum
annum existebat, quodque de hiis tempore eiusdem contracti matrimonii
erat et postea fuit et est communis opinio et credulitas hominum dictorum locorum, et publica vox, et fama, et eadem erant publica et notoria
in eisdem locis.

[**26**] ¶ Item ponit et probare intendit quod uterque predictorum, scilicet
/95// dominus Karolus et domina Blancha, propter deffectum etatis et
tenuitatem corporis ⁹⁶erant impotentes ad carnis copulam tempore dicti
matrimonii contracti quodque de hiis erat et ante fuerat vox et fama
publica, et adhuc est et erant premissa notoria et publica dicto tempore
in locis predictis.

[**27**] ¶ Item ponit et probare inten- /96// -dit quod dictum matrimonium inter dictos dominum Karolum et dominam Blancham contractum fuit contractu omissis bannis de iure introductis ad opponendum
impedimenta que erant contra ipsum matrimonium contrahendum; et
fuerunt sollempnitates omisse que debent et consueverunt servari super
⁹⁷matrimoniis contrahendis; quodque /97// ipsum matrimonium inter
eosdem dictum dominum Karolum et dominam Blancham fuit clandestine contractum, et de hiis est publica vox et fama.

[**28**] ¶ Item ponit et probare intendit quod dictum matrimonium fuit
contractum, licet clandestine, alibi quam in locis et parrochiis unde erant
prefati dominus Karolus et domina Blancha ori- /98// -iundi et alibi quam
in ecclesiis de quarum parrochiis ipsi vel ipsorum alter existerent, et
non per curatos suos seu alterius eorumdem, et etiam absque licentia
eorumdem curatorum, et sunt et fuerunt premissa notoria tempore dicti
matrimonii et post et est et fuit de ipsis publica vox et fama in locis
predictis.

[**29**] ¶ Item ponit /99// et probare intendit quod adveniente tempore pubertatis utriusque ipsi dominus Karolus et Blancha absque alia
⁹⁸sollempnitate in ⁹⁹matrimoniis solito facienda, et absque novo alio seu
expresso consensu, in predicta coniunctione sic illicita remanserunt, et
de hoc est et fuit communis opinio, publica vox et fama, in locis et /100//
tempore predictis.

---

⁹⁵ dictos . . . predictam] *sic ms.*
⁹⁶ erant impotentes ad] *apparently after correction, and preceded by mark which may have
indicated need for it.*
⁹⁷ matrimoniis contrahendis] matrimon' contrahend' *ms.*
⁹⁸ sollempnitate] sollepnitate *ms.*
⁹⁹ matrimoniis solito facienda] matrim' solit' faciend' *ms.*

[**30**] ¶ Item ponit et probare intendit quod predicta domina Matildis, mater prefate domine Blanche fuit presens personaliter in baptismo dicti domini Karoli, ipsumque tenuit supra fontes baptismales, [100]et fuit eius matrina, una cum quibusdam [101]aliis, et alias egit circa dictum baptismum, et fecit taliter, quod cognatio spiritualis [102]sequta fuit et /101// contracta inter predictam dominam Matildim et predictam dominam Blancham ex una parte [103]et parentes dicti domini Karoli, et ipsum etiam dominum Karolum [104]ex altera, sic quod idem dominus Karolus contrahere non potuit [105]cum predicta domina Blancha, et sunt et fuerunt hec publica et notoria, et pro veris habita, et communiter reputata, et est et fuit de ipsis communis opinio, publica vox, et /102// fama in locis predictis.

[**31**] ¶ Item ponit quod de omnibus supradictis, tam coniunctim quam divisim, et de quolibet eorumdem, est communis opinio, publica vox et fama.

(l) Et insuper [106]protestatur procurator prefatus dicti domini Karoli quod possit positiones et articulos declarare predictos corrigere et reformare /103// si opus fuerit, et alios dare, quodque non [107]astringit ad probanda omnia supradicta nisi dumtaxat ad ea que sibi sufficient de premissis ad propositum consequendum. /104//

. . .

> The following passage seems to show the legal team of Blanche putting up some resistance. To find it, go to the third membrane, which, after the notarial signs: 'Et fuerunt per nos singulariter et secrete examinati.' To make it easier to identify the relevant passage in the document I start the line numbering not from the start of the document but from the beginning of this third membrane.

(m) /44// 'Procurator autem dicte domine Blanche dixit se velle proponere deffensiones suas secundum quod presens dies requirebat et predictas suas deffensiones /45// proposuit et tradidit sub hiis verbis. [108]Coram vobis, reverendo in Christo patre domino [109]Stephano [110]divina providentia episcopo Parisiensi excipiendo proponit Aymericus Mazerant procurator et nomine procuratorio nobilis domine domine Blanche de Burgundia contra /46 // procuratorem excellentissimi et potentissimi principis domini Karoli dei gratia Francie et Navarre regis [111]dicens quod non obstantibus consanguinitatibus quibus prefatus dominus rex

---

[100] et fuit eius matrina] *between lines.*   [101] aliis, et alias] al' et al' *ms.*
[102] sequta] *between lines.*   [103] et parentes dicti domini Karoli] *between lines.*
[104] ex altera] *between lines.*   [105] cum predicta domina] *after* cum predicto domin *deleted.*
[106] protestatur] protestatus *could be read.*   [107] astringit] *read* astringit se *or* astringitur?
[108] Coram] *preceded by double dot.*   [109] Stephano] *preceded by double dot.*
[110] divina] *otiose abbreviation in ms.?*   [111] dicens] *between lines.*

et domina Blancha predicta ad invicem sunt coniuncti nec aliis propositis per partem prefati pro- /47// -curatoris dicti domini regis ex quibus petit matrimonium olim contractum inter prefatos dominum regem et dominam Blancham pronuntiari nullum esse et fuisse et dari dicto domino regi licentiam cum altera contrahendi, dictum matrimonium est et fuit ratum, validum et /48// canonicum, nec potest nec debet quomodolibet annullari nec etiam esse nullum quomodolibet declarari, pro eo et ex eo quia super predictis impedimentis ex quibus predictum matrimonium asseritur esse nullum fuit per felicis recordationis dominum [112]Clementem quintum sacrosancte [113]et /49// et universalis ecclesie summum pontificem [114]ex certa scientia, [115]secundum mentem suam et ex iustis causis que ipsum induxerunt ad dispensationem huiusmodi faciendam, rite et canonice et de sue plenitudine potestatis, sicut sibi licuit, dispensatum, prout ex litteris ipsius summi pon- /50// -tificis super dispensatione [116]predicta [117]factis plenius poterit apparere, pretextu cuius dispensationis [118]prefati dominus rex et Blancha matrimonium contraxerunt et [119]insimul longo tempore steterunt, et liberos suceperunt palam et publice bona fide, quare dicit dictum matrimonium non fore pronuntiandum nullum nec etiam /51// domino regi cum altera contrahendi licentiam [120]dandam esse. – Quibus petit pro parte dicti domini regis responderi, et si negentur, ad probandum se admitti, offerens de premissis facere promptam fidem. Et ibidem procurator dicti domini regis negavit super predictis consanguinitatibus /52// quibus constat ipsos adinvicem attinere et super spirituali [121]cognatione per quam etiam sunt coniuncti et super aliis impedimentis per que dictum matrimonium ipso iure est et a principio fuit nullum esse vel fuisse per predictum dominum Clementem seu per quemlibet alium dispensatum et [122]etiam si /53// aliqua dispensatio super impedimentis aliquibus fuit facta, dicit quod predicta dispensatio est et a principio tamquam subreptitia fuit nulla, vel si tenuit, dicit quod impedimenta dictam nullitatem inducentia quomodolibet non includit, et [[123] ... /54// ...] sicut obtulit idem procurator immediate proponere

---

[112] Clementem] *preceded by double dot.*   [113] et/48// et] *sic ms.*

[114] ex certa scientia . . . mentem suam] *possibly written over erasure.*

[115] secundum mentem . . . dispensare] *or emend thus:* [dispensatum] secundum mentem suam et ex iustis causis que ipsum induxerunt ad dispensationem huiusmodi faciendam, rite et canonice et de sue plenitudine potestatis, sicut sibi licuit dispensare [dispens' *ms.*]: *evidence of correction undertaken at the beginning of this passage suggests how a word might have dropped out while the scribe was modifying what he had originally written.*

[116] predicta] predictis *ms.?*   [117] factis] *between lines.*

[118] prefati . . . contraxerunt et] *possibly written over erasure.*   [119] insimul] *between lines.*

[120] dandam] dand' *ms.*   [121] cognatione] *smudged in ms.*

[122] *Supplied in margin, preceded by an omission mark whose counterpart I cannot find in the text, and hard to read: the transcription and position are guessed from sense and context.*

[123] . . . /54// . . .] *deleted words – preceded by* 'va' *for* 'vacat' *in ms.:* 'adhuc si secundum suum tenorem potuisset, sicut non /55// potest, nichilominus, attenta forma ipsius et hec que

et docere, exhibita dicta dispensatione per quam excipiebat pars adversa, procuratore dicte domine Blanche contrarium asserente et protestante. Et cum [124]idem procurator dicte domine Blanche non /55// haberet in promptu probationes paratas super superius exceptatis, petiit ad hoc sibi brevem terminum aliquem assignari ad probandum. Et altercato huic et inde super predictis [125]propositis a qualibet partium predictarum, attendentes quod in causa presenti procedendum erat summarie et de plano et quod ni- /56// -chilominus pars utraque habuerant multas dilationes, volentes negotio brevem finem imponere sed maturum sicut et personarum et negotii qualitas exigebat, de voluntate et assensu procuratorum partium predictarum ordinavimus in hunc modum, videlicet quod procurator dicte domine Blanche /57// probet quicquid probare voluerit de premissis infra diem martis que erit ante festum Annunciationis Dominice inclusive, et quod interim mittamus apud Creodelium pro predictis testibus audiendis . . . /58// . . . /63// . . . Item anno quo supra predicta die martis ante festum Adnuntiationis Dominice superius assignata comparuerunt procuratores qui supra [126]ubi supra, et nominibus quibus /64// supra, coram nobis, presentibus reverendis patribus et notariis sepedictis, et tunc procurator prefate domine Blanche ad probandum ea que per viam exceptionis proposuerat exhibuit et produxit pro vera et autentica quamdam litteram papalem, cum vera bulla plumbea impendenti /65// in serico, non abolitam nec vitiatam, ut prima facie apparebat, dictam dispensationem continentem. Cuius tenor noscitur esse talis: [127]'Clemens episcopus . . . '

The conclusion of the document

The passage transcribed below starts towards the end of the fifth line from the end of the document, above the notarial signs.

(n) Acta sunt hec anno, inditione, mense, die / et pontificatu predictis, apud castrum Gaillardi, Rothomagensis diocesis, presentibus [names follow] . . . In quorum testimonium nos prefatus Parisiensis episcopus coram / quo omnia predicta sunt facta sicut superius per ordinem continentur; et nos prefatus Iohannes divina miseratione Belvacensis

---

circa dictum [*ms.* dominum] matrimonium non iuvasset'. *The deletions and additions in this very formal document around the point when the dispensation argument is used suggest that there was some disarray and redrafting.*

[124] idem /55// procurator dicte domine Blanche] *written over lines* /54// *and* /55// *and also in the margin. The marginal words are scarcely legible but, minus the* 'dicte', *appear to duplicate – or to have been replaced by – the words interlined.*

[125] propositis] *between lines, preceded by strokes, possibly* s *but possibly part of the omission sign.*
[126] ubi supra] *added between lines.*   [127] Clemens] *preceded by double dot.*

episcopus, et Gauffridus de [128]Pleeio, qui premissis interfuimus, ad preces et requisitionem predicti reverendi patris domini Parisiensis Episcopi, sigilla nostra premissis omnibus / in assertionem et testimonium veritatis, videlicet in cordis quibus quatuor rotuli predicti totum processum, coram dicto reverendo patre factum nobis presentibus, continentes, ad invicem sunt ligati, et in cordellis de serico ultimo rothulo adherentes.

---

[128] Pleeio] *read* Pleyio *or* Plexio? *At any rate this must be the Geoffrey de Plexey to whom Pope John XXII several times refers in his definitive sentence.*

Appendix 2   Paris, Archives nationales, J.682.2

Physical description

Parchment: long strip folded rather than in roll form, consisting of sheets of parchment fastened together. Width *c.* 42.5 cm; length *c.* 690 cm (!); ruled in pencil; paraph marks in the margin: together with large capitals, they mark out depositions of new witnesses. On verso of first sheet: 'Attestationes testium examinatorum in causa divortii mota inter ¹dominum Karolum Franc(orum) et Navarre regem et dominam Blancham de Burgundia filiam comitisse attrebatensis'.

Note: In the transcription, ¶ = paraph mark, in margin unless otherwise specified. In the apparatus criticus, '*ms.*' = Paris, Archives nationales, J.682.2. The paragraphing is editorial; its purpose is to help readers match up the English translation with the Latin.

(a) Sequntur depositiones testium productorum per procuratorem excellentissimi principis domini Karoli dei gratia ²Francie et Navarre regis, contra dominam Blancham de Burgondia et eius procuratorem super causa nullitatis matrimonii olim inter ipsos /1// de facto, sicut dicitur, contracti, qui testes in presentia partium coram nobis Parisiensi Episcopo presentibus et assistentibus reverendis patribus dominis Belvacensi episcopo, et magistro Gaufrido de Plexeyo, notario domini pape, iuraverunt super articulis infra- /2//- scriptis deponere veritatem, et fuerunt examinati per nos in presentia predictorum reverendorum patrum, et notariorum infrascriptorum, et deposuerunt ut in sequentibus continetur . . .

(lines 1–3)

Resuming line 521:

(b) ¶ Dominus Radulphus de Mullento canonicus Parisiensis etatis lx annorum vel circa, interrogatus super primo articulo deposuit per suum Iuramentum super eo de auditu dici super contentis in eo prout in

¹ dominum] *added above line.*
² Francie] Franc' *ms., here and below, but Francie is spelled out in full once in* J.682.1.

dicto articulo continetur et de ³hoc fuit fama tempore /521// suo prout
dixit. Et idem deposuit de contentis in secundo articulo, sed adiecit
quod vidit dictum sanctum Ludovicum et duos fratres suos, videlicet
Comitem Andegavensem et Comitem Pictavensem, non tamen vidit dictum dominum Robertum primum, sicut dixit, sed erat fama /522// dicto
tempore quod fuerat frater predicti sancti Ludovici et quod fuerat mortuus apud ⁴Lamassorr' in primo passagio quod fecit sanctus Ludovicus.
Interrogatus super iiiᵒ, iiiiᵒ, vᵒ, viᵒ, viiᵒ, viiiᵒ, xiᵒ, xiiᵒ, xiiiᵒ, xiiiiᵒ, xvᵒ, et
xviᵒ ⁵articulis ipsis sibi /523// ⁶singulariter et sigillatim expositis, dixit per
iuramentum suum se vidisse pluries personas in predictis articulis contentas et designatas – excepto hoc quod dicitur in xiᵒ articulo et in dicto
xiiᵒ articulo de dicto Roberto primo et de dicta domina /524// Mathildi
uxore sua, quos non recolit se vidisse – se gerere et habere et haberi
publice et reputari communiter ab omnibus qui habebant temporibus
eorum notitiam de eisdem pro coniunctis secundum modum et formam
in predictis ⁷articulis contentas et ut /525// in ipsis continentur, et hoc
deposuit seriatim super quolibet de predictis articulis. Item, interrogatus super xviiiᵒ dixit per iuramentum suum ⁸quod ⁹pronepotes stipitis,
quando unus descendit per unam ¹⁰lineam usque ad tertium gradum a
stipite /526 // computando, et alius per aliam lineam transversalem in
eodem tertio gradu, esse coniunctos in tertio gradu ex utroque latere,
sicut sunt predicti dominus Karolus et Blancha in ea consanguinitate in
qua dominus Robertus primus ¹¹ponitur pro stipite; /527 // ¹²abnepotes
autem, id est ¹³filios pronepotum, coniunctos esse in quarto utroque
latere, sicut sunt predicti dominus Karolus et Blancha in consanguinitate in qua fit computatio a patre sancti Ludovici sumpto pro stipite, et
illos qui descendunt ¹⁴impariter /528// videlicet 'pronepos' et 'abneptis',
coniungi in duobus gradibus, videlicet in tertio et quarto; et iste modus
¹⁵erat computandi et reputandi ¹⁶coniunctos in dictis gradibus in regno

---

³ hoc] *the abbreviation used is more commonly used for* 'hec' *but in this document the context
repeatedly indicates* hoc.

⁴ *Italicised letters unclear: but this refers to Mansoura.*

⁵ articulis] articul' *ms.:* articulo *is also possible but except where it is spelled out, as at line 569,
I have guessed at a plural extension of this repeated abbreviation.*

⁶ *Between 523 and 524 there is a large blank space. Just before the writing begins again at line
524, in the left-hand margin there is an* 'viii'.

⁷ articulis] *between lines.*

⁸ quod . . . esse coniunctos] 'quod' *clause ungrammatically turns into an accusative and infinitive construction.*

⁹ pronepotes] pronepote *ms.?*

¹⁰ *Followed by hairline and space – possibly a hole invisible on microfilm.*

¹¹ ponitur] *corr. from* ponen.   ¹² abnepotes] abnepot' *ms.*

¹³ filios] fil' *ms.*   ¹⁴ impariter] impart' *ms.*   ¹⁵ erat] *conjecture: om. ms.*

¹⁶ coniunctos] *out of context, abbreviation would be extended as* coniunctis.

Francie secundum quod tempore suo computavit et ab aliis audivit computari. Idem /529 // testis interrogatus super xxx° articulo dixit se nescire
pro certo, nisi de auditu dici. Dixit tamen quod communiter dicitur ita
esse sicut in predicto articulo continetur, et hoc ipse audivit dici a multis,
sicut dixit. Super ceteris articulis nec etiam /530// super istis nichil aliud
pertinens [17]dixit. Dixit per suum iuramentum quod non deposuit timore,
odio, comodo vel amore, sed pro dicenda veritate, prout dixit. /531//

(c) ¶ Magister Aldricus, iurisperitus, canonicus Metensis, oriundus
de Ytalia, interrogatus super xviii° articulo, super quo tantummodo fuit
productus, dixit per suum iuramentum quod, secundum modum et com-
putationem communem et notoriam in partibus Ytalie, illi qui /532// a
stipite [18]descendunt quilibet per suam lineam in tertio gradu ex suo latere
vocantur et reputantur coniuncti in tertio gradu ex utroque latere; et illi
quorum quilibet descendit in quarto gradu per suam lineam vocantur et
reputantur /533// coniuncti in quarto gradu ex utroque latere; et illi quorum unus in suo latere descendit in tertio gradu et alter, qui in alio latere
descendit, [19]in quarto, vocantur et reputantur coniuncti in comparatione
eiusdem stipitis; et hoc /534// reputat idem testis certum et notorium in
partibus Ytalicis, et sic vidit et audivit toto tempore suo computari et
reputari, nec vidit nec audivit quod aliter computaretur, sicut dixit idem
testis. /535//

(d) ¶ Dominus Amanuel, iurisperitus, canonicus sancti Marcelli, testis
iuratus et diligenter interrogatus super xviii° articulo, super quo tantummodo fuit productus, dixit per iuramentum suum quod in partibus Ytalie
unde traxit originem in computatione gra- /536// -duum, ad sciendum in
quo gradu aliqui sunt coniuncti computatur gradus videlicet tertius ex
utroque latere quando duo in transversalibus lineis quilibet per latus sue
linee descendit a communi stipite in tertio gradu, et in quarto gradu ex
utroque quando quilibet per suum /537// [20]latus descendit in quarto, et
[21]illi [22]in tertio quando unus descendit ex uno latere in tertio, alius ex
alio in quarto – ipsum [*end of passage inserted between lines*] quod [23]nepos
unius lateris et abneptis [24]alterius lateris – et ita appellantur et reputantur esse in tertio ex utroque latere, vel in quarto ex utroque latere, vel
in tertio et quarto, et [25]hoc communis computatio et communis modus
loquendi in partibus illis /538// sicut in istis partibus, et hoc vidit et audivit

---

[17] dixit] *om. ms. and supplied from sense.*   [18] descendunt] descendu' *ms.*
[19] in quarto, vocantur] *read* in quarto, in tertio et in quarto vocantur? *Error by eyeskip.*
[20] latus . . . in quarto – ipsum] *between lines.*   [21] illi] ¹i *ms., so* ibi *also possible.*
[22] in tertio] *read:* in tertio et in quarto?   [23] nepos] *read:* pronepos?
[24] alterius] *from sense: otiose stroke in ms.?*
[25] hoc] hec *could be read: the abbreviation is the same with this scribe and neither can be excluded*
grammatically.

pluries idem testis, ut dixit, et est hoc notorium in predictis partibus inter
omnes quando computant consanguinitates suas vel aliquorum qui vol-
unt inter se contrahere, secundum quod gradus accidit /539// equaliter
vel inequaliter. Interrogatus unde est oriundus, dixit quod de civitate
Placentie.

(e) [26]¶ Guillelmus de Placentia, testis iuratus et diligenter examina-
tus super predicto xviii° articulo ipso sibi /540// exposito dixit se pro
certo credere contenta in predicto articulo vera esse, et quod aliqui
[27]reputabantur esse coniuncti in tertio ex utroque latere vel in quarto
ex utroque vel in tertio et quarto secundum quod in predicto articulo
continetur. /541//

(f) ¶ Domina Ysabellis de [28]Soyziaco testis iurata et diligenter exam-
inata super quibusdam articulis qui sequuntur, super quibus fuit petita
examinari, et primo super xx° articulo. Dixit per iuramentum suum quod
dictus dominus Karolus habuit /542// in die veneris ante festum beati
Iohannis Baptiste preteritum xxvii annos et non amplius, et hoc scit quia
nutrivit et [29]ablatavit eum a principio, et quod xiiii anni fuerunt preteriti inter festum nativitatis Domini et festum Purificationis /543// beate
Marie preterita quod [30]cuntraxit cum dicta domina Blancha, et sic dicto
tempore non habebat xiiii annos, et de hoc perfecte recordatur, ut dixit,
et fuit dictum matrimonium dicto tempore factum [31]a [32]Hedyn. Super
xxi° articulo interrogatus dixit per suum /544// iuramentum quod dictus
dominus Karolus erat simplex et sine malitia et indiscretus presertim
pro querenda sibi decenter uxore et secundum conditionem suam et
secundum etatem, ut dixit. Super xxii° articulo dixit se pro certo /545//
credere quod et de nominatis in dicto articulo et de aliis reperisset sibi
eque faciliter ita decentem sicut erat dicta domina Blancha, et adiecit
se credere per ea que audivit ante tempus [33]antedicti matrimonii, tempore quo domina Iohanna /546// mater sua vivebat, quod dicta mater
numquam permisisset, si vixisset, quod contraheret cum dicta domina
Blancha. Super aliis articulis nichil aliud pertinens dixit. /547//

(g) ¶ Magister Iohannes Hellequin magister in medicina, interrogatus super xx° articulo, dixit per iuramentum suum quod dictus dominus
Karolus habebit xxvii annos vel xxviii ad plus circa festum Trinitatis
venturum, sed melius cre- /548// dit de xxvii; et dixit quod habebat in
scriptis diem et datam quam in die nativitatis eius [34]scripxit, et hoc recordatur quia fuit loco nativitatis sue dicto tempore. Interrogatus super xxi°

[26] *Same line.*   [27] reputabantur] *or* reputantur.
[28] Soyziaco] *E. A. R. Brown corrected my original reading of this as* Soyriaco.
[29] ablatavit] *sic for* ablactavit.   [30] cuntraxit] *sic for* contraxit.
[31] a] *French vernacular.*   [32] Hedyn] Hedy *ms.? The place must be Hesdin.*
[33] antedicti matrimonii] ai' mat' *ms.*   [34] scripxit] *sic ms.*

articulo, dixit per iuramentum suum contenta in predicto /549// articulo vera esse. Interrogatus quomodo scit, dixit quod ex eo quia a cunabulis habuit curam de ipso et bene scit quod erat valde simplex, sine tali discretione et notitia quod sciret vel posset secundum statum in quo erat sic providere /550// vel querere decentem uxorem. Interrogatus super xxii° articulo, dixit quod meliorem et magis decentem uxorem reperisset, vel alteram de nominatis in predicto articulo vel aliam, quia, sicut dixit, nulla dedisset repulsam quin libenter cum ipso contra- /551// - xisset. Super xxiii° articulo, dixit esse verum prout in articulo continetur, quia etiam sufficientius contraxisset cum altera illarum quam cum ista, ut dixit. Super xxvi° articulo interrogatus dixit quod utrumque predictorum, domini Karoli et domine Blanche, no- /552// -verat et conditionem et complexionem eorum, quia medicus erat regis et puerorum ipsius et quod pro certo existimat secundum quod poterat ex etate et alias apparere quod erant impotentes ad carnis copulam. Super xxviii° et xxix° articulis dixit /553// per iuramentum suum quod licet dicto tempore esset de domo regis et fuerit in locis ubi matrimonium tractabatur et ubi [35]fuit factum, numquam audivit loqui de dictis bannis nec quod licentia contrahendi a curatis eorum vel ab aliis episcopis /554// fuerit petita, quare credit ut dixit sicut in predictis articulis continetur. Super xxx° articulo interrogatus dixit per iuramentum suum quod ipse testis tunc temporis morabatur cum Comitissa de Dampno Martino, que fuit mandata quod iret /555// ad baptismum dicti domini Karoli, et ivit dicta comitissa et idem testis, qui loquitur, cum ea, et fuit presens quando dictus dominus Karolus fuit aportatus ad ecclesiam, que est in castro de [36]Creel, pro baptismo recipiendo, et ivit ad /556// fontes cum dicta Comitissa de Dampno Martino, et ibidem dum dictus puer aportaretur super fontes, dicta domina Mathildis, que tunc erat Comitissa Burgondie – et adhuc est etiam Comitissa Attrebatensis – sicut dixit, venit ante dictum /557// baptismum ad fontes de versus illam partem versus quam erat idem testis valde impetuose, et retraxit ipsum a dictis fontibus, et in retrahendo dixit sibi talia verba: 'Sire prestre, que faites vous yci? Vous ne /558// serez mie compere' – credens ipsum testem esse presbiterum, licet non esset. Et tunc idem testis respondit sibi: 'Domina, presbiteri bene debent esse in talibus', et in dicendo dictis verbis, ipse testis se retraxit ad retractionem ipsius /559// comitisse, et ipsa transivit ad fontes baptismales immediate, et posuit se inter illas que fuerunt commatres, inter quas non erat aliqua tanti status quod recordetur sicut ipsa, ex quibus existimat pro

---

[35] fuit] fuut *ms? Bibliothèque Mazarine 1986 and Bibliothèque nationale de France, Lat. 8935 transcribe as* 'fuerit'.

[36] Creel] *spelled in several ways – not normalised – in this document.*

certo quod dicta domina /560// Mathildis fuit una de principalioribus commatribus et matrina dicti domini Karoli. Interrogatus [37]fuit si dictus dominus Karolus posset cum dicta domina Blancha in matrimonio absque gravi scandalo remanere, et respondit /561// quod firmiter credebat et existimabat quod non. Interrogatus si odio, comodo vel amore, favore vel timore deposuerat aliquid de predictis, dixit per iuramentum suum quod non, sed pro veritate dumtaxat. /562// Super aliis articulis non fuit interrogatus, et nichil aliud pertinens dixit. /563//

(h) ¶ Dominus Robertus de Brisol', miles, etatis xlvii annorum, qui moratus fuit cum domina Blancha, id est matre domine Regine Iohanne matris domini regis per aliqua tempora, super primo, secundo et tertio articulis deposuit per suum /564 // iuramentum se audivisse dici prout in dictis articulis continetur. Interrogatus a quibus audivit, dixit a domina Katherina de [38]Riginaco matre sua et domino Guidone de Roisiere, alias dicto Quatre Soulz, miles qui fuit cum /565// dicto domino Roberto primo de quo fit mentio in primo dicto articulo apud Massoria[39] ubi fuit mortuus dictus dominus Robertus sicut audivit dici a predictis. Premissa etiam audivit a pluribus aliis, de quibus non recolit quo ad /566// presens. Interrogatus quid credit, dixit per suum iuramentum quod prout in predictis articulis continetur, et per ea que predixit, et quia vidit dictum dominum Philippum primum qui se gerebat pro filio predicti sancti Ludovici, et sic successit [40]tanquam suus /567// filius, prout in toto regno Francie [41]notorie reputabatur. Item interrogatus super iiii°, v°, vi°, vii°, viii °, xi°, xii °, xiii °, xv °, et xvi ° articulis, ipsis sibi sigillatim et seriatim expositis, dixit per iuramentum suum – excepto hoc /568// quod in v° et vi° [42]articulo de dicto domino Roberto primo et in xi° et xii° articulis de eodem domino Roberto primo et de domina Mathildi uxore sua asseritur, de quibus nescit pro veritate deponere, sed credit quod dictus dominus Robertus primus /569// fuit frater sancti Ludovici et pater domini Roberti secundi et dicta domina Mathildis mater, quia sic audivit dici pluries et a multis, ut dixit – quod omnes alias personas in predictis articulis nominatas vidit pluries se gerere et habere et haberi /570// et reputari pro coniunctis et attinentibus, prout in dictis articulis continetur, et propter hoc credit ut dixit quod ad invicem prout in predictis articulis continetur insimul attinebant. Interrogatus super ix° articulo, eo sibi exposito, et computatis /571// personis utriusque lateris, dixit verum esse

---

[37] fuit] *followed by space in ms.*
[38] Rigniaco] *suggested by E. A. R. Brown, and preferable to* Riginaco *(my initial attempt),* Rigmaco *or* Regmaco.
[39] i.e. Mansoura.   [40] tanquam] *in full, with* n.   [41] notorie] *or* notorium: notor' *ms.*
[42] articulo] *in full: but it has seemed best on balance to extend the frequently recurring* articul' *as* articulis *when it occurs with more than one ordinal number.*

prout in dictis articulis continetur. Interrogatus de causa, dixit quia ita computaret ipse et audivit in similibus computari. Super x° articulo interrogatus, respondit famam esse de predictis a se depositis. Super /572// xiiii° articulo interrogatus, expositis sibi personis prout per [43]utranque lineam a domino Roberto primo ascendebant, secundum modum quem computat gradus et audivit [44]semper computari, dixit verum esse prout in predicto articulo continetur. Interrogatus super xviii° /573// articulo deposuit per suum iuramentum quod secundum quod ipse audivit communiter computari et reputari aliquos in gradu seu gradibus esse coniunctos, dictus articulus continet veritatem secundum modum computandi in Francia, alias nescit, ut dixit. /574// Interrogatus super xx°, dixit per suum iuramentum se firmiter credere secundum tempus etatis sue et tempus matrimonii quod non compleverant xiii annum. Super xxi° articulo, non credit quod haberet discretionem talem que sufficeret /575// ad discernendum ea que [45]continet idem articulus, [46]ymmo erat nimis simplex et indiscretus, etiam secundum etatem suam, et quod ex hoc vocabant eum 'orson', [47]et [48]contemnebatur propter simplicitatem suam etiam a matre sua, ut dixit. Super xxii° articulo /576// interrogatus, credit eum, alias nescit pro certo. Super xxiii° articulo interrogatus, credit contenta in eo quia vidit in aliis casibus quod recipiebant filii [49]regum aliquas non maiores illis et hoc vidit de domino Valesii et de aliis. Super xxv° articulo /577// [50]interrogatus, credit contenta in eo, alias nescit veritatem. Super xxvii° et xxviii° articulis, dixit se nescire. Super xxx° articulo dixit dictum articulum verum esse. Interrogatus quomodo scit, dixit quia presens fuit in baptismo. Interrogatus ubi, /578// dixit quod apud Creeill, in ecclesia canonicorum sancti [51]Evremundi, que est infra castrum dicti loci. Interrogatus quid ibi vidit, dixit per suum iuramentum se vidisse quod dicta domina Machildis recepit puerum, scilicet dictum dominum Karolum /579// et tradidit eum domino Comiti Valesii nudum super [52]fontes ad recipiendum dictum baptismum. Item vidit, ut dixit, quod dicta domina Mathildis in baptismo apposuit manus sicut alie commatres, ut est moris, et tenuit eum supra /580// fontem dum baptizaretur, ipsum tangendo a manibus, et tenendo una cum aliis supra fontes. Interrogatus quare venerat ibi, dixit quod morabatur cum domino Guichardo abbate

---

[43] utranque] *when abbreviation conceals* n/m *I normalise with the scribe to* m, *or use italics to indicate that it could be either, but here the* n *seems to be indicated.*
[44] semper] super *ms.*   [45] continet] contine; [= contineet] *ms.*
[46] ymmo] *or* ymo, *depending on whether the superscript is an abbreviation or a diacritical stroke.*
[47] *Presumably pejorative.*
[48] contempnebatur] contempnebantur *ms., probably influenced by the plural* vocabant.
[49] regum] regnum *ms.*   [50] *In right-hand margin: 21 (modern?).*
[51] Evremundi] *variant spellings – not normalised – in this document.*   [52] fontes] font' *ms.*

tunc monasterii Celle iuxta Trecas, qui postmodum fuit /581// Episcopus
Trecensis, et recordatur quod stetit idem abbas et ipse cum eo in villa
de Montataire iuxta Credolium per mensem unum et ultra expectantes
quod dicta domina peperisset, quia dictus dominus Guichardus volebat
esse in baptismo /582// predicto et demum dicto domino Karolo nato
yverunt ad dictum locum de Creell, et ibi vidit predicta, de quibus perfecte dixit se recordari. Interrogatus de personis presentibus, dixit quod
recordatur quod ibi fuit presens Comes Flandrie, /583// scilicet dominus
Guido, pater istius comitis qui est hodie, et vidit quod tenebat unum
baculum quod cum dentibus ruminabat. Item vidit dominum Karolum
Comitem Valesii, qui tenuit dictum puerum. Vidit etiam ibidem Guillelmum de Sancto /584// Marcello et dominos archiepiscopum Senonensem
et episcopum Belvacensem, qui erant pro tempore, et Comitem Sancti
Pauli, et multos alios manus tenentes ad puerum pro dicta compater-
nitate. Interrogatus de tempore, dixit quod circa festum beati Iohannis,
/585// et recordatur quod ivit apud Claromontem prope duas leucas pro
piscibus, quia in villa de Creeill, propter multitudinem magnatum qui
erant ibi, non potuerunt [53]pisces reperiri. Interrogatus de aliis commatribus, dixit quod Comitissa de Ioigny /586// et fuit ibi etiam comitissa de
Dompmnomartino et multe alie de quibus bene non recordatur. Interrogatus quot anni possunt esse, dixit quod xxvii vel circa, secundum quod
recordatur. Et nichil aliud pertinens dixit. [54]Et per suum iuramentum si
odio /587// vel amore, timore, subornatione, vel pro comodo quocunque
non deposuit aliquid de predictis, sed pro veritate dumtaxat, ut iuraverat.
/588//

(i) ¶ Thomas de Rogueta prepositus de [55]Arbelliaco in ecclesia Sancti
Aniani Aureliensis, Ytalicus [56]Assensis dyocesis interrogatus super xviii°
articulo dixit per suum iuramentum illum esse modum computandi in
Lombardia coniunctos in tertio gradu ex [57]/589// utroque latere vel in
tertio ex uno latere et quarto ex alio vel in quarto ex utroque latere prout
in eodem articulo continetur, et dixit hoc se scire quia sic vidit pluries et
a pluribus computari et est notorium in partibus illis, ut dixit. Super aliis
non fuit interrogatus. /590//

(j) Matheus dictus de Moncell', lombardus, mercator diocesis [58]V'ren'
in partibus ultramontanis interrogatus super dicto xviii° articulo: vocant,
ut dixit, gradus consanguinitatis genu, [59]unde deposuit quod [60]illos qui
descendunt a stipite per tres personas, sic quod ipse sit /591// tertius a

---

[53] pisces] pices *ms.*
[54] Et . . . iuraverat] *words missing from Latin, probably through carelessness.*
[55] Arbelliaco] *or* Arbilliaco.   [56] Assensis] Assen' *ms.*   [57] ex] ex /589// ex *ms.*
[58] V'ren'] Veronensis?   [59] unde deposuit] *over erasure?*
[60] illos] *read* illi (*unless the hybrid 'quod' + accusative and infinitive construction is intentional*).

stipite, non computato dicto stipite, et alius qui in alia linea est in pari descensu, dicuntur et reputantur in tertio gradu seu genu ex utroque latere, et [61] illi qui descendunt per quattuor personas, in quarto ex utroque latere, et quando unus per tres personas in suo latere, alius per quattuor /592// tunc reputantur et habentur pro coniunctis in tertio et quarto in partibus ytalicis, et ita vidit tempore suo haberi et computari et reputari in Ytalia publice et notorie, ut dixit. /593//

(k) ¶ Ascelanus dictus Taire, lombardus Astensis dyocesis, interrogatus super dicto xviii° articulo, idem deposuit de modo loquendi et computandi in Ytalia sicut testis proximus. /594//

(l) ¶ Iordanus de Calochio Parisiensis dyocesis etatis xl annorum vel circa, lumbardus mercator, idem [62] deposuit in effectu quod testis proxime precedens et sicut Matheus de Moncell'. /595//

(m) ¶ Matheus [63] Scarempus Astensis dyocesis xx annorum lombardus mercator testis iuratus et interrogatus super dicto xviii° articulo, dixit quod in Ytalia in tertio gradu vocant consanguineos secundos, in quarto consanguinitatis, consobrinos, in quarto et tertio unum consan-/596//-guineum secundum et unum consobrinum, et ita vidit et audivit computari in partibus illis. De aliis contentis in predicto articulo nichil scit. /597// [64]

(n) [65] Guillelmus de Sancto Marcello burgensis de Pruvino testis iuratus et diligenter [66] [interrogatus] super primo et [67] secundo articulis dixit per iuramentum suum se credere contenta in predictis articulis vera esse. Interrogatus quare credit, dixit quod ideo quia sic au-/598//-divit dici a pluribus fidedignis prout in predictis duobus articulis continetur, et hoc, tempore sancti Ludovici, quem vidit idem testis, ut dixit, [68] notorium reputabatur. Interrogatus super tertio et quarto articulis, dixit per iuramentum suum se vidisse omnes perso- /599// -nas in predictis articulis contentas se gerere et habere et ab aliis communiter et publice haberi et reputari secundum quod in predictis articulis continetur, scilicet sanctum Ludovicum et Philippum primum pro patre et filio, et Philippum primum et Philippum secundum pro /600// patre et filio, et Philippum secundum et dominum Karolum nunc Regem Francie pro patre et filio, et hoc certum et notorium fuit reputatum temporibus eorum, ut dixit, et tales esse communiter ab omnibus suis temporibus dicebantur, et adhuc dicuntur. Super /601// vi° articulo interrogatus, dixit se non vidisse dictum dominum Robertum primum, sed vidit dictum dominum

---

[61] illi qui . . . latere et] *between lines.*   [62] deposuit] depouit *ms.?*
[63] Scarepnus] Scaremp[us] *ms.*   [64] *Large space follows.*   [65] *In right hand margin:* 22.
[66] interrogatus] *om. ms.*   [67] secundo] *barely legible.*
[68] notorium] *or:* notorie: notor' *ms.*

Robertum secundum, qui dicebatur ab omnibus fuisse filius illius, et pro tali se gerebat, et sibi successerat in comitatu Attrebatensi, ut communiter dice- /602// -batur, et hoc verum et indubitatum reputat etiam idem testis. Et vidit etiam quod idem dominus Robertus secundus et dominus Philippus primus se reputabant consanguinei filii, scilicet duorum fratrum dominorum Ludovici sancti et Roberti primi. /603// Interrogatus super vii° et viii° articulis, dixit per iuramentum suum se vidisse personas de quibus fit in [69]ipsis mentio unam ab altera descendentem et pro sic se coniunctis gerentes et reputantes esse prout in predictis articulis continetur. Item interrogatus super /604// xi° articulo dixit se credere contenta in eo vera esse, quia sic audivit a multis prout in eodem articulo continetur, [70]maxime temporibus iam elapsis. Interrogatus super xii° articulo dixit se scire quod predicti dominus Robertus secundus et domina Blancha que fuit /605// mater domine Iohanne regine Francie, matris dicti domini Karoli, se reputabant, et [71]reputabantur frater et soror, filii predictorum domini Roberti primi [72]et domine Mathildi de Brebantia, et hoc vidit et audivit pluries, ut dixit, et in locis pluribus, et notorium /606// et indubitatum reputabatur temporibus eorumdem. Et alia contenta in dicto articulo credit per ea que predixit esse vera. Interrogatus super xiii°, xiiii° xv° et xvi° articulis, dixit per iuramentum suum se vidisse sepius omnes personas /607// in predictis articulis contentas se gerere et habere et haberi et reputari pro sic coniunctis ut in predictis articulis continetur. Cetera in dictis articulis contenta credit esse vera, quia ita certum et notorium reputabatur temporibus eorumdem. Item super xxx° /608// articulo interrogatus dixit per iuramentum suum quod adveniente [73]tempore nativitatis dicti domini Karoli aliquantulum ante ipse ivit apud Credolium cum abbate monasterii Celle qui vocabatur Richardus, et fuit postmodum episcopus Tricensis, et /609// quia dicta domina regina non peperat, expectavit abbas predictus et idem testis cum eo quasi per tres septimanas in quodam loco prope Credolium nativitatem dicti pueri, hoc excepto quod idem testis interdum dicto tempore ivit in aliquibus locis et /610// mox redibat. Demum autem, nato dicto domino Karolo, quidam vocatus Lambertus, qui erat scisor pannorum domine regine venit ad significandum nativitatem dicto abbati, et dedit sibi xx. lb. Par', et retinuit eum de raubis suis. /611// Et postmodum in die baptismi ivit cum dicto abbate ad ecclesiam que est in castro de Credolio, et ibi vidit quod dictus puer fuit apportatus ad portam ecclesie, et dum fierent ea que sunt consueta fieri in ianuis quando puer /612//

---

[69] ipsis] *barely legible.*   [70] maxime temporibus] *barely legible.*
[71] reputabantur] repu^tur *ms.*   [72] et] *illegible on microfilm.*
[73] tempore] *physical damage in ms.*

debet baptizari. Vidit ibidem, ut dixit, dominam [74]Mathildim Comitissam Burgondie prope dominum Karolum Comitem Valesii, qui tenebat dictum puerum et postmodum intraverunt ecclesiam et in ecclesia vidit quod dicto puero /613// pannis exsoluto dicta Domina Mathildis recepit eum inter manus suas, et totum nudum tradidit eum supra fontes domino Karolo predicto ad tenendum eum in baptismo, et postquam ipsum tradidit ut predixit, vidit ipsam ad fontes /614// prope puerum et tenentem manus ad ipsum sicut commater supra fontes dum baptizabatur; et de hoc dixit se habere memoriam quia bene congnoscebat dictam comitissam, et volens videre baptizari filium regis, respiciebat /615// ut melius poterat. Item dixit quod dicto puero baptizato iterum recepit eadem domina dictum puerum, et pannis involvit cum aliis, et involutum dicto domino Karolo reddidit. Interrogatus de tempore, dixit quod fuit circa festum Trinitatis eo tempore /616// quo sunt nundine de Landit[75] prope sanctum Dyonisium et hoc recordatur quia, dum dictus abbas expectabat ortum ipsius domini regis, idem testis venit interdum [76]Parisius et transibat per nundinas predictas que tunc erant. Interrogatus quot sunt anni /617// dixit quod erunt [77]xxviii° anni circa festum Trinitatis, prope festum beati Iohannis Baptiste, ut sibi videtur pro certo. Interrogatus de personis presentibus, dixit de Comite Flandrie qui tunc erat, et de Archiepiscopo tunc Narbonensi et Senonensi, et Episcopo Suessionensi /618// et de domina Mathildi predicta et aliis de quibus predixit, et de domino Roberto de Brisoles et de multis aliis, et adhuc recordatur, ut dixit, quod quidam puer ceciderat in aqua que fuit ibi, et mater voverat eum, et fuerat habitus /619// pro mortuo, et revixerat miraculose, ut dicebat, et dum Comes Flandrie et abbas predictus et multi prelati et alii expectarent in ecclesia predicta quod dictus puer apportaretur ad baptizandum, voluerunt videre illum /620// in cuius persona fuerat miraculum, [78]et fecerunt eum ibi venire. Interrogatus si odio vel amore, comodo, favore, vel timore deposuerat aliquid, dixit quod non, sed quia veritas sic se habebat ut dixit. /621//

(o) ¶ Dominus Radulphus de Paredo etatis lxxii annorum Cantor Meldensis, magister quondam hospitii [79]puerorum domini Philippi et domine Iohanne regine, parentum domini regis, tam domini regis moderni [80]quam fratrum suorum, deposuit quantum ad primum /622// et secundum articulos de auditu et de credulitate sua, et quod dictus Ludovicus fuit mortuus apud Montpancier,[81] et audivit ita dici ut in dictis

---

[74] Mathildim] Mathildam *could be read.*   [75] i.e. 'Lendit'.   [76] Parisius] Par' *ms.*
[77] xxviii° anni] *sic ms.*   [78] et] *unclear but supplied from sense.*
[79] puerorum] principorum *Bibliothèque Mazarine 1986, Bibliothèque nationale de France, Lat. 8935.*
[80] quam] quod *ms.?*   [81] *i.e.* Montpensier.

articulis continetur, et [82]domina Margareta, relicta sancti Ludovici, cum qua moratus fuit per xv annos. /623// Item interrogatus super omnibus articulis tangentibus consanguinitates, tam in consanguinitate descendente a predicto domino Ludovico patre sancti Ludovici, in qua asseruntur dictus dominus Karolus et dicta domina Blancha esse in quarto ex utroque latere, /624// quam in alia consanguinitate descendente a predicto domino Roberto primo fratre sancti Ludovici, deposuit per suum iuramentum quantum ad hoc [83]quod persone in dictis articulis contente sic se habent et habentur prout in articulo continetur, excepto dicto domino /625// Roberto primo, quem non vidit – sed de ipso audivit a pluribus fidedignis sicut in predicto articulo continetur; sed omnes alios vidit, et novit et vidit quod [84]notorie reputabantur, et habebantur prout sic communiter, et sic inter [85]se se habebant prout /626// in dictis articulis est contentum. Item super xviii° articulo, deposuit, quantum est de modo computandi, prout in articulo continetur sic audit et audivit sepius, sicut dixit. Super xxii° articulo interrogatus deposuit per suum iuramentum prout /627// in articulo continetur. Interrogatus de causa, dixit quod audivit dici quod ipse potuisset habere sororem ducis [86]Britanie, de qua fit mentio in dicto articulo, cum comitatu de Pertico, qui sibi fuisset datus in valore decem /628// milium librarum redditus, et cum L. milibus libr' in pecunia, et ideo [87]etc. – quia non credit quod aliqua dedisset sibi repulsam, ut dixit. Super xxx° articulo interrogatus, dixit per suum iuramentum se nescire veritatem, quia non fuit /629// presens. Nichil aliud pertinens deposuit super articulis predictis de quibus interrogatus fuit. Si odio etc. /630//

(p) Dominus Guido de Joyaco, miles, testis iuratus et interrogatus super dicto xxx° articulo, deposuit quod tempore dicti baptismi erat de domo domine regine et quod comitissa Burgondie erat in villa [88]de Credolio, sed non /631// fuit ipse testis in dicto baptismo, sicut dixit, [89]quia [90]remanxit in camera dicte domine regine, sed post baptismum videtur sibi pro certo quod [91]dicta Mathildis Comitissa Burgondie [92]reportavit puerum ad cameram, et quod dixit /632// se commatrem esse dicte domine Iohanne regine, et ad suam conscientiam si iuraret assertive quod fuit commater non haberet [93]conscientiam lesam,

---

[82] domina] *read* de domina?   [83] quod] *between lines.*

[84] notorie] *or:* notorium: notor' *ms.*   [85] se se] *corr. from* se?

[86] Britanie] *superscript probably goes with the* i *rather than marking a missing* n.

[87] etc.] e' *ms.:* etiam *could be read.*

[88] de] de de *ms.*   [89] quia] *between lines.*

[90] remanxit] *probably sic (for* remansit*) though the ink is faint.*

[91] dicta] *concealed by physical damage:* domina *also possible.*

[92] reportavit] *last letters illegible on microfilm.*

[93] conscientiam lesam] *partly concealed by physical damage.*

et hoc postmodum etiam audivit interdum dici a multis quod tenuerat dictum dominum /633// Karolum super fontes, et credit hoc esse verum quod ipsum [94]tenuerit per suum iuramentum, et aliud [95]impertinens non deposuit. Interrogatus [96]si odio, timore, comodo, vel amore deposuerat, [97]vel dixerat aliquid quod deposuerit /634// et dixerit, [98]dixit quod non, per suum iuramentum, sed pro veritate dicenda. /635//

(q) ¶ Richardus le Poissonnier, burgensis de Credolio, etatis lx [99]annorum productus et iuratus, super dicto xxx° articulo dixit [100]quod per iuramentum suum vidit dominam Mathildim iuxta fontes dum baptizaretur idem dominus Karolus prope /636// ipsum puerum, et erat maior domina que esset ibi, ut sibi videtur, sed non potuit discernere utrum apposuerit manus ad eum tenendum, sed credit pro certo quod fuit commater, et hoc iuraret citius [101]quam aliud, et vidit in dicto baptis- /637// -mo Comitem Burgondie maritum suum. Interrogatus de personis astantibus, dixit de domino Karolo Valesii, de Comite Flandrie, de Comitissa de [102]Iongny, et de multis aliis de quibus non recolit, et de predictis Comite /638// Burgondie et Comitissa interrogatus si credit quod tenuerit supra fontes dictum Karolum, dixit quod sic, quia vidit eam inter commatres, sicut dixit, et erat suo iudicio maior domina inter alias. Et aliud pertinens non dixit. /639//

(r) ¶ Colardus Heitie etatis liii annorum testis iuratus et diligenter interrogatus super predicto xxx° articulo, dixit per suum iuramentum quod fuit presens in ecclesia sancti [103]Ewremundi de Credolio quando dictus dominus rex fuit baptizatus, et /640// vidit ibidem dictam dominam Mathildim Comitissam Burgondie prope dominum Karolum Comitem Valesii, qui tenebat dictum puerum supra fontes. Interrogatus si vidit quod dicta domina Mathildis teneret dictum dominum Karolum /641// supra fontes, dixit quod non recordatur perfecte, quia in pressura erat et non poterat bene videre omnia que fiebant. Interrogatus quid credit, dixit quod credit pro certo quod fuit [104]matrina dicti domini Karoli, per ea que predixit, et quia hoc /642// tunc audivit dici a domina Comitissa de [105]Iongny cui operabatur de opere peletarie et a quadam domicella domine regine [106]I. matris dicti domini regis que vocabatur Amabilete, que [107]portabat signum secretum dicte regine ut dixit /643// et a multis

---

[94] tenuerit] *or* tenuerat?   [95] impertinens] *read* pertinens?
[96] si] sed *ms.*?   [97] vel] u^e *or* n^e *ms.: scribe may have wrongly intended* nec.
[98] dixit] *between lines.*   [99] annorum productus] *partly concealed by physical damage.*
[100] quod] *between lines.*   [101] quam] quem *ms.*?   [102] Iongny] *sic.*
[103] Ewremundi] *unclear on microfilm.*
[104] matrina] *also spelled* marrina *in this document.*   [105] Iogny] *unclear on microfilm.*
[106] I. matris] *between lines and unclear on microfilm.*
[107] portabat] portabatur *ms., probably influenced by the immediately preceding passive.*

aliis dicto tempore, plusquam a xl in predicta villa de Credolio et in domo dicte domine regine. Interrogatus ad quid venerat ibi quando vidit predicta, dixit quod quia morabatur et adhuc moratur in dicta villa de Credolio /644// et volebat videre baptizare filium regis. Interrogatus de fama, dixit per iuramentum suum quod fama fuit et erat in dicta villa et in domo regine quod dicta domina Mathildis fuerat commater dicte domine regine et marrina [108]dicti /645// domini Karoli. Et aliud pertinens non dixit. Interrogatus si odio, amore, favore, comodo vel timore deposuit aliquid de predictis, dixit quod non per iuramentum suum, sed quia veritas sic se habet. Super aliis articulis non fuit /646// petitus interrogari. /647//

[Space in ms.]

(s) Nobilis et potens [109]vir dominus Galcherus de [110]Castellione constabularius Francie, testis iuratus et diligenter interrogatus super primo, ii°, iii°, iiii°, v°, vi°, vii°, viii°, xi°, xii°, xiii°, xiiii°, xv°, et xvi° articulis, ipsis sibi seriatim /648// expositis, respondit, videlicet quantum ad parentes sancti Ludovici, de quibus fit mentio in primo et ii° articulis, nec etiam quantum ad dominum Robertum primum et dominam Mathildim de Brebant', [111]se nescire de veritate deponere, cum ut dixit non viderit /649// supradictos, sed pluries et a pluribus [112]fidedignis audivit dici contenta in predictis articulis, quo ad ea que de predictis personis asseruntur vera esse, et ita credit, ut asseruit idem testis. Alias autem personas in predictis articulis contentas dixit se vi- /650// -disse, et quod una descendit ab alia sicut in predictis articulis continentur, per ordinem, scilicet: a sancto Ludovico, quem vidit, Philippus primus; a Philippo primo, Philippus secundus, a Philippo secundo, dominus Karolus nunc rex. Item a domino Roberto secundo, quem vidit, domina /651// Mathildis, et a dicta domina Mathildi, dicta domina Blancha. Item a domina Blancha uxore regis Navarre que erat soror domini Roberti secundi descendit domina Iohanna regina Francie [113]mater dicti regis [114]Karoli et a dicta domina Iohanna [115]descendit dominus rex predictus, et vidit /652// quod dictus dominus Robertus secundus et dominus Philippus primus se reputabant consanguineos germanos, filios duorum fratrum, scilicet sancti Ludovici et Roberti primi, et quod domina Regina Navarre et domina Mathildis predicta se reputabant germanas, scilicet

---

[108] dicti] dci' *with two extra strokes, apparently otiose.*
[109] vir] *followed by* homo, *probably deleted.*
[110] Castellione] *unclear, between lines, over* Casteillon, *probably deleted.*
[111] se nescire] *corr. from* senescire.
[112] fidedignis] *with possible otiose stroke.*   [113] mater dicti regis Karoli] *between lines.*
[114] Karoli] K. *ms. (unclear in microfilm).*   [115] descendit] *between lines.*

fratris et sororis [116]filias /653// videlicet predictorum domini Roberti secundi et domine Blanche Regine [117]Navarre; et premissa reputabantur et adhuc inter habentes notitiam de temporibus [[118]reputantur] certa et indubitata. Super xxx° articulo interrogatus deposuit per iuramentum suum se recordari quod domina Io- /654// -hanna mater dicti domini regis tempore partus ipsius domini regis erat apud Credulium, et rex Philippus veniebat ibi, et ipse testis qui loquitur, et multi alii cum ipso, et fuit significatum domino domino Philippo regi [119]per dictum [120]Malengrene, valletum camere, quod dicta domina Iohanna uxor sua, [121]regina, pepere- /655// -rat, et tunc dictus dominus Philippus rex mutavit iter suum et ivit [122]Sanctum Christophorum in Halata apud Silvan',[123] et precepit ipsi testi quod [124]iret ad baptismum dicti domini Karoli, et ivit ibi et vidit quod dominus Karolus Comes Valesii [125]tenuit ipsum dominum Karolum nunc regem supra fontes bap- /656// -tismales, et ibidem vidit Comitissam Burgundie, scilicet dictam dominam Mathildim et multas alias personas, et fuit dictus testis unus de parrinis dicti domini Karoli, et compater parentum eiusdem. Et predicta domina Mathildis fuit una de marri- /657// -nis in dicto baptismo ipsius domini Karoli, et commater parentum eiusdem. Interrogatus quomodo scit, dixit quia sic vidit et [126]audivit. Vidit enim, ut dixit, quod predicta domina Mathildis tenuit – una cum domino Valesii qui tenebat dictum [127]puerum principa- /658// -liter, et cum ipso teste et aliis parrinis et marrinis ibi presentibus – dictum dominum Karolum [128]nunc regem super fontes baptismales dum baptizabatur. Interrogatus de loco, dixit quod in ecclesia [129]sancti Evvremondi de Credulio. Interrogatus de personis presentibus, dixit de predictis domino Valesii et domina /659// Mathildi. Et videtur sibi pro certo sicut dixit quod Comes Burgundie maritus ipsius domine Mathildis et pater dicte Blanche fuit ibi, et Comes Flandrie et multi alii nobiles et prelati. Interrogatus si odio, amore, favore, commodo, vel timore /660// deposuit aliquid de premissis, dixit quod non, per iuramentum suum, sed dumtaxat pro veritate quam iuraverat se dicturum. Super aliis non fuit interrogatus, unde nichil aliud pertinens dixit. /661//

---

[116] filias] *in margin.*   [117] Navarre] Novarre *ms.?*
[118] reputantur] *om. ms.*   [119] per… camere] *between lines.*
[120] Malengrene] *or* Malengreve.   [121] regina] *between lines.*
[122] Sanctum Christophorum in Halata] *between lines, unclear, and supplied from Bibliothèque nationale de France, Lat. 8935 and Bibliothèque Mazarine, 1986.*
[123] *Cf.* E. Guillemot, Les forêts de Senlis: étude sur le régime des forêts d'Halatte, de Chantilly et d'Ermonville au Moyen Age et jusqu'à la révolution *(Paris, 1905), p.* 96, *note* 2.
[124] iret] *from sense – letter forms unclear.*   [125] tenuit] *between lines.*
[126] audivit] *corr. from:* audivit et.   [127] puerum] *corr. from* dominum Karolum.
[128] nunc regem] *between lines.*   [129] sancti Evvremondi] *between lines.*

(t) Magnificus et potens princeps dominus Karolus Comes Valesii et Andegavie, testis iuratus et diligenter interrogatus super xxx° articulo, dixit per iuramentum suum se tenuisse dictum dominum Karolum regem in baptismo ipsius [130]domini regis et quod bene recordatur quod /662 // dicta domina Mathildis Comitissa Burgundie tunc, et nunc [131]Artesii, fuit ibi presens in ecclesia de Credulio ad fontes baptismales dicte ecclesie – que est [132]nunc intra castrum dicti [133]loci – dum predictus dominus Karolus rex fuit baptizatus; sed non recordatur perfecte si /663// tenuit eum, sed plures fuerunt qui tenuerunt manus ad dictum dominum regem in dicto baptismo, sed non perfecte recordatur qui. Interrogatus quid credit: – an credit quod tenuerit manus et fuerit marrina vel non – dixit per iuramentum suum quod credit quod fuerit marrina /664// et quod tenuerit manus ad ipsum in baptismo, et hoc per iuramentum suum magis quam aliud. Interrogatus de tempore, dixit quod circa festum beati Iohannis Baptiste erunt circiter xxviii anni. Et nichil aliud pertinens dixit super contentis in articulo predicto. Sed super /665// etate in qua erant predicti dominus Karolus et Blancha tempore matrimonii inter eos contracti, dixit quod dictus dominus Karolus rex non habebat xiiii annos, immo deficiebant sibi v menses vel circa. Item quod dicta domina Blancha non habebat xii annos /666// completos; et [134]hoc scit quia utrumque tenuit supra fontes, ut predixit. Et recordatur etiam de tempore matrimonii, quia fuerunt elapsi xiiii anni circa festum purificationis beate Marie preteritum. Super aliis non fuit interrogatus, et nichil /667// aliud pertinens dixit. /668//

(u) Dominus P. de [135]Argento Cantor [136]ecclesie Meledunensis interrogatus super xxx° articulo, super quo tantummodo fuit productus deposuit per suum iuramentum quod fuit presens dum dictus dominus Karolus fuit apportatus pro baptizando ad ecclesiam sancti Evremundi de Credulio et /669// ibidem vidit et audivit quod frater Iohannes de [137]Granchy Elemosinarius Regine Iohanne matris dicti [138]domini Karoli, qui, dum puer pararetur ad tradendum baptismo, legit quamdam cedulam in qua erant scripta nomina illorum et illarum qui debebant /670// esse compatres et commatres, et inter alios fuit nominata dicta domina Mathildis comitissa Burgundie, que ibidem erat presens. Et videtur sibi quod nominata fuit prima vel secunda inter alias, et statim vidit ut dixit quod dicta domina Mathildis /671// recepit de gremio domine

---

[130] domini] *between lines.*
[131] Artesii, fuit] *corr. from* Artesiifuit; *otiose abbreviation on* Artesii?
[132] nunc] *between lines. Ms.* num?
[133] loci] *stroke added in ms., possibly punctuation.*   [134] hoc] *or* hec.
[135] Argento] dictus Dar'gens/Dar'gent *written above.*   [136] ecclesie] *between lines.*
[137] Granch'] Geranch' *ms.?*   [138] domini] *concealed by damage and supplied from sense.*

Iohanne [139]obstetricis dictum dominum Karolum, et portavit eum inter suas manus nudum supra fontes baptismales, et ibi tradidit ipsum domino Karolo comiti Valesii, qui fuit principalis compater, et fuit dicta domina Ma- /672// -thildis continue ad fontes baptismales quamdiu dictus puer fuit baptizatus, ut dixit. Tanta tamen erat pressura, sicut deposuit, quod non potuit videre appositionem [140]manuum [141]compatrum et commatrum qui tenuerant eum, sed dicebatur communiter /673// in domo regine post dictum baptismum quod ipsa fuerat commater. Interrogatus quare erat ibi dixit quod ideo quia erat capellanus dicte domine regine et morabatur cum ea et venerat cum ipsa ad dictam villam de Credulio et venerat /674// tunc ad dictam ecclesiam pro videndo baptizari dictum dominum Karolum. Interrogatus si vidit quod dicta domina Mathildis apponeret manus ad tenendum dictum puerum ex quo tradidit ipsum dicto domino Valesii, dixit quod non recordatur nec de ipsa nec de aliis, /675// excepto de dicto domino Karolo [142]Comite Valesii, quia pressura erat, et non potuit se ita appropinquare quod illud bene posset videre. Interrogatus quid tenuit fama, dixit quod tenuit quod [143]dicta domina Mathildis comitissa Burgundie erat commater, ut supra deposuit. /676// Et nichil aliud pertinens dixit. Et non deposuit odio, amore, commodo vel timore, sed pro veritate, ut dixit. /677//

(v) Dominus Ger' de Saponhia, sacerdos, canonicus de Roya, testis iuratus et diligenter interrogatus super dicto xxx° articulo, super quo tantummodo fuit productus, dixit per iuramentum suum quod ipse vidit et audivit quod dicta domina Mathildis fuit nominata inter /678// alias que debebant esse commatres per elemosinarium dicte domine Iohanne Regine Francie in ecclesia de Credulio ubi idem dominus Karolus fuit baptizatus. Vidit etiam quod dicta domina Mathildis tunc Comitissa Burgundie recepit dictum /679// puerum nudum inter manus suas et tradidit eum supra fontes dicto domino Karolo Comiti Valesii, et vidit quod erat prope dictum dominum Karolum ad fontes baptismales dum dictus puer baptizaretur. Interrogatus si vidit quod teneret eum supra fon- /680// -tes, dixit per suum iuramentum quod non, quia propter pressuram que erat ibi non potuit hoc videre, sed firmiter credit quod fuit commater per ea que deposuit. Interrogatus si dicebatur postea quod fuisset commater, dixit se non recordari. Interrogatus ubi vidit /681// predicta, dixit quod in ecclesia de Credulio ubi fuit baptizatus idem dominus Karolus Rex Francie, ut predixerat. Interrogatus quare ibi venerat, dixit quod ex eo quia erat clericus capelle dicte domine Iohanne Regine, et venerat ad

---

[139] obstetricis] *corr. from* austetricis.   [140] manuum] *between lines.*
[141] compatrum] *corr. from* compatruum.   [142] Comite Valesii] *between lines.*
[143] dicta] *corr. from* dictan?

villam [144]eam /682// cum ea et iverat ad ecclesiam sicut alii ad videndum dictum baptismum. Et non deposuit odio vel amore, etc. /683//

(w) Dominus Nicolaus de Fara sacerdos, canonicus de Roya, testis iuratus et diligenter interrogatus super xxx° articulo super quo tantum fuit productus dixit, per iuramentum suum, quod vidit quod dicta domina Mathildis, in porta ecclesie de Credulio, in qua /684// fuit dictus puer baptizatus, recepit dictum puerum et portavit eum prope fontes. Et postmodum vidit quod dicta domina Mathildis puerum totum nudum pannis exsolutum tradidit domino Karolo Comiti Valesii supra fontes. Et vidit etiam, /685// ut dixit, quod predicta domina Mathildis tenuit supra dictos fontes dictum puerum per unum de pedibus ipsius pueri dum [145]baptizaretur. Interrogatus de fama, dixit [146]per suum iuramentum quod communiter dicta die dicebatur in dicta villa de Cre- /686// -dulio et in domo regine specialiter quod dicta domina Mathildis fuerat commater et quod pro tali habebatur. Interrogatus quare erat ibi, dixit quod erat clericus capelle domine regine, et venerat ad ecclesiam pro videndo dictum baptismum. /687// Item adiecit quod dicta Mathildis fuerat mandata per dictam dominam reginam per Michaelem le Flamenc qui missus fuerat ad ipsam ut veniret ad baptismum dicti domini Karoli. Et aliud pertinens non dixit. Et deposuit premissa /688// pro veritate que sic se habet ut dixit et non odio vel amore, commodo vel timore. /689//

[Depositions continue].

---

[144] eam] *final* m *strangely shaped.*   [145] baptizaretur] *followed by* eum (?), *deleted.*
[146] per] *between lines, corr. from* quod.

Appendix 3 London, British Library, Add. 20917

Louis XII and Jeanne de France: passages from the trial omitted in de Maulde's edition

The manuscript is one of the original official notarised copies of the trial proceedings. How it came to the British Library is obscure. It is parchment, 345 mm in height, 240 mm in width (written space: height 220 mm, width 145 mm); last written page 204r. (Cf. de Maulde, *Procédures politiques*, p. 803, for other manuscripts.)

The king's oath

> Passages in bold are supplied from the manuscript, whereas passages in ordinary type are printed in the edition.

[**fol. 77v**]: Anno domini **millesimo quadringesimo nonagesimo octavo, indictione secunda, mensis vero decembris die martis quarta pontificatus sanctissimi in Christo patris et domini nostri domini Alexandri divina providencia pape sexti anno septimo, nos, Philippus miseracione divina titulo(tt) sanctorum Petri et Marcellini sacrosancte Romane ecclesie presbiter cardinalis de Lucemburgo episcopus Cenomannensis, Ludovicus Albiensis et Fernandus Septiensis episcopi, iudices a sancta sede apostolica delegati** – insequendo appunctuamentum per nos **in causa nullitatis matrimonii inter Christianissimum Ludovicum Francorum regem, actorem, ex una, et illustrissimam dominam Iohannam de Francia, ream, ex altera partibus coram nobis pendente et mota, die lune precedenti datum, una cum scientificis viris magistris Petro de Bellessor, Officiali Parisiensi, et Roberto Lalongue, Officiali Archidiaconi Paris', assessoribus nostris in hac causa assumptis,** a villa Ambasie . . . [**fol. 77v**].

> Continues as in de Maulde, except that where the edition has 'et (*sic*) iuramentum', the ms. has the correct reading 'ut iuramentum'.

285

The next omission is in the edition, p. 932, after the words: 'nos, Philippus, Ludovicus et Fernandus, episcopi, judices antedicti, pro tribunali sedentes'. In the manuscript the words that follow are on fol. 78v, lines 4 ff.:

in presentia nobilis viri Karoli de Preux procuratoris dicte domine Iohanne literatorie fundati prestationi iuramenti veritatis in ipsa villa de Ligeul, expresse consentiente, prefatum Ludovicum regem, tactis sacrosanctis ewangeliis, et in verbo regio, preposita tamen prius et exhibita representatione Ihesu Christi, capite eius cum reverentia discooperto, iuramentum de dicendo veritatem super ipsis articulis per ipsam ream quotatis delatum et per ipsum dominum regem susceptum prestari fecimus quod, premissis sic ut premittitur gestis, prestitit petendo et requirendo huiusmodi articulos sibi legi, asserendo quod pro quacunque re mundi non vellet deierare, quodque ipse super ipsis articulis diceret veritatem. Quo iuramento sic prestito, obtemperando requeste dicti domini nostri regis, nos iudices prefati, per prefatum magistrum Petrum de Bellessor officialem Parisiensem, alterum assessorum, dictos articulos eidem Ludovico regi de longo ad longum et verbis galicis legi et exponi fecimus. Quibus lectis et expositis, ipsum dominum Ludovicum regem super omnibus et singulis articulis quotatis ipsius domine Iohanne de Francia, presente prefato Karolo de Preux procuratore dicte domine Iohanne interrogavimus. Quiquidem Ludovicus rex tunc requisivit huiusmodi articulos sibi communicari ut ad partem peramplius videret et certius et verius super ipsis respondere posset. Cuius petitioni [1]annuentes nos iudices, cum assessoribus ac aliis, ad alium locum retraximus, ac post spacium unius hore aut eocirca erga eundem [fol. 79r] Ludovicum regem nobis revertentibus et pro tribunali[2] sedentibus, prefatus Ludovicus rex, presente dicto Karolo procuratore dicte domine Iohanne, cuilibet articulorum sigillatim respondit,[3] quam scripto redactam legi fecit, et exinde se subscribendo illam tradidit prout et [4]quemadmodum in fine cuiuslibet articuli continetur et habetur. Et primo sequitur tenor decimi quinti et responsionis super eo . . .

(fols. 78v–79r)

fol. 79v: [seventeenth article] Item quod ipse actor singulis annis bina aut trina vice veniebat apud dictum locum de Ligniers ad

---

[1] annuen' *ms.*   [2] seden' *ms.*   [3] *i.e.* quam responsionem?   [4] q,ᵃdmodum *ms.*

ipsam ream suam uxorem videndum[5] et ibidem morabatur per
decem aut duodecim aut plures dies, et cum eadem pernoctebat,
solus cum sola, nudus cum nuda, debitum coniugale per carnalem
copulam reddendo, risus, oscula, amplexus et alia signa appetitiva experiencie copule coniugalis, ymo etiam veracis copule,
prout decet inter coniuges, aperte manifestando, prout manifes-
tavit antedictus actor, et hoc fuerat et erat tunc tenporis verum,
publicum, notorium et manifestum. Super quo decimo septimo
articulo [6]respond quil a este a lignieres, mais que respond . . . [fol.
80r] . . . nu a nu (fols. 79v−80r).

fol. 80r: Item quod ipse actor cum ex lecto coniugali surg-
eret pluries dixit et se iactavit coram pluribus quod [80r] necesse
habebat bibere et gentari eo quod ipsam ream ter aut quarter cog-
noverat carnaliter, dicens verbis gallicis: 'Jay bien gaigne a boyre
pource que jay chevauche ma femme la nuyt troys ou quatre foiz',
loquendo de ipsa rea. Super quo articulo decimo octavo [7]affirmat
iuramento quil net pas vroy.

> Passage added above, p. 215 n. 178 from British Library, Add. 20917,
> fol. 203v:

'quandam tortuositatem in orificio vulve adeo quod virga eius
non poterat ingredi, sed caleficiendo se emittebat semen inter
seu supra crura ipsius domine Iohanne'.

> Cf. the deposition of another medical doctor, Jean Bourgeois, in de
> Maulde, *Procédures politiques*, p. 1033; the bowdlerised words are sup-
> plied by Destefanis, *Louis XII et Jeanne de France*, p. 161, on the basis
> of the manuscript he used (they are also in British Library, Add. 20917,
> fol. 157v):

He heard it said by the same present king, at that time the Duke of
Orleans, that he had tried very hard to have intercouse with her, and that
he had not sown in the field of nature, but after much effort and great
agitation he used to sow his seed between the hips, as the same king
believed and reported to him.

---

[5] *Sic for* videndam?
[6] *Remainder of response printed by de Maulde,* Procédures politiques, *pp. 932–3: British
Library, Add. 20917 varies only trivially.*
[7] affirmat . . . vroy] *printed by de Maulde, who has* vray *not* vroy.

Appendix 4   London, British Library, Add. 37154

This eighteenth-century transcription is full of minor errors, most of which were then corrected. For approximately the first 1,000 words I record these minutiae in the apparatus, to give an idea of the character of the manuscript, but after that I pass over them in silence.

The first transcription is an extract from Catherine's appeal to have the case transferred to Rome. It includes the two papal dispensations on which her case for the validity of her marriage to Henry rested. Passages more or less common to the two dispensations are in italics.

fol. 8r—
Tenor vero mandati [1]procurationis ac substitutionis procuratorum publicorum instrumentorum unde supra fit mentio, sequuntur et sunt tales:

[2]Katarina Regina
Universis [3]Christifidelibus ad quos presentes littere sive hoc presens [4]procuratorii [5]protestationis, reclamationis et discensus instrumentum [6]pervenerit Catherina Dei gratia Anglie regina et invictissimi [7]principis Henrici illius nominis post conquestum [8]octavi Anglie et Francie [9]reges moderni consors, uxor, et [10]ligittima coniux, salutem in visceribus Ihesu Cristi.

Ad [11]notitiam vestram deduco, et [12]deduci volo per presentes, quod [13]Artherus, cuius [14]anime [15]commisse Deus condonet, pubes me puberem duxit in uxorem, et mecum per aliquot noctes concubuit, citra

---

[1] procurationis] *after two deletions.*
[2] Katherina . . . Regina] *underlined: in left hand margin:* (Mandatum serenissime domine Catharine Regine Anglie principalis in quo magnificus Dominus de Mayo).
[3] Christifidelibus] *corr. to* Cristifidelibus? *In the document we find both* Christ- *and* Crist-.
[4] procuratorii] *after corr.*   [5] protestationis] *after corr.*
[6] pervenerit] perveneritit *ms.*   [7] principis] *after deletion.*   [8] octavi] ortam *ms.*
[9] reges] *read* regis.   [10] ligittima] *sic ms.*   [11] notitiam] *after corr.*
[12] deduci] *between lines, after* Deum *deleted.*   [13] Artherus] *corr. from* Arthurus.
[14] anime] *probably corr. from* animo.   [15] commisse] commisso *ms.? See trans.*

288

tamen carnalem copulam; post cuius mortem et sepulturam prefatus
illustrissimus rex Henricus octavus [16]eiusdem Arthuri frater naturalis,
cum vix duodecim annorum esset etatis, mecum sponsalia contraxit, ac
nostri postea parentes ut nobis ad invicem matrimonium de presenti non
obstante [**fo. 8ᵛ**] affinitatis impedimento [17]contrahere liceret apostolicas
obtinuerunt dispensationes, quarum tenor sequitur, et est talis de [18]verbo
ad verbum:

{**Iulius Episcopus servus** servorum dei dilecto filio Henrico charissimi in Cristo filii nostri Henrici Anglie regis illustris nato, et dilecte in
Christo filie nostre Catherine, charissimi in Cristo filii nostri Ferdinandi
regis et charissime in Christo [19]filiae nostre Elizabet Regine Hispaniarum
et Sicilie, catholicorum, nate, illustribus, salutem et [20]apostolicam benedictionem. *Romani pontificis [21]precellens auctoritas [22]concessa sibi [23]desuper
utitur potestate prout personarum negotiorum, et temporum qualitate pensata
id in Domino conspicit salubriter expedire. Oblate nobis nuper pro parte vestra
peticionis series continebat [24]quod, cum alias [25]tu, [26]filia Catherina, et tunc in
humanis agens Arthurus, [27]carissimi in Cristo [28]filii [29]nostri Henrici Anglie
regis [30]illustris primogenitus, pro conservandis pacis et amicitie nexibus et federibus inter carissimum in Cristo filium nostrum Ferdinandum et carissimam
in Christo filiam nostram Elisabeth Hispaniarum et Sicilie catholicos, et prefatum Anglie reges et reginam, matrimonium per verba legittime de presenti
contraxissetis, illudque carnali copula forsan consumassetis, [31]dictus Arthurus prole ex huiusmodi matrimonio non suscepta, discessit,* cum autem sic
ut eadem petitio subiungebat, [**fol. 9ʳ**] [32]ab hoc ut huiusmodi vinculum
pacis et amicitie inter prefatos reges et reginam diutius permaneat, cupi-
atis *matrimonium inter vos per verba legittime de presenti contrahere,* supplicari nobis fecistis ut vobis in premissis de opportuna *dispensationis gratia
providere de benignitate apostolica dignaremur. Nos igitur qui inter singulos
Cristi fideles presertim catholicos reges et principes pacis et concordie ameni-
tatem vigere intensis desideriis affectamus,* vosque et quemlibet vestrum a
quibuscumque [33]excummunicationis, suspensionis et interdicti aliisque
ecclesiasticis sententiis, censuris et penis a iure vel ab homine quavis

---

[16] eiusdem] *after deletion.*   [17] contrahere] *after corr.*
[18] verbo . . . servus *underlined: in margin:* (insertio brevis apostolici).
[19] filiae] *the eighteenth-century transcriber is not quite consistent with the orthography of* ae/e.
[20] apostolicam] aplicam *ms., without abbreviation mark.*
[21] precellens] percellens *ms.*   [22] concessa] *corr. from* commissa.
[23] desuper] desupre *ms., altered. from* desupere.   [24] quod] *corr. from* quam.
[25] tu] *added later?*   [26] filia] *after double correction.*   [27] carissimi] *corr. from* carissimus.
[28] filii] *corr. from* filius.   [29] nostri] *corr. from* noster.
[30] illustris] *corr. from* illtustris.   [31] dictus] *corr. from* dicens.   [32] ab] *read* ad?
[33] excummunicationis] *sic ms., and corr. from* excummunationis.

occasione vel causa latis, si quibus quomodolibet innodati existis, ad effectum presentium dumtaxat consequendum harum serie [34]absolventes et absolutos fore censentes, *huiusmodi* [35] *supplicationibus inclinati, vobiscum ut impedimento affinitatis huiusmodi ex premissis proveniente* ac constitutionibus et ordinationibus apostolicis ceterisque contrariis nequaquam obstantibus matrimonium per verba legittime de presenti *inter vos contrahere, et in eo postquam contractum fuerit etiam si* [36] *iam forsan hactenus de facto publice vel clandestine contraxeritis, ac illud carnali copula consumaveritis,* [37] *licite remanere valeatis, auctoritate apostolica* [38]tenore presentium [39]de specialis dono gratie *dispensamus,* ac *vos et quemlibet vestrum,* si contraxeritis ut prefertur, *ab excessu* [**fol. 9v**] [40] *huiusmodi ac excommunicationis sententia quam propterea incurristis eadem auctoritate absolvimus, prolem ex huiusmodi matrimonio sive contracto sive contrahendo susceptam forsan vel suscipiendam legittimam decernendo,* proviso quod tu, filia Catharina, propter hoc rapta non fueris. [41] *Volumus autem quod, si huiusmodi matrimonium de facto contraxistis, confessor per vos, et quemlibet vestrum eligendus, penitentiam salutarem propterea vobis iniungat, quam adimplere teneamini.* Nulli ergo omnino hominum liceat hanc paginam nostram absolutionis, dispensationis, et voluntatis infringere vel ei ausu temerario [42]contraire. Si quis autem hoc attemptare presumpserit, indignationem omnipotentis dei ac beatorum Petri et Pauli apostolorum eius se noverit incursurum. Datum Rome apud Sanctum Petrum anno incarnationis Dominice millesimo [43]quingentesimo tertio, septimo kal. ianuarii pontificatus nostri anno primo. [44]Sigismundus signavit.}

{ [45]Dilecte [46]fili et dilecta filia salutem et [47]appostolicam benedictionem. *Romani pontificis precellens auctoritas commissa sibi desuper utitur potestate prout personarum negotiorum et temporum qualitate pensata id in Domino conspicit salubriter expedire. Oblate nobis nuper pro parte vestra petitionis* [48] *series continebat quod cum alias tu filia Catharina et tunc in* [49] *humanis agens quondam* [**fol. 10r**] *Arthurus* [50] *charissimi in Cristo* [51] *filii nostri Henrici Anglie regis illustris primogenitus, pro conservandis pacis et amicitie nexibus et federibus* inter prefatum [52] *Anglie et charissimum in Christo filium nostrum* [53] *Ferdinandum regem et charissimam in Cristo filiam nostram*

---

[34] absolventes] absolvem'(?), *corr. from* absolvemus.   [35] supplicationibus] *after corr.*
[36] iam] *over curious looped underlining.*   [37] licite] *after corr.*   [38] tenore] *after* t *deleted.*
[39] de] *after deletion.*   [40] huiusmodi] *written into a space left blank?*
[41] Volumus] *written over* vel minus *deleted.*   [42] contraire] *after corr.*
[43] quingentesimo] *after corr.*   [44] gismundus signavit . . . fili et] *underlined.*
[45] *In margin:* (Insertio alterius brevis).   [46] fili] *after corr.*   [47] appostolicam] *sic ms.*
[48] series] *corr. from* fuere.   [49] humanis] *corr. from* germanis.
[50] charissimi] *corr. from* charissimus.   [51] filii nostri] *corr. from* filius noster.
[52] Anglie] *read* Anglie regem?   [53] Ferdinandum] *after corr.*

reginam [54]*catholicos Hispaniarum et* [55]*Sicilie matrimonium per verba legittime de presenti contraxeritis, illudque carnali copula consumaveritis,* quia
tamen *dictus Arthurus prole ex huiusmodi matrimonio non suscepta discessit,*
et huiusmodi vinculum pacis et connexitatis inter prefatos reges et reginam ita firmiter verisimiliter non perduraret nisi etiam illud alio affinitatis vinculo confoveretur, et confirmaretur, ex hiis et aliis certis causis
[56]*desideratis matrimonium inter vos per verba legittime de presenti contrahere,*
sed [57]quia desiderium vestrum in premissis adimplere non potestis dispensatione apostolica desuper non obtenta, nobis propterea humiliter
[58]supplicari fecistis ut vobis providere in premissis *de dispensationis gratia et benignitate apostolica dignaremur. Nos igitur, qui inter singulos Cristi
fideles presertim inter catholicos reges et principes pacis et concordie ameni-
tatem vigere intensis desideriis affectamus,* hiis et aliis causis animum nostrum moventibus, *huiusmodi supplicationibus inclinati vobiscum* ut *aliquo
impedimento* [59]*affinitatis huiusmodi* [**fol. 10v**] *ex premissis proveniente non
obstante, matrimonium inter vos contrahere et* [60]*in eo postquam contractum
fuerit* [61]*remanere* libere et licite *valeatis auctoritate* [62]*appostolica* per presentes *dispensamus,* et quatenus *forsan iam matrimonium inter vos de facto
publice* [63]*vel* [64]*clandestine contraxeritis ac carnali copula consumaveritis vos
et quemlibet vestrum ab excessu huiusmodi* [65][ac] excommunicationis sententia quam propterea incurristis eadem auctoritate absolvimus ac etiam
vobiscum ut in huiusmodi matrimonio sic de facto contracto seu illud de
novo [66]inter vos contrahere libere et licite valeatis similiter dispensamus,
*prolem ex huiusmodi matrimonio sive contracto sive contrahendo suscipiendam
legittimam decernendo. Volumus autem si huiusmodi* [67]*matrimonium de facto
contraxistis confessor per vos, et quemlibet vestrum eligendus, penitentiam quam
implere teneamini propterea* [68]vobis iniungat. Datum Rome apud sanctum Petrum sub annulo Piscatoris die vigesima sexta Decembris millesimo quingentesimo tertio pontificatus nostri anno primo. Sigismundus.
Superscriptio talis est: Dilecto filio Henrico charissimi in Cristo [69]fili
nostri Henrici Anglie Regis illustris [70]nato illustri et dilecte in Cristo filie
Catharine cha- [**fol. 11r**] -issimi etiam in Cristo filii nostri Ferdinandi
regis et charissime in Cristo filie nostre Elisabet Hispaniarum et Sicilie

---

[54] catholicos] *after corr.*   [55] Sicilie] *after corr.*   [56] desideratis] *after corr.*
[57] quia] *after corr.*   [58] supplicari] *corr. from* supplicare.   [59] affinitatis] *after corr.*
[60] in eo] *after* inire *deleted.*   [61] remanere] *after corr.*   [62] appostolica] *after corr.*
[63] vel] *after corr.*   [64] clandestine] *corr. from* occulte.
[65] ac] *om. ms., supplied from sense.*   [66] inter] *letters added and deleted.*
[67] matrimonium] *after corr.*   [68] vobis . . . apud] *underlined.*
[69] fili] *sic.*   [70] nato] *after corr.*

catholicorum [71]nate illustri, et inter [72]immargine [73]affixus est annulus [74]piscatoris.}

[Note: from this point trivial corrected errors in the manuscript are not noted.]

– quorum vigore interim mecum sponsalia contraxit circiter annum duodevicesimum tunc etatis habens, in quibus per quatuor annos fuimus; tandem prefatus illustrissimus rex Henricus octavus me ad matrimonium sollicitavit; nuptie inter nos solempnizantur ex more publice, interim perlecta dispensatione; ut vir et uxor per octodecim annos viximus et cohabitavimus, prout in presenti vivimus et cohabitamus, proles suscepimus et habebamus, quarum una superstes filia manet. Nuper tamen, quod dolenter fero, apud multos de valore illius matrimonii inter nos ut prefertur contracti et consumati dubium vertebatur, et quin ut pretenditur illustrissimus rex Henricus octavus maritus meus amantissimus ex hoc matrimonio conscientiam habet lesam. Plurimi sunt qui divortium inter nos fieri ambiunt, et ut facilius id apostolica auctoritate consequantur, suggerunt summo pontifici quod ego divortium inter me et prefatum regem illustrissimum Henricum octavum fieri cupio, et ut sic fiat consentio, et quod religionem ingredi ea de causa [**fol. 11v**] polliceor; pluraque alia eque ficta et falsa meo nomine narrant et explicant, cum revera ego nunquam assensum meum ad tale divortium celebrandum prebui, nec religionem ea aut alia quacumque de causa unquam ingredi decrevi, nec mandatum procuratorum aut potestatem aliquam ad id suggerendum summo pontifici dedi, feci, aut alicui concessi, ymmo ab omnibus et singulis factis et dictis quibus huiusmodi divortium fieri, et procurari potuit dissentiebam, et reclamavi quam cito aliquid tale ad meam pervenit noticiam, prout in presenti tenore presentium dissentio, et reclamo, protestando prout protestor palam, publice, et aperte per hec mea scripta, quod nunquam ut huiusmodi divortium fiat assentiam, sed quantum de iure potero, reluctabor . . .

The queen's proctor presented her side's articles, set out fols. 43r–47v. In the transcriptions below I have moved the article numbers from the margin to before the article in question. They are a selection of the articles which seem especially relevant legally. The variant spellings of Catherine's name are in the manuscript.

---

[71] nate] *corr. from* nato?   [72] immargine] *after corr.;* inmargine *could be read.*
[73] continuatio mandati] *in margin*; affixus . . . quorum *underlined.*
[74] piscatoris] *after corr.*

We should note the claim that the dispensation covered both public honesty and affinity.

fol. 45v: XVI. [75]Item quod prefatus felicis recordationis Iulius Papa secundus, visa importantia pacis federis et amicitie inter dictos Hispanie, et Anglie reges conservande, et ad occurrendum scandalis, controversiis et discordiis inter eosdem reges, si que verisi | militer [**fol. 46r**] oriri formidabantur, aliisque ex causis et [76]eorum intuitu [77]Henricus Octavus et serenissima Caterina reges predicti publice honestatis et affinitatis si que contracte forte [78]fuisset impedimentis non obstantibus matrimonium inter se contrahere et in illo permanere possent potiori pro cauthela dispensavit, prout in litteris apostolicis desuper confectis quas procurator predictus hic dat loco positionum et articulorum quatenus pro se dictaque parte sua et contra partem adversam faciant aut facere videantur et non alias aliter nec alio modo de quo expresse protestatur plenius continetur. (fols. 45v–46r)

Note also the stress on the fact that the dispensation was well known to Henry and Catherine before they contracted marriage:

fol. 46r–XVII. [79]Item ponit quod dispensatio ut premittitur per felicis recordationis Iulium Papam Secundum Henrico octavo et serenissime Catherine regibus predictis ut premittitur concessa fuit in regno Anglie publica et notoria et tempore quo Henricus et Catharina reges predicti matrimonium publice in facie ecclesie contraxerunt ibi lecta et publicata atque plene intellecta prout testes qui interfuerunt dicere et deponere poterunt ac dicent et deponent palam et publice et sic fuit et est verum.

XVIII. [80]Item quod illustrissimus Henricus octavus et serenissima Catherina Anglie reges ante tempus et tempore inter eos contracti et confirmati matrimonii | (**fol. 46v**) sciverunt et sciebant huiusmodi dispensationem eis ad contrahendum inter se matrimonium a sede apostolica concessam et de illa plenam noticiam habuerunt et habebant palam et publice, et sic fuit et est verum.

XIX. [81]Item quod prefatus illustrissimus Henricus octavus et serenissima Catherina Anglie reges previa dicta dispensatione publice in eorum presentia lecta et publicata in legittima etate ad contrahendum matrimonium constituti matrimonium per verba de presenti publice et in facie sancte matris ecclesie presentibus populi multitudine et magnatibus et prelatis regni Anglie . . . contraxerunt . . . (fol. 46r–v)

---

[75] Item . . . recordationis] *underlined.*   [76] eorum] *followed by a line-filler or deletion.*
[77] Henricus] *read* ut Henricus?   [78] fuisset] *read* fuissent.
[79] Item . . . premittitur] *underlined.*
[80] Item . . . Octavus] *underlined.*   [81] Item . . . Henricus] *underlined.*

After many twists and turns in the formal proceedings, Henry's representative, not a formal proctor, said that the king wanted to appear in person, not through a proctor – but that it was difficult for him to do so at that time.[82]

fol. 61r: [83]Item similiter constare dicit et constat quod ex causis et rationibus predictis ipsius domini Enrici Regis minus interest sibique tamquam melius et magis scienti informato et instructo importat et expedit si et ubi agatur ipsa causa personaliter et per se ipsum non autem per procuratorem illi interesse, assistere et instruendos instruere et informandos informare prout etiam in iure fuit et est clarum, et sic fuit et est verum, publicum, notorium et manifestum . . . [**fol. 61ᵛ**] . . . [84]Item quod veritas fuit et est quod retroactis temporibus regibus et principibus a regnis et principatibus ipsorum recedentibus [**fol. 62r**] et ad loca remota se conferentibus et absentantibus – presertim regibus Anglie – ob eorum recessum et absentiam, in dictis regnis et principatibus, et presertim in regno Anglie, insurrexerunt seditiones, tumultus, scandala, questiones, rixe, et discordie, que tetenderunt in maximum [85]exilium et gravem [86]iacturam et enormissimum dampnum tam dictorum regnorum et principatuum quam eorum regum et principum ac regnicolarum habitatorum et in eis incolarum, et sic fuit publicum, manifestum, et notorium.

(British Library, Add. 37154, fols. 61r −62r)

The next passage develops the same point about the danger of leaving the kingdom. Where all this leads is to the claim that Henry needs to be present, but he cannot come: the implication is that the trial in Rome is unfair.

---

[82] *Surtz*, Henry VIII's Great Matter, *vol. II, pp. 987–8: 'the court register . . . enters under January 30, 1531, the appearance of* Odoardus Karne *. . . [p. 988] . . . who asserted and produced certain defensory and excusatory matters to prevent procedure against the King. . . . Carne's points . . . were written into the record (foll. 60–64v)'. Surtz goes on to summarise them. I transcribe points 4 and 6, omitting the marginal numbers.*

[83] *In margin:* Item . . . constat] *underlined.*

[84] *In margin:* Item . . . retroactis] *underlined.*

[85] exilium] *read* exitium?   [86] iactura] factura *ms.*

Appendix 5   Glossary of technical terms

This short alphabetical glossary of technical terms is intended for the documents edited and/or translated in this volume. It is in a way a problem that the English translations tend to conceal the technicality of the Latin, in order to make it intelligible to the reader, so the purpose of the mini-lexicon is to flag up the presence of professional legal language as well as to explain it. The procedure followed here is designed to both to identify and explain technicality. It is to pick out legal language lemmata from the translations of proctorial statements, to put them together with the Latin (as I have often also done in notes to the translation), and to give a short gloss where appropriate.

This informal guide is no substitute for proper dictionaries, among which the following are especially convenient (for readers of German at least): E. Habel and F. Gröbel, *Mittellateinisches Glossar* (Paderborn, 1989), and Albert Sleumer, *Kirchenlateinisches Wörterbuch* (Hildesheim 2006 facsimile of Limburg an der Lahn, 1926 edn). Though it is not specifically for canon law, R. E. Latham, *Revised Medieval Latin Word-List from British and Irish Sources* (London, 1965), is very handy. There is in fact a larger lexicon purporting to meet this need: Konrad Eugen and Franz Rosshirt, *Manuale Latinitiatis Juris Canonici: Rerum Moralium et Theoligicarum, Brevessimis Annotationibus et Probationibus Instructum, quo Lexici Juris Canonici Lineamenta Proponere Studuit* (Schaffhausen, 1862). But this is less helpful for our documents than its title suggests, and of course it is all in Latin. The admirable analyses of canon law procedure by R. H. Helmholz, *The Spirit of Classical Canon Law* (Athens, GA, 1996) and Brundage, *Medieval Canon Law*, are perhaps the best preparation for an informed reading of the more technical documents.

accept jurisdiction of a judge who might not otherwise have cognisance]
  iurisdictionem iudicis prorogandi: see Adrianus den Bandt, *Specimen Iuridicum Inaugurale De Prorogata Jurisdictione* (Lugduni Batavorum, 1852), p. 2 'Therefore we think that the prorogation of juristiction is

that which is exercised outside the limits of its competence, either by the consent of the parties, or by order of the law' (my translation).

affinity] *affinitas*: an impediment to marriage arising if one has previously consummated marriage, or had sexual intercourse, with someone related within the forbidden degrees of consanguinity.

annulment] *divortium*: the Latin word covers a wide range, including annulment, legal separation, and divorce in the modern sense (possible for non-consummated marriages in the Middle Ages).

apostolic letter] *litterae apostolicae*: papal bull (in the broad loose sense).

apostolic: papal.

apostolic blessing] *apostolicam benedictionem*: from language meaning 'greetings' from the pope.

articles] *articuli*: propositions to be put to witnesses. In practice *articuli* and *positiones* seem sometimes to be used interchangeably. Note also *articulandum* for 'to formulate articles'.

authenticate] *in fidem*: seal is affixed 'in fidem' of the statements made in the document.

burden of giving satisfaction] *onus satisdandi*: the grantor of power of attorney may guarantee that the proctor will be free from this burden.

calumny, oath of] *iuramentum de calumnia*: very broadly, an oath not to pervert the cause of justice, that the case is being brought or contested in good faith, and that 'the litigants will employ no fraudulent means to win their suit':[1] goes beyond the common law oath to tell the truth, the whole truth, etc. (which also had a canon law counterpart). Cf. Linda Fowler-Magerl, *'Ordines iudiciarii' and 'libelli de ordine iudiciorum': From the Middle of the Twelfth to the End of the Fifteenth Century* (Turnhout, 1994), p. 44.

canonical conclusion] *fine canonico*: an ending in accordance with the law of the Church.

certain knowledge] *ex certa scientia*: the document has been issued with the personal knowledge of the pope or other authority issuing it (as opposed to by the administration without his specific knowledge); such a document outranks a document without such a formula (see d'Avray, *Medieval Religious Rationalities*, pp. 144–5, for further references).

contumacious] *contumax*: refusing to take part in a trial.

---

[1] This element of the definition was supplied by Emily Corran, who has made a study of the term.

de facto, marriage contracted] *matrimonium de facto contractum*: a union with the appearance but, by implication, not the reality of a marriage.

definitive sentence] *sententia diffinitiva*: final verdict. Cf. Brundage, *Medieval Origins*, pp. 442–3.

delay] *dilatio*: an adjournment.

dissolution: *see* annulment.

document] *instrumentum*: a document with legal force, especially one drawn up by a notary.

due process] *ordo iuris* or *ordo iudiciarius*: following the formal legal procedures.

each of them entirely] *in solidum*: in the language of the common law, power of attorney held jointly and severally, so that each proctor can take up what another has begun.

full and unlimited power] *plenam et liberam potestatem*: there are echoes of the papal *plena potestas* or sovereignty. There are no implicit limits to what the proctor can do in the place of the person he represents.

guaranteed by] *hypotheca*: [goods] pledged as guarantee [that costs will be paid].

in the eyes of the Church] *in facie ecclesiae*: marriage legitimate in the Church's view (probably rather than 'at the Church door').

instrument] *see* document] *instrumentum*.

interlocutory sentence] *sententia interlocutoria*: interim judgement, especially on objections (*exceptiones*) or procedural rulings: cf. Brundage, *Medieval Origins*, pp. 161, 432.

judge delegate, papal] *delegatus, iudex delegatus*: a judge who can exercise the office of the pope with respect to a particular lawsuit – often in conjunction with one or more other delegates.

libellus: virtually equivalent to an English common law writ, in the sense of a document by which a plaintiff starts a case against a defendant, though the associations of 'writ' with England are too strong for it to be an appropriate translation.

litis contestatio: the formal opening of the trial, at which the plaintiff's case (as refined after the pre-trial back and forth) is stated and denied, and the oath of calumny (q.v.) taken.

objection] *exceptio*: generically comparable to 'objections' in modern common law jurisdisctions. For an analysis of medieval specificities, see *Brundage, Medieval Origins*, pp. 431–2.

Official] *officialis*: bishop's deputy.[2]

---

[2] My pupil Aaron Hope has in hand a study of the development of this office in England.

on my soul] *in nostram animam*: when a proctor takes an oath on his client's soul, it is as if the client has sworn it, so that the client is morally responsible.

plea] *accusatio*: lawsuit.

positiones: *see* articles; *ponendi* = stating *positiones* to be put to witnesses.

proctor] *procurator*: lawyer legally empowered to act in place of his client; person with power of attorney.

publicly available form] *forma publica*: an official public notarial record.

publish depositions] *depositiones publicare*: 'After all the witnesses had been questioned and copies of their depositions prepared, the court scheduled a further hearing for the "publication" of their testimony. Both parties had to be present to certify that they did not intend to call any further witnesses and to petition jointly that the recorded testimony be made public. When the judge granted their petition, he directed his notary to read the depositions (or at least some of them) aloud, after which he furnished copies to each party and scheduled a further session to hear and adjudicate any exceptions the parties might wish to raise concerning the fitness of the witnesses to testify or the content of their evidence.'[3]

records] *acta*: the official record of proceedings, especially in a legal context.

records] *gesta*: official record of a trial; 'acts' is a synonym.

records] *acta* or *gesta*: official record of a trial. Another possible translation for 'records' would be 'acts'. In some contexts *acta* could also be translated as '[legal] deeds'.

replication] *replicatio*: a formal reply, embodying an objection, by the plaintiff (see Brundage, *Medieval Origins*, p. 157); cf. *Oxford English Dictionary*: replication is 'any response made by one party to the other's argument', etc.; 'In traditional English pleadings: a claimant's answer to a defendant's plea.'

security for costs] *iudicatum solvi*: the person granting power of attorney guarantees that the proctors will not be liable for costs.

summarily, straightforwardly, and without without judicial commotion and formalities] *summarie et de plano et sine strepitu iudicii et figura*: an abbreviated and simplified legal procedure. Cf. Brundage, *The Medieval Origins of the Legal Profession*, pp. 449–51; and Brundage, *Medieval Canon Law*, p. 139 (I adapt his translation). See also C. Lefebvre, 'Les origines romaines de la procédure sommaire aux XIIe

---

[3] Brundage, *Medieval Origins*, p. 438.

et XIIIe siècles', *Ephemerides iuris canonici* 12 (1956), pp. 149–56, cited Brundage, *Medieval Canon Law*, p. 139, note 24.

with procuratorial commission from] *nomine procuratorio*: acting with power of attorney.

with the advice of his brothers] *de fratrum suorum consilio*: with the counsel of the college of cardinals.

withdraw formally] *renuntiandi*: cf. *Oxford English Dictionary*, 'renounce', under 'Etymology'.

Bibliography

Airlie, Stuart, 'Private Bodies and the Body Politic in the Divorce Case of Lothar II', *Past and Present* 161 (1998), pp. 3–38.

Annales Xantenses et Annales Vedastini, ed. B. de Simson (*MGH*, SS rer. Germ. 'in usum scholarum' XII; Hannover, 1909).

Anton, E., '"Handfasting" in Scotland', *Scottish Historical Review* 37 (1958), pp. 89–102.

Aubery, [le sieur] *L'histoire du Cardinal Duc de Ioyeuse, a la fin de laquelle sont plusieurs Memoires, Lettres, Dépéches, Instructions, Ambassades, Relations, & autres pieces non encore imprimées* (Paris, 1654).

Aurell, Martin, *Les noces du comte: mariage et pouvoir en Catalogne (785–1213)* (Paris, 1995).

Auvray, Lucien, *Les registres de Grégoire IX: recueil des bulles de ce pape publiées ou analysées d'après les manuscrits... du Vatican* (Bibliothèque des Écoles Françaises d'Athènes et de Rome; Paris, 1896).

Baldwin, John W., *Masters, Princes and Merchants: The Social Views of Peter the Chanter and his Circle*, 2 vols. (Princeton, NJ, 1970).

Bauer, Thomas, 'Rechtliche Implikationen des Ehestreites Lothars II.: Eine Fallstudie zu Theorie und Praxis des geltenden Eherechts in der späten Karolingerzeit. Zugleich ein Beitrag zur Geschichte des frühmittelalterlichen Eherechts', *Zeitschrift der Savigny Stiftung f. Rechtsgeschichte, kanonistische Abteilung* 80 (1994), pp. 41–87.

Baumgartner, Frederic J., *Louis XII* (Stroud, 1994).

Bedouelle, Guy and Le Gal, Patrick, *Le 'divorce' du roi Henry VIII: études et documents* (Geneva, 1987).

Berger, E., *Les registres de Innocent IV*, vol. I (Bibliothèque des Écoles Françaises d'Athènes et de Rome; Paris, 1884).

Bischoff, Georges, 'Maximilien 1er, roi des Romains, duc de Bourgogne et de Bretagne', in Jean Kerhervé and Tanguy Daniel (eds.), *1491: la Bretagne, terre d'Europe*. International conference, Brest, 2–4 October 1991 (Brest, 1992), pp. 457–71.

Bouchard, Constance Brittain, 'Eleanor's Divorce from Louis VII: The Uses of Consanguinity', in Bonnie Wheeler and John Carmi Parsons (eds.), *Eleanor of Aquitaine, Lord and Lady* (New York, 2002), pp. 223–35.

Bouquet, Martin and Delisle, Leopold, *Recueil des historiens des Gaules et de la France*, vol. XV (Paris, 1878).

Bourel de la Roncière, C., de Loye, J., de Cenival, P. and Coulon, A., *Les registres d'Alexandre IV*, vol. II (Bibliothèques des Écoles Françaises d'Athènes et de Rome, 2nd series; Paris, 1917).

Bruguière, M. B., 'Canon Law and Royal Weddings, Theory and Practice: The French Example, 987–1215', in S. Chodorow (ed.), *Proceedings of the Eighth International Congress of Medieval Canon Law* (Monumenta Iuris Canonici, Series C, Subsidia IX; Vatican City, 1992), pp. 473–96.

'Le mariage de Philippe-Auguste et d'Isambour de Danemark: aspects canoniques et politiques', in Université des Sciences Sociales de Toulouse (ed.), *Mélanges offerts à Jean Dauvillier* (Toulouse, 1979), pp. 135–56.

Brundage, James A., 'The Canon Law of Divorce in the Mid-Twelfth Century: Louis c. Eleanor of Aquitaine', in Bonnie Wheeler and John Carmi Parsons (eds.), *Eleanor of Aquitaine, Lord and Lady* (New York, 2002), pp. 213–21.

Medieval Canon Law (Harlow, 1995).

The Medieval Origins of the Legal Profession: Canonists, Civilians and the Courts (Chicago, 2008).

Buchanan, Patricia Hill, *Margaret Tudor Queen of Scots* (Edinburgh, 1985).

Bullarium Cyprium, vol. I: *Papal Letters Concerning Cyprus, 1196–1261*, ed. Christopher Schabel, with introduction by Jean Richard (Cyprus Research Centre: Texts and Studies in the History of Cyprus LXIV; Nicosia, 2010).

Burns, Robert I., 'The Spiritual Life of Jaume the Conqueror of Arago-Catalonia, 1208–1276: Portrait and Self-Portrait', *Catholic Historical Review* 62 (1976), pp. 1–35.

Canteaut, Olivier, 'L'annulation du mariage de Charles IV et de Blanche de Bourgogne: une affaire d'État?', in Emmanuelle Santinelli (ed.), *Répudiation, séparation, divorce dans l'Occident médiéval* (Recherches Valenciennoises XXV; Valenciennes, 2007), pp. 309–27.

Cazel, Fred A. Jnr and Painter, Sidney, 'The Marriage of Isabelle of Angoulême', *English Historical Review* 63 (1948), pp. 83–9.

'The Marriage of Isabelle of Angoulême', *English Historical Review* 67 (1952), pp. 233–5.

Chaplais, P., *Medieval Diplomatic Practice*, part I, vol. I (London, 1975).

Cheney, C. R. and Jones, Michael, *Handbook of Dates for Students of English History* (Cambridge, 2000).

Colección de docmentos ineditos para la Estoria de Espana, vol. XL, ed. Marqueses de Pidal y de Miriaflores y D. Miguel Salva (Madrid, 1862).

Collard, Franck, 'Les scandaleux divorces des rois de France', *L'Histoire* 189 (1995), pp. 56–61.

Contamine, Philippe, 'Un aspect de la "tyrannie" de Louis XI: variations sur le thème du "roi marieur"', in Michel Rouche and Jean Heuclin (eds.), *La femme au Moyen Age: Actes du colloque de Maubeuge (1988)* (Ville de Maubeuge, 1990).

Cottineau, L. H., *Répertoire topo-bibliographique des abbayes et prieurés*, 2 vols. (Macon, 1939).

Coulon, A., *Lettres secrètes et curiales du pape Jean XXII (1316–1334) relatives à la France* (Bibliothèque des Écoles Françaises d'Athènes et de Rome; Paris, 1906).

d'Avray, D. L., 'Authentication of Marital Status: A Thirteenth-Century English Royal Annulment Process and Late Medieval Cases from the Papal Penitentiary', *English Historical Review* 120 (2005), pp. 987–1013.

Medieval Religious Rationalities: A Weberian Analysis (Cambridge, 2010).

'Papal Authority and Religious Sentiment in the Late Middle Ages', in Diana Wood (ed.), *The Church and Sovereignty, c. 590–1918: Essays in Honour of Michael Wilks* (Studies in Church History Subsidia IX; Oxford, 1991).

Davidsohn, R., *Philipp II. Augustus von Frankreich und Ingeborg* (Stuttgart, 1888).

de Chevanne, M. J. Robert, 'Charles IV le Bel et Blanche de Bourgogne', *Bulletin philologique et historique (jusqu'à 1715) du Comité des travaux historiques et scientifiques, années 1936 et 1937* (Paris, 1938), pp. 313–50.

de la Figanière, Frederico Francisco, *Memorias das Rainhas de Portugal* (Lisbon, 1859).

de Maulde, M. (ed.), *Procédures politiques du règne de Louis XII* (Collection de documents inédits sur l'histoire de France, first series: Histoire; Paris, 1885).

Destefanis, Abel, *Louis XII et Jeanne de France: étude historique et juridique sur une cause en nullité de mariage à la fin du XVe siècle (1498)* (Avignon, 1975).

Digard, Georges Alfred Laurent, *et al.* (eds.), *Les registres de Boniface VIII*, 4 vols. (Paris, 1884–1939).

Donahue, C., *Law, Marriage, and Society in the later Middle Ages* (Cambridge, 2007).

Du Mont, J. J., *Corps universel diplomatique du droit de gens*, vol. III, Part II (Amsterdam, 1726).

Duby, Georges, *The Knight, the Lady and the Priest: The Making of Modern Marriage in Medieval France* (Harmondsworth, 1983, 1984).

Medieval Marriage: Two Models from Twelfth-Century France, trans. Elborg Forster (Baltimore, MD, 1978).

Eaves, Richard Glen, *Henry VIII and James V's Regency, 1524–1528: A Study in Anglo-Scottish Diplomacy* (Lanham, MD, 1987).

Ehses, S., *Römische Dokumente zur Geschichte der Ehescheidung Heinrichs VIII. von England 1527–1534* (Quellen und Forschungen aus dem Gebiete der Geschichte II) (Paderborn, 1893).

Emond, K., 'The Minority of King James V, 1513–1528' (PhD thesis, University of St Andrews, 1988).

Eugen, Konrad and Rosshirt, Franz, *Manuale Latinitatis Juris Canonici: Rerum Moralium et Theologicarum, Brevessimis Annotationibus et Probationibus Instructum, quo Lexici Juris Canonici Lineamenta Proponere Studuit* (Schaffhausen, 1862).

Faucon, M., 'Les arts à la cour d'Avignon sous Clément V et Jean XXII (1307–1334)', *Mélanges d'archéologie et d'histoire* 2 (1882), pp. 36–83.

Feret, P., 'Nullité du mariage de Henri IV avec Marguerite de Valois', *Revue des Questions historiques* 11ième année, 39e livraison (1876), pp. 77–114.

Fleisch, Ingo, *Sacerdotium – Regnum – Studium: der westiberische Raum und die europäische Universitätskultur im Hochmittelalter: prosopographische und rechtsgeschichtliche Studien* (Berlin, 2006).

Flori, Jean, *Aliénor d'Aquitaine: la reine insoumise* (Paris, 2004).

Fowler-Magerl, Linda, '*Ordines iudiciarii*' and '*libelli de ordine iudiciorum*': *From the Middle of the Twelfth to the End of the Fifteenth Century* (Turnhout, 1994).

Gams, Pius Bonifacius, *Series Episcoporum Ecclesiae Catholicae* (Graz, 1957 reprint).

Gane, Robert and Billot, Claudine, *Le chapitre de Notre-Dame de Paris au XIVe siècle: étude sociale d'un groupe canonial* (Saint-Étienne, 1999).

Guiraud, Jean, *Les registres d'Urbain IV (1261–1264)*, vol. I: *Registre dit Cameral* (Paris, 1899/1900 [1901 on title page]).

Heidecker, Karl, *The Divorce of Lothar II: Christian Marriage and Political Power in the Carolingian World*, trans. Tanis M. Guest (Ithaca, NY, 2010).

Helmholz, R. H. *Marriage Litigation in Medieval England* (Cambridge, 1974).

The Spirit of Classical Canon Law (Athens, GA, 1996).

Hinkmar of Reims, *De Divortio Lotharii regis et Theutbergae reginae, MGH Concilia 4*, supplementum 1, ed. Letha Böhringe (Hannover, 1992).

Hlawitschka, Eduard, 'Weshalb war die Auflösung der Ehe Friedreich Barbarossas und Adelas von Vohburg möglich?', *Deutsches Archiv für die Erforschung des Mittelalters* 61 (2005), pp. 509–36.

Hoensch, Jörg K, *Premysl Otakar II. von Böhmen: der goldene König* (Graz, 1989).

Holleger, Manfred, *Maximilian I. (1459–1519): Herrscher und Mensch einer Zeitenwende* (Stuttgart, 2005).

Howell, Margaret, *Eleanor of Provence: Queenship in Thirteenth-Century England* (Oxford, 1998).

Jasper, Detlev and Fuhrmann, Horst, *Papal Letters in the Early Middle Ages* (History of Medieval Canon Law; Washington, DC, 2001).

Kelly, Henry Ansgar, *The Matrimonial Trials of Henry VIII* (Stanford, CA, 1976).

Knoll, Paul W., *The Rise of the Polish Monarchy: Piast Poland in East Central Europe, 1320–1370* (Chicago, 1972).

Kottje, Raymond, 'Kirchliches Recht und päpstlicher Autoritätsanspruch. Zu den Auseinandersetzungen über die Ehe Lothars II.' in H. Mordek (ed.), *Aus Kirche und Reich. Studien zu Theologie, Politik und Recht im Mittelalter. Festschrift für Friedrich Kempf zu seinem fünfundsiebzigsten Geburtstag und fünfzigjährigen Doktorjubiläum* (Sigmaringen, 1983), pp. 97–103.

Kroppmann, Hubert, *Ehedispensübung und Stauferkampf unter Innozenz IV.: Ein Beitrag zur Geschichte des päpstlichen Ehedispensrechtes* (Abhandlungen zur Mittleren und Neueren Geschichte LXXIX; Berlin, 1937).

Labande-Mailfert, Yvonne, *Charles VIII et son milieu (1470–1498): la jeunesse au pouvoir* (Paris, 1975).

Lalou, Elisabeth, 'Le souvenir du service de la reine: l'hôtel de Jeanne de Navarre, reine de France, en juin 1294', in J. Paviot and Jacques Verger (eds.), *Guerre, pouvoir et noblesse au Moyen Âge: mélanges en l'honneur de Philippe Contamine* (Cultures et civilisations médiévales XXII; Paris, 2000), pp. 411–26.

Latham, R. E., *Revised Medieval Latin Word-List from British and Irish Sources* (London, 1965).

Lhospice, Michel, *Divorce et dynastie* (Paris, 1960).

Linehan, Peter *Spain, 1157–1300: A Partible Inheritance* (Oxford, 2011 edn).

Lobineau, Gui Alexis, *Histoire de Bretagne*, 2 vols. (Paris, 1707).

Mackenzie, George, *The Lives and Characters of the Most Eminent Writers of the Scots Nation*, vol. II (Edinburgh, 1711).

MacLean, Simon, *History and Politics in late Carolingian and Ottonian Europe: The Chronicle of Regino of Prüm and Adalbert of Magdeburg* (Manchester, 2009).

Marshall, Rosalind K., *Scottish Queens, 1034–1714* (East Linton, East Lothian, 2003).

Matarasso, Pauline, *Queen's Mate: Three Women of Power in France on the Eve of the Renaissance* (Aldershot, 2001).

Mayer, H. E., 'Ibelin versus Ibelin: The Struggle for the Regency of Jerusalem 1253–1258', *Proceedings of the American Philosophical Society* 122, no. 1 (1978), pp. 25–57.

Martène, E. and Durand, U., *Thesaurus Novus Anecdotorum*, vol. II (Clementis Papae Epistola CCXXX; Paris, 1717).

MGH Concilia, vol. VI: *Die Konzilien Deutschlands und Reichsitaliens 916–1001*, ed. Ernst-Dieter Hehl, Part 2: *962–1001* (with Carlo Servatius) (Hannover, 2007).

Minois, Georges, *Anne de Bretagne* (Paris, 1999).

Nelson, Janet L., *Charles the Bald* (Harlow, 1992).

Ninth-Century Histories, vol. I: *The Annals of St-Bertin* (Manchester, 1991).

Nicholas I, 'Epistolae', ed. E. Perels (*Monumenta Germaniae Historica, Epistolarum* VI; Berlin, 1925).

Owen, D. D. R., *Eleanor of Aquitaine, Queen and Legend* (Oxford, 1993, 1996).

Oxford Dictionary of the Christian Church, 3rd edn, ed. E. A. Livingstone (Oxford, 1997).

Pedersen, Frederik, 'The Danes and the Marriage Break-up of Philip II of France', in Paul Brand, Kevin Costello and W. N. Osborough (eds.), *Adventures of the Law*, Proceedings of the Sixteenth British Legal History Conference, Dublin, 2003 (Dublin, 2005).

Marriage Disputes in Medieval England (London, 2000).

Perels, Ernst, *Papst Nikolaus I. und Anastasius Bibliothecarius: ein Beitrag zur Geschichte des Papsttums im neunten Jahrhundert* (Berlin, 1920).

Perry, Maria, *Sisters to the King* (London, 2002).

Peters, Edward, *The Shadow King: Rex Inutilis in Medieval Law and Literature 751–1327* (New Haven, CT, 1970).

Pigaillem, Henri, *Anne de Bretagne: épouse de Charles VIII et de Louis XII* (Paris, 2008).

Pitts, Vincent J., *Henri IV of France: His Reign and Age* (Baltimore, MD, 2009).

Post, Gaines, *Studies in Medieval Legal Thought* (Princeton, NJ, 1964).

Rapp, Francis, *Maximilien d'Autriche: souverain du saint empire romain germanique, bâtisseur de la maison d'Autriche, 1459–1519* (Paris, 2007).

Regino of Prüm, *Reginonis Abbatis Prumiensis Chronicon cum Continuatione Treverensi*, ed. F. Kurze (*MGH SS. rer. Germ.* L; Hannover, 1890).

Richardson, H. G., 'King John and Isabelle of Angoulême', *English Historical Review* 65 (1950), pp. 360–71.

'The Marriage and Coronation of Isabelle of Angoulême', *English Historical Review* 61 (1946), pp. 289–314.

Rider, Catherine, *Magic and Impotence in the Middle Ages* (Oxford, 2006).

Roelker, Nancy Lyman, *One King, One Faith: The Parlement of Paris and the Religious Reformations of the Sixteenth Century* (Berkeley, 1996).

Rolker, Christopher, *Canon Law and the Letters of Ivo of Chartres* (Cambridge, 2010).

Rüdiger, Jan, 'Married Couples in the Middle Ages? The Case of the Devil's Advocate', in Per Andersen et al. (eds.), *Law and Marriage in Medieval and Early Modern Times: Proceedings of the VIIIth Carlsberg Academy Conference on Medieval Legal History* (Copenhagen, 2012).

Rymer, Thomas, *Foedera*, vol. V, part 3 (The Hague, 1741); vol. VI, part 1 (The Hague, 1741).

Sayer, Jane, *Original Papal Documents in England and Wales from the Accession of Pope Innocent III to the Death of Pope Benedict XI (1198–1304)* (Oxford, 1999).

Scarisbrick, J. J., *Henry VIII* (London, 1968, 1997).

Schwennicke, Detlev, *Stammtafeln zur Geschichte der Europäischen Staaten*, vol. II: *Die Ausserdeutschen Staaten: die regierenden Häuser der übrigen Staaten Europas* (Marburg, 1984).

Skinner, Quentin 'The Principles and Practice of Opposition: The Case of Bolingbroke versus Walpole', in Neil McKendrick (ed.), *Historical Perpectives: Studies in English Political Thought and Society* (London, 1974), pp. 93–128.

'Some Problems in the Analysis of Political Thought and Action', *Political Theory* 2 (1974), pp. 277–303.

Visions of Politics, vol. I: *Regarding Method* (Cambridge, 2002).

Slavin, Arthur J., 'Defining the Divorce: A Review Article', *Sixteenth Century Journal* 20 (1989), pp. 105–111.

Smith, Charles Edward, *Papal Enforcement of Some Medieval Marriage Laws* (Baton Rouge, LA, 1940, reissued Port Washington, NY, 1972).

Smith, Damian J., *Innocent III and the Crown of Aragon: The Limits of Papal Authority* (Aldershot, 2004).

Stone, Rachel, *Morality and Masculinity in the Carolingian Empire* (Cambridge, 2012).

Surtz, Edward, *Henry VIII's Great Matter in Italy: An Introduction to Representative Italians in the King's Divorce, Mainly 1527–1535*, 2 vols. (Ann Arbor, University Microfilms, 1975, 1982).

Surtz, Edward and Murphy, Virginia, *The Divorce Tracts of Henry VIII* (Angers, 1988).

Tanon, T., *Histoire des justices des anciennes églises et communautés monastiques de Paris* (Paris, 1883).

Tenbrock, R. H., 'Eherecht udn Ehepolitik bei Innocenz III.' (doctoral dissertation for the University of Münster, Dortmund-Hörde [1933?]).

Toudouze, Georges-Gustave, *Anne de Bretagne: duchesse et reine* (Paris, 1938).

Tremlett, Giles, *Catherine of Aragon: Henry's Spanish Queen* (London, 2010).

Turner, Ralph V., *Eleanor of Aquitaine, Queen of France, Queen of England* (New Haven, CT, 2009).

Ubl, Karl, *Inzestverbot und Gesetzgebung: die Konstruktion eines Verbrechens (300–1100)* (Millennium-Studien XX; Berlin, 2008).

Vincent, Nicholas, 'Isabella of Angoulême: John's Jezebel', in S. D. Church, *King John: New Interpretations* (Woodbridge, 1999), pp. 165–219.

Vincke, J., 'Der Eheprozeß Peters II. von Aragon (1206–1213), mit Veröffentlichung der Prozeßakten', in H. Finke *et al.*, *Gesammelte Aufsätze zur Kulturgeschichte Spaniens: Spanische Forschungen der Görresgesellschaft*, series 1, vol. V (Münster in Westfalen, 1935), pp. 108–89.

von Isenburg, Wilhelm Karl Prinz, *Stammtafeln zur Geschichte der Europäischen Staaten*, vol. II: *Die außerdeutschen Staaten*, 2nd edn (Marburg, 1953).

Vones-Liebenstein, U., 'Mathilde', article 5, in R. Auty (ed.), *Lexikon des Mittelalters*, vol. VI (Munich, 1993), cols. 392–3.

Vouters, Eugène, *Essai juridique et historique sur un procès en annulation de mariage au XVème siècle: Louis XII et Jeanne de France* (Lille, 1931).

Weir, Alison, *Eleanor of Aquitaine: By the Wrath of God, Queen of England* (London, 2000).

Wiesflecker, Hermann, *Kaiser Maximilian I.: das Reich, Österreich und Europa an der Wende zur Neuzeit*, vol. I: *Jugend, burgundisches Erbe und Römisches Königtum bis zur Alleinherrschaft 1459–1493* (Vienna, 1971).

Wooding, Lucy, *Henry VIII* (Abingdon, 2009).

Index of manuscripts

London, British Library (BL),
    Add. 20917, 194, 214–16, 219,
    285–7
London, British Library (BL), Add.
    37154, 229–38, 288–94

Paris, Archives nationales (AN),
    J.682.1, 124, 125, 130, 143,
    145, 168, 173, 235, 249–66,
    267

Paris, Archives nationales (AN), J.682.2,
    123, 125, 145–63, 168, 267–84
Paris, Archives nationales (AN),
    J.934.1/27, 241–5
Paris, Archives nationales (AN),
    J.934.1/29, 246–7
Paris, Bibliothèque Mazarine 1986, 271,
    277, 281
Paris, Bibliothèque nationale de France
    (BNF), Lat. 8935, 252, 271, 277, 281

General index

Acre, kingdom of, 99
Adelheid of Hesse, 5, 186
affinitas, 117, 296
Agnes of Meran, 1, 58, 60, 108
Albigensian Crusade, 69
Aldricus, Master, canon of Metz, 146
Alexander IV, 99–107
Alexander VI, 186, 198–200, 216
Alfonso III of Portugal, 1, 108–11
Amanuel, canon of St Marcellus, 147
Annales Xantenses, 23
Anne of Brittany, 1, 2, 6, 183–9, 190
Antoine de Lestang, 201
Antoine de Stagno, 206, 217
archers, Scottish, as guard of French king, 214–15
Archibald, Earl of Angus, 220–6
articles. *See* propositions (*articuli/ positiones*)
articuli. *See also* propositions (*articuli/positiones*)
Ascelanus called 'Taire', 154
Aubery, le sieur, 241, 246
Aurell, Martin, 70
Aymeri Mazerant, 123, 124, 126, 129, 130, 142, 164, 176, 178, 181, 249, 263

Baldwin, John, 51, 61
Balian, husband of Plaisance, queen of Cyprus, 99–107
banns, before marriage, 4, 120, 129, 134, 141, 149, 174
Barbiche, Bernard, 241
Baudouyn, Jean, 242–4
Baumgartner, Frederick J., 194
Beatrice of Lomanges, 74, 75
Beaugency, Council of, 50, 62
Bedouelle, Guy, 230
Bertha, and Robert II, 44–6
Bertrada, and Philip I of France, 47–9

Binns, Jim, 39
Blanca of Aragon, 2
Blanche of Burgundy, 1, 116–82
Blanche of Burgundy's legal team, efforts of, 142–5
Blanche of Castile, 135
Boniface VIII, 116–18
Bouchard, Constance Brittain, 51
Brittany, 6, 183, 190
Brown, E. A. R., 120, 122, 123, 125, 148, 165
Bruguière, M. B., 60–1
Brundage, James A., 8, 51, 65, 166, 209
Burchard of Worms, 44
Burgundy, alliance with Francis II of Brittany, 190
Burgundy, duchy of, breaks up, 183
Burns, Robert I., 76–7

calumnia, 127, 166, 296
calumny, 83, 105, 127, 134, 170, 175, 179, 180, 181, 296, 297
Calvinism in France, 239
Canteaut, Olivier, 123–4
Carne, Edward, 237, 238, 294
Casimir of Poland, 5
Catherine of Aragon, 227–38
Cazel, Fred A., 54–5
Celestine III, 58, 63
chapter bar, in the close of Notre Dame of Paris, 242, 244
Charles Faye. *See* promotor, in annulment suit
Charles IV of France, 119–82
Charles V, Holy Roman Emperor, 183
Charles VIII of France, 183, 184, 185, 186, 187–9, 190, 194, 198
Charles de Preux, 213, 217
Charles of Anjou, 110, 145
Charles of Valois, 152, 156, 158, 160, 161, 162, 163

Charles the Bald, 16, 20, 28
Chateau Gaillard, 132, 178
chronicle, at Saint Denys, as evidence of genealogy, 95
civil law, 165. *See also* Roman law
clandestine marriage, 112, 129, 141
Clement IV, 112–15
Clement V, 123, 143, 174
Clement VII, 222, 226, 235
Clement VIII, 247
Clermont, Council of, 1095, 47
Colard Heitie, 158
Coligny, Admiral, 239
Collard, Franck, 194
consummation, 183, 190–219, 227, 230, 236
Contamine, Philippe, 193–4
contumacy, 65, 90, 91, 97
Corpus Iuris Canonici
　Clem.2.1.2, 209
　Clem.5.11.2, 209
　Decretum Gratiani C.33.q.2.c.4, 66
　VI.2.2.1, 200
　VI.4.3.3, 118
　X.1.3.28, 200
　X.1.6.54, 180
　X.2.1.13, 210
　X.2.25.4, 209
　X.4.11.7, 117
　X.4.11.8, 117
Corran, Emily, 127, 296
Council at Soissons, 58
Council of Beaugency, 50
Council of Pavia. *See* Pavia, Council or Synod of
Council of Rome 998–9, 46
Crawford, Michael, 246
Cyprus, 99–107

Davidsohn, R., 59
Dawson, Jane, 220
de Chevanne, M. J. Robert, 122
de facto, 5, 70, 72, 80, 89, 91, 95, 96, 98, 101, 105, 107, 109, 126, 129, 130, 139, 164, 174, 175, 179, 198, 202, 206, 224, 232, 233, 250, 252, 253, 260, 267, 290, 291, 297
de Maulde, M., 191, 194–219
Denmark, 61, 65
Destefanis, Abel, 193
dispensation, for Catherine of Aragon to marry Arthur Tudor, 227, 228, 232–4
dispensation, fresh consent required after, 99–107

dispensations, 121, 124, 125, 143–4, 145, 167, 169, 172, 173, 194–7, 211, 234, 239
　Council of Trent's new rule for, 239, 240, 246, 248
divortium, 56, 80, 173, 188, 224, 234, 292, 296
Donahue, Charles, xi, 112
double dot, significance of, 83
Duby, Georges, 45, 48, 59–60
due process, 8, 12, 62, 63, 64, 67, 82, 84, 86, 87, 99, 104, 132, 229

Eaves, Richard Glen, 221, 222
Edict of Nantes, 240
Edward, son of Henry III of England, 81, 82
Ehses, S., 235
Eleanor of Aquitaine, 1, 3, 50–2, 62
Eleanor of Castile, 82
Eleanor of Provence, 81, 82
Emond, Ken, 220, 221
Enrique IV of Castille, 2
Erchembald, archbishop of Tours, 46
Eugenius III, 50, 52, 191
ex certa scientia, 73, 133, 143, 175, 177, 256, 264, 296
exceptio, 72

Faye, Charles, 242. *See* promotor, in annulment suit
Feret, P., 241
Fernand, bishop of Ceuta, 198–216
Fleisch, Ingo, 108
Flodden, battle of, 220, 222
forbidden degrees, 4, 50, 60–1. *See also* godparenthood; kinship; spiritual kinship
formal legal rationality, 7, 8, 116
Fourth Lateran Council, 4, 61, 76
Fowler-Magerl, Linda, 105, 296
Francis Behoulat, 204
Francis II of Brittany, 190
Frederick Barbarossa, 51, 62–3
French royal family, desirability of marrying into, 149

Gabrielle, mistress of Henri IV of France, 240
Gallicanism, 241
Gaspar, bishop of Modena, 242, 247
Gaucher de Châtillon, 159
Gaude-Ferragu, Murielle, 194
Gaudemet, Jean, 117
genealogies, 82

Geoffrey de Plessy, 125, 165
Ger. de Saponhia, 162
godparenthood, 116–18, 121–42, 153,
  190, 198. *See also* spiritual kinship
Gondi, cardinal de, 248
Gouvanh. *See* Pierre Gouvanh
Gregory V, 44, 45
Gregory XIII, 243, 244
Guichard, 152, 155
Guillaume de Piacenza, 147
Guillaume de Saint Marcel, 153, 154
Guillaume Feydelli, 201, 213
Guillaume Soubut, 126
Guise family, 239
Gunther, 20, 21, 22, 23, 28, 29, 30, 32,
  33, 35, 36, 38, 41, 64
Guy de Jouy, 158

Hageneder, O., 62, 67
Hautecombe, abbot of, 89
Hautecombe, prior of, 82, 87, 88, 89, 91,
  97
Helmholz, R. H., 8, 112, 295
Henry II of England, 50
Henri II of France, 239, 247
Henry III of England, 1, 4, 81–98
Henri IV of France, 1, 6–7, 191, 192,
  239–48
Henry VIII of England, 1, 6, 220, 227–38,
  240
Hlawitschka, Eduard, 51
Hoensch, Jörg K., 2
Horace, archbishop of Arles, 242, 247
Howell, Margaret, 82
Huguenot. *See* Calvinism in France

Ibelin, 99, 100, 103, 104
impotence, 2, 190–219
in facie ecclesiae, 297
in nostram animam, 127, 175, 251, 298
indissolubility doctrine, theological
  underpinnings of, 235
Ingeborg of Denmark, 4, 54, 58–68,
  191
Innocent III, 2, 4, 7, 54, 58–68, 69–75
Innocent IV, 79–80, 81–98
Isabel of Soisy, Lady, 148
Isabella of Gloucester, 1, 53–7, 62
Isabelle of Angoulême, 1, 53
iudex delegatus, 297. *See also* judges delegate
iurisdictionem iudicis prorogandi, 295
ius commune, 207

Jaffé, Elspeth, 116, 117
James IV of Scotland, 220

Jane of Traquair, 220, 222–3
Jaume I of Aragon, 76–8, 112–15
Jean de Essartis, 130, 132
Jean de Molins, 92–3, 94
Jean des Essartis, 133
Jean Hellequin, 148–50
Jeanne of France, 190–219
Jeanne of Ponthieu, afterwards queen of
  Castile, 1, 81–98
John, king of England, 3, 53–7, 62, 63
John XXII, 5, 116, 120–1, 163–73
John Capelli, 82, 89, 90, 91, 96
John of Arsur, 99, 100
John of Jaffa, 99, 100
John of Salisbury, 10, 51–2
Jordan de Calochio, 154
Joyeuse, cardinal de, 242, 247
judges delegate, 55, 71, 72, 82, 86, 88, 89,
  91, 95, 96, 99, 100, 200, 204, 213,
  216, 242
Julian, cardinal priest of St Peter in
  Chains, 195
Julius II, 231

Kelly, Henry Ansgar, 229
King John. *See* John, king of England
kinship, degrees of, how reckoned in Italy,
  146–7, 153–4
Knut VI of Denmark, 65
Kroppmann, Hubert, 53

La Guesle, 191–2, 240
La Reine Margot. *See* Marguerite de Valois
Lalou, Elisabeth, 122–3
Lambert of Arras, 48–9
Las Navas de Tolosa, 69
Le Gal, Patrick, 230
le Ratif, Amis/Amisius, 132, 165, 176,
  178
legal formality, 7–10. *See also* formal legal
  rationality
legitimation, 2
  of children, 5
Leviticus, and Henry VIII, 228
Lhospice, Michel, 191
libellus, 29, 105, 133–4, 166, 172, 173,
  179, 181, 297
Linehan, Peter, xi, 108, 186
litis contestatio, 72, 105, 131, 297
Lord Ralph de Paredo, 157
Lothar II, 2, 3, 9, 11–43, 64, 191
Loüet, George, 242, 248
Louis, bishop of Albi, 198–216
Louis VII of France, 1, 3, 50–2, 62, 63
Louis VIII of France, 60

Louis IX of France, 81, 135, 145, 154, 155
Louis X of France, 119
Louis XI of France, 183, 190, 191, 193, 198, 199, 211
Louis XII of France, 183, 184, 190–219
Lyonor, wife of Jaume I of Aragon, 76–8

MacLean, Simon, 12, 29
magic, as cause of impotence, 191–205
Mahaut, countess of Artois, as godmother, 150, 152, 155–6, 161
    name on written list, 161
Mansoura, 145, 150
Marco Travers, 201
Margaret of Scotland, 1, 6, 220–6
Marguerite of Burgundy, 119
Marguerite of Valois, 1, 6, 191, 239–48
Maria of Montpellier, 4, 69–75
Mary Tudor, daughter of Henry VII of England, 183, 184
Matarasso, Pauline, 194
Mathilda of Boulogne, 108–11
Matthew 'de Moncell', 153
Matthew 'Scarempnus', 154
Maximilian of Habsburg, 1, 2, 6, 183–9, 190
Mayer, H. E., 99, 100, 103, 104
Mécia Lopes de Haro, 79–80
'Mentia Lupi'. See Mécia Lopes de Haro
Murphy, Virginia, 229
Murray, Alexander, 194

Napoleon, and Josephine, 191
Nelson, Janet, 18, 20, 22, 37, 39
Nicholas I, 2, 11–43, 58, 64

onus satisdandi, 296
ordo iuris, 297. See also due process
Ottokar of Bohemia, 2

Painter, Sidney, 54–5
Parlement de Paris, 241
Pavia, Council or Synod of, 44, 45
Pederson, F., 112
Pere II of Aragon, 1, 4, 69–75
Perels, Ernst, 13
Peter of Aigueblanche, bishop of Hereford, 81, 82, 84, 85–98
Peters, Edward, 79
Philip, cardinal priest, and bishop of Le Mans, 204–16
Philip I of France, 3, 47–9, 191
Philip II of France, 3, 4, 54, 58–68, 191
Philip III of France, 136

Philip IV of France, 119, 136
Philip V of France, 119
Philip Augustus. See Philip II of France
Pierre Borelli, 201
Pierre de Bellessor, 201, 213, 216
Pierre Duban, 201
Pierre Gouvanh, 125, 126, 129, 173, 176, 179
Pitts, Vincent J., 241
Plaisance, queen of Cyprus, 1, 7, 99–107
plenitude of power, 84, 109, 172, 174
polygamy, 3
positiones, 73, 105, 127, 131, 135, 142, 166, 169, 170, 176, 180, 181, 205, 209, 213, 229, 236, 238, 247, 257, 263, 296, 298
pre-contract, as grounds for annulment, 220–3
proctors, 71, 72, 74, 82, 91, 96, 123, 128, 130–2, 144, 169, 201–2, 206
procurator. See proctors
procuratorial commission, 125, 129, 133, 143, 168, 169, 172, 173, 175, 179, 181, 202, 299
promotor, in annulment suit, 242
propositions (articuli/positiones), 104, 127, 131, 135, 142, 170, 180, 181, 190, 203–14, 236, 237, 247
proxy marriages, 5, 81, 183–4
puberty, 129, 134, 139, 141, 149, 174, 184, 198, 211
public honesty, 119, 185, 188, 197, 227, 230, 236

Rabikauskas, P., 164
Ralph of Coggeshall, 53, 57
Ralph of Diceto, 53, 56
Ralph of Mullento, 145
rationality, formal. See formal legal rationality
resuscitation, miraculous, of small boy, 156
Richard 'le Poissonnier', 158
Richard, bishop of Troyes. See Guichard
Richardson, H. G., 54–5
Rider, Catherine, 2
Robert II of France, 44–6, 191
Robert de Brisol, knight, 150
Robert La Longue, 201, 213
Robert Salomon, 201
Roelker, Nancy Lyman, 241
Roger of Howden, 53, 55, 57
Rolker, Christopher, 48
Roman law, 8, 51, 63, 165
Rome, Council or Synod of 998–9, 44, 46
Rossignol, Christophe, 242, 248

Rozala, and Robert II of France, 44
Rüdiger, Jan, 4

Salomon de Bombelles, 193, 214
Sancho II of Portugal, 79–80
Sanmark, Alexandra, 60
Sayers, Jane, 83
Scarisbrick, J. J., 227, 230
Schabel, Christopher, 100, 102, 104
Schwennicke, Detlev, 110
Sens, 48, 82, 86, 88, 89, 90, 91, 95, 96, 97
Sext, the, canon law compilation of
    Boniface VIII, 116–18
Sixtus IV, 196
Skinner, Quentin, 2
Slavin, Arthur J., 229
Smith, Charles Edward, 45, 48
Smith, Damian J., 70
Smith, Marc, 245
Soissons, Council of, 58
Soubut. See Guillaume Soubut
Spalletti, Joseph, 229
spiritual kinship, 116–18, 121–42, 159,
    160, 166, 190. See also godparenthood
St Bartholemew's Eve, massacre, 7, 239
St. Andrews, Consistorial Court of, 222
Stone, Rachel, 13, 15
summary procedure, 134

Surtz, Edward, 229, 230, 231, 236, 237
Synod. See Council

Tenbrock, R. H., 59
Teresa Gil de Vidaure, wife of Jaume I of
    Aragon, 76, 112–15
Theutberga, 2, 3, 11–43, 64
Theutgaud, 20, 21, 22, 23, 26, 28, 29, 30,
    32, 35, 36, 38, 41
Thinot, Adrien, 244, 245, 246
Thomas de Rogueta, 153

Ubl, Karl, 44, 45, 51
Urban IV, 108–11
Urban V, 5

Valois dynasty, 190
Veldtrup, Dieter, 5
Vincent, Nicholas, 56
Vincke, J., 69, 70–5
Violant, wife of Jaume I of Aragon, 76
Vones-Liebenstein, U., 108
Vouters, Eugène, 191–2

Waldrada, 3, 11–43, 64
Willigis, archbishop of Mainz, 44
Wolsey, Cardinal, 227, 228, 230
Wooding, Lucy, 220, 230

30192090R00185

Printed in Great
Britain
by Amazon